Supply Chain Redesign

Transforming Supply Chains into Integrated Value Systems

ISBN 0-13-060312-0

9 780130 603128

Supply Chain Redesign

Transforming Supply Chains into Integrated Value Systems

Robert B. Handfield

*Bank of America University Distinguished Professor
of Supply Chain Management and
Director, Supply Chain Resource Consortium
College of Management
North Carolina State University*

Ernest L. Nichols, Jr.

*Associate Professor of Supply Chain and Operations Management
Fogelman College of Business and Economics and
Director, Center for Supply Chain Management
FedEx Technology Institute
The University of Memphis*

FINANCIAL TIMES
Prentice Hall

Prentice Hall PTR
Upper Saddle River, NJ 07458
phptr.com

Library of Congress Cataloging-in-Publication Data

Handfield, Robert B.
   Supply chain redesign : converting your supply chain into an integrated value system /
  Robert B. Handfield, Ernest L. Nichols, Jr.
    p. cm. -- (Financial Times Prentice Hall)
  Includes index.
  ISBN 0-13-060312-0 (alk. paper)
    1. Business logistics 2. Industrial marketing. I. Nichols, Ernest L. II. Title. III. Financial Times
Prentice Hall books

HD38.5 .H364 2002
658.7'2--dc21

                                      2002016449

Production Supervisor: Wil Mara
Acquisitions Editor: Jim Boyd
Editorial Assistant: Allyson Kloss
Marketing Manager: Bryan Gambrel
Manufacturing Manager: Alexis Heydt-Long
Buyer: Maura Zaldivar
Cover Designer: Anthony Gemmellaro
Composition: Pine Tree Composition

© 2002 by Financial Times Prentice Hall
An imprint of Pearson Education, Inc.
Upper Saddle River, NJ 07458

The publisher offers discounts on this book when ordered in bulk quantities. For more information
contact: Corporate Sales Department, Prentice Hall PTR, One Lake Street, Upper Saddle River, NJ 07458.
Phone: 800-382-3419; FAX: 201-236-7141; E-mail: corpsales@prenhall.com.

Company and product names mentioned herein are the trademarks or registered trademarks of their
respective owners.

Printed in the United States of America

10 9 8 7 6 5 4 3 2 1

ISBN 0-13-060312-0

Pearson Education LTD.
Pearson Education Australia PTY, Limited
Pearson Education Singapore, Pte. Ltd
Pearson Education North Asia Ltd
Pearson Education Canada, Ltd.
Pearson Educación de Mexico, S.A. de C.V.
Pearson Education—Japan
Pearson Education Malaysia, Pte. Ltd
Pearson Education, Upper Saddle River, New Jersey

FINANCIAL TIMES PRENTICE HALL BOOKS

For more information, please go to www.ft-ph.com

Dr. Judith M. Bardwick
  Seeking the Calm in the Storm: Managing Chaos in Your Business Life

Thomas L. Barton, William G. Shenkir, and Paul L. Walker
  Making Enterprise Risk Management Pay Off:
  How Leading Companies Implement Risk Management

Michael Basch
  CustomerCulture: How FedEx and Other Great Companies Put
  the Customer First Every Day

J. Stewart Black and Hal B. Gregersen
  Leading Strategic Change: Breaking Through the Brain Barrier

Deirdre Breakenridge
  Cyberbranding: Brand Building in the Digital Economy

William C. Byham, Audrey B. Smith, and Matthew J. Paese
  Grow Your Own Leaders: How to Identify, Develop, and Retain
  Leadership Talent

Jonathan Cagan and Craig M. Vogel
  Creating Breakthrough Products: Innovation from Product Planning
  to Program Approval

Subir Chowdhury
  The Talent Era: Achieving a High Return on Talent

Sherry Cooper
  Ride the Wave: Taking Control in a Turbulent Financial Age

James W. Cortada
  21st Century Business: Managing and Working
  in the New Digital Economy

James W. Cortada
  Making the Information Society: Experience, Consequences,
  and Possibilities

Aswath Damodaran
  The Dark Side of Valuation: Valuing Old Tech, New Tech,
  and New Economy Companies

Henry A. Davis and William W. Sihler
  Financial Turnarounds: Preserving Enterprise Value

Sarv Devaraj and Rajiv Kohli
  The IT Payoff: Measuring the Business Value
  of Information Technology Investments

CONTENTS

Chapter 3

Internal Integration—Managing Information Flows within the Organization 83

Chapter 4

The Financial Impacts of SCM—Finding the "Sweet Spot" 113

Chapter 8
Navigating the Business to Business (B2B) E-Commerce Landscape 253

Chapter 9

Creating Information Visibility 293

PREFACE

Integrated supply chain management is now recognized as a core competitive strategy. As organizations continuously seek to provide their products and services to customers faster, cheaper, and better than the competition, managers have come to realize that they cannot do it alone; rather, they must work on a cooperative basis with the best organizations in their supply chains in order to succeed. When pressed to identify how to achieve this strategy, however, the path forward for managers is not clear. Numerous "solution providers" offer the "magic bullets" to supply chain integration; yet the results are never guaranteed.

In this book, we focus on the concept of the value system. We propose that by integrating the flows of information, materials, technology, and resources in a supply chain, a true system of creating value for the end customer can be created. This book shares insights gained from our research, which has brought us in contact with managers in engineering, purchasing, operations, logistics, information systems, and sales functions across a range of industries. These experiences have been synthesized to create a managerial perspective of the core tasks and challenges required to transform supply chains into high-performing value systems. This text is unique in that it describes a phenomenon that has been rapidly evolving yet never fully deployed by any single organization. Although other books have dealt with the individual processes associated with developing new products, buying materials, transforming them, and shipping them to customers, we believe our treatment of the topic from an integrated managerial perspective is unique.

Because supply chain management involves all functions within organizations, this book has been written for a general audience and provides insights into the conceptual foundations of supply chain management. It also presents a topical discussion of what a supply chain is, why it is important, and what types of challenges are implicit in managing supply chains. In sum, this book will enable readers to better understand—

- The contribution of supply chain management to creating value, in the form of increased profitability, technology leadership, and market share in the modern organization
- Requirements for analyzing and improving supply chain business processes

- The benefits of integrating major functional activities, including product design, purchasing, information systems, manufacturing planning and control, inventory management, human resource development, financial planning, forecasting, sales, quality management, distribution, transportation and other areas via internal information systems
- Understanding the "sweet spot", or area of greatest value to focus resources in organizational supply chains
- Strategies for creating collaboration and trust among supply chain participants
- The contribution of customers and suppliers to collaborative product/processs/service design
- Strategies for achieving significant shared cost reductions among supply chain partners
- Latest developments in B2B standards and applications that facilitate supply chain integration and creation of value systems
- Recent technologies that enable visibility of end customer requirements for multiple tiers of OEM's and suppliers in a supply chain
- A detailed case study of a major change management initiative at General Motors that illustrates the critical success factors required to create an integrated value system, as well as the challenges in deploying a value system initiative

These points are illustrated through multiple examples from a variety of industries and settings, based on extensive research over many years. The concepts are presented in an easy to understand narrative that is intended for any reader interested in learning about supply chain management.

ACKNOWLEDGEMENTS

The authors wish to acknowledge the contributions of many students, executives, faculty, and others in writing this book. Thomas Putvin, CEO of Putvin Enterprises, provided a number of significant insights into the historical background of the events at General Motors discussed in Chapter 10, based on his 30 years of experience with the company. Other executives from GM who contributed include Dick Alagna, John Calabrese, Tom Fabus, Bo Andersson, Bob Burkhart, Anton Meurer, and others. Dr. Arun Gupta provided invaluable insights into information technology updates. Other executives who provided insights into this book included Bruce Corbett and Phil McIntyre from Milliken & Company, Nancy Walker from American Airlines, Art Rowe and Greg Kern from Deere & Company, John Kinney from Solectron, Brandy Maranian from Sonoco, Laura Covitz of Nortel Networks, Tom Allen, Kent Hudson of Indus, Mike Clem of GKN Automotive, John Dalton, Ross Prior, Frank Elliott, and Larry Ford of Bechtel, Stephanie Miles of BridgePointe, Tina Claps and Steve Brandt, Sam Straight from GlaxoSmithKline, Tom Mariner from ABB, Dana Lane from Freemarkets, Adrian Despres from J.D. Edwards, and countless others. Faculty members who contributed to the book include Fay Cobb-Payton and Debra Zahay (North Carolina State University), Dan Krause, Robert Monczka, and Ken Peterson (Arizona State University), Phil Carter (Center for Advanced Purchasing Studies and Arizona State University), Bob Trent (Lehigh University), and others. Steve Edwards, Managing Director of the Supply Chain Resource Consortium at North Carolina State University directed a number of student teams who contributed to the various benchmarking studies described in book. Participating student included: Ajith Kumar Parlikad, Amit Heblikar, Anand Kosur, Karthik Gandlur, Manjiri Kaundinya, Rohit Razdan, Srinivas Balisetti, Uday Rao, Steven Edwards, Meenakshi Lakshman, Michel Diab, Mark Lenhart, Luther Beverage, Anshu Gupta Yunsheng Huang, Courtney Mudd, Brett Schonberg, Sandeep Sehgal and Asmita Barve. Lisa Carl provided an invaluable service in reviewing the manuscript in its roughest form. We also wish to thank Laura Edwards (The University of Memphis) and Christine Nichols for reviewing the manuscript and their valuable suggestions. Support provided by the FedEx Center for Cycle Time Research at The University of Memphis and by the Global Procurement and Supply Chain Benchmarking Initiative at Michigan State University is also appreciated. Finally, we are both very grateful for the ongoing support of our families.

Robert B. Handfield and Ernest L. Nichols, Jr.

ABOUT THE AUTHORS

Robert B. Handfield is the Bank of America Distinguished University Professor of Supply Chain Management in the College of Management at North Carolina State University. He is the founder and Director of the Supply Chain Resource Consortium at NC State (http://scrc.ncsu.edu). Handfield is recognized for his expertise in supply chain management, new product development, and collaborative systems. He serves as the Editor-in-Chief of the Journal of Operations Management, Associate Editor of Decision Sciences Journal, Editorial Columnist on supply chain management for APICS: The Performance Advantage, and Editorial Advisor for the Supply Chain Management Review.

Ernest L. Nichols, Jr. is Associate Professor of Supply Chain and Operations Management in the Marketing and Supply Chain Management Department of the Fogelman College of Business and Economics at The University of Memphis. He also serves as Director of the Center for Supply Chain Management in the FedEx Technology Institute at The University of Memphis. His research, teaching, and consulting activities interests address a range of integrated supply chain management issues. He is Editor of Cycle Time Research, Associate Editor of the Journal of Operations Management, and a member of the Editorial Review Board for the Journal of Supply Chain Management.

1

Supply Chain Management: Transforming Supply Chains into Integrated "Value Systems"

Two years after taking on a challenging job as director of business processes in advance purchasing, Rick Calabra[1], a General Motors executive, stretched back in his chair thinking about what had transpired between him and the group vice president of Worldwide Procurement (WWP). Rick had been nominated to lead the cluster called "Sourcing and Supplier Management" in General Motor's (GM's) major "Order to Delivery (OTD)" initiative. This new initiative would radically re-define the business processes at GM. In a presentation, the VP had challenged him to develop a supply base that "can transform end customers' clicks" on GM's Buyer Power Website into technology and demand requirements that are "sensed" by suppliers throughout GM's supply chain via Supply Power (an Internet-based technology for sharing information with key suppliers). A cross-functional team consisting of 50 people representing seven clusters had been put together to take the automotive giant's OTD initiative forward.

GM defines its OTD initiative as:

"The engine that will deliver the promise of e-business to our customers and shareholders by:

- Helping to transform GM from a traditional make-and-sell company (push system) to a dynamic sense-and-respond company (pull system)
- Integrating and streamlining the entire supply chain (supply, manufacturing, and distribution)
- Enabling GM to meet dealer and customer requirements rapidly and reliably."

One of the challenges of the OTD initiative was to develop the capability to quickly deliver customized vehicles to customers ordering them from the GM Buyer Power website. This task was daunting, as GM's order to delivery lead times for customized orders have historically been 12 to 16 weeks. Rick had been assigned responsibility for the supply part of the initiative. Although this was an exciting project, Rick also realized he had a tough job ahead of him. The problem was complex. How would he get 12,000 suppliers to collaborate on this effort?

Rick realized that the first step involved establishing a dialogue with suppliers. This would help him discover what problems they faced with the OTD initiative. Then, he could recommend solutions to improve supply chain reliability and responsiveness and align it with OTD's vision of "sense and respond."

It was 6 p.m. on a cold winter evening. As Rick looked out of his window, it was snowing. The office building was silent, as most employees had left early due to a snow storm warning. Rick rested his face on his palms and thought to himself, "Where do I start? Will I get cooperation from the suppliers? Can I complete my task within three years?" He was known in GM as a go-getter; the new assignment was a challenge and he had to find the answers.

In the last two decades, managers have witnessed a period of change unparalleled in the history of the world in terms of advances in technology, globalization of markets, and stabilization of political economies. With the increasing number of world-class domestic and foreign competitors, organizations have had to improve their internal and external processes rapidly in order to stay competitive.

In the 1960s–1970s, companies began to develop detailed market strategies focused on creating and capturing customer loyalty. Organizations also realized that strong engineering, design, and manufacturing functions were necessary to support these market requirements. Design engineers had to be able to translate customer needs into product and service specifications, which then had to be produced at a high level of quality and at a reasonable cost. As the demand for new products escalated in the 1980s, manufacturing organizations were required to become increasingly flexible and responsive to modify existing products and processes or to develop new ones in order to meet ever-changing customer needs. In the 1990s, as internal manufacturing capabilities improved, managers realized that material and service inputs from suppliers had a major impact on their organizations' ability to meet customer needs. This led to an increased focus on the supply base and the organization's sourcing strategy. Managers also realized that producing a quality product was not enough. Getting the products to customers when, where, how, and in the quantity that they wanted, in a cost-effective manner, constituted an entirely new type of challenge. More recently, the "Logistics Renaissance" was also born, spawning a whole set of time-reducing information technologies and logistics networks aimed at meeting these challenges.[2]

The rules of business have changed. In today's environment, new products are launched and businesses are born every day. Customers are increasingly difficult to keep and costly to replace. Companies face intense competition from traditional powerhouses and new players, and must continue to find new revenue opportunities and increase efficiencies. The effects of September 11, 2001 have made the global market environment even more volatile, with added security concerns for global travel and logistics. Today more than ever, businesses depend on strategic relations with their customers and suppliers to create value systems that will provide a competitive edge in the market. In effect, there is a new network economy emerging where companies trade with suppliers and customers over the Internet in real time. The virtual corporation is now a reality, with companies outsourcing a wide range of functions including design, manufacturing, distribution, and others so that they can focus on their core competencies. However, ensuring a seamless, consistent customer experience requires real-time automation of interorganizational business processes that span across trading partners. Traditional business practices, such as e-mail, faxes, and voice mail introduce delays and often require data to be re-entered multiple times. Hence, the need for dynamic business-to-business (B2B) integration that can automate business processes that encompass a diverse range of packaged and legacy applications and systems within the corporation and among supply chain member organizations. The ability to develop these B2B relationships and realize their potential in the shortest possible time is critical to the long-term success of any modern business. Indeed, no business can afford not to efficiently automate business processes with trading partners.

Businesses are continually forging closer relationships with their customers. Customers expect to be informed from contact to completion of transaction, 365 days a year, 7 days a week, 24 hours a day. Rather than adding the costly human resources that would traditionally be required to maintain such a level of service, customers now interact directly with company information systems via automated e-mail systems, self-service Web sites, and information portals. Companies are empowering their customers to help themselves to their information. Customers not only expect their interaction to be real time, but also to be personalized, with information that represents their specific history with the company.

In order to meet these demands, businesses must be able to integrate their information systems and applications with those of their suppliers and customers reliably, securely, and in a timely manner. Not surprisingly, this has led to a tremendous growth in B2B integration as companies look for ways to automate and accelerate their business processes and become e-businesses, responding to customer demands immediately and making changes as market opportunities shift.

e-business integration significantly improves organizational performance by supporting the key principles of business success:

- Faster to market with new products and services
- Better service
- Better sales process
- Lower operational costs
- Lower production costs
- Lower inventory costs

However, e-business also adds a significant amount of complexity (e.g., security, reliability, fault tolerance, government regulations, etc.) not to mention the money and time required to integrate an organization's business applications. Companies are undertaking significant restructuring initiatives to be able to function in the new era of electronic commerce. Presented with a deluge of information on "dot-coms," servers, B2B requirements, and online customer and supplier linkages, many executives are now struggling to develop a comprehensive strategy for this new market environment.

This book is intended to provide a roadmap for managers to develop a strategy for integrating and improving their supply chains, while understanding the limitations of current B2B applications. After the initial wave of excitement about e-business, many companies are recognizing that beneath the Web, there must still be a physical distribution and sourcing structure. All of a sudden, supply chain management (SCM) is back in vogue. However, these discussions often overlook a critical point. SCM is concerned with more than just the movement of materials from point A to point B. The goal of SCM is the creation of value for the supply chain member organizations with a particular emphasis on the end customer in the supply chain. For this reason, we will refer to these "new and improved" supply chains that have been designed and developed to create the maximum value for supply chain members as "value systems."

The need to create a new system of managing supply chains has become even more apparent since the events of September 11, 2001. In response to the terrorist attacks, organizations have imposed a number of measures, including deep discounting to sustain profitability (i.e., the automotive industry), significant downsizing of the workforce, changes in leadership, and even appeals to the federal government to restrict international competition (textiles).

The impact on many organizations has been predictable: there are fewer people around to take on an increasing workload, significant cost pressures, high inventory levels, plant closings, and increasing conflicts between customers and suppliers. In some industries, such as telecommunications, companies are using the term "deferred commitments" to reflect the fact that they are not willing to purchase agreed-upon forecasted quantities from their suppliers. In response to these events, some organizations have reverted to the traditional adversarial approach to managing supply chain relationships.

On the other hand, the impact of 9/11 has forced many managers to confront an important message: the old model of managing supply chains is broken and simply doesn't work. In fact, the recent downturn in the economy has, more than ever, reinforced the need to improve performance across the entire supply chain. In industries such as automotive, electronics, transportation, industrial equipment, and many others—senior executives realize that raising prices is no longer an option, and neither is the possibility of dramatically increasing sales in a flat economy. This leaves only one option: reducing costs across the supply chain.

A manager at GM noted, "Our only opportunity left is to take out cost, and work better with our suppliers. One outcome of the downturn has been a strong signal to our top management team that a new model for managing customers and suppliers is needed." General Motors is not the only organization to realize this fact. Many companies today are realizing that in the future, managing costs across multiple enterprises in the supply chain is the only real path to sustained growth. To succeed in difficult as well as good economic times, organizations in a supply chain will need to concurrently "step on the brakes," or "step on the gas" in a collaborative manner.

Jeff Trimmer, a former executive at Daimler–Chrysler and currently the Director of the National Initiative for Supply Chain Integration, describes this evolution as the "Third Phase of Industrial Renewal:"

- Phase 1: Optimization of individual functions
- Phase 2: Optimization of cost and quality between individual organizations
- Phase 3: Management of entire supply chains with synchronized goals and involved managers

Trimmer notes that as long as humans have traded goods, supply chains have existed. The real issue is whether companies will choose to manage their supply chains, or abdicate this responsibility to other entities. For thousands of years, businesses have depended on Adam Smith's "invisible hand" to optimize supply chains. From the silkworm farmer in China to the cloth merchant in Venice, each element of the supply chain tried to optimize his individual gain by negotiating with direct suppliers to keep his costs down, and with individual customers to maximize his income. Today, we have countless examples of how managing the multiple links of a supply chain can improve performance by significant amounts.

The principles of the new model are threefold:

1. The only entity that puts money into a supply chain is the end customer. Until the end customer decides to buy a product, the rest of us are shuffling his money back and forth among supply chain members.
2. The only solution that is stable over the long term is one in which every element of the supply chain, from raw material to end customer, profits from the business. It is shortsighted for businesses to believe they can solve their cost problems by punishing suppliers and customers. Shifting costs and problems without solving root causes is inherently unstable and unsuccessful over the long term. The best supply chains will solve problems, implement the best solutions, and share the benefits among their members.
3. Supply chain management is about economic value added. SCM is not just about cost. It's about the total content of a final product or service, including quality, technology, delivery, and after-sales service. If we can't manage the total content, we will be unable to meet the needs of our customers.

To achieve these goals, supply chain management strategy should be an inherent part of any corporate strategy; just as product strategy, marketing strategy, and financial strategies are elements. Managers who have been working in this area are not surprised by these developments.

We are not the first authors to emphasize the importance of partnering with customers and suppliers, linking systems, and sharing information as the foundation for an integrated supply chain and future deployment of e-business applications. However, our approach is unique; we emphasize that the entire supply chain must be re-evaluated from start to finish in order to turn it into a true "value system." Much of the content of this book is based on research by the authors over the last ten years with three major consortiums: The Global Procurement and Supply Chain Benchmarking Initiative at Michigan State University, the FedEx Center for Cycle Time Research at the University of Memphis, and the Supply Chain Resource Consortium at North Carolina State University. Through this research, we will provide an understanding of the enablers and tools needed to ensure that SCM applications are successful—involving the physical systems, relationships required, and software applications.

It has become obvious in the last five years that making money on the Web is becoming increasingly difficult. Many of the big Customer-to-Business (C2B), Customer-to-Customer (C2C), and Business-to-Customer (B2C) companies such as Priceline, Amazon, and E-bay have experienced significant reductions in their stock prices. Investors, aware of the inability of these companies to produce a profit, have punished them in the market. Amazon's distribution system has experienced very low turns, while Priceline's business has dropped due to Webvan's failure and lack of capacity in airline seating. After the initial furor over the promise of B2B e-commerce and the ridiculous valuations that accompanied this frenzy, the B2B sector cooled significantly. All of a sudden, people recognized that business processes were in many cases not yet improved enough to enable the use of the technology.

It seemed like everyone wanted to get on the B2B bandwagon without really understanding the full impact on the business and ensuring that the business processes were changed to get to the "value" provided by these systems. There is no question that many of the strategies pursued by supply chain organizations will rely on e-business solutions. However, before this occurs, organizations will need to re-think their entire supply chains to optimize performance and value as they seek to better integrate with suppliers and customers, share information, link information systems processes, and outsource manufacturing, logistics systems, on-site engineering, and maintenance activities. These strategies will require new e-commerce channels, Web-based applications to enable information sharing, and mass customization applications, but most importantly, an effective order fulfillment process with rapid delivery. While many solution providers promise these capabilities, they are, in fact, extremely difficult to deploy and execute. Why? Because of the reluctance of organizations to give up their investments in existing business applications resulting in a heterogeneous system that often gets very difficult and expensive to integrate and validate.

We contend that the B2B software industry has at times dramatically overstated its capabilities. In interviews with key managers, the most common complaint is the lack of a fundamental set of standards and proven capabilities. Many application service providers are coming forward with "The Answer," using terms such as "end-to-end solutions." Yet, upon being asked to provide demonstrated successes with prior customers, they are unable to do so. Worse yet, many have a limited understanding of fundamental materials management principles such as bills of materials, inventory control, and order-fulfillment processes. To complicate matters, a lack of software standards and a growing set of niche players often results in significant systems integration challenges that are costly and time consuming. In other companies, organizations developed homegrown solutions pieced together to meet a pressing immediate need; such solutions were never integrated into other applications, yet never relinquished. In an effort to capture a piece of this lucrative market, suppliers announce new versions before being ready for market.

In order to place the whole B2B software application market in context, we will review some basic concepts in this chapter, including supply chains, supply chain management, and value systems. Next, we present a technology roadmap for integrating B2B applications into the supply chain, beginning with basic Electronic Data Interchange (EDI), then the evolving virtual private networks, and future capabilities in supplier-centric and customer-centric e-commerce. Finally, we introduce the notion of "value systems," and present the framework for the remainder of the book.

Defining Supply Chains

Faced with the challenge of the current e-commerce-powered competitive environment, organizations now find that it is no longer enough to manage their own business but also the supply chain. They must be involved in managing the network of all upstream firms that provide input (directly or indirectly), as well as the network of downstream firms responsible for delivery and after-market service of the product to the customer. For purposes of this book, we define the terms supply chain and supply chain management as follows:

The *supply chain* encompasses all organizations and activities associated with the flow and transformation of goods from the raw materials stage, through to the end user, as well as the associated information flows. Material and information flows both up and down the supply chain.

Supply chain management (SCM) is the integration and management of supply chain organizations and activities through cooperative organizational relationships, effective business processes, and high levels of information sharing to create high-performing value systems that provide member organizations a sustainable competitive advantage.

If we consider an individual firm within the context of this definition, we must include both its upstream supplier network and its downstream distribution channel (see Figure 1–1). In this definition, the supply chain includes managing information systems, sourcing and procurement, production scheduling, order processing, inventory management, warehousing, customer service, and after-market disposition of packaging and materials. The supplier network consists of all organizations that provide inputs, either directly or indirectly, to the focal firm. For example, an automotive company's supplier network includes the thousands of firms that provide items ranging from raw materials such as steel and plastics, to complex assemblies and subassemblies such as transmissions and brakes. As shown in Figure 1–1, the supplier network may include internal divisions of the company as well as external suppliers. A given material may pass through multiple processes within multiple suppliers and divisions before being assembled into a vehicle. A supplier for this company has its own set of suppliers that provide input (called second-tier suppliers) that is also part of this supply chain. The beginning of a supply chain inevitably can be traced back to "Mother Earth," that is, the ultimate original source of all materials that flow through the chain (e.g., iron ore, coal, petroleum, wood, etc.). Supply chains are essentially a series of linked suppliers and customers; every customer is, in turn, a supplier to the next downstream organization until a finished product reaches the end user.

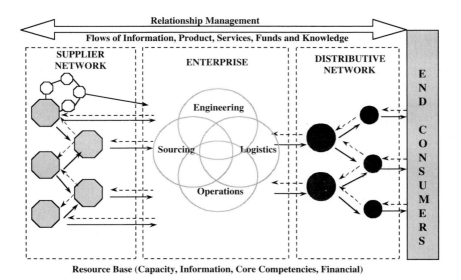

Figure 1–1   The Integrated Supply Chain

From the focal firm's perspective, the supply chain includes upstream suppliers, internal functions, and downstream customers. A firm's *internal functions* include the different processes used in transforming the inputs provided by the supplier network. In the case of an automotive company, this includes all of its parts manufacturing (e.g., stamping, power train, and components), which are eventually brought together in actual automobiles. Coordinating and scheduling these internal flows is challenging, particularly in a large organization such as an automotive company. For example, order-processing managers are responsible for translating customer requirements into actual orders, which are put into the system. In the case of an automotive company, these individuals work primarily with the extensive dealer network to ensure that the right mix of automobiles and service parts are available so that dealers can meet the needs of their customers. Order processing also may involve extensive customer interaction, including quoting prices, discussing delivery dates and other shipment requirements, and after-market service. Another important internal function is production scheduling, which translates orders into actual production tasks. This may involve working with materials requirements planning (MRP) systems, scheduling work centers, employees, capacity planning, and machine maintenance.

The second major part of supply chain management involves *upstream external* supply chain members. In order to manage the flow of materials between all of the upstream organizations in a supply chain, firms employ an array of personnel who ensure that the right materials arrive at the right locations at the right time. The purchasing function serves as the critical interface with the upstream supplier. Purchasing managers are responsible for ensuring that: 1) the right suppliers are selected; 2) suppliers are meeting performance expectations; 3) appropriate contractual mechanisms are employed; and 4) an appropriate relationship is maintained with all suppliers. They may also be responsible for driving improvement in the supply base and acting as liaisons between suppliers and other internal members (engineering, accounting, etc.). Materials managers are responsible for planning, forecasting, and scheduling material flows between suppliers in the chain. Materials managers play an important role coordinating a wide range of activities. Materials managers work closely with production schedulers to ensure that suppliers are able to deliver the materials on time to the required locations, and that they have some visibility regarding future requirements so that they can plan ahead of actual production and delivery dates.

Finally, a firm's *external downstream* supply chain encompasses all of the downstream organizations, processes, and functions that the product passes through on its way to the end customer. In the case of an automotive company's distribution network, this includes its finished goods and pipeline inventory, warehouses, dealer network, and sales operations. This distribution channel is relatively small.

Other types of supply chains may have relatively small internal supply chains, but extensive downstream distribution channels. Within the downstream portion of the supply chain, the logistics function is responsible for moving materials between locations. Logistics activities typically include network design, packaging, warehousing, transportation, order processing, materials handling, and finished goods inventory management.

An important recent trend in supply chain management is the recovery, recycling, or reuse of products from the end user. Organizations are now extending their distribution channels beyond the end customer to include the acceptance and disassembly of final products for reuse in new products. Organizations are seeking to close the loop and eventually transform used products into new products and/or materials that can be recycled without harming the environment. In other cases, organizations have developed extensive repair networks to handle warranty and quality problems that occur with products returned by customers. This function may include after-sales service, maintenance services, and other activities related to the continued satisfaction of the customer. Here again, organizations are actively working to improve their "reverse logistics" functions, to manage the flow of products moving backward through the supply chain.

All organizations are part of one or more supply chains. Whether a company sells directly to the end customer, provides a service, manufactures a product, or extracts material from the earth, it can be characterized within the context of its supply chain. Until recently, however, organizations focused on their direct customers and internal functions and placed relatively little emphasis on other organizations within their supply chain network. Three major developments in global markets and technologies have brought supply chain management to the forefront of executive management's attention:

1. Ever-increasing customer demands in areas of product and service cost, quality, delivery, technology, and cycle time brought about by global competition.
2. The emergence of and greater acceptance of higher-order cooperative interorganizational relationships.
3. The information revolution.

Each of these has fostered the emergence of an integrated supply chain management approach. In doing so, a new concept has emerged—that of the "value system." A *value system* is defined as follows:

"A connected series of organizations, resources, and knowledge streams involved in the creation and delivery of value to end customers. Value systems integrate supply chain activities, from determination of customer needs through product/service development, production/operations and distribution, including (as appropriate) first-, second-, and third-tier suppliers. The objective of value systems is to position organizations in the supply chain to achieve the highest levels of customer satisfaction and value while effectively exploiting the competencies of all organizations in the supply chain."

Some of the trends in customer requirements, interorganizational relationships, and information systems that have brought the concept of interorganizational value systems to the forefront are presented in the following section.

Increasing Customer Demands for Value Across the Supply Chain

The first major trend facing organizations today is the demand of ever-greater levels of value in the form of responsiveness and shorter defined cycle times for deliveries of newly developed high-quality goods and services at lower prices. A variety of changes occurring throughout global markets have resulted in an increasingly competitive environment. The rate of change in markets, products, technology, and competitors is occurring at an increasingly rapid pace, leading to a condition in which managers must make decisions on shorter notice, with less information and with higher penalty costs. At the same time, customers are demanding quicker delivery responsiveness.

These same customers require products that incorporate state-of-the-art technology and features. Products are becoming less standardized as customers are demanding custom-tailored options. In many market segments, only those firms that have the ability to "mass-customize" are successful. Computers are assessed based on their speed and cost, automobiles on their safety and reliability, and long-distance telephone carriers on price competitiveness. This means that such products are becoming more complex, have a greater variety of options, and must be tailored to a greater number of smaller market "niches." In some industries, product life cycles are shrinking from years to a matter of two or three months. In one sense, many global markets are becoming increasingly similar to the fashion industry, in which products go in and out of style in a season.

Managers throughout the supply chain are feeling the full effect of these changes. Cutbacks in staffing are forcing managers to handle a greater number of channels with fewer people, while cost pressures require that they do so with fewer inventories. Because of the ever-increasing levels of competition found in many markets, supply chain–related mistakes leading to lost sales cannot be easily dismissed. Furthermore, both customers and suppliers are becoming better at measuring performance, so that these mistakes are more easily detected. Customers are demanding "perfect orders," requiring a supply chain that is quick, precise, and provides a top-quality product and support every time. Despite the imposing challenges of this competitive environment, some organizations are thriving. Such firms have embraced these changes and have integrated quick response and flexibility into their culture and their operations. They are managing by paying attention to *time*. For example, the reduction of delivery times both in the marketplace and throughout the supply chain has earned such firms as Cisco, Dell, and, Toyota, reputations as "time-based competitors."

Entire industries have changed to reflect time-based capabilities. For instance, Johnson Controls can now receive a seat order release from Ford and deliver the order four hours later, starting from the raw materials stage. Another auto supplier producing stamped metal parts has reduced its finished goods inventory to two hours' worth of goods, yet is faced with a penalty of $10,000 per minute if it delivers late to its customer's assembly line.

A number of "buzzwords" have emerged to describe time-based capabilities: *throughput time reduction, delivery speed, fast cycle capability, quick response or resupply time, lead-time reduction,* and *time compression.* Unlike many management fads, however, time-based competition is here to stay because of its direct linkage to profits. The advantages achieved by time-based competitors enable them to grow faster and earn higher profits relative to other firms in their industry, increase market share through early introduction of new products, control overhead and inventory costs, and move to positions of industry leadership.

A number of firms, including Wal-Mart, Procter and Gamble, Flextronics, and Dell have significantly improved corporate performance, whether measured using return on assets, return on net assets, or return on sales as a result of their focus on cycle time. All of these firms were able to link corporate performance to several market factors. First, they were able to translate time into profits by satisfying their "impatient" customers. These customers are willing to pay a premium if they can get their goods and services very quickly. Customers will award their business to time-based competitors because doing so means that they too can reduce their inventory levels while saving time and money. In a well-managed integrated supply chain, the amount of inventory held throughout the chain decreases, such that inventory is now "flowing" between parties in the chain with only minor delays (as shown in Figure 1–1).

Organizations such as Bose, Black and Decker, Ford, and others have developed "dock-to-stock" delivery systems. Supplier deliveries of component parts that are made directly to the plant floor end up in finished products by the end of the day!

There is a secondary effect for companies that achieve time-based capabilities: reduction in delivery lead time translates not only into less inventory, but also into less re-work, higher product quality, and less overhead throughout the supply chain. Each of these improvements has a direct impact on financial performance. In many cases, these benefits are shared by all of the parties within a given supply chain.

Both internal and external benefits are associated with being a time-based competitor. The external effects refer to benefits enjoyed by time-based organizations in the marketplace relative to their competitors (higher quality, quicker customer response, and technologically advanced products). The internal benefits are found within and between the different functional areas in the firm. These include more effective processes, shorter planning periods, increased responsiveness, better communication, coordination, and cooperation between functions.

These capabilities become even more important when considered on a global scale. In order to sustain growth, many organizations must increase market share on a global basis. Simultaneously, these same organizations must vigorously defend their domestic market share from a host of world-class international competitors. To meet this challenge, managers are seeking ways to rapidly expand their global logistics and distribution networks in order to ship products to the customers who demand them in a dynamic and rapidly changing set of market channels. This requires strategic positioning of inventories so that the right products are available when customers (regardless of location) want them, in the right quantity and for the right price. This level of performance is a continuous challenge facing organizations and can occur only when all parties in a supply chain are operating on the "same page". The management of inventory in a supply chain is discussed in Chapter 2.

Supply Chain Relationships

This leads us to the second, and perhaps most challenging aspect of effective supply chain management shown in Figure 1–1: supply chain relationships. The concept of creating value for customers is relatively well understood and the processes associated with cycle time reduction have been successfully implemented and continue to evolve in many organizations. However, without a foundation of effective organizational relationships among supply chain member organizations, efforts to manage the flow of materials or information across the supply chain are likely to be unsuccessful.

Of the critical activities associated with supply chain management, relationship management is perhaps the most fragile and tenuous and is therefore the most susceptible to breakdown. A poor relationship at any link in the supply chain can have disastrous consequences for the entire supply chain. For example, an undependable source of parts can virtually cripple a plant, leading to inflated lead times, higher costs, and resultant problems across the supply chain—all the way to the final customer.

To avoid such problems, organizations must develop a better understanding of their processes, as well as of their suppliers' quality and delivery performance in order to find better ways to serve their customers. To ensure a solid working relationship, communication links with customers and suppliers must be established, maintained, and used regularly. Nevertheless, many organizations continue to view suppliers and customers as adversaries who are not to be trusted and with whom long-term relationships should be avoided. This approach is reflected in the practices of the procurement and logistics functions of many organizations. These functions often have no strategic role and are viewed as merely "buying" or "shipping" materials. In many cases, materials management is considered a separate activity and personnel have little or no communication with other internal functions, suppliers, or customers. Many of these individuals want to maintain the status quo, are protective of their "turf," and focus on individual transactions rather than on establishing and maintaining an on-going supply chain relationship. Performance measures in the organizations are very often efficiency-based and rely on metrics such as "purchase orders processed per buyer" or "dollars purchased per buyer," rather than on time-based or cost-based measures of overall supply chain effectiveness. Finally, most purchasing and logistics functions have a manufacturing and supply orientation, with almost no input into critical new-product design, pipeline inventory reduction, quality improvement, information systems, or process re-engineering initiatives. Buyers and logistics managers in many organizations choose suppliers and carriers on the basis of one criterion only—price. (Note that this criterion does not include other factors that account for the total cost but rather reflects only the bottom-line price, which includes both the supplier's/carrier's cost and profit.) As such, suppliers are often played against one another, are dropped on a moment's notice, and are chosen from a large pool on an order-by-order basis. Increasingly, organizations are attempting to develop closer relationships with their major customers and suppliers, and in some cases are going beyond the first tier to do so. Given the dependence of firms on supplier performance, some organizations are adopting strategies that can help foster improvement, including greater information sharing between parties and the development of "co-destiny" relationships. The latter refers to the commitment of the focal firm to using a single or dual source of supply over an extended period of time. In such cases, the focal firm makes a set of long-term strategic decisions focusing on improved supplier relationships.

Similarly, the evolution of "customer relationship management" (CRM) dictates that companies focus on a few major customers, offering them superior service and value. In many companies today the objective is to become a "preferred customer," that is, a customer allowed special insights into technology and access to materials in critical periods of shortages, etcetera. As the degree of trust between customers and suppliers in the supply chain develops, a smoother flow of both materials and information among the organizations within the supply chain occurs. The contrary scenario, observed often, is one in which the focal firm generally distrusts its suppliers, provides uncertain schedules, and maintains high levels of inventory to safeguard against the possibility of "non-performance." Similarly, a firm that attempts to provide the same level of service to all its customers may be suddenly surprised when customers with major accounts decide to go to a competitor. Such adversarial supply chain strategies do not consider the long term. Surprisingly, given the benefits observed from establishing closer relationships, many supply chain managers continue to adopt an adversarial, open market view of suppliers and customers.

A key element of improved customer-supplier relationships is the use of an objective performance measurement system which helps ensure that all parties operate according to expectations and are meeting stated objectives. In addition, parties must clearly establish objectives, expectations, and potential sources of conflict in order to facilitate communication and joint problem solving. As a result of this communication, trust between buyers and suppliers begins to grow, leading to further improvements.

Supply chain member organizations must recognize that power in a broad array of channels has shifted downstream toward the customer or end-user. As the customer "calls the shots" in the marketplace, the manufacturer and the intermediaries must be nimble and quick or face the prospect of losing market share. To effectively implement integrated supply chain management, however, a relationship based on mutual benefits and trust must exist. This means that downstream buyers must also be *"good customers."* Major customers must provide supply partners with the information they need to meet performance expectations.

The improvement of supply chain relationships occurs through a great deal of communication and problem-solving activities between organizations, including joint improvement projects, shared training programs, co-location of personnel, workshops presenting corporate plans, as well as meetings between the respective organizations' personnel at all levels of the organization from top management to hourly employees. Organizations also are beginning to hold regular meetings of supply chain councils, which include representatives from all major suppliers and customers in a supply chain. Such councils can provide supply chain management executives with insights regarding changes in policies, information systems and standards, and other suggestions that can remove costs from the supply chain and eliminate non-value-added activities.

As the frequency of communication between customers and suppliers increases, organizations often witness an expansion in the type of information that is shared. Managers and engineers from supplying organizations may be invited to customer facilities to address possible improvements in the supplying process. Firms may share different types of production and forecasting data, including product-level and part-level material requirements planning schedules. Companies may even share cost data in order to identify non-value-added cost drivers (such as re-work, scrap, excess inventory, etc.), which could be reduced through joint efforts.

In many American industries, true supply chain networks like those found in Japan may not develop as readily. American firms are often geographically distant, and do not have as many small suppliers as in Japan.

In the case of high-tech firms, many components may be sole-sourced to overseas suppliers who are proprietary owners of the required technology. In these environments, selecting a few suppliers becomes more important; the way is paved for informal interaction and information sharing that can foster time-based improvements.

Information Systems and Supply Chain Management

The final variable enabling companies to create integrated value systems is the evolution of information technology. In the early 1960s, when business computing first emerged, corporations such as IBM used mainframe computers that filled an entire room. With the development of the integrated circuit, computer size and cost decreased radically, while computer speed increased exponentially. Today, a laptop computer weighing five pounds exceeds the power of an old mainframe by several orders of magnitude.

In the early stages of linking supply chain member organizations, many adopted Electronic Data Interchange (EDI):

- Traditional EDI typically spans many different standards and often results in expensive "hard-coded" technology driven by the consumer goods industry; not all partners can or will participate.
- The EDI process is secure, but different versions of the software may result in transmission errors.

In working with one set of suppliers in a supply chain, we discovered that parties utilizing different versions of the software were comparing their EDI transmissions to faxed orders, and discovering discrepancies in order quantities. The reason? The different versions of software translators were manipulating the data packets, and essentially changing the requirements in the process! The result: inaccurate orders, wrong quantities shipped, and mass confusion. In the end, everyone went back to relying on faxes, with the funds invested in EDI essentially lost.

The "new" EDI is communicated over Virtual Private Networks (VPNs) via the Internet. This form of EDI is typically much less expensive, involves fewer standards issues, and generally requires a common platform on either end. Yet the new EDI still has to deal with tunneling protocols to address security issues.

With VPNs, industry standards are again important. The issue of emerging standards in the B2B era will be addressed later in this book. With the emergence of the personal computer, optical fiber networks, and the explosion of the Internet and the World Wide Web, the low cost and availability of information resources allows for easy linkages and eliminates information-related time delays in any supply chain network. This means that organizations are moving toward a concept known as *electronic commerce,* in which transactions are completed via a variety of electronic media. E-commerce does not refer to the Internet only; in reality, a variety of electronic media communicate information between companies, including EDI, electronic funds transfer (EFT), bar codes, fax, automated voice mail, CD-ROM catalogs, and Web portals. Leading-edge organizations no longer require paper purchase requisitions, purchase orders, invoices, receiving forms, or a manual accounts payable "matching" process. All required information is recorded electronically, and associated transactions are performed with a minimum amount of human intervention. Recent developments in database applications allow part numbers to be accumulated, coded, and stored in databases, and electronically ordered. This means that with the application of the appropriate information systems, the need to constantly monitor inventory levels, place orders, and expedite orders will soon be a thing of the past. A lot of tools exist that can make this happen. However, businesses need to understand the impact these tools will have and be willing to re-engineer their business processes.

The proliferation of new telecommunications and computer technology also has made real-time, online communications throughout the supply chain a reality. These systems are now being linked between suppliers, manufacturers, distributors, retail outlets, and ultimately, customers, regardless of location. These technologies are supply chain "enablers." They can substantially reduce paperwork, improve communication, and reduce lead-time and non-value-added activities if properly implemented.

Managers developing information systems should not visualize information as a set of repetitive transactions between entities such as buyers and suppliers, or distributors and retailers. Rather, an ideal system should span all functions and organizations throughout the supply chain.

The ideal supply chain information system is shown in Figure 1–1 (information flows between organizations are indicated by the dotted arrows). Note that information is available to any party within the chain. Note also the number of feedback loops defining a totally integrated system. These linkages are critical, as they allow just-in-time (JIT) deliveries to occur between every linkage in the chain, inventories to be minimized, and entities to respond to fluctuations in a timely and effective manner. Point-of-sale data is transferred immediately throughout the supply chain, allowing managers to spot trends, plan capacity requirements, allocate materials, and notify suppliers throughout the chain. The information flows also permit inter-organization payments for goods and services through electronic fund transfers, which ensures quick payment for supply chain members. With all these elements in place, supply chain members have access to the information that they need, when they need it, allowing for improved decision-making, and quicker action. Although some would claim that this vision of the future is imminent, in reality changes are happening in gradual stages. One of the real benefits of the Internet was that it eliminated many of the difficulties associated with traditional B2B transactions. Early applications of the Internet to B2B e-commerce included the development of VPNs. Today, the Internet is used largely for viewing and entering data. However, the set of applications that lies in the future goes far beyond this approach. The Internet is becoming a more interactive tool that enables applications to not only view, but also to make active use of data. As this transition occurs, business systems will evolve from supplier-centric to customer-centric systems. We can think of four stages of progression toward increased integration of buyers and suppliers via B2B electronic commerce: 1) Web presence; 2) e-commerce; 3) data delivery; and 4) automation. The first two stages are supplier-centric; the second two are customer-centric.[3]

Web Presence—Today's Internet is largely a supplier-centric computing environment. The World Wide Web allows suppliers to create a Web presence for providing product and service information directly to their customers. This phenomenon, a form of dis-intermediation, adds value by enabling businesses to communicate directly with customers in addition to such established channels of communication as sales and marketing or customer service (see Figure 1–2). For example, a customer can go directly to a computer software vendor to download the latest version of a program or to view "Frequently Asked Questions" (FAQs) about the product with no human intervention. The Web server is usually outside the company's firewall, and is not linked with any existing business systems. Many businesses establish this type of Web presence through an Internet Service Provider (ISP).

E-Commerce—Stage 2 entails a higher level of integration than Stage 1. On the World Wide Web today, suppliers go beyond electronic brochures describing their products, services, and company information. Suppliers offer e-commerce services that allow their customers to place orders directly with them by linking to an internal line of business systems (Figure 1–3). An example is Barnesandnoble.com, which uses a Web presence for e-commerce that ties into its pre-existing fulfillment systems supporting their catalog sales. We

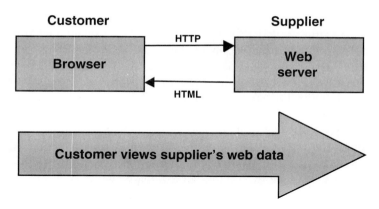

Figure 1–2 Stage 1 - Web Presence (Supplier-Centric)

also have seen the rise of a new set of middlemen who consolidate information made available from a number of external Web sources to provide a single consolidated supplier-information site for their customers. If Stage 1 was the stage of dis-intermediation, this is the stage of re-intermediation (a new intermediary is involved in the supply chain). An example of re-intermediation is Travelocity.com, a travel site that incorporates information from other Web sources to provide its travel customers services such as airline tickets, hotel room, and rental car reservations.

Stages 1 and 2 are supplier-centric models. In supplier-centric computing, customers go to suppliers to get one-size-fits-all data. All customers receive the same data (no personalization). There are still many suppliers without a Web presence today. We will continue to see explosive growth in Stages 1 and

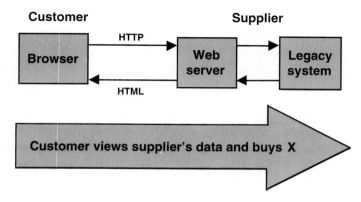

Figure 1–3 Stage 2 - E-commerce (Supplier-Centric)

2, since these models provide new ways for suppliers to advertise, market, and sell their products and services.

Data Delivery—For tomorrow's Internet, we will see a significant transition to customer-centric computing. Customer-centric computing is about the shift from customers using their browser to obtain data from their suppliers, to suppliers enabling their customers by delivering personalized data directly to them. Suppliers will begin to deliver data that can be integrated into their customers' and suppliers' business systems (see Figure 1–4). For example, the supplier might supply a component that automatically updates the customer's system whenever an order status changes. Having this data delivered allows the customer to take the necessary steps to deal with issues like inventory shortages or missed delivery windows.

The major difference between supplier-centric and customer-centric computing is that in the former case, if you want information, you must go looking for it. In customer-centric computing, data is shipped to you to make your job easier, and is transported directly from multiple sources into your organization's business applications. The advantage of data delivery is that it helps to improve a customer's decision support capability. For example, customers can check inventory to determine whether they will be able to fill a sales order on time. The ability to order data across multiple systems and suppliers means available inventory is not limited to what the customer's business system says is available in the warehouse. Stage 3 combines information from both internal and external business systems. It also initiates a radically different relationship between suppliers and customers—one in which suppliers compete

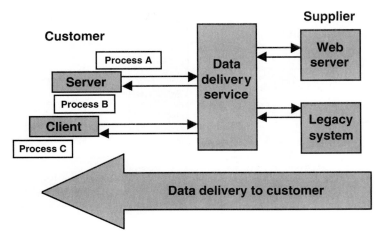

Figure 1–4   Stage 3 - DataDelivery (Customer-Centric)

on the basis of how effectively they can integrate their information systems with that of their customers and suppliers to create a positive service experience. Suppliers win orders by not only accelerating, automating, and optimizing their own business systems and decision-making environments, but also by delivering information that helps customers and suppliers accelerate, automate, and optimize their decision-making.

Automated   Inter-Business   Processes   (Machine-to-Machine M2M)—In Stage 4 (Figure 1–5), process integration between the decision-making systems of businesses, their suppliers, and their customers becomes bi-directional and tightly integrated. This is sometimes referred to as M2M—machine-to-machine integration. Supply chain members can interact dynamically and can initiate business processes within each other's information systems by pre-defining business rules that trigger events across systems. This means that physical supply chains can become at least partially automated. For example, when an order comes to a supplier, orders to the supplier's suppliers to replace committed stock are automatically generated causing a ripple effect through the supply chain. Less human intervention is required at each step as inter-business processes become more automated and rules-based.

As this stage evolves, customers and suppliers are able to make more intelligent business decisions. For example, if one supplier's price drops below that of other suppliers, the customer's application might automatically move that supplier up in the "supplier of choice" list based on the business rules engine. The customer consulting the "supplier of choice" list before ordering would see the supplier at the top of the list and place an order with that

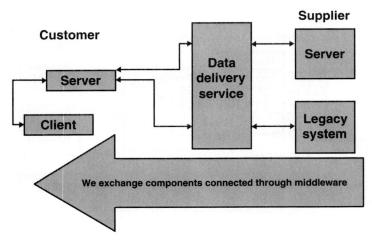

Figure 1–5   Stage 4 - Automated Inter-Business Processes

supplier. Other applications of automation of decision-making processes between businesses would also occur. For example, a supplier application sends a customer application a component that includes pricing information and services that let that customers automatically place orders. If the supplier's price drops to a level designated in the business rules, it triggers the customer's inventory control system to start ordering stock (without human intervention) from that supplier, rather than from the competition (this is, in effect, automated supplier selection). Another potential application is dynamic pricing; price to the customer on the web is based on the price of the raw material. If the raw material price goes down, so does the price of the finished item. The key value of Stage 4 is rich connections which convey more than information between businesses. The rapid two-way flow of information accelerates the business cycle, enables just-in-time delivery, reduces transaction costs, and streamlines the flow of materials through the supply chain.

To summarize, the e-business transition of today's supplier-centric data-view environment to a customer-centric environment is one in which suppliers:

- Use the universal communications medium of the Internet to tightly link their business information systems.
- Win customer loyalty and increase the value of their supply chain by using their own information systems and technology to increase their customers' and suppliers' decision-making effectiveness.

Customer-centric e-business suppliers will compete not only on the price and quality of their products and services, but also on the quality of their information services and e-business links. Suppliers who operate within intelligent supply chains will be able to reduce inventory, be more responsive, and improve customer service.

Although these Internet capabilities may materialize, it is not clear that organizations will be prepared to exploit them. Many companies' lack the fundamental supply chain infrastructure required to apply these technologies across multiple tiers of customers and suppliers. To learn to crawl before learning to walk and then run, organizations must address the flaws in their existing supply chains and *only then* build these B2B applications around these re-engineered networks. There is also a "trust" factor; sharing critical data between functions and partners requires a fundamental change in organizational culture. A Web-based application cannot fix the problems associated with a large and poorly performing supply base, a fragmented logistics and distribution network, adversarial relationships with key supply chain members, and an unwillingness to share information owing to a lack of trust. In order to succeed in the value system world, organizations must be willing to share risks and rewards, and to build the underlying infrastructure to apply B2B software tools.

This is easy to say, yet difficult to accomplish. Let's take a look at a step-by-step roadmap for developing a supply chain infrastructure.

A Process Model:
SCM for Value System Creation

Figure 1–6 shows the process model around which this book is written. The process model represents a series of activities and strategies that must be implemented in order to successfully create integrated value systems. The numbers in the arrows correspond to the chapters that are dedicated to each respective set of activities and strategies.

Process Mapping—The first step involves optimizing the coordination between business functions. Purchasing, operations, and distribution must have aligned business strategies, common performance metrics, and an understanding of where the organization is going. Basic processes (order fulfillment, sourcing strategies, logistics flows) must be analyzed and improved. The total business across all global units should be documented, with established commodity strategies in place for all major purchases. In addition, the fundamental network structure of suppliers and customers must be optimized (in most cases through supply base/customer base reduction). This requires that managers understand with whom they are doing business, and in some cases, requires going beyond the first tier of the supply chain network.

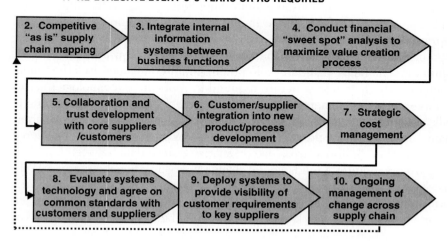

Figure 1–6   Integrated Value Chain Creation – Process Roadmap (Numbers Correspond to Chapters in Book)

Although most companies believe they are well beyond this level of integration, we are prepared to challenge this assumption. Our personal experience in consulting and research has revealed that many highly regarded companies still have a lot of work to do in this regard. The good news is that this activity can provide significant benefits: better value creation and cost savings. Many of the projects in which we have engaged companies through our faculty/student projects have helped provide the fundamental stepping-stones for building a supply chain infrastructure.

Given the number of initiatives on most managers' plates, it is difficult to find the resources to assign personnel to carry out this painstaking and detailed type of analysis. However, the time taken to understand the "as is" status of your business processes is the critical starting point for effective value system creation. Chapter 2 provides detailed information on how to carry out supply chain mapping.

Internal Integration Between Business Functions

In this phase of integration, organizations must focus on ensuring internal integration among their functional areas. Enterprise resource planning (ERP) systems are integrated business transaction processing and reporting systems that many companies have implemented in recent years. ERP software applications support the re-engineering of business processes and form the foundation for an integrated organizational value system. A basic definition of ERP is a system that tracks transactions that, in turn, trigger business processes involving organizational resources (people, materials, and technology).

Understanding the resources consumed allows an organization to leverage these resources more productively and, in theory, achieve a competitive advantage. ERP systems serve as the organization's "backbone," providing fundamental decision-making support. ERP systems add a "process logic" to an organizational information system and create a fundamental discipline in business processes. In the past, managers in one functional area often made decisions independent of other functional areas but ERP systems provide decision-makers with a unified view of the organization and effectively force people to interact in a single system, even if they would prefer not to! ERP systems help integrate the areas of customer order management, manufacturing planning and execution, purchasing, and financial management and accounting. ERP systems enable people in these very different parts of the business to communicate and share information with one another.

The new ERP holds the promise of being able to effectively link the organization's functions and key business processes together. ERP systems are integrated business transaction processing and reporting systems designed to look at business transactions from a process rather than a functional view. When they were first developed, ERP systems held the promise of being able to sit "on top" of legacy systems, or alternatively, data from legacy systems were migrated over to ERP databases. Extracting data from the legacy systems and making it available in a desired format to all people in all functional areas increased visibility to transactional data throughout the business.

The problem of disparate systems being used by different functional groups and business units is an on-going problem. One company we worked with comes immediately to mind. As with many organizations, this company had grown through acquisitions, and had many global locations with disparate software systems, databases, and decentralized buying activities. The company may have had the same supplier supplying different locations, yet was unable to leverage these purchases owing to a lack of data. An important step for this company would be to "scrub" its data, and apply data warehouses to consolidate purchase data to enable better coordination between the units. This should lead to an optimization of the supply base considering the total cost of supplying key commodities to different locations using a combination of local and international suppliers. Similarly, this company's distribution network should be configured to optimize inventories, spare parts, commonality in product designs, and improved coordination between sales and distribution units within the global organization. A detailed discussion of internal integration systems across business functions is provided in Chapter 3.

Collaboration with Suppliers and Customers

In the next stage of evolution, a company must change the nature of its alignment and collaboration not only with first-tier customers and suppliers, but throughout its supply chain. In the future, the best supply chains will win and managers must be aware of the actions and requirements for critical customers and suppliers in the network. Accessing this information is difficult unless the scope and nature of relationships with key supply chain member organizations is established and maintained. This is not to say that every relationship should (or can) be a "long-term strategic alliance." However, the relative importance of the supplier/customer on value and overall supply chain performance should be determined. This assessment should be a primary determinate of the type of organizational relationship that should be pursued for the organization in question. This means that one should have a basic understanding of the performance metrics for the key supply chain member, based on technology, potential for growth, and profitability. It means that the performance of key suppliers in terms of quality, delivery, and technology should be described in financial terms that directly relate bottom-line impact. It also means that key supply chain partners should be aligned with your organization's internal strategies in order to exploit their expertise and knowledge in creating value. Finally, collaborative sharing of forecasting and demand information can better help plan long-term capacity, inventory, and human resource requirements. In Chapter 4, we detail the financial realities of supply chains, and address how companies can discover the financial "sweet spot" within their supply chain to produce the highest returns given their intellectual and physical assets. In Chapter 5, we discuss the core processes required to create and manage critical supply chain relationships, by developing trust between individuals and organizations, and creating the basis for agreement on sharing information via collaborative means. Until such fundamental issues as trust and information sharing are resolved with key suppliers and customers, no B2B technology is likely to ever have any significant impact on business processes.

Once these stepping-stones have been put in place, a number of opportunities arise for creating greater value. One of these is in the collaborative design and development of new products in the supply chain, a topic discussed in Chapter 6. The reality in many markets today is that 40 percent or more of revenues are from new products introduced in the previous year. Thus, unless supply chain members can create a continuous stream of fresh and innovative technologies and products, customers take their business elsewhere.

In addition to creating new products, collaboration between supply chain participants also affects another critical element in the value equation: cost. The area of strategic cost management is addressed in Chapter 7. Cost management again involves taking a supply chain-wide perspective on costs and working in a collaborative manner with supply chain partners to reduce costs without damaging required profits and rates of returns for key stakeholders in the supply chain. By working collaboratively, supply chain members can reduce costs of doing business, providing a means to improve profitability and/or to pass on the savings to end customers, and benefit from higher market share. Here again, we believe that collaborative activities between supply chain members in assessing core competencies, developing new products, and managing costs represents a fundamental opportunity for improvement.

B2B Integration: The Final Step.

The final stage of deployment involves a full commitment to deploying B2B applications across the supply chain structure. Based on our research, we believe that jumping into B2B applications, before fully understanding the nature of the supply markets, customer needs, technology roadmaps, cost drivers, and internal business functional processes is a MAJOR MISTAKE. Although many organizations jump into this technology blindly, there is a sound set of reasons for not taking this course of action.

A primary factor that companies should understand in the B2B environment is their relative positioning vis-à-vis business requirements (see Figure 1–7). Although there are many advocates of exchanges, as well as "end-to-end applications" provided by multiple software vendors, we argue that businesses also

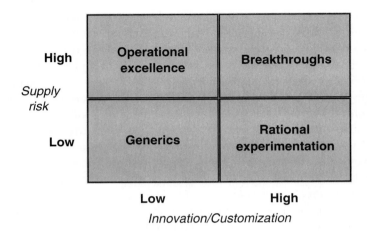

Figure 1–7   Structuring B2B Applications Around Supply Chain Structures

need to understand the basic nature of the types of products and services being managed in the supply chain. The framework we present here is broad enough to apply to almost any organization and provides a set of actionable guidelines.

Generics are common commodities that have little technological risk and little to no supply risk (Figure 1–7). These are usually good candidates for public marketplaces. Many suppliers can produce these items. The supply and distribution strategies often will involve greater standardization and coordination across business units to leverage spend and reduce the cost of acquisition. Such systems can optimally be sourced through online forward or reverse auctions–in which a community of many buyers and sellers comes together. Third-party logistic providers who ensure that the products get to the right people can manage these auctions. Industry-specific independent exchanges such as Covisint, Pantellos, and AeroExchange are examples of such exchanges. Allowing users to directly order these requirements reduces the total delivery cost. Typically these are private marketplaces and everyone is not allowed to enter. Examples of commodities that may fall into this category include office products, temporary services, corrugated packaging, electrical components, bulk chemicals, etc. These types of products are entirely suitable for exchanges where multiple buyers and sellers can operate.

A second category (rational experimentation) involves highly customized products/services that may have a high technology content, yet many potential suppliers. The primary goal in such cases is to expand the role of innovation to ensure that a broader universe of qualified suppliers can provide potential solutions. Price is not the issue, so an auction is not appropriate. The real challenge is to create a forum in which the performance and design specifications can be communicated to as many qualified organizations as possible in an interactive manner and to obtain input into alternative designs that are creative and technologically superior. Because the sourcing decision may change on these types of purchases, committing to a single source and establishing an expensive set of customized systems linkages is not appropriate. Examples of such purchases are programming services, certain types of electronics, engines, pumps, certain construction materials, customized RAM's, and uniforms. In the future, this category may include utility services such as electricity.

Some companies, such as Ford, use e-steel to source stampings. This is a company-specific exchange set up for its suppliers. Ford purchases steel on behalf of all its stampers, and uses the e-steel site to facilitate this exchange. The potential payoff? Lower administrative costs, plus better matching of suppliers with product specifications, less inventory, reduced complexity, and increased product velocity in the supply chain.

In certain markets, the product or service may be an industry standard with little customization, yet relatively few suppliers (operations excellence). If possible, buyers will want to develop preferred suppliers who can execute orders quickly. The primary cost drivers may often be the logistics costs, not the product piece price. By automating the purchasing process, supply chain specialists can free up their time to focus on critical items, letting users order directly from the provider. Note that only qualified suppliers must be allowed to supply users through these mechanisms. Examples might include aircraft and vehicle components, steel, transformers, specialty chemicals, and so on.

The final set of products and services that should be considered include those items with a high technological or customized requirement, and relatively few suppliers (breakthroughs). Supply chain strategies for these types of items should seek qualified suppliers and initiate strategic alliances with defined metrics, collaboration on design and order fulfillment, process improvement, supplier development, and on going sharing of risk and rewards. A variety of B2B applications may be appropriate with these strategic partners. For example, online customer/supplier suggestions programs, shared cost systems, and technology roadmaps can help ensure improved communication on multiple levels between the companies from both a business and a technical perspective. Companies also are exploring dedicated systems that may provide a joint awareness of engineering changes, design shifts, and end-of-life strategies. Examples include contract manufacturing, product and process design, construction, maintenance services, and third-party logistics.

The following illustrate potential best cases, as well as abuses, of B2B applications.

The first is a negative result. An automotive company, jumping on the exchange bandwagon, decided to purchase tires through an online auction, thereby getting major price reductions. This was an inappropriate application for an online auction: the product was highly engineered and has a major impact on noise, vehicle performance, and most importantly, vehicle safety. Five tire manufacturers participated–at the end of 12 hours, they were still bidding! The market tension in this case was very different. The supplier also was supplying the product at a price that was below their cost of manufacture. Were shortcuts taken? Perhaps. However, if squeezing prices is the most significant result of trade exchanges, then they have fallen short of their potential. They should ideally represent a "win" for all parties involved, and drive systemic costs out of the supply chain.

A positive case is also worth mentioning. SMTC is a Canadian-based producer of PC boards that supports a wide variety of customers, including Dell, IBM, Compaq, and others. SMTC, along with other suppliers in the electronics industry, is facing an increasing number of supply chain challenges, including short product lifecycles, constant new product introduction, continuous engineering changes, demand volatility, demand for greater product variety, increasing levels of customer service, and high volatility in component prices and availability.

One of SMTC's largest customers, Dell Computer, developed the business model to sell computers on the web. When they place their orders via Dell's Website, customers can configure their computers to include different types of monitors, modems, CD-ROMs or DVDs, memory, and microprocessors. Once the customer places the order and pays for the computer, Dell orders the specific components from its suppliers, performs the final assembly and tests the product (in a few hours) once supplier shipments arrive. In essence, Dell carries no inventory and does not order it until it has the customer's payment. This approach provides Dell with superior Return-on-Assets performance. Many other large computer manufacturers and even automotive manufacturers are seeking to mimic the Dell model.

SMTC produces PC boards, and is responsible for improving supply chain performance, managing supply problems associated with components, developing collaborative forecasts for their suppliers, and dealing with the impact of orders changed on short notice. Meanwhile, customers such as Dell seek to reduce inventory, expediting, and order-to-delivery cycle with improved customer service. This means that each of SMTC's eight manufacturing sites also must meet these same objectives and require their suppliers to do the same. In fact, Dell requires SMTC to carry 150 percent of its inventory requirements at all times to ensure availability. Dell requires this of all its suppliers.

With a complex supply chain consisting of more than 50 customers and 700 suppliers, SMTC decided to create an e-supply chain hub that would provide greater visibility to their supply chain planning system and improved communication with its suppliers. At the time, SMTC was one of the few Dell suppliers to develop such a site. One major supplier connected to the hub was Philips Electronics, a supplier of microchips to SMTC.

Early in 1999, due to market conditions, Philips managers warned SMTC that a chip shortage was imminent. Philips advised SMTC that they should increase their inventory of chips to avoid possible shortages. SMTC informed Dell of this situation and let Dell know that they should increase inventory and plan for possible shortages of certain types of PC boards. Managers at Dell were skeptical. The company checked with other suppliers and was told that there would be no problem in obtaining microchips. Five days later, the shortage occurred as SMTC and Philips had predicted. Although SMTC was able to meet Dell's requirements during this period due to their foresight in increasing inventory of microchips, several other Dell suppliers were caught by surprise and were unable to meet their order commitments.

As a result of this event and of SMTC's innovations, Dell decided to reward SMTC with more business. Following this event, SMTC increased its customer satisfaction ratings with Dell, increased its business with Dell fivefold, and increased revenues from $200 million to $1.2 billion. Today, Dell considers SMTC one of its best suppliers, along with Philips Electronics. By moving quickly to establish a B2B Web-based presence and by collaborating with its partners in the supply chain, SMTC has become a major player in the electronics supply chain.[4]

What lies in store for the future? Although it is difficult to predict what evolving future systems will look like, we can make a few observations based on current events. First, an effective understanding of the business processes and information standards that enable buyer-to-seller communication to occur is critical. Chapter 8 deals with navigating one's way through the standards, emerging markets and exchanges, and new technologies that lie in the B2B landscape.

Second, Internet-based supply chain-enabling information systems and technology is a reality today, but significant work will be required for effective deployment. There is no question that companies who adapt early can help drive the agenda yet they need to do so in a manner that considers the design of the supply chain, and in some cases, the redesign of these chains. The Internet also has given us a communication platform from which a multi-tiered supply chain should be able to operate. However, to-date, real-time collaboration has been largely limited to "one-on-one" communication between supply chain members. Batch mode applications allow for one buyer to disseminate information to multiple suppliers, but the promise of the Internet does not lie in a time-delayed background batch process. The end goal must be to increase efficiency throughout the supply chain by allowing one buyer to collaborate with many suppliers or many buyers to collaborate with many suppliers to simultaneously share information—enabling real-time collaboration. This means providing an Internet-accessible, real-time forum where buyers and their suppliers can communicate and share inventory and forecasting information, and allow for the effective dissemination of engineering change orders (ECOs) throughout the supply chain. The nature of the changes that must take place to exploit the potential of B2B e-commerce with supply chain partners is explored in Chapter 9. We discuss how organizations can fine-tune their supply chain processes by enabling their suppliers to develop manufacturing schedules that will best meet just-in-time demands, and also minimize inventory holdings. The architecture of such a system should be easily deployable via the Web and should provide capabilities that support collaborative planning and forecasting, visibility to end customer build schedules, real-time updates, capacity and inventory planning, and standard Purchase Order/Accounts Payable transaction information. The real potential of such systems can be enhanced through a visual supply chain map with wireless and browser graphic interfaces that can be easily configured to changing supply chain conditions.

Change Management: The Challenge Facing Supply Chain Managers

Although the topic of integrated supply chain management appeals to many practitioners, consultants, and academics, the difficulty involved in implementing this strategy is evident. The integrated management of information and materials across the supply chain offers the benefits of increasing the value-added by supply chain members, removing waste, reducing cost, and improving customer satisfaction. However, deploying and managing this strategy is a challenging and significant endeavor.

In many cases, problems occur in the implementation of information systems so that the appropriate information is not readily available to the people who need it. In other cases, the information is available but supply chain members are reluctant to share it, due to their lack of trust and their fear that the information will be revealed to competitors.

Inventory management from a supply chain perspective is no less difficult. Although inventory systems are continuously improving, the need to expedite late shipments never seems to disappear. There are always delays in shipments for a variety of reasons. Slowdowns resulting from customs when crossing international borders, adverse weather conditions, poor communication, and, of course, simple human error are inevitable. With the double-edged sword of lower inventory levels and increasing demand for improvements in fill rates and on-time delivery performance, managing inventory throughout a supply chain becomes increasingly complex and demanding. Finally, establishing trust between parties in a supply chain is perhaps the greatest challenge. Legal staffs may produce "airtight" contractual agreements that fail to include mechanisms for addressing the inevitable conflicts short of legal action. This can result in a situation where an organization may win the legal battle at a future point in time but be eliminated from the marketplace in the interim. Conflict management in inter-organizational relationships is becoming an increasingly difficult task. The fragile bond of trust, once broken, becomes extremely difficult to repair and some supply chain relationships eventually break under the strain.

The authors have worked with companies that have attempted to implement significant change within their supply chains. Many organizations struggle to complete even one link in the chain. The challenge of integrating information requirements and inventory flows across multiple tiers of suppliers and customers proves immense. To provide additional insights about how these strategies are being deployed, we have included case examples throughout the book that illustrate how to succeed. The cases were developed through in-depth interviews with leading-edge firms implementing integrated supply chain management. In some of the cases, the names of the firms are disguised to avoid confidentiality problems. These cases are instrumental in illustrating the concepts described in the earlier chapters and provide a template to guide managers and students. Change will come in many forms. The critical success factors for the B2B world will require: 1) a solid global supply chain organization; 2) appropriate levels of integration and standardization; and 3) executive support of these initiatives. Implementing these systems may require additional training and cultural changes on the part of suppliers, customers, and internal functions.

In Chapter 10, we discuss the change management experience of a major Fortune 500 company, General Motors, and discuss the "lessons learned" from this company. We also provide a brief overview in this chapter of what the future holds for supply chain management.

However, let's begin with the first step: mapping out what your supply chain looks like!

Endnotes

[1]Fictional name.

[2]*World Class Logistics: The Challenge of Managing Continuous Change*, prepared by The Global Logistics Research Team, Michigan State University (Oak Brook, IL: Council of Logistics Management, 1995).

[3]George Moakley, "eCommerce Requires Intelligent Supply Chains," *Achieving Supply Chain Excellence Through Technology*, pp. 188–190, Anderson Consulting, 1999.

[4]Source: Dan Russell, Strategic Technologies, presentation at North Carolina State University, March 2000.

2

Understanding and Improving Supply Chains and Key Supply Chain Processes

SlurryTech's[1] Order Fulfillment Process

SlurryTech (ST) is a young company started four years ago by six people who put together the technology and the equipment for a new chemical mechanical planarization process. The process was introduced to a single customer which subsequently worked with SlurryTech to help bring the product to market. Once the ST team convinced the customer to adopt the technology, it was able to convince others to do so as well. ST developed a silicon-based slurry that allows the different planes of a microchip to be planed flat between layers, and thereby improve the performance capabilities of chips, improve yields, and reduce their size. Because of its rapid growth, the same marketing mentality of "just get the customer's business and don't worry about the production and logistics details" pervades the thinking of many people in the company. In some respects, the company is still a make-to-order small batch manufacturer that reacts to each order using jump-through-hoops technology to make it happen.

An important challenge facing SlurryTech is to identify their goals and vision as their customer base and market grows. Although the company has $160 million in sales today, it is projected to be a $1 billion company in three years. In effect, ST's supply chain challenge is: how can a high-tech company with demanding customers operate in a commodity-based supply chain with low levels of performance in raw material production, warehousing, packaging, and transportation? This challenge is a function of the constraints in the operating environment ST now finds itself in.

First, ST's roots are with its parent company that produces commodity-type chemicals. The parent is a typical large-volume chemical manufacturer with "loose" production specifications and capabilities. The parent also happens to be ST's only source of fumed silica, the primary raw material used in its slurries. ST was spun off from its parent in April 2000 due to its growth. This required a fundamental shift in organizational culture: the parent company is in many ways a commodity-driven organization in a high volume industry, driven to reduce price, where quality is often not the order-winning criteria. ST, on the other hand, is faced with a zero tolerance quality requirement, and must deal with its parent company as the primary supplier of silica. Furthermore, 95 percent of ST's requirements from its parent company come from a single plant.

A second related problem is that ST's customers are extremely demanding, and have grown used to dictating what they want from them as a supplier. There is very little co-development or integration of ST's R&D personnel into their customers' new product development processes. To some extent, this is due to the "copy exactly" mentality that has filtered through much of the semi-conductor industry. One of the outcomes of this approach is that any change to the process, including switching of suppliers, requires a full re-qualification, which may take up to 120 days to complete.

Finally, because of their rapid growth, ST has developed an internal production and order-fulfillment system that was never properly designed from start to finish. The system essentially grew in an ad hoc manner as capacity was rapidly added and people were hired without a formal training program or consideration of interdependencies between the stages of production. A full 70 percent of non-conforming orders are non-product related, and of these, 50 percent are in the area of documentation accompanying the shipment.

In response to these problems, ST formed the "Order Fullfillment Team." The need for the order fulfillment team stemmed from a review of non-product complaints for 1999 and 2000. Results of Pareto analysis suggests that in 1999, approximately 82 percent of errors were caused by incorrect inputs and miscommunication between different stages in the process (customer service, quality, production/filling, and shipping). In 2000, data suggest that 60 percent of the incidents resulted from these causes. Although this number is down from previous years, this may be due to the large number of errors attributable to other sources during this same period. Analysis revealed more than half the errors could be avoidable with the right process in place.

The team used the following approach to address the problem:

- Develop detailed process map of existing process
- Develop the "should be" process based on input and discussion
- Define policy guidelines for acceptance of "emergency" customer requests in less than two week leadtimes
- Design contingency planning scenarios for process breakdowns
- Conduct scenario / "what if" analysis using simulation package
- Identify constraints – to help define the future system and implementation of enterprise resource planning system
- Define key criteria for future system
- Define requirements for web-based linkages to customers and suppliers in future supply chain
- Determine and provide potential solutions for constraints imposed by customers (e.g. "copy exactly")

Recommendations

Following this process, the team came up with the following recommendations:

Should be process:

- Customer places order via fax, phone or email
- Review the order via checklist (packaging, quality, pricing, lead-time)
- Enter the order into the system
  - Review default notes
  - Order available for review by appropriate internal personnel
  - Print acknowledgement and fax and mail to customer

Major changes

- Re-define standards and create new order entry template with specific sections for sales, logistics, production, R&D, quality, and shipping
- Create a set of "default standards" that automatically generates defaults for all of the above areas
- Fax details to shipping and quality and integrate with production
- Recommend to customers how to ship the product (e.g., this is how we label and package our product for you). Have manufacturing and quality review these standards prior to implementation
- Picklist re-designed to include information for each area. This means that the requirements for each area must be re-designed as well to use common language that everyone will understand
- Integrate forecasts from the customer by part number and size on a weekly basis. Although this will always be a make-to-order system, improved forecasting is still important for capacity planning and scheduling of orders within the system
- Create a liaison in R&D to understand the timing of future requirements as they work with customers and communicate regarding timing of new products

The team's efforts were rewarded. In January 2001, non-compliant product errors were reduced to less than one percent of all shipments. The team was able to effectively identify the problems, and by working together across functions, identify an approach that would eliminate the root causes. As SlurryTech continues to grow, the learning that took place on this initiative will be applied to many other areas of the company.

Introduction

To survive, many organizations today must increase market share on a global basis in order to sustain growth objectives. Simultaneously, these same organizations must vigorously defend their domestic market share from a host of "world-class" international competitors. To meet this challenge, managers are seeking ways to rapidly expand their global logistics and distribution networks, in order to ship products to the customers who demand them in a dynamic and rapidly changing set of market channels. This requires the strategic positioning of inventories so that products are available when customers want them, in the right quantity and for the right price. This level of performance is

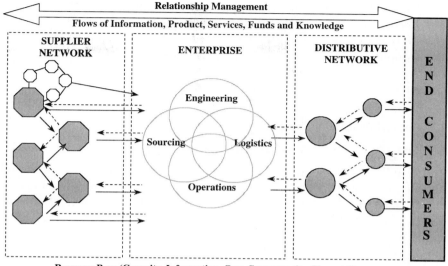

Figure 2-1 The Integrated Supply Chain

a continuous challenge, and can occur only when all parties in a supply chain are on the same "wavelength".

Corporate executives and academics alike have in recent years recognized the importance of effectively managing the flow of materials across the supply chain to achieve global growth objectives and generate financial returns (see Figure 2–1). The cost associated with this flow of materials has particularly interested these executives. Industry experts estimate not only that total supply chain costs represent the majority share of operating expenses for most organizations but also that, in some industries, these costs approach 75 percent of the total operating budget.[2] In a 1995 article in *IIE Solutions*, H. Donald Ratliff writes, "According to the U.S. Department of Commerce, companies are spending more than $600 billion annually on logistics-related services and activities."[3] One main promise that supply chain management holds is the opportunity to improve this flow of materials across the supply chain from the perspective of the end user, while reducing supply chain costs.

Establishing integrated supply chains that provide end customers and supply chain member organizations with the materials required, in the proper quantities, in the desired form, with the appropriate documentation, at the desired location, at the right time, and at the lowest possible cost lies at the heart of supply chain management. As organizations attempt to create and manage these integrated supply chains, several key issues need to be addressed, including:

- Understanding existing supply chains and mapping the network
- Recognizing the critical role of cycle time in the supply chain
- Re-engineering supply chain logistics
- Establishing a performance measurement system for the supply chain

Each of these issues is addressed in this chapter.

Understanding Supply Chains through Process Mapping

Adopting and implementing a value system requires considerable effort and represents a quantum change in direction for many organizations. Prior to embarking into the promising, but largely uncharted, world of SCM, organizations must have a detailed understanding of current supply chains and associated processes. This understanding will serve the organization well in its efforts to determine the relative importance of its various supply chains and to identify those processes most in need of improvement. In this section, we describe several tools and techniques managers employ to fully understand their organizations' supply chains.

Multiple Supply Chains

Most organizations are simultaneously members of multiple supply chains. Organizations typically offer a number of products and services, purchase materials from a wide range of suppliers, and sell to multiple customers. From the perspective of a typical organization, each of its supply chains has both internal and external linkages. However, it is unlikely that all of the organization's supply chains will be part of formal inter-organizational SCM initiatives. An organization must, therefore, focus its SCM efforts on those supply chains most critical to the organization's success. By critical, we mean those supply chains, related processes, suppliers, and customers that offer the greatest potential for achieving a competitive advantage and that, therefore, hold the greatest promise for the organization's ongoing success. In discussing supply chains, we will first discuss basic process mapping issues then differentiate between internal and external supply chains.

Process Mapping

Process mapping is a fundamental tool for understanding supply chains. A process is defined as "a logical series of related transactions that converts input to results or output." A business process is "a chain of logical connected repetitive activities that utilizes the enterprise's resources to refine or transform an object (physical or mental) for the purpose of achieving *specified and measurable results or output* for internal or external customers."[4]

All business processes have a customer, either internal or external to the company. Examples of common business processes include:

- New product development
- New customer identification
- Procurement
- Inbound logistics
- Production planning and control
- Manufacturing and assembly
- Sales
- Customer order processing
- Outbound logistics
- Customer service and after-sales support
- Product research and development

Improving business processes is at the very core of supply chain management. For one thing, the performance level of most processes tends to decrease over time, unless forces are exerted to maintain it. In addition, if an organization does not improve its business processes, its competitors surely will. Finally, today's customers are becoming more and more demanding. The quality of currently available products and services is improving. This causes customer expectations to rise. Thus, what a customer might have considered quite satisfactory a few years ago, today may not meet his or her requirements. It is therefore irrelevant to discuss whether we *must* improve processes; the question is rather *how much* and *how fast* the improvement should be.

How do we go about improving processes? The process improvement cycle "plan, do, check, act" developed by W. Edward Deming provides an effective approach:

- In the "plan" phase, the firm identifies and analyzes the problem and plans activities to remedy it.
- In the "do" phase, the firm carries out the activities planned in the previous phase. The purpose is primarily to experiment with the solution.
- In the evaluation, or "check" phase, the firm measures whether the corrective activities had the desired effect on the problem.
- Finally, in the "act" phase, the firm modifies the process to fit the activities that were confirmed to give results. After the firm has performed the four phases, the process is considered improved.

Deming noted that in the first phase of the process improvement activity, the firm must document the process. As a general rule, if you want to improve something, you must first determine current performance. If you do not truly understand the process and its current performance, it will be very difficult to know which improvement initiatives can be started and whether they will ever work at all. Documenting the process should therefore always be the first step in any improvement activity. A key part of understanding and documenting a process is accomplished through the development of a "process map." Development of a process map serves several purposes:

- It creates a common understanding of the content of the process: its activities, results, and who performs its different steps.
- It defines the scope of the process, as well as the boundaries of the process relevant to adjacent processes.
- It provides a baseline against which to measure improvements in the future.

Understanding the Process "AS IS"

Once we understand the process as it is today, we may more easily speculate on improvements and the way the process should be. The "should be" part comes later, however. For now, we are simply concerned with understanding the way the process currently works. The following two-step approach is often used to document a process:

1. Define and describe the process in qualitative terms using a technique called *relationship mapping*. This involves answering questions including:
   a. Who are the customers of the process and what is the output from it?
   b. Who are the suppliers to the process and what is the input to it?
   c. What are the requirements for the input and output of the process?
   d. What is the internal flow of activities of the process?
2. Construct a *flow chart* that shows all the activities in the process in a more detailed map.

These activities are presented in the following section.

Relationship Mapping[5]

Before constructing a detailed flow chart of a process, we need to create a broad picture to understand which people are involved in the process, and what relation they have to one another. This can become very complicated when processes involve multiple individuals, departments, or organizations. For example, the process of receiving orders and shipping goods to the customer is a complicated process that involves many different people and several functional areas. Relationship mapping can be helpful as a first step in such cases.

A relationship map does not consider specific activities, but looks at flows among major groups. The map is constructed by placing on a blank sheet the different units, functions, departments, or individuals expected to participate in or impact the process. For the process of order receipt and delivery, logical participants would be the sales, planning, production, and procurement departments, as well as customers and suppliers. We might also include the finance department and external transport companies. Once potential participants are established, each relationship among them is defined by type. Different types of arrows are suitable for this purpose. Any groups that do not have any arrows going in or out of them in the end are removed from the map. After the arrows are roughed out on the first copy of the map, a second copy is re-drawn that provides a good overview about the relationships between participants in the process. A relationship map may not contain all of the details of the process–we are concerned with the overall patterns of flows between participants, so minimal time should be spent perfecting this map.

Example—A large corporation was formed with one central manufacturing site covering the entire United States. Local dealerships carried their own finished goods inventories in a number of states. There were clear indications that the supply process, including communicating needs from the local dealers and distribution to these dealers, was not working satisfactorily. The company therefore wanted to improve the material flow, starting with the main manufacturing site. To obtain a better idea of how information and goods were flowing, the firm decided to create a relationship map. The following information was collected from all involved parties regarding the firm's most important transactions:

- Local dealers based their demand forecasts on quarterly sales meetings with their main customers. Customers share their requirements for the next three-month quarter, as well as forecasts for the following quarter.
- Based on aggregated information from these meetings, the firm transmitted its expected forecasted demand for the different product families to the manufacturing unit for the upcoming quarter, as well as for the following quarter.
- Information from all the dealers was further aggregated to a set of consolidated forecasts for the next three to six months.
- These forecasts were shared with suppliers, forming the basis for negotiations regarding price and delivery terms for the following quarter.

- Detailed orders were issued by the local dealers every month with a three-week fixed delivery time from the manufacturing site.
- The ordered products were either taken from a small finished goods inventory or manufactured before they were sent by truck to the dealers. Local dealers were invoiced only when the goods had been sold to end customers.

The relationship map that the company developed is shown in Figure 2–2.

Process Flow Charts

While relationship maps are a good first step in establishing the broad flows of materials and information, they do not describe what happens below the surface. In other words, relationship maps provide a "10,000-foot view" of the process but what is needed in some cases is a "100-foot view" to understand what is happening at a more detailed level. Flow charts, or graphic depictions of the flow of activities in a process, serve this purpose.

Let's look at a smaller part of the relationship map: order processing at the manufacturing site (as indicated by the box and magnifying glass in Figure 2–2). The manufacturing plant manager has been receiving many complaints from dealers regarding the amount of time required to process their orders

Figure 2–2   Relationship Map

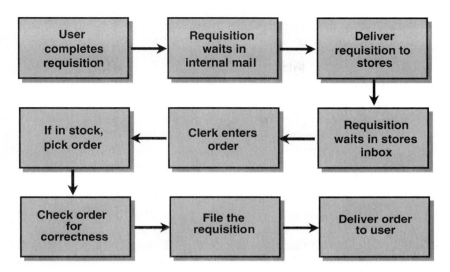

Figure 2–3   Stores Requisition Process

through its storage warehouse. The firm has decided to study the process in more detail, and has interviewed people involved in the process to describe a "typical" ordering process below (See Figure 2–3).

The customer speaks to the dealer in the field, who completes a requisition. The requisition is put in the mail, and is eventually delivered to finished goods stores at the manufacturing location. Once at stores, the requisition waits in the "inbox" until retrieved by a clerk. The clerk enters the order into the system. If the product requested is in stock, the order is picked and put into a box by an employee. An inspector then checks the order for correctness. The requisition is filed by the clerk and the order is delivered to the user. If the order is not in stock, the dealer is notified and the order is passed on to production scheduling.

A simple block diagram may be used (Figure 2–3), but often does not provide enough information. In creating flow charts, we recommend the use of a set of graphical symbols to represent what is happening. Although there are a variety of flow charting approaches, the American National Standards Institute (ANSI) symbols are frequently used. Examples of common ANSI symbols include the following:

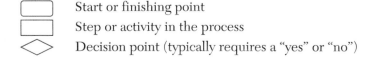

Start or finishing point
Step or activity in the process
Decision point (typically requires a "yes" or "no")

Input or output (typically data or materials)

Document created

Delay

Inspection

Use of the ANSI symbols provides additional information beyond that conveyed by the block diagram approach.

There are some important points to remember here. First, you want to document the process as it is, not the way you remember it to be. This means you may have to physically walk through the process, or "staple yourself to an order" in this case! Second, you will have to decide which parts of the process you want to address. Areas beyond the scope of control of the manager or not directly relevant to the problem may not be included in the process map. In this example, we assumed that the order is in stock, but the flow chart does not detail what happens if the product is not in stock, other than that the dealer is notified and the order is passed on to production. (Production scheduling is a different process, and should be considered separately from this process, with the linkages nevertheless established.) Finally, you must decide how much detail is required. This is a matter of judgment that is best left up to the manager working on the problem.

Once the process has been documented using these symbols, a manager may decide to include such additional information as:

- Information flows
- Time requirements for process elements
- Distance moved
- Resources required
- Capacity

For example, Figure 2–4 now shows detailed information on the average amount of time required to process an order. Based on this information, we know that the average time is about 7.1 hours, but can range from 2 hours to 14.3 hours (and that assumes that the item is in stock). If the item is not in stock, producing and delivering it will take even longer!

Once we have completed the process map, we can consider ways to improve the process. Some general guidelines for identifying potential opportunities to improve the process and cut cycle times include:

1. Examine each decision symbol: $\diamondsuit$
   - Is this a checking activity?
   - Is this a complete check, or do some errors go undetected?
   - Is this a redundant check?

2. Examine each rework loop (arrows that go back to a previous process):
   • Would we need to perform these activities if we had no failures?
   • How "long" is this rework loop (steps, time lost, resources consumed, etc.)?
   • Does this rework loop prevent the problem from reoccurring?

3. Examine each delay symbol: ⬭
   • What causes the delay?
   • What problems occur as a result of the delay?
   • How long is the delay?
   • How could we reduce the delay or its impact?

4. Examine each activity symbol: ☐
   • Is this a redundant activity?
   • What is the value of this activity relative to its cost?
   • How have we prevented errors in this activity?

5. Examine each document or database symbol: ⬭
   • Is this necessary?
   • How is this kept up to date?
   • Is there a single source for this information?
   • How can we use this information to monitor and improve the process?

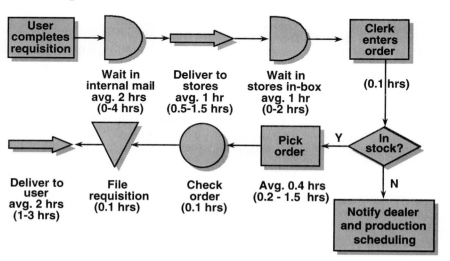

Figure 2–4   Flow Process Chart: Stores Requisition Process

There are typically multiple opportunities for improving a business process, once we clearly understand the current state. In our example, perhaps the information could be sent via e-mail to a central dispatcher who would dispatch the orders to order-pickers working in stores. This would eliminate many delays.

Process mapping is used across manufacturing and service industries. For example, the Massachusetts General Hospital used process flow diagrams in its patient billing process, and noted the following:

> *"Both the process of developing the flow diagram and the diagram itself enhanced each department's understanding of how one area impacts the next in the production of a "clean bill." The flow chart clearly identified areas where the process can falter."*[6]

Internal Supply Chains

It is generally a good idea to develop process maps of your internal supply chain before extending the analysis to inter-organizational processes. The internal supply chain is that portion of a given supply chain that occurs within an individual organization. Internal supply chains can be quite complex. Given the multidivisional, international organizational structures found in many businesses, it is not uncommon for the internal part of a supply chain to have multiple "links" that span the globe. Developing an understanding of the organization's internal supply chain is often an appropriate starting point for firms considering an SCM initiative. In these multidivisional structures, the employees of one division often view the "other" divisions in much the same manner as they would external suppliers or customers. In some cases, "turf wars" between divisions make integrating cross-divisional functions and processes very difficult.

Developing supply chain process maps (flow charts) for major supply chains and their related processes helps establish an understanding of the internal supply chain. Process map development is best accomplished through the use of cross-functional teams comprised of personnel from all parts of the organization included in the supply chain under review. Team members must be knowledgeable regarding their part of the supply chain and also must understand how their part interfaces with the other supply chain members.

To facilitate the process mapping activity, each team member should be provided with instructions about the mapping convention to be utilized, along with other information requirements. The objective of this exercise is to develop supply chain maps that present all supply chain entities along with key processes. Examples of key processes and associated entities include order transmittal (sales), order entry (materials planning), order preparation (purchasing, manufacturing, warehousing), and order shipment (distribution and transportation). Each team member documents the steps in its portion of the supply chain along with current performance information.

Once team members have completed the process maps for their part of the supply chain, the entire cross-functional team meets to develop the overall internal supply chain map. It is beneficial to conduct this step in a workshop session because considerable learning often takes place when the team members present their portion of the supply chain. It is interesting to note during the workshops the different (and in some cases limited) levels of understanding that individuals have regarding "what happens" outside their part of the process.

External Supply Chains

Once one understands the internal supply chain, the next step is to extend the analysis to the external portion of the supply chain (i.e., key suppliers and customers). The greatest opportunities for improvement often lie at the interfaces between the various supply chain member organizations. This step also adds a greater level of complexity, given that multiple organizations and their representatives are now participating in the analysis. At this point in the analysis, the organization needs to focus its efforts on those supply chains that are most important to the organization's success.

Once the key supply chains have been identified, one must identify the supply chain member organizations that are considered most *critical* to the organization's supply chain management efforts. These key suppliers and customers are likely to provide the greatest benefits to the SCM initiative. Organizations must be important members of the supply chain because the time and effort required for a significant SCM program is not warranted for "minor players." In selecting external members, several issues should be addressed. First, one must identify the competitive situation that exists between prospective SCM members. SCM endeavors are likely to be more productive if participating organizations are not direct competitors. There may be limits to collaborative supply chain efforts when both buyer-supplier and competitor relationships exist between participating organizations (i.e., company A is supplier to company B in one market, but A and B are direct competitors in several other markets). Second, all organizations and their representatives must be pursuing similar goals. This does not mean that each organization should have identical goals, but that their respective goals must be compatible with the overall SCM initiative. Third, SCM efforts have limited potential for success unless all organizations feel their involvement is beneficial. In an internal setting, participants may be able to survive situations where individual business units or functional areas may feel like "losers" (in terms of loss of planning authority, responsibility, resources, etc.) as a result of decisions considered optimal for the overall organization. An external SCM initiative is unlikely to be successful unless all members from each organization involved feel they are benefiting from participation.

Once the external participants have been identified, the development of the external supply chain process map is conducted in the same manner as discussed earlier for the internal supply chain. However, the team's composition is now both cross-functional and inter-organizational. This team should include representatives from all functional areas and all member organizations in the supply chain under consideration. Here again, the inter-organizational workshop sessions have been found to be an effective means to complete the development of the external supply chain process maps. As with the internal supply chain workshops, significant learning takes place during these sessions.

Benefits of Interorganizational Supply Chain Collaboration

External supply chain workshop participants indicate that a number of benefits are associated with these sessions in addition to documenting existing supply chain processes. Specific benefits include: 1) establishing valuable contacts across the supply chain; 2) gaining insights into current organizational practices; and 3) identifying opportunities for joint projects among supply chain members. This phenomenon is consistent with other research findings in the area of inter-organizational collaboration.[7]

Establishing Contacts across the Supply Chain

External supply chain workshops provide participants with an opportunity to become acquainted with key personnel from other supply chain member organizations. Establishing this network within the supply chain provides organizations with "real person" contacts within the other organizations. These contacts can be extremely valuable when organizations are presented with future supply chain problems (or opportunities). Supply chains that include an established network will be better positioned to respond to these situations than their counterparts who do not have these contacts.

Gaining Insights into Current Organizational Practices

Simply giving organizations a forum in which to discuss their current practices with the entire supply chain membership is very productive. These sessions often lead to the discovery of problems as well as the idenification of potential remedies to correct these problems. For example, in a workshop facilitated by the authors, one organization discovered it was ordering a key component from its supplier considerably later than necessary. The buying organization knew its order requirements for the component after the completion of an intermediate stage in the production process. However, the buying organization was not communicating this requirement to its supplier until the production process was completed, *approximately two weeks later!*

In another case, a supplier measured its customer order fulfillment performance on the basis of the time period from placement of the customer's order through order shipment. According to this measure, the supplier believed it was doing a "good" job. However, this organization's customer did not share this view. The customer measured order-fulfillment performance from its order placement through order receipt. On the basis of this measure, the supplying organization was late approximately 75 percent of the time. Further investigation revealed that 60 percent of the time that orders were late the problems were shipping-related. Prior to discussing this situation with its customer, the supplying organization was not even aware that there was a problem.

Joint Projects between Supply Chain Members

Often, opportunities for joint projects between "subgroups" of the supply chain organizations are identified and projects initiated during the workshop sessions. Although these projects do not focus on the entire supply chain, they often address issues that improve overall supply chain performance. For example, in one project in which the authors participated, an internal consulting group within one organization conducted detailed studies of the linkages between its organization and the organizations adjacent to it in the supply chain—that is, its supplier and its customer. This approach helped identify the level of process variability and its causes. Once the sources of variability were identified, the organization made efforts to remove the root causes of variability or to determine the appropriate location and quantity of inventory required to protect against this uncertainty. In another project, the two organizations that discovered the order-fulfillment problem discussed in the preceding section established a joint project team to address this problem. Now an interorganizational cross-functional team from these organizations holds weekly conference calls and meets monthly. The group's objective is to continually improve the processes between the two organizations.

Supply Chain Performance

In order to accurately assess the performance of an existing supply chain and its related processes, one must have objective performance information. Ideally, this information should cover the full range of performance areas, including, but not limited to:

Products and services offered	Delivery
Sales	Cycle times
Market share	Assets utilized
Cost	Responsiveness
Quality	Customer service
Inventory holdings	

Developing and maintaining a supply chain performance measurement system represents one of the more significant challenges faced in SCM initiatives. However, if supply chains are to be improved, decisions need to be based on objective performance information and will require sharing of this type of information with key supply chain members. Organizational willingness to share information with other supply chain members is a critical selection criterion for SCM membership. An organization that is willing to receive information from other supply chain members but is reluctant to share information is a poor candidate for inclusion in an SCM initiative.

Role of Benchmarking

Benchmarking analysis has been shown to be an effective means of determining the supply chain's performance relative to those of other organizations. Cook (1995) defines benchmarking as "the process of identifying, understanding, and adapting outstanding practices from within the same organization or from other businesses to help improve performance. This involves a process of comparing practices and procedures to those of the 'best' to identify ways in which an organization (or organizations) can make improvements. Thus new standards and goals can be set which, in turn, will help better satisfy the customer's requirements for quality, cost, product and service."[8]

The steps typically found in the benchmarking process include:[9]

1. Identify and understand current processes.
2. Form a benchmarking team.
3. Determine what to benchmark.
4. Identify benchmarking partners.
5. Collect data.
6. Analyze data and identify performance gaps.

7. Take actions to improve.

8. Review results.

Benchmarking provides a means to focus the supply chain management efforts on those areas most in need of improvement. One of these areas that spans multiple areas of the supply chain is process cycle time.

The Importance of Time in Creating High-Performance Supply Chains

Superior cost, quality, delivery, and technological performance do not guarantee success for a supply chain. Organizations must also be able to compete on the basis of time. This does not mean that cost, quality, delivery, and technology considerations are no longer important; they are critically important. However, individual organizations and supply chains must be competitive in these areas and be able to get their products and services to their customers faster than the competition.

Increasingly, organizations are realizing that they are competing on the basis of time. In fact, reducing the time required to provide the end customer with products or services is one of the major forces leading organizations to participate in supply chain management initiatives. Adopting an integrated supply chain management approach provides the means to make significant reductions in the cycle time required to move materials among supply chain members and to the end customer. Several authors have shown time to be a highly effective area in which to focus overall improvement efforts within an organization.[10] The opportunity for improvement appears to be even greater in an inter-organizational supply chain environment. This time-sensitive environment presents new challenges and opportunities for the individual organizations and their supply chains. This section introduces the concept of cycle time, presents common causes of "long" cycle times, discusses an approach for making cycle time improvements, and presents several critical success factors that should be considered as part of the cycle time reduction initiatives.

Cycle Time Overview

Cycle time is the total elapsed time required to complete a business process. All too often only a small percentage (e.g., three to five percent) of the total elapsed time required to complete a process has anything to do with "real work." The rest of the time is typically devoted to a wide range of counterproductive, time-consuming activities and events. Identifying, improving, and/or eliminating these time-consuming activities represent one of the major SCM opportunity areas. However, cycle time reduction is not just about completing a process quickly (i.e., speed for the sake of speed); it is concerned with completing the given process effectively. By focusing on key processes, supply chain member organizations can significantly improve cycle time performance, improvements that can provide a source of competitive advantage for the supply chain.

Causes of Long Cycle Times[11]

A number of causes of long process cycle times can be found in a supply chain environment. In examining supply chain processes, typically one or more of the following causes will be present.[12] Several common causes of long process cycle times and key issues that should be addressed when these situations are encountered include, but are not limited to, the following:

Waiting—In many multi-step processes, significantly more time is devoted to waiting between process steps than is spent in all of the processing steps combined! Where are the longest waits occurring in the process? What are the causes of these delays? What actions can be taken to reduce or eliminate the time spent waiting? Does the organization or supply chain need additional capacity in terms of facilities, equipment, or personnel?

Non-Value-Added Activities—The key processes found in many supply chains have existed for many years. When examining supply chain processes, it is worthwhile to determine the value that is being added by the overall process and individual process activities. It is not uncommon to find processes or activities within a process that were essential at one time, but that now add little or no value. Is this process necessary? Do all activities in the process add value? Activities that do not add value should be eliminated. If the process activity is adding value, is it being conducted in the best possible way given current practices and available technologies? For example, does the organization conduct quality inspections of purchased materials upon receipt, or does it utilize high-performing suppliers that certify that the materials they ship meet all specifications?

Serial versus Parallel Operations—Many supply chain process activities are conducted serially (i.e., first complete activity 1, then complete activity 2, and so on through activity N). Are there opportunities in the process for activities to take place in a parallel (i.e., simultaneous) manner as opposed to the currently used serial or sequential fashion? For example, within a manufacturing organization in the supply chain, are new products and the processes that will be used to manufacture these products developed concurrently, or is the product designed and then thrown "over the wall" to the manufacturing group? Are the manufacturing organization's key supplier and customer partners in the supply chain involved early in the new-product development process?

Repeating Process Activities—A significant cause of poor supply chain cycle time performance is having to repeat process steps due to product or service quality problems. There are few situations that can increase product cycle times (in terms of both average cycle times and variability) more than this condition. Are parts of the process repeated owing to an inability to get it right the first time? What are the causes of these problems? What actions are necessary to resolve these problems?

Batching—Batching occurs when some quantity of materials or orders is accumulated at one step in the process or organization in the supply chain before it is released to the next process step or supply chain member organization. What is the rationale for batching? Make certain that the rationale is economic rather than "that's how we have always done it." For example, a firm might wish to take advantage of lower transportation rates by batching orders to create larger shipment quantities. In such circumstances, however, the firm should periodically revisit the economics of the situation to ensure that the savings associated with the batch approach are worth the additional time required.

Excessive Controls—How much time is spent and potentially wasted following the rules and regulations governing processes within and among supply chain member organizations? A common internal example of this situation is seen in purchase order (PO) processing. How many signatures are needed for a PO? How many of these signatures are merely being "rubber stamped"? We do not mean to imply that all controls should be abandoned. However, organizations would be well served to periodically review the controls it uses to govern both internal and external supply chain processes, and determine if the level of control provided is worth the associated cost. A periodic cost/benefit analysis for intraorganizational and interorganizational controls as they apply to the supply chain is likely to be time well spent. Many organizations discover that their rules and regulations serve only to increase their response time to internal and external customers, and that many of these control mechanisms are more of a burden than a benefit.

Lack of Synchronization in Materials Movement—Are materials being moved across the supply chain in the most effective manner? Are product movements across the supply chain managed so as to ensure that the right quantity of the right product is getting to the right location at the right time? Or are materials arriving at the customer's location too early, causing additional storage and materials handling activities, or too late, disrupting the customer's operations and in so doing damaging the supplier's reputation?

Ambiguous Goals and Objectives—Do all supply chain member organizations clearly understand the overall supply chain goals and objectives? Do all supply chain members understand what their organization must contribute for the overall supply chain to be successful?

Poorly Designed Procedures and Forms—Do the procedures and forms associated with a specific process lead to the efficient completion of the process? Or do they significantly increase the time required to complete the process by creating more work while adding little value?

Outdated Technology—Are the supply chain member organizations making the best use of available technology? How is key information communicated across the supply chain? For example, are purchase orders transmitted from the buying organization to the supplying organization by fax, EDI, the Internet, or are they mailed? Are warehousing operations within the supply chain utilizing a high level of automation or are they primarily manual operations?

Lack of Information—The cycle time for supply chain decision making is often lengthy owing to the time needed to gain access to the information required to make decisions. It should be recognized that the required information may originate within the decision-maker's organization or in one or more of the other supply chain member organizations. Do decision makers have the information they need, when they need it, and in the desired format? How much time is being spent identifying, collecting, and manipulating the information required to make a decision versus making the actual decision?

Poor Communication—Intra-organizational and inter-organizational communication are critical to overall supply chain performance. Have the necessary lines of communication been established across the supply chain member organizations? Do managers within supply chain organizations know whom to contact in other functional areas within their own organization, as well as in the other supply chain organizations, if there are problems? A list of key contacts in different organizations across the chain is a very simple but valuable problem-solving resource.

Limited Coordination—Coordinating supply chain processes is another important factor in determining supply chain performance. Do all parties involved in a given process have a clear understanding of their respective roles and associated responsibilities? Are the inter-organizational processes effectively coordinated? Are there formal rules of engagement to ensure that the desired level of coordination is maintained?

Limited Cooperation—Are all supply chain member organizations truly committed to the supply chain management initiative? If not, it is time to re-evaluate the membership of those organizations that lack the required level of commitment. Cycle time and overall supply chain performance hinges on the cooperative efforts of the member organizations. Do all organizations have the appropriate cooperative philosophy?

Lack of/Ineffective Training—Proper training reduces the time for people to become proficient in their jobs and also can lead to ongoing improvements. Have all people involved in supply chain processes and activities received adequate training for their specific jobs? Are there ongoing training opportunities for employees that focus on supply chain performance improvement in general and cycle time reduction in specific?

Opportunities for Cycle Time Reduction across the Supply Chain

Very few organizations do not have significant opportunities for cycle time improvement from a supply chain process perspective. As customers increasingly focus on time-based performance, supply chain member organizations must be able to meet this challenge. SCM represents a challenge that is much like the game of golf: no matter how well you perform, there is always room for improvement. (It is also similar to golf in that your customers are not terribly impressed by your organization's past performances. To be competitive, the organization must be the top performer every week.) As for future expectations, the level of importance associated with time will only increase.

Given this challenge, where should the supply chain member organizations begin in their quest for cycle time reduction? Opportunities for cycle time reduction exist on both an intra-organizational and inter-organizational basis. Although it requires considerable effort, an examination of the entire supply chain—from raw materials through receipt by the end customer—is usually warranted. If a complete analysis cannot be performed, specific supply chain activities that are possible candidates for review include:

Materials planning and scheduling	Customer order processing
Purchase order cycle	Warehousing operations
Inbound transportation	Outbound transportation
Material receipt/inspection	Return materials/reverse
Material review activities	logistics
Manufacturing processes	

How can the cycle times for key supply chain processes be reduced? It would be great if there were a "secret weapon" that guaranteed significant cycle time reductions. Unfortunately, the secret weapon has yet to be discovered (at least by the authors). Furthermore, there is no one right way to reduce supply chain process cycle times, but rather there are many viable approaches. The specific tools and techniques required will depend upon the current state of affairs within the supply chain.

An approach that has been utilized by the authors in a variety of cycle time reduction projects is presented in the remainder of this section. This approach is adapted from the process-improvement approach presented by Harrington[13] and is focused on cycle time performance. It consists of the following steps:

1. Establish a cycle time reduction team.
2. Develop an understanding of the given supply chain process and current cycle time performance.
3. Identify opportunities for cycle time reduction.
4. Develop and implement recommendations for cycle time reduction.
5. Measure process cycle time performance.
6. Conduct continuous improvement efforts for process cycle time reduction efforts.

Establish a Cycle Time Reduction Team (CTRT)—The first step in this process is to identify the people who are going to conduct the cycle time reduction effort. The composition of this team is extremely important as it will have a significant effect on the probability of success for the initiative. The CTRT should include representatives of each functional area and organization involved in the given process. Therefore, the CTRT will be cross-functional and, if the process includes more than one organization, inter-organizational in its composition. Furthermore, the CTRT members must possess a thorough understanding of their part of the process. This point cannot be overemphasized. The authors have found that in some cases people assigned to CTRTs have a general understanding, but not a detailed understanding of the process. Without a detailed understanding, identifying opportunities for cycle time reduction and making significant improvements in the process is difficult.

Understand the Given Supply Chain Process and Current Cycle Time Performance—Once the CTRT is established, the next task is to develop an understanding of the current process and its associated cycle time performance characteristics. A highly effective approach to this task is through a process map (flow chart) by the CTRT in a "workshop" format. Each functional area and/or organization represented on CTRT is responsible for researching, documenting (i.e., mapping), and presenting its part of the process to the CTRT. The overall process map is then developed and is a composite of each of these various parts of the process. Current cycle time performance for the overall process as well as the activities that make up the process are also required. Specific measures should include, but are not limited to, average cycle time, minimum cycle time, maximum cycle time, and standard deviation of the cycle times. Worksheets can be used in this activity to help ensure that all key information is addressed. A sample worksheet is presented in Figure 2.5.

Identify Opportunities for Cycle Time Reduction—Once the CTRT has an understanding of the process and its current performance, the next task is to identify opportunities for cycle time reduction. If this is the initial examination of the process, a number of opportunities for improvement

Describe the current customer order-fulfillment process that exists between your customers and your firm for the period from customer order placement to receipt of product by the customer.

1. Develop a process flow chart that provides an overview of the current order-fulfillment process that exists between your customers and your firm.

2. Describe each of the activities (e.g., order placement, order changes, transit etc.) in the current order-fulfillment process. For each activity, please provide the following information:

   A. Activity description

   B. Frequency of activity

   C. Individual or group responsible for activity

   D. Information required to conduct activity (including source, how and when provided)

   E. Average activity cycle time

   F. Minimum activity cycle time

   G. Maximum activity cycle time

   H. Causes of activity cycle time variability

   I. Activity-specific performance measures and current performance levels

3. What performance measures does your firm currently utilize to assess overall customer order-fulfillment performance?

4. What impact does the current customer order-fulfillment process performance have on your firm?

5. Describe the type (e.g., raw materials, WIP, finished goods) and amounts (e.g., dollar value, quantities, and days of supply) of inventory held within your organization's portion of the supply chain.

6. For the inventory held within your organization's portion of the supply chain, indicate why this inventory is held.

7. How is the product transported from your organization to the customer? Which organization (e.g., your organization, the customer, third party, etc.) manages this in-transit portion of the supply chain?

8. What potential actions could be taken by your firm to improve the customer order-fulfillment process cycle time?

9. What potential customer actions could be taken to improve customer order-fulfillment process performance?

Figure 2–5   Customer Order Fulfillment Process Worksheet

are often readily apparent. The CTRT should attempt to focus its efforts on the parts of the process with the longest average cycle times and those parts of the process that have the highest levels of cycle time variability.

Develop and Implement Recommendations for Cycle Time Reduction—Having identified specific parts of the process that offer opportunities for cycle time reduction, the CTRT must develop and implement recommendations for cycle time reduction. This is the creative part of the CTRT's task. Specifically, for the opportunities identified in the previous step, the CTRT must determine what can be done to improve the process cycle time performance, given its resource constraints. At this point, the CTRT should remember that although it is charged with improving cycle time performance, this is not time strictly for time's sake. Rather, the CTRT is striving for cycle time improvements that recognize the cost, quality, and technology requirements of the marketplace. It is also imperative to understand the effects of any process changes for all parts of the system in question. Computer modeling the process and proposed changes is highly beneficial.

It is beyond the scope of this book to provide a detailed discussion of specific approaches to process cycle time reduction. However, several works are available on this topic. A helpful list of approaches for cycle time reduction is presented in Wetherbe's 1995 article, "Principles of Cycle Time Reduction: You Can Have Your Cake and Eat It Too."[14] This article provides an effective summary of 45 techniques that have been demonstrated to reduce process cycle times. These cycle time reduction approaches address the areas of:

- Organization design and management
- Human resources
- Product management
- Operations
- Inter-organizational issues

Once the specific recommendations are developed, the CTRT will present these recommendations to the management responsible for the areas involved. Actual implementation of the changes will typically require people and resources beyond the charter of the CTRT. However, CTRT member participation in the actual implementation is often worthwhile. These individuals provide valuable context for the implementation effort as well as detailed process knowledge.

Measure Process Cycle Time Performance—After the initial recommendations have been implemented, the effects of the changes on the actual process cycle time performance should be determined. Have the average process cycle times decreased? What effects do the implemented changes have on process cycle time variability? Key performance measures must be implemented if they do not already exist. These measures need to be monitored on an ongoing basis to determine process performance.

Conduct Continuous Improvement Efforts for Process Cycle Time Reduction—Process cycle time reduction is not a one-time event, but rather an ongoing activity. Once the process or part of a process has been examined and improved, it is time to move on to the next process or attempt to improve further the one at hand.

Critical Success Factors for Cycle Time Reduction

In conducting research with organizations that have successfully completed cycle time reduction efforts in a variety of supply chain management areas, several critical success factors have been identified:

- Top management support
- A commitment to significant cycle time reduction goals
- Use of cross-functional teams with team members that possess thorough process knowledge
- Application of Total Quality Management (TQM) tools (e.g., process mapping, Pareto analysis, fishbone diagrams, etc.)
- Training in cycle time reduction approaches
- Establishing, monitoring, and reporting formal cycle time performance measures
- Application of information systems and technology
- Collaboration with supply chain members[15]

Re-Engineering Supply Chain Logistics

Many companies have spent enormous amounts of money to decrease the lead times *within* their organizations, only to discover that their customers never saw much benefit because of long shipping times. These same companies are now concentrating intensively on the logistics systems that link them to their customers. Since logistics systems often interface directly with the customer, they can have considerable impact on overall customer satisfaction.

Consider the experience of Ford Motor Company, which had to radically re-engineer their entire system of delivering vehicles to dealerships. Why was this necessary? Quite simply, customer expectations exceeded the performance of Ford's old logistics system. Ford dealers would often complain that consumers were "spoiled" by their experience with package delivery companies such as Federal Express, which allowed them to track packages. Dealers, however, couldn't tell customers when a vehicle would arrive at a dealership! Until recently, once a vehicle left Ford's factory, a dealer didn't know where it was until it arrived at the lot. Many consumers, unwilling to wait to find out whether the car they wanted was on its way, simply went elsewhere for a car.[16] In February 2000, however, Ford struck a deal with UPS. Under the agreement, UPS uses its advanced logistics capabilities to track Ford's vehicle shipments, so that dealers can find the exact location of a particular vehicle by logging onto the UPS website. The system is a major improvement in the way Ford does business.

In studying the existing supply chain processes and attempting to reduce cycle time, organizations (such as Ford) may realize that the entire logistics system has major flaws. In such cases, the entire supply chain may need to be re-designed or "re-engineered." This subject is discussed in the next section.

Logistics as a Source of Competitive Advantage for the Supply Chain

Logistics is defined by the Council of Logistics Management (CLM) as " . . . the process of planning, implementing and controlling the efficient, effective flow and storage of goods, services and related information from the point of origin to the point of consumption for the purpose of conforming to customer requirements." Another author defines logistics as "the design and operation of the physical, managerial, and informational systems needed to allow goods to overcome time and space."[17] Logistics entails the planning and control of all factors that will have an impact on getting the correct product where it needs to go, on time, and at the optimum cost. Superior logistical performance is a primary area in which organizations participating in an integrated SCM initiative can make significant improvements. Logistical management is vital not only to manufacturing and assembly industries but also to retailing, transport, and other distribution or service-oriented industries. Owing to intensive competition in global markets, logistical management is considered an important source of competitive advantage. David Gertz, the author of *Grow to Be Great: Breaking the Downsizing Cycle*, says, "Supply chain and logistics are critical components of any successful growth strategy."[18] A study done by CLM found that "world-class firms are more apt to exploit logistics as a core competency than their less advanced competitors."[19] This logic can certainly be extended to interorganizational supply chains. The CLM study identified what the best-of-the-best logistics firms do to achieve world-class status. Key focus areas include:

1. Positioning concerning the selection of strategic and structural approaches to guide logistics operations.

2. Integration of internal achievement of logistical operating excellence and boundary-spanning development of solid supply chain relationships.

3. The firm's agility with respect to relevancy, accommodation, and flexibility.

4. Measurement of internal and external performance.

In this section, we describe the types of changes organizations are making to improve their logistics capabilities across the entire supply chain.

SCM and Logistics

Integrated SCM will only increase the importance of logistics activities. SCM allows supply chain members to optimize logistical performance at the inter-organizational level. At its limit, this means integrated management of the movement of materials from the raw materials supplier across the chain to the end customer. This represents a major departure from current logistics practices of many companies, often characterized by independent efforts with limited coordination between organizations.

Logistics professionals will continue to be challenged to manage the movement of products across the supply chain in a timely and cost-effective manner that meets customers' service requirements. Meeting this challenge requires a logistics strategy that encompasses the entire supply chain. This overall strategy will be the primary driver for the specific logistics strategy within each of the supply chain member organizations. Distribution networks, transportation modes, carrier management, inventory management, warehousing, order processing, and all other related activities need to be addressed. The scope of the logistics strategy is now the entire supply chain (not just each individual unit in the chain). It will no longer be necessary or desirable for each supply chain member organization to manage its logistics activities independently.

Role of Third-Party Logistics Service Providers

Partnership is defined as a tailored business relationship featuring mutual trust, openness, and shared risk and reward that yields strategic competitive advantage. Often the formula for success in logistics is the one that leads to partnership. According to a 1996 CLM study into the market positioning and development of the third-party logistics industry, partnerships with third parties add value for a growing number of companies. Fully 72 percent of respondents used third-party logistics providers with outbound transportation as their most frequently outsourced service, followed by warehousing at just under 60 percent. In the future, freight consolidation and distribution were the logistics activities thought most likely to be outsourced (by 22.1 percent of respondents), followed by warehousing and inbound transportation and/or freight bill auditing/payments (18.2 percent and 16.6 percent of respondents, respectively). Outsourcing of logistics activities was considered to be extremely successful for the customers of 38 percent of respondents. Another 52 percent of respondents' customers considered outsourcing somewhat successful.[20]

Many firms engaged in international business also use external logistics service providers to handle most of their logistics needs. This clearly shows the need for these companies to establish a close relationship with their service providers. These partnerships reduce uncertainty and complexity in an ever-changing global environment and minimize risk while maintaining flexibility. Research by Daugherty, et al. on international third-party service providers shows that partnerships are extremely important for minimizing problems associated with information flow that can easily damage the supplier—customer relationship.[21]

Third-party partnership provides the advantages of ownership without the associated burden, allowing organizations to take advantage of "best-in-class" expertise, achieve customer service improvement, respond to competition, and eliminate assets. However, according to Daugherty, "partnerships are not the way to go in all cases. They may not always be feasible or appropriate. Partnerships are complex relationships demanding corporate cultural compatibility, a strong perspective of mutuality, and symmetry between the two sides. To succeed, partnerships must include components that management controls and can put in place, like planning, joint operating controls, risk/reward sharing, trust/commitment, contract style, expanded scope, and financial investment."[22]

As organizations adopt integrated SCM approaches, the role of third-party logistics service providers is likely to expand. This will be the case particularly for those third-party service providers that function effectively as part of the overall supply chain team. Third-party service providers will increasingly be sought out for their SCM expertise.

International Considerations

Relative to domestic supply chains, international supply chains often entail the following: 1) greater geographic distances and time differences; 2) multiple national markets; 3) multiple national operations locations; and 4) greater opportunities because of diversity of supply and demand conditions.[23] Additional costs are also associated with global supply chains. Major costs categories for a global supply chain include:

- Manufacturing costs—purchased materials, labor, equipment charge, and supplier's margin

- Movement costs—transportation cost, inventory in pipeline and safety stock cost, and duty
- Incentive costs and subsidies—taxes and subsidies
- Intangible costs—quality costs, product adaptation or performance costs, and coordination
- Overhead costs—total current landed costs
- Sensitivity to long-term costs—productivity and wage changes, exchange rate changes, product design, and core competence.[24]

Global supply chain performance improvement by leading organizations has involved the following: 1) rationalizing supply chains by changing locations and transportation modes; 2) reducing the buffers of inventory and time between successive steps in the supply chain; 3) increasing the geographic and international scope of the supply chains; and 4) increasing the sophistication of the goods and services accessed through supply chains.

Changes in government regulations and policies also may create the need for changes in supply chain strategy. In Europe, for example, the deregulation of European Community (EC) economic, financial, and operational barriers have meant that companies have to rethink their logistics strategies.[25] The single market environment allows greater flexibility in supplier sourcing and customer deliveries. Many companies are re-engineering and rationalizing their logistical networks to take advantage of the reduction in, or elimination of, numerous artificial barriers that previously affected logistics decisions.

In addition to regulations, organizations must recognize the cultural differences found in many countries where they do business. One group of logistics researchers notes that. "Seemingly small cultural differences among Asian countries are only an indication of the complexity of the task of managing logistics within the region." Performance standards may vary from region to region or by organization. Therefore, global supply chains require a detailed understanding of a foreign supply chain partners' capabilities as well as regional performance standards and regional infrastructure. Managers attempting to create global supply chains must be sensitive to specific local conditions and modify their strategies accordingly.

Re-Engineering Challenges and Opportunities

As organizations embark on various initiatives to manage supply chains, they need to recognize that these efforts provide an opportunity to do much more than merely align their current logistical processes with those of their supply chain partners. SCM provides a platform to make significant improvements in logistical performance across the supply chain. These improvements may be the result of changes in roles of the supply chain member organizations. Organizations that ignore this re-engineering opportunity will likely make only incremental improvements.

DeRoulet and Kallock[26] suggest the need for logistics to re-engineer. They argue that "new approaches to business partnerships, dramatic innovations in technology, and reinvented supply chain strategies all result in new logistical expectations, none of which are attainable through mild-mannered, incremental tweaks to an existing process."[27] Whirlpool and Hewlett-Packard are among those companies that have successfully re-engineered their logistics functions. At Whirlpool the re-engineering process relies on computer systems and third-party partners that enable the company to fill orders within 24 hours. The Hewlett-Packard re-engineering process takes the form of an improved delivery strategy, which was formulated and prototyped to meet the needs of the company.

The Council of Logistics Management suggests that companies consider the following issues when working to improve their supply chains:[28]

1. Help customers become more knowledgeable about logistics.
2. Eliminate any logistics activities that do not add customer value.
3. Remove the barriers among the members of the supply chain to improve customer focus, make better and faster decisions, improve supply chain efficiency, and achieve sustainability.
4. Manage partnerships with third parties.

Organizations are recognizing that their current logistical processes and practices may not be the best approach within the context of an interorganizational supply chain. Although organizations recognize the danger of functional or departmental sub-optimization within the context of a single organization, this logic must now be applied to the supply chain to avoid "suboptimizing" performance at the organizational level. This means that the level of analysis for the re-engineering effort is the entire supply chain, and it is this larger system that the member organizations must attempt to optimize.

Although internal corporate process improvements can lead to significant performance gains, managers and academicians alike have realized that re-engineering must extend beyond the organization to include other members of the supply chain. This outward-focused approach to re-engineering not only aligns corporate actions with the customer's desire for on-time provision of goods and services, but in most cases can also significantly improve profitability. One study, for example, found that supply chain re-engineering can boost profits by 150 percent to 250 percent and can reduce order cycle time by up to 70 percent.[29] Supply chain process improvements also may significantly reduce the cost of doing business for supply chain members, particularly in the areas of administration, inventory control, warehouse management, and transportation. Grocery industry managers, for example, believed they could cut $30 billion—10 percent of total operating budgets—via supply chain re-engineering.[30]

Firms such as Dow Chemical, SC Johnson Wax, National Semiconductor, Merle Norman, Levi Strauss, and Xerox[31] are but a few of the growing list of organizations to reap the vast benefits of total supply chain re-engineering. The main obstacles keeping others from realizing similar benefits are top management's limited understanding of the process, a general resistance to change, the persistence of rigid department-based organizational structures, and lack of a customer perspective.[32]

The cost of not re-engineering can be high. For example, Compaq Computer estimated that it lost between $500 million and $1 billion in sales in the first 10 months of 1994 because its products were not available when and where customers wanted them.[33]

The Supply Chain Operations Reference Model (SCOR)

Managers responsible for supply chain process improvement planning, implementation, and measurement received a much needed framework to guide their efforts in November 1996 when the then 69-member Supply chain Council introduced its Supply Chain Operations Reference Model (SCOR). Member companies, including such diverse industry leaders as Dow Chemical, Merck, Texas Instruments, Compaq, and Federal Express, worked together for over six months to develop the model. Specifically, they defined common supply chain management processes, matched these processes against "best practice" examples, and benchmarked performance data as well as optimal software applications. The result was a tool for (1) measuring both supply chain performance and the effectiveness of supply chain re-engineering, as well as (2) testing and planning for future process improvements.[34] This model was tested both in a mock supply chain situation and internally at Rockwell Semiconductor Systems with highly positive results.

At the core of the SCOR model is a four-level pyramid that guides supply chain members on the road to integrative process improvement. Level One consists of a broad definition of the four key supply chain process types (i.e., plan, source, make, and deliver) and is the point at which supply chain competitive objectives are established. Level Two defines the 26 core supply chain process categories established by the Supply Chain Council with which supply chain partners can jointly present their ideal or actual operational structure. Level Three provides partners with information useful in planning and setting goals for supply chain process improvement. Level Four focuses on implementation of supply chain process improvement efforts.

The major benefit of SCOR is that it gives inter-organizational supply chain partners a basis for integration by providing them, often for the first time, with something tangible to talk about and work with. According to Vinay Asgekar, manager of Business Process Re-Engineering at Rockwell Semiconductor, "Various departments are now talking the same language . . . that's a notable achievement. The framework helped to break down functional silos and allowed people to look at real issues and practices holding back supply chain management improvements. It gave people the chance to look at the supply chain with company-wide needs in mind."[35]

Supply Chain Performance Measurement

The importance of performance measurement in the context of SCM cannot be overstated. Timely and accurate assessment of overall system and individual system component performance is paramount. An effective performance measurement system (1) provides the basis to understand the system, (2) influences behavior throughout the system, and (3) provides information regarding the results of system efforts to supply chain members and outside stakeholders. In effect, performance measurement is the glue that holds the complex value-creating system together, directing strategic formulation as well as playing a major role in monitoring the implementation of that strategy. In addition, research findings suggest that measuring supply chain performance in and of itself leads to improvements in overall performance.[36] In one study of U.S.-Mexican manufacturing operations, performance improvements were found in order cycle time reduction, routing and scheduling, and effective handling of border crossings of outbound freight.[37] Another study found that implementation of performance measurement systems led to improvements in process cycle time, cost, quality, and delivery performance.[38] Despite its importance, however, prior to 1990, supply chain performance often was measured in oversimplified and sometimes counterproductive (cost-reduction-based) terms.[39] Lack of an appropriate performance measurement system has been cited as a major obstacle to effective supply chain management.[40]

Developments in Supply Chain Performance Measurement

The concept of SCM requires measuring overall supply chain performance rather than just the performance of the individual chain members. It is the combined performance of the supply chain, the final outcome of the efforts of all integrated members, that is of greatest importance from a measurement perspective. Although measures of supply chain performance differ in terms of individual indicators employed, virtually all have one overriding focus: continual improvement of end-customer service.[41] After all, the final customer of the supply chain must be satisfied for the overall supply chain to succeed long-term. These customers care little about the time required to move materials between intermediate supply chain members or about the cost associated with this activity. The customer is concerned with the time required to meet its demands and the cost of doing so. This fundamental concern is reflected most generally in a desire to continually reduce total cycle time.[42]

A good performance measurement system also is "actionable." It allows managers not only to identify but also to eliminate causes of supply chain operational problems so that relationships with customers are not permanently harmed.[43] Beyond these general customer-oriented aspects of effective supply chain performance measurement, researchers have stressed the desirability of assessing a wide variety of phenomena indicative of overall supply chain performance. These include measurement of (1) changes in both the average volume of inventory held and frequency of inventory turns across the supply chain over time,[44] (2) the adaptability of the supply chain as a whole to meet emergent customer needs, and (3) the extent to which intra-supply chain relationships are based on mutual trust.[45] Finally, effective measurement of supply chain performance entails looking beyond the integrated chain itself in a variety of ways. For example, key members of some integrated supply chains employ outside auditors to conduct random customer-satisfaction surveys at supply chain members' operational facilities in order to ensure objectivity in the measurement process.[46] In addition, managers responsible for performance assessment should continually engage in supply chain benchmarking wherein they compare the results of internal supply chain performance with that of other target supply chains in a wide variety of industries, including their own.[47]

The "Balanced Scorecard" Approach to Supply Chain Performance Measurement

Supply chain management requires that member organizations have a means to assess the performance of the overall supply chain to meet the requirements of the end customer. In addition, it is necessary to be able to assess the relative contribution of the individual member organizations within the supply chain. This requires a performance measurement system that can operate not only at several different levels but also can link or integrate the efforts of these different levels to meeting the objectives of the supply chain. In their 1996 work, *The Balanced Scorecard: Translating Strategy into Action*,[48] Kaplan and Norton present a promising approach for performance measurement that can be applied to the supply chain. The "balanced scorecard" approach incorporates both financial and operating performance measures that are used at all levels of the supply chain. In an inter-organizational supply chain environment, the supply chain level represents the starting point for the balanced scorecard.

The balanced scorecard formally links overall supply chain objectives and the strategies undertaken to meet these objectives with supply chain-wide performance measures. Objectives, strategies, and performance measures at the supply chain level can then be linked to the organizational levels. Here individual organizations develop organizational level objectives, the strategies to achieve these objectives, and associated performance measures. This process is then repeated at the functional level within the individual supply chain member organizations. For example, the procurement function within a manufacturing supply chain member organization will develop its functional objectives, strategies, and performance measures, which are based on the organization's objectives, strategies, and performance measures. This process is then taken to the team or individual level within the various functions where the teams or individuals develop their own objectives, strategies, and performance measures based on those of their respective functional area.

At each level, the balanced scorecard addresses four key performance areas: 1) financial; 2) customer; 3) business process; and 4) learning and growth. Within each of these areas, key objectives are identified that are driven by the objectives and strategies of the next higher level in the scorecard hierarchy; specific performance measures associated with the objectives, performance targets, and initiatives to achieve the targets are then developed. Table 2–1 presents the balanced scorecard framework.[49]

What Should We Measure?

Considerable debate has focused on the specific performance measures required to manage an integrated supply chain. Organizations recognize that future competition is likely to pit supply chain against supply chain in pursuit of the end customer's business. Therefore, it is critical to assess and continuously improve the performance of the entire chain. Recognizing the importance of this issue, a consortium of businesses, academics, and consultants developed a comprehensive group of performance measures for supply chain manage-

Table 2–1 Balanced Scorecard Framework

Financial Area

Objectives	*Measures*	*Targets*	*Initiatives*

Customer Area

Objectives	*Measures*	*Targets*	*Initiatives*

Business Process Area

Objectives	*Measures*	*Targets*	*Initiatives*

Learning and Growth Area

Objectives	*Measures*	*Targets*	*Initiatives*

[71]Robert S. Kaplan and David P. Norton, "Using the Balanced Scorecard as a Strategic Management System," *Harvard Business Review,* January–February 1996, pp. 75–85

Figure 2–6   Balanced Scorecards for Supply Chain Management

ment.[50] These measures address four broad performance areas: 1) customer satisfaction/quality; 2) time; 3) costs; and (4) assets. For each of these areas, the consortium identified primary and secondary performance measures. These performance measures are presented in Figure 2–6.

The specific measures necessary to manage supply chain performance will vary according to customer type, product line, industry, or other factors. However, maintaining an end-customer perspective (i.e., addressing issues that are truly important to the supply chain's ability to cost-effectively satisfy the end-customer requirements) when developing these measures is critical. Researchers have identified several supply chain characteristics and activities that significantly increase the likelihood that performance objectives will be attained. Most important is the integration, across the entire channel, of information systems that allows the sharing of information and also facilitates the measurement of performance.[51]

Summing It Up: The Perfect Order Versus Total Cost

In order to understand the real impact that logistics has on customers, more and more companies are measuring logistics performance in terms of "perfect order" and "total cost." The first measure assesses how *effective* the logistics organization is in servicing the customer. The second measure assesses how *efficiently* it is servicing those customers. Each measure is important, and one cannot consider either independently.

The Perfect Order

The perfect order represents the ability of the supply chain to provide 100 percent availability in a timely, error-free manner. One company defines the perfect order as:

- On-time to the buyer's requested delivery date
- Shipped complete
- Invoiced correctly
- Not damaged in transit

For example, consider the following data from an organization's logistics records from one year:

- 5.4 million orders were processed
- 30,000 were delivered late
- 25,000 were incomplete
- 15,000 were damaged
- 20,000 were billed incorrectly
- 90,000 "defective" orders out of 5.4 million

The percentage of perfect orders in the example above is (5,400,000 - 90,000)/5,400,000 = 98.3 percent perfect orders.

Procter and Gamble's Perfect Order System

At Procter and Gamble, the "perfect order" concept has driven major changes in the organization. P&G's mission is to "Improve the lives of the world's customers." That means providing value by reducing product costs. Ralph Drayer, Vice President of Global Logistics at P&G, estimates that supply chain costs today are at least two to three times higher than they should be. P&G's goals are to double their unit volume in ten years, increase market share, simplify the shopping experience, and integrate their supply chain. The company's objectives are to be a true global company and to have all of their global business units supported by geographic marketing organizations with global business services groups helping to simplify transactions such as order fulfillment.

In 1992, P&G began to measure their "perfect orders," defined as arriving on-time, complete (as ordered), and billed correctly (payable as invoiced). Initially, managers were shocked to discover that the number of perfect orders was only 75 percent. Since that time, P&G has achieved substantial improvements through continuous replenishment, having customer service representatives work closely with major customers, and improved information systems (see Table 2–2).

Total Cost

Another major driver that companies must consider is the total logistics systems costs. Obviously, having "non-perfect orders" also has costs associated with it. Procter and Gamble estimates that every imperfect order costs approximately $200, as denoted as follows:

On time:

- Cost of redelivery

Delivered complete:

- Lost revenue of cut cases
- Damaged cases
- Warehouse and shipping costs
- Back orders

Invoiced accurately:

- Price and allowance deductions
- Quantity adjustments
- Deductions P&G honored based on a lack of accurate data

However, a number of other costs are associated with maintaining a high level of customer service. A total cost analysis of a business logistics system assesses the interrelationship among transportation, warehousing, inventory, and customer service, and suggests that a decision made in one area of logistics may impact other areas of the firm. Decisions made in the transportation area, for

Table 2-2 P & G's Perfect Order Performance History

	92/93	93/94	94/95	95/96	96/97	97/98
Perfect Orders	75%	75%	80%	82%	86%	88%
On Time	87%	87%	94%	92%	94%	94%
Delivered Complete	91%	88%	88%	91%	94%	96%
Billed Accurately	88%	91%	92%	93%	95.6%	96.6%

example, have an impact on the cost of warehousing and inventory, product marketability, and the cost of lost sales and damaged/obsolete goods.

Some of the tradeoffs that may be considered in a total cost approach include:

- Different modes of transportation
- Warehousing versus transportation costs
- Centralized versus decentralized warehouses
- Higher inventory costs versus increased sales
- Cost of inventory versus cost of stopping a production line

Although it is beyond the scope of this chapter to provide a detailed model for calculating total cost, we can employ the following basic equation to calculate the total cost associated with the movement of material through a supply chain.

Price per unit
+   Containerization cost
+   Transportation freight costs
+   Duties and premiums
=   Landed cost
+   Incoming quality control
+   Warehouse costs
=   Dock-to-stock cost
+   Inventory carrying costs
+   Defective materials
+   Factory yield
+   Field failures
+   Warranties
+   Service
+   General and administrative costs
+   Lost sales and customer goodwill
=   Total cost

By applying this approach, managers can effectively identify the cost of providing a given level of customer service. They can also develop ways to reduce costs without reducing service.

Summary

Although many organizations are involved in a variety of initiatives with key suppliers and customers, relatively few have taken the broader supply chain perspective. Organizations may realize that collaborative supply chain initiatives are the "right" thing to do, but many organizations are not entirely certain how to proceed. This chapter addressed several areas important to the management of supply chain material flows. Understanding current supply chains, reducing cycle times, re-engineering logistical processes, and measuring performance are all key to supply chain management.

Organizations must understand current supply chain processes prior to implementing changes. This is an extremely important step in any SCM initiative. Although organizations have experienced over a decade of process re-engineering, many organizations do not clearly understand their intra-organizational or inter-organizational supply chain processes.

In many cases, inter-organizational processes are the product of evolution rather than the result of a precision design effort. Re-engineering inter-organizational processes across the supply chain may hold benefits of an even greater magnitude to those associated with internal re-engineering efforts. However, as with internal re-engineering, the appropriate application of information technology enables the re-engineering of processes.

Organizations must realize that overall supply chain performance ultimately affects their own individual performance. Furthermore, supply chains are only as strong as the weakest link in the chain. For example, the process linkages between the supply chain manufacturing organization and suppliers may be functioning at world-class levels. However, if the links between the manufacturing organization and the retailing organization are not functioning at a desired level then the supply chain is not performing well. The critical linkage for the ultimate success of the supply chain is sales to the end customer. It matters little that performance at earlier stages of the supply chain is outstanding if the product is not available to support retail sales.

The critical question to ask when establishing or improving supply chains is, "What are the effects on the end customer and other supply chain members?" If you cannot demonstrate that the proposed change is going to lead to an improvement from the end customer's perspective or that the change will somehow improve the process for the supply chain while not having negative effects on the end customer, don't do it!

Will supply chains be faced with the challenges of time-based competition? The answer for most supply chains is yes. An equally important question: is the supply chain going to be dragged into the fray in a reactive manner or will it meet this challenge proactively? This choice faces many supply chains. For supply chains that have not undertaken formal cycle time reduction efforts there is no time like the present. The challenges are there but the opportunities for significant cycle time improvement are plentiful.

Supply chain performance measurement was also presented in this chapter. Many supply chain initiatives are currently addressing this area. A balanced scorecard approach that includes both financial and operational performance at various levels of the supply chain (i.e., supply chain, organizational, functional, and team levels) holds promise for many SCM initiatives.

Organizations that can successfully incorporate the aforementioned areas into their supply chain management initiatives will be well positioned to succeed.

Endnotes

[1]SlurryTech is a fictional name used to disguise the name of the real company used in this example.

[2]Francis J. Quinn, "What's the Buzz? Supply Chain Management; Part 1," *Logistics Management 36* (February 1997), 43; and *Business Wire*, "Supply Chain Management Becoming Leading Strategic Concern in Chemical Industry, New A. T. Kearney Study Shows," June 1997, p. 30.

[3]H. Donald Ratliff, "Logistics Management: Integrate Your Way to an Improved Bottom Line," *IIE Solutions 27*, No. 10 (October 1995), p. 31.

[4]Adapted from Anderson, 1999.

[5]Ibid.

[6]Massachusetts General Hospital, *NDP on QI in Health Care*, *1990*, American Society of Quality, Milwaukee, WI.

[7]Benjamin Gomes-Casseres, "Group Versus Group: How Alliance Networks Compete," *Harvard Business Review 72*, No. 4 (July–August 1994), pp. 62–74; Rosabeth Moss Kantner, "Collaborative Advantage: The Art of Alliances," *Harvard Business Review 72*, No. 4 (July–August 1994), pp. 96–108.

[8]Sarah Cook, *Practical Benchmarking: A Manager's Guide to Creating a Competitive Advantage* (London: Kogan Page Limited, 1995), p. 13.

[9]Ibid, p. 17.

[10]Joseph D. Blackburn, *Time-Based Competition: The Next Battle Ground in American Manufacturing* (Homewood, IL: Richard D. Irwin, 1991); and George Stalk, Jr. and Thomas M. Hout, *Competing Against Time: How Time-Based Competition Is Reshaping Global Markets* (New York: The Free Press, A Division of Macmillan, 1990); Christopher Meyer, *Fast Cycle Time: How to Align, Purpose, Strategy, and Structure for Speed* (New York: The Free Press, 1993); Robert B. Handfield, *Reengineering for Time-Based Competition* (Westwood, CT: Greenwood Publishing Group, 1995).

Ernest L. Nichols Jr., Mark N. Frolick, and James C. Wetherbe, "Cycle Time Reduction: An Interorganizational Supply Chain Perspective," *Cycle Time Research, vol. 1*, no. 1 (1995), pp. 63–84.

[11]Adapted from Ernest L. Nichols Jr., "It's About Time!" *Purchasing Today*, November 1996, pp. 29–31.

[12]Ken Kivenko, "Cycle Time Reduction," *APICS—The Performance Advantage*, February 1994, pp. 21–24.

[13]H. James Harrington, *Business Process Improvement: The Breakthrough Strategy for Total Quality, Productivity, and Competitiveness* (New York: McGraw-Hill, 1991).

[14]James C. Wetherbe, "Principles of Cycle Time Reduction: You Can Have Your Cake and Eat It Too," *Cycle Time Research* 1, no. 1 (1995), pp. 1–24.

[15]Nichols, Frolick, and Wetherbe, "Cycle Time Reduction;" Thomas E. Hendrick, *Purchasing's Contribution to Time-Based Strategies* (Tempe, AZ: Center for Advanced Purchasing Studies, 1994); G. Tomas M. Hult, Mark N. Frolick, and Ernest L. Nichols Jr., "Organizational Learning and Cycle Time Issues in the Purchasing Process," *Cycle Time Research* 1, no. 1 (1995), pp. 25–39.

[16]Fara Warner & Rick Brooks, "Ford is Hiring UPS to Track Vehicles As They Move From Factories to Dealers," *WSJ*, 2/2/00, p. A6.

[17]Huan Neng Chiu, "The Integrated Logistics Management System: A Framework and Case Study," *International Journal of Physical Distribution & Logistics Management* 25, no. 6 (1995), pp. 4–22. As quoted from M. S. Daskin, "Logistics: An Overview of the State of the Art and Perspectives on Future Research," *Transportation Research* 19A, no. 5/6 (1985), pp. 383–398.

[18]Helen Richardson, Sarah Bergin, Perry Trunick, and Lisa Harrington, "New Life Through Logistics," *Transportation & Distribution* 37, no. 12 (December 1996), p. 46.

[19]Helen Richardson and Perry A. Trunick, "Breakthrough Thinking in Logistics," *Transportation & Distribution* 36, no. 12 (December 1995), p. 34.

[20]Richardson et al., "New Life Through Logistics," p. 46.

[21]Patricia J. Daugherty, Theodore P. Stank, and Dale S. Rogers, "Third-Party Logistics Service Providers: Purchasers' Perceptions," *International Journal of Purchasing & Materials Management* 32, no. 2 (Spring 1996), pp. 23–29.

[22]*Ibid.*, p. 52.

[23]M. Therese Flaherty, *Global Operations Management* (New York: McGraw-Hill, 1996), p. 286.

[24]*Ibid.*, p. 288.

[25]Jack Berry, Herve Mathe, and Cynthia Perras, "Planning for the Long Haul: The Single Market Reroutes Logistics Management," *Journal of European Business 4*, no. 1 (September/October 1992), pp. 32–36.

[26]David G. DeRoulet and Roger W. Kallock, "Logistics Drives Dramatic Innovations," *Transportation & Distribution* 33, no. 11 (November 1992), pp. 40–44.

[27]*Ibid*, p. 40.

[28]Richardson et al., "New Life Through Logistics," pp. 44–53.

[29]Gary Gagliardi, "Tightening the Flow," *Manufacturing Systems* 14 (October 1996), pp. 104–110; and "From the Editor: Manufacturers Must Strengthen Weak Links in Supply Chain," *Manufacturing Automation* 8 (May 1995), pp. 111–115.

[30]Ronald Henkoff, "Delivering the Goods," *Fortune*, November 28, 1994, p. 64.

[31]Robert L. Cook and Robert A. Rogowski, "Applying JIT Principles to Continuous Manufacturing Supply Chains," *Production & Inventory Management Journal* 37, no. 1, (1996), pp. 12–17. Tom Andel, "Forge a New Role in Supply Chain: Modern Warehousing," *Transportation & Distribution* 37 (February 1996), p. 107. Henkoff, "Delivering the Goods." "Supply Chain Makeover Doubles Company's Inventory Accuracy," *IIE Solutions* 28 (May 1996), pp. 72–74. "Reengineering, the Sequel: A New Tool for Growth," *Investor's Business Daily*, March 19, 1996, p. A4. Tim Minahan, "Xerox Plots a Plan Worth Copying," *Purchasing* 120, no. 11 (1996), p. 90.

[32]Robert W. Kallock, "Logistics Process Reengineering: Getting Started," *Transportation & Distribution* 35 (October 1994), p. 86.

[33]Henkoff, 1994.

[34]"69 Manufacturers Launch First Cross-Industry Framework for Improved Supply chain Management," *PR Newswire*, November 12, 1996; and Dianne Trommer, "Reference Model on Its Way—Allows Firms to Evaluate Supply Chain Processes," *Electronic Buyers' News*, October 14, 1996, p. 59.

[35]Trommer, 1996.

[36]Daniel C. Bello and David I. Gilliland, "The Effects of Output Controls, Process Controls, and Flexibility on Export Channel Performance," *Journal of Marketing* 61 (Winter 1997), p. 22; and Theodore P. Stank and Charles W. Lackey Jr., "Enhancing Performance Through Logistical Capabilities in Mexican Maquiladora Firms," *Journal of Business Logistics* 18, no. 1 (1997), pp. 91–123.

[37]Stank and Lackey, 1997.

[38]Ernest L. Nichols Jr. and Robert M. Monczka, "Value of Supplier Performance Measurement," working paper from the Global Procurement and Supply chain Benchmarking Initiative at Michigan State University, 1997.

[39]Thomas A. Foster, "It Pays to Measure Performance: Logistics Performance Compensation Programs," *Chilton's Distribution* 90 (September 1991), p. 4.

[40]See Hau L. Lee and Corey Billington, "Managing Supply chain Inventory: Pitfalls and Opportunities," *Sloan Management Review* 33, no. 3 (1992), pp. 65–73.

[41]Stank and Lackey, 1997 and Garland Chow, Lennart E. Henriksson, and Trevor D. Heaver, "Strategy, Structure, and Performance: A Framework for Logistics Performance." *The Logistics and Transportation Review 31* (December 1995), p. 285.

[42]Chow, Henriksson, and Heaver, "Strategy, Structure, and Performance."

[43]Stank and Lackey, 1997.

[44]Ibid.; and Lee and Billington, "Managing Supply Chain Inventory," p. 65.

[45]Bello and Gilliland, "The Effect of Output Controls, Process Controls, and Flexibility."

[46]Toby B. Gooley, "Partnerships Can Make the Customer-Service Difference," *Traffic Management* 33 (May 1994), p. 40.

[47]Stank and Lackey, 1997.

[48]Robert S. Kaplan and David P. Norton, *The Balanced Scorecard: Translating Strategy into Action* (Boston: Harvard Business School Press, 1996).

[49]Robert S. Kaplan and David P. Norton, "Using the Balanced Scorecard as a Strategic Management System," *Harvard Business Review*, January–February 1996, pp. 75–85.

[50]PTRM Consulting, "Integrated-Supply chain Performance Measurement: A Multi-Industry Consortium Recommendation" (Weston, MA: PTRM, 1994).

[51]Tom Richman, "Logistics Management; How 20 Best-Practice Companies Do It," *Harvard Business Review*, September–October 1995, p. 11; Ryan Mathews, "CRP Moves Toward Reality: Continuous Replenishment Will Either Be a Blessing or a Curse Depending on How the Process Is Managed on Both Sides of the Table," *Progressive Grocer* 73 (July 1994), p. 43; and Lee and Billington, 1992.

3

Internal Integration— Managing Information Flows within the Organization

Managers at Herman Miller are justifiably proud of their furniture plant in Holland, Michigan. The place is so bright and airy that it's called the "Greenhouse." But best of all is the plant's performance. A sign near the front door boasts that workers there have not shipped a single late order in 70 days. Indeed, the factory has managed to solve a host of problems plaguing office furniture makers. Herman Miller, the country's second-largest manufacturer of office furniture, built the plant five years ago, to serve a new division: "Simple, Quick, Affordable" (SQA). Key to the effort was that all sales and purchasing operations were linked via the Internet—something Herman Miller's competitors are only now starting to do. "No one is going to lead in this industry without leading in technology," said CEO Michael Volkema.

The SQA division was founded in 1995 to serve small and medium-sized businesses of 5 to 150 employees, a market Herman Miller had largely ignored. A top priority of those customers is speedy delivery of their furniture. So SQA set a goal of delivering anything in its product line within two weeks, compared with six to eight weeks for the rest of the company. To do this, the unit had to scale back the choices it offered customers. Chair finishes, for example, come in only gray or black, compared with 11 color selections in the broader Herman Miller line. To accommodate demand for fast turnaround and lower prices, the company turned to an Internet-based system. This cut inventory, reduced costs, and slashed delivery times. The SQA process works as follows. First, SQA sends a salesperson equipped with design software to a customer's office. The software runs on the salesperson's laptop, allowing the customer to select furniture from a limited range, and to choose colors, configurations, and styles. Variants are shown on the laptop screen in "3-D," and the program calculates the cost of various options. Next, the customer selects an office layout. The salesperson generates a final bill, logs onto the Internet, and transmits the order to Herman Miller factories in Michigan or California. Within two hours, the customer receives e-mail confirmation of the order and a scheduled delivery date. Scheduling software reserves the time and day for production, and space is reserved on a delivery truck. Another e-mail notifies the local dealer to schedule a crew to install the order. On the manufacturing day scheduled by the system, the order is broken down into components, and employees on various production lines start work at the same time. Factory workers gather parts for the order, staple fabrics on chairs and screens, and assemble the furniture. When the delivery truck arrives, components are brought together on the loading dock. Several times a day, suppliers of the components and materials check the SQA Web site for order volumes, in case their inventory requires restocking. Finally, between three days and two weeks after the date of sale, the furniture is installed on the customer site. This system provides nearly 99 percent on-time deliveries. Herman Miller also is setting up EZ-Connect, a dedicated Web site for top customers like Nationwide Insurance and Viking Range. Now clients around the world can order furniture from a limited menu at previously negotiated prices. And EZ-Connect also transmits a bill to the customer's accounts payable department via the Internet.

The company has developed another program to give its network of more than 500 suppliers access to its ordering system on the Web. That means companies that make chair coverings or laminated surfaces can check what the factory's needs will be weeks in advance. As soon as inventories are expected to drop below a certain level—usually a day's worth of production—the supplier sends more. To provide an incentive for meeting deadlines, each supplier receives a daily rating based on punctuality of deliveries and quality of goods sold. Suppliers that perform consistently below expectations are warned and eventually face termination of their contracts.

Source: Rocks, David, "Reinventing Herman Miller," *Business Week E. Biz*, April 3, 2000, pp. 92–96.

During the 1980s and 1990s, almost every major company went through some form of re-engineering and restructuring, as thousands of workers and managers were shed in a variety of efforts to increase productivity and reduce costs. In conjunction with these efforts, organizations implemented information systems to perform tasks previously performed by these workers. They installed systems such as Material Requirements Planning (MRP), Distribution Requirements Planning (DRP), and Enterprise Resource Planning (ERP). Worries about the Year 2000 (Y2K) bug required careful analysis of "legacy" systems to determine if any computer programming bugs existed as companies entered the new millennium.

No sooner was this over than a new challenge loomed—restructuring to function in the new era of electronic commerce. Presented with a deluge of information on "dot.coms," servers, B2B requirements, and on-line customer and supplier linkages, many organizations now have to struggle to catch up to this new business requirement. At the same time, organizations continue to reduce staffing levels and managers face the challenge of performing at higher levels with fewer resources. For many organizations, the key to improved productivity and decision-making is the expanded use of information systems. Such systems can help to improve the *internal integration* of business functions.

Internal integration of business information systems is a critical step in SCM. Unless an organization can communicate information effectively among internal business functions, information flows with external supply chain partners are unlikely to succeed. As one manager we interviewed said, "We need to be able to improve our own business processes and link them to our databases. Otherwise, we're simply pumping our garbage over the Internet to our customers and suppliers!" Indeed, the problem of internal data integration and data validity continues to be a significant problem for organizations in almost every industry. One big issue companies struggle with is data quality and data collection. The essential problem is the need to get down to detailed "data dictionary" levels in order to define specific business processes. Recently, a consulting company hosted a session to assign business process events to specific information system terms. The group spent more than two hours defining the term "on-time arrival!" Before deploying any B2B system, companies must begin at the basic level and define their business processes carefully. Then they must assign specific meaning to data elements based on events known to occur within these business processes. Data integration is becoming increasingly problematic for companies attempting to link their information systems with customers and suppliers Companies must begin with this level of detail before tackling larger "visionary" B2B supply chain issues. This is one of the most difficult lessons learned from the "dot.com" era. Without fully comprehending the need for data standards, companies purchased new B2B software based on fuzzy objectives. When companies realized the Herculean effort required to implement these applications, the money suddenly stopped flowing; so did the stock prices of the software vendors involved.

Before we embark on this discussion, let's review the evolution of information systems, and discuss why internal information integration is so critical to SCM.

A Historical Perspective

The use of computers range from systems that focus on structured repetitive tasks, to interactive systems capable of imitating human thought. Over the last 50 years, computer technology has stressed different applications, and the use of information in organizations has also evolved (see Figure 3–1). Each new information era has built upon the structure of previous applications. The first era, electronic data processing (EDP), lasted from the 1950s to the mid-1960s, and focused on the routine performance of structured tasks, often involving the automation of clerical tasks to realize greater operating efficiency such as the processing of accounting transactions. These new systems were justified on the basis of cost savings.

The next phase of computer technology, management information systems (MIS), provided information processing and data manipulation to support operational needs and reporting. This phase lasted from the mid-1960s through the mid-1980s.[1] For example, a system may convert actual historical usage data into projected forecasts of material requirements. Other tasks involved

---

- Data Processing (1950s–60s)
  - –Current data
  - –Transaction and word processing
  - –Primary justification: cost/benefit
- Management Information Systems (60s–80s)
  - –Current and historical databases
  - –Integrated data/text/graphics
  - –Primary justification: cost/benefit and value in planning and control
- Electronic Commerce (80s–present)
  - –Current, historical and future data
  - –Subject and relational databases
  - –Primary justification: creating market equilibrium rapidly and quick response to changing requirements to create advantage

---

Figure 3–1   Evolution of Information Systems

managing current and historical databases. The primary data forms included integrated data, text, and graphics.

More recently, new systems such as ERP and B2B Web-based communications as a vehicle for massive business change have been implemented. The systems often include future planning data, and apply decision-support tools that use subject and relational databases. With decision-support tools, a user and the system interact to support decision-making in a complex environment. Information systems provide the information a manager requires to make decisions; decision-support systems provide the information and assist in the decision-making process, using the Web as a vehicle for joint decision-making among supply chain partners. The types of data include not only text, but also image and voice data. In this regard, information becomes an asset for strategic planning and revenue generation. With the introduction of the World Wide Web across the Internet, organizations and individuals can access databases all over the world in a point-and-click environment, using only a personal computer, and an Internet connection.

It is not our intention to convert supply chain managers into information systems experts, as this is the role of the information systems group. However, it is important that supply chain managers have an appreciation of the functionality of currently available information systems and technology "tools." Moreover, supply chain managers need to recognize the important role that these tools play in both internal and external integration. Therefore, we will focus on the functionality of several of these tools.

Drivers of Supply Chain Systems and Applications

To be successful in the new virtual electronics-based economy (e-economy), even companies in traditional "rust-belt" industries are recognizing the need for new information systems. New systems provide a distinct advantage: they promote the flow of information instantaneously up and down the supply chain. Survival in the e-economy requires fluid and swift supply chains whose primary competitive advantage is speed and excellence of execution.

Several drivers are behind this new e-economy. These include:

- Strategic integration (internal and external)
- Globalization of markets
- Availability of powerful information systems and technology
- The need for new business processes
- The need to replace obsolete systems
- The need to continually reduce cost throughout the supply chain (strategic cost management).

As shown in Table 3–1, organizations are implementing several information systems and technologies to meet these challenges.

Internal and External Strategic Integration

As supply chain members begin to work together, integration must occur between functions both *internal* to the organization (i.e., purchasing, engineering, manufacturing, marketing, logistics, accounting, etc.) and *external* to the organization (i.e., end customers, retailers, distributors, warehouses, transportation providers, suppliers, agents, financial institutions, etc.). *Internal strategic integration* requires that all company members have access to an integrated information system, spanning multiple functions and locations. This is often accomplished through a company-wide ERP system, which links internal groups via a single integrated system. *External integration* refers to the systems that link external suppliers and customers to the focal company. External integration allows all supply chain members to share critical information such as forecast demand, actual orders, and inventory levels across the

Driver	Applications			
	Enterprise Resource Planning	Data Warehouses	Customer Relationship Management	Decision Support Systems
Internal Integration	x	x	x	x
External Integration			x	x
Globalization	x	x	x	x
Data Information Management		x	x	
New Business Processes	x	x	x	
Replace Obsolete Systems	x		x	
Strategic Cost Management	x	x	x	x

Table 3–1   Information System Drivers and Applications

supply chain. Systems used to integrate supply chain members include advanced planning systems, Internet linkages, network communications, and Electronic Data Interchange (EDI).

Globalization of Markets

While the notion of a global market is easy to envision, conducting business in different cultures and geographies is extremely challenging. Companies require systems that enable them to: 1) manage suppliers and customers all over the world; 2) allow total global logistics costs calculations; 3) increase leverage and component standardization worldwide; and 4) improve communication of strategies across all of a company's global business units and supply chain partners. Although English is becoming the universal language of the Internet, supply chain systems must be able to communicate in a variety of languages. Training users in different global locations to use these systems is an essential requirement for success.

Availability of Powerful Information Systems and Technology

New forms of servers, telecommunication and wireless applications, and software are enabling companies to do things that were once never thought possible. These systems raise the accuracy, frequency, and speed of communication between suppliers and customers, as well as for internal users. With this capability comes another problem, however: a deluge of data from many sources. Information systems must be able to effectively filter, analyze, and "mine" this data to enable effective decision-making. Users must be able to enter databases and extract the information they need to make better supply chain decisions. This is often achieved through systems known as data warehouses, and associated decision-support systems.

Several well-known firms involved in supply chain relationships owe much of their success to the systems utilized to share information with one another. Among the most notable examples are P&G and Wal-Mart. Through a series of agreements with giant retail customers; P&G has made a major commitment to developing dedicated customer teams to handle their major accounts. A primary objective of these teams is to facilitate information sharing between the firms. These teams typically address a full range of logistics, finance, accounting, information systems, and supply issues.

According to Bowersox and Closs, timely and accurate information is now more critical to American business than ever before. Three factors have fostered this change in the importance of information. First, pleasing customers has become something of a corporate obsession. Serving the customer in the best, most efficient and effective manner has become critical, and information about issues such as order status, product availability, delivery schedules, and invoices has become a necessary part of the total customer service experience. Second, information is crucial to managers' abilities to reduce inventory and human resource requirements to a competitive level. Finally, information flows are essential to strategic planning for and deployment of resources.[2]

Enable New Business Processes

Although many companies underwent re-engineering efforts in the 1980s and 1990s, these changes are not one-time events. Companies are constantly modifying their business processes in response to rapidly changing external events. Such processes include customer order management, supplier evaluation and selection, and new product development. These processes are being mapped, studied, and changed in order to reduce redundancies, delays, and waste. In so doing, organizations can create a "rapid response" capability that allows them to quickly adapt to their customers' ever-changing requirements in an effective and efficient manner. Information systems such as computer networks and ERP are enabling companies to link these processes more effectively.

Key to using information systems to develop and maintain successful supply chains is the need for virtually seamless linkages within and between organizations. This means creating intra-organizational processes and links to facilitate delivery of required information between marketing, sales, purchasing, finance, manufacturing, distribution, and transportation internally, as well as inter-organizationally, to customers and suppliers across the supply chain. More pointedly, it means that a firm must alter its way of seeing its business at the highest level. This involves alterations like aligning corporate strategies with the information technology (IT) paradigm; providing incentives for functions to achieve common goals through the sharing of information; and implementing the technologies to redesign the movement of goods to maximize channel value and lower cost.

Replace Obsolete Systems

In the past, as companies adopted new information systems, it was often done on a functional basis. Each function (e.g., accounting, purchasing, engineering, human resources) had its own system that was not linked to the other functional systems. These systems (often called "legacy systems") are now being integrated into a single enterprise-wide system used by everyone. ERP systems promise to solve incompatibilities that existed before, and to reduce excessive maintenance and programming costs. The systems are also being adopted to exploit the new hardware technologies emerging in computer net-working, telecommunications, and Web-based applications.

Strategic Cost Management

Throughout the supply chain cycle, from order fulfillment to purchasing and order payment, millions of transactions take place among different parties. In order to determine specific cost drivers behind different business processes, companies often estimated costs based on outdated cost accounting systems. New systems promise to automate data capture throughout the supply chain, thereby automating the transactions that occur in the traditional procurement cycle. This will not only reduce the costs of operating, purchasing, and logistics departments, but also will enable allocation of resources and reductions in inventory held throughout the supply chain. Prior to the 1980s, a significant portion of information flows among functional areas within an organization, and among supply chain member organizations, were paper-based. In many instances, these paper-based transactions and communications were slow, unreliable, and error-prone. Conducting business in this manner was costly and constrained a firms' ability to design, develop, procure, manufacture, and distribute their products in a timely manner. This approach also impeded efforts to develop and capitalize on successful inter-organizational ventures. During this period, information was often overlooked as a critical competitive resource because its value to supply chain members was not clearly understood. However, firms now embarking upon supply chain management initiatives recognize the vital importance of information and the various technologies that make this information available. Increased use of information systems within SCM-related areas can result in the following benefits:

- Increased productivity that, in turn, allows people to focus on value-adding activities, rather than "pushing paper."
- Expanded, more accurate and timely information to streamline the flow of materials both up and down the supply chain.
- Ability to manipulate multiple variables to support complex decision-making through detailed simulation and decision-support systems.
- Ability to modify data to determine the impact on a decision.
- Improved linkages across functions within organizations and among supply-member organizations.
- The ability to consolidate global purchase requirements. For example, an organization that was able to fully leverage its purchases as a result of implementing a global commodity database, leading to cost reductions of approximately $1 million in the first year the system was implemented.[3]

- Lower total operating costs. An example of this benefit includes the elimination of routine paper transactions. Purchasing transaction systems have reduced the cost per transaction by 30 percent to 50 percent, while reducing the procurement cycle from weeks to days.[4]
- Improved supplier performance measurement. Organizations that have implemented computerized supplier performance measurement systems have achieved significant improvements in both supplier quality (e.g., 20 percent reduction in defective parts per million) and delivery performance (e.g., improvement in shipments received on time from 60 percent to 95 percent).[5]

Developing and implementing supply chain information systems is costly. Without proper planning, the system can fail to meet the user's needs, and development costs can quickly escalate beyond budgeted volumes. Top management must provide the vision, leadership, and resources to support information systems development throughout the process. They must also make certain that all supply chain "stakeholders" participate and remain actively involved throughout the process. Although the use of new information systems can lead to significant improvements, internal functions and supply chain partners must be willing to commit the resources to properly plan, develop, implement, train for, and use the system. If these conditions are not met, the resulting system may simply automate existing ways of doing business and fail to generate the expected benefits.

Information technology infrastructures required to support a firm's communication networks, databases, and operating systems is complex, comprehensive, and critically important. In fact, according to an article in *Sloan Management Review*, "IT infrastructure capabilities underpin the competitive positioning of business initiatives such as cycle time reduction, implementing redesigned cross-functional processes, utilizing cross-selling opportunities and capturing the channel to the customer."[6] These infrastructures also support the development, management, and maintenance of inter-organizational supply chains.

In a sense, the information systems and the technologies utilized in these systems represent one of the fundamental elements that link the organizations of a supply chain into a unified and coordinated system. In the current competitive climate, little doubt remains about the importance of information to the ultimate success of any supply chain management initiative.

When all of these applications work as they should, the result is a shared information system that spans all functions along the supply chain with the following characteristics:[7]

- Centralized coordination of information flows, but cross-functional/cross-organizational decision-making.
- Total logistics management—integrating all transportation, warehousing, ordering, and manufacturing systems.
- Customer fulfillment systems that trigger a cascading series of modifications to production schedules, logistics plans, and warehouse operations.
- Coordinated transportation resources across business units and national boundaries.
- Global inventory management—the ability to locate, track, and predict the movement of every component or material anywhere upstream or downstream in the supply chain.
- Global sourcing—consolidation of the purchasing function across organizational lines, facilitating purchasing leverage and component standardization across business units and across multiple continents.
- Cross-organizational information access—clarity of production and demand information residing in organizations both upstream and downstream throughout the supply chain, but secure from competing members of the supply chain.
- Data interchange between affiliates and non-affiliates through wireless communication.
- Data capture—the ability to acquire data about an order at the point of origin, and to track products during movement and as their characteristics change.
- Transformation of the business from within—managers who can see the "big picture" and accept the new forms of business processes and systems.
- Higher levels of trust between supply chain partners to justify investments in shared information systems.

Although the promise of these globally linked information systems is great, ERP applications such as those offered by Baan, J. D. Edwards, Peoplesoft, Oracle, and SAP, are difficult to implement and very expensive. Many companies are in the very early stages of deploying these technologies. Nevertheless, major benefits can accrue even when isolated modules are implemented. These benefits range from the routine improvement of clerical functions to increased decision-support involving multiple variables.

In the remainder of the chapter, we provide an overview of four important forms of information systems used in managing internal supply chain activities: ERP, data warehouses, Customer Relationship Management (CRM), and decision-support systems.

Enterprise Resource Planning (ERP)

ERP systems are integrated business transaction processing and reporting systems that focus on business processes. A simple definition of an ERP system is that it is a system for managing organizational resources, including:

- People
- Processes
- Technology

Understanding the resources consumed allows an organization to leverage these resources more productively. In the words of one ERP consultant, the system serves as the organization's backbone, in terms of providing the fundamental decision-making support throughout. ERP systems add a "process logic" to an organizational information system; they create a fundamental discipline in business processes. Whereas decisions in the past were made independent of other functional areas, ERP systems effectively "force" people to interact in a single system, even if they would prefer not to. As shown in Figure 3–2, ERP systems also create a process logic among the closely related areas of customer order management, manufacturing planning and execution, purchasing processes, and financial management and accounting. In effect,

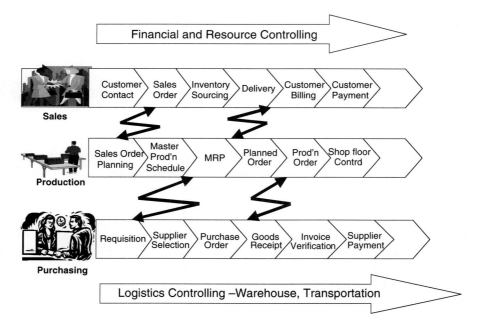

Figure 3–2   Business Process Integration in ERP

ERP systems enable people in these very different parts of the business to communicate.

An ERP system allows a salesperson in the field to take a customer's order, log onto the company system, and access the sales order planning and master production schedule. The salesperson can view inventory records to determine products that are "available-to-promise." Once the customer's order is entered into the system, the salesperson can answer a customer's inquiry about when they can expect a potential order to be delivered. The master production schedule, in turn, electronically drives the material requirements system (MRP), which automatically generates purchase orders to ensure that suppliers deliver parts, components, and services in time to produce the customer's order. The MRP-scheduled order releases are converted into purchase requisitions, which are then electronically sent to selected suppliers. When the supplier delivers the components, this information is passed to the scheduling system, which ensures that the components are linked to the specific production order on the shop floor. Once production begins, the salesperson in the field also knows that the order will soon be delivered to the customer. Once the order is delivered, customer billing is also automatically generated by the ERP system.

The concept of a single information system that links sales, production, transportation, warehousing, and purchasing appears to be an inherently obvious way to manage these different business processes. However, the evolution of information systems in most organizations reveals that until recently, such integrated systems were not common. Moreover, most of the functional areas described here utilized their own individual systems that typically did not communicate with one another. Each of these individual information systems were able to fulfill the requirements of information needs of sales, purchasing, production, etc., but were not linked to one another in any way. The different systems often did not communicate with the accounting or financial reporting systems in the firm. This made it difficult, if not impossible to be able to extract cost data related to indirect and support functions, in order to more accurately allocate overhead costs to different parts of the business. Thus, companies were unable to determine the true costs of serving the customer. Deciding how much to charge one customer with high service requirements over another customer with low service requirements became very difficult. In legacy systems, decisions in each functional area and in each business process were made independently, based on a limited perspective of the "big picture" across the entire enterprise.

The new ERP systems hold the promise of providing a unified, organization-wide view of business processes and associated information, rather than the isolated functional perspective of these legacy systems. A typical ERP system is designed around four primary business processes, shown in Figure 3–2.

1. Making a product: Manufacturing Planning and Execution process
2. Buying a product: Procurement process
3. Selling a product or service: Customer Order Management Process
4. Costing, paying the bills, collecting: Financial/Management Accounting and Reporting process

While ERP systems hold great promise, conversion from multiple functional legacy systems to an integrated ERP system is a significant task typically requiring several years to complete.

ERP systems facilitate the integration of these processes by adopting a single customer, product and supplier database. One master record with multiple views is used for the enterprise. All processes use a common database. Furthermore, information is captured only once, reducing the possibility of inaccurate data entering the database. Information is provided to the affected business process in real time, eliminating delays as a result of information sharing. Specific transactions taking place in each business process are visible to everyone in the organization; theoretically, if anyone wants to find out where an order is in the process, or whether a supplier has been paid, etc., he or she can do so. Furthermore, all business processes are linked with the workflow, such that standard workflow templates for entering information about transactions are provided every step of the way.

Implementing ERP Systems

All of this makes such good sense, it seems as if companies should have done this a long time ago! However, the actual process of implementing a new ERP system in an environment where people have grown accustomed to using their familiar legacy systems has proven to be a monumental task in many organizations. Many implementation efforts have turned into multi-million-dollar projects involving multiple consultants residing on-site for months and even years. Why is ERP implementation proving to be so difficult and expensive?

The answer lies in the fact that when businesses implement ERP, they must adhere to a more rigorous set of business processes. In Chapter 2, we discussed process mapping as a tool to identify what happens within any given business process. Before organizations implement ERP, they must first create a process map for every key business process. An example of a process map for a typical requisition process is shown in Figure 3–3. Many companies who formally define their business processes for this purpose are doing so for the first time! When companies map the process, often they discover it is very different than they originally believed. In some cases, no formal process exists since everyone in the organization has always done it their own way! When it comes time to create an information system around the business processes, many companies

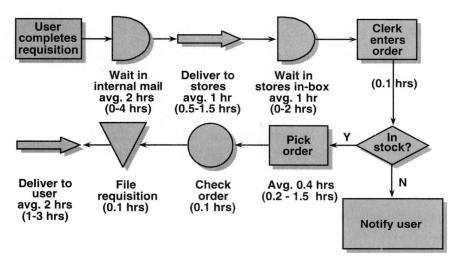

Figure 3–3   Process Flow Chart: Stores Requisition

discover that they need to "re-engineer" their business processes before they can build the information system around it. In some cases, changing these business processes requires major organizational and cultural change.

In order to effectively implement an ERP system, a company must ensure that its business processes are in good order. Only then should the ERP system be designed around the process. The steps in the process of implementation are:

1. **Define the current process "as is."** An ERP implementation team of subject-matter experts should be used to document the current process. This means that the ERP implementation team must actually "staple themselves" to a customer order or purchase requisition, and discover how the current process takes place. For example, in the process shown in Figure 3–3, the team may be surprised to learn that a stores requisition spends a significant amount of time waiting to be delivered via internal mail. Once the product reaches the stores area, the team may also discover that the requisition sits in the stores mailbox for several hours. In the process of developing the "as is" picture of any given business process, the team seeks to understand the delays and inefficiencies in the process that need to be addressed.
2. **"Design Phase"**—determine the "best-in-class" approach for the process under consideration. At this point, the team must understand the final objective of the process. Furthermore, they must understand what the ERP system will replace, and how the benefits are likely to

occur. Although companies typically employ consultants to provide "best practices" and various types of assistance throughout the process, it is the internal team that must ultimately decide what the re-engineered process will look like, because they are the ones that are going to have to live with the end result.

3. "Construction"—Actual development of the system. This is an iterative process in which consultants work with managers who are most familiar with the business processes in question. Most ERP packages consist of different "modules," including MRP/Master Production Schedule/Activity Control, Distribution, Finance, Human Resource, Project Management, and Purchasing. The construction phase involves selection of modules to be implemented and configuration to meet process requirements. For instance, the process shown in Figure 3–4 would perhaps be included in the Distribution module and would require that a specific screen come up for each of the decisions involved in this process. Obviously, the delays would be minimized, perhaps by having a "notice" automatically generated to the user instead of having the requisition sit in a "mailbox." At any rate, a well-defined and re-engineered process requires that users be involved and specific barriers addressed.

4. In the final phases of ERP implementation, the team will typically test the system and conduct pre-production runs. Next, it will run in the new process parallel to the existing systems and, finally, "flip the switch" to a fully operational state.

ERP "Meltdowns"

Although ERP systems provide the means for increased functional integration and improved business performance, some companies are finding the implementation process to be expensive, and in some cases, ineffective. Consider, for instance, the case of Hershey Foods. In 1999, just a few days before Halloween, the biggest candy sales period of the year, one of Hershey Foods' largest warehouses in Michigan displayed empty shelves where there should have been Hershey's candies. The trouble: an order for 20,000 pounds of candy placed by the regional distributor had not arrived. In fact, the distributor had not received any orders for five weeks! The $4.4 billion candy maker had flipped the switch on a $112 million system that was supposed to automate and modernize everything from candy orders to putting pallets on trucks. The project called for 5,000 personal computers, as well as network hubs and servers and applications from several different vendors.

What happened? Despite the complexity of the system, Hershey decided to go on line with a huge piece of it all at once—a so-called "big bang" that computer experts say is rare and dangerous. Initially, the confectioner planned to start up in April, a slow period. Development and testing weren't complete, and the date was pushed to July, when Halloween orders generally begin to arrive. The system had trouble receiving customer orders and transmitting the details of those orders to warehouses for fulfillment. System problems were exacerbated by the fact that Hershey had increased its product offerings through an acquisition of the candy maker, Leaf North America, while adding variations to its existing products. The proliferation of candies seemed to be increasing sales but made the systems issues even more challenging. The result of this serious mistake: Net income dropped 19 percent in the third quarter of 1999, and market share was also lost to competitors. Unfortunately, Hershey also lost out on a good portion of its Christmas 1999 sales as well.[8]

Implementing an ERP system is a huge undertaking that requires major change in processes and organizational culture. Companies should not expect external consultants to define business processes for them. Their best people should be assigned to work on the implementation teams. This can be a major challenge, as internal employees are often resistant to change and prefer to use the legacy systems.

Another important lesson to be learned from the Hershey experience is that ERP systems may be very good for integrating internal business processes, but often are not capable of linking suppliers and customers in the supply chain. In many respects, ERP systems should be installed before linked information systems are put in place with outside parties. There is no point providing inaccurate information to suppliers and customers. Many ERP systems cannot yet provide the type of support required for the following types of supply chain processes:

- Demand planning
- Advanced order management
- Transportation planning
- Electronic procurement
- Electronic commerce

Many current SCM-related systems have been developed as "bolt-ons" to ERP systems. Moreover, ERP systems are not the "silver bullet" that will integrate parties in the supply chain. As one expert, Dan Wecker, from Manugistics noted: "If you are planning to run ERP using inaccurate data, you have a worthless system. ERP is in place to record transactions, but not to facilitate decision-making in the supply chain. To truly drive collaboration and integration in the supply chain, process change is required. Companies need to overcome their suspicion of consultants and software and adhere to a rigorous set of timeframes and project objectives. Finally, companies need a clear business strategy which drives their goals and performance metrics to guide their ERP implementation effort."[9]

Supply Chain ERP Modules

This section describes the basic modules and features of an ERP system that are unique to supply chain processes. The supply chain modules are typically integrated into a single system used by multiple functions in the organization. This represents one of the greatest challenges to information systems developers. Many information systems have grown in increments, with different divisions and functions developing their own systems and applications. ERP systems designed to integrate these legacy systems provide a means of linking sources. Supply chain processes require information from a variety of sources including:

- Current inventory and order status
- Cost accounting
- Sales forecasts and customer orders
- Manufacturing capacity
- New product introductions
- Computer-aided design (CAD) drawings
- Product and quality specifications
- Supplier capabilities
- Transportation rates
- Foreign currency exchange rates
- Competitive benchmark analysis

The role of these modules throughout the order fulfillment cycle is described next:

Inventory Management And Control—The purpose of this module is to provide control and visibility to the status of individual items maintained in inventory. The main functions of this module are to maintain inventory record accuracy and to generate material requirements for all purchased items. The system should also be able to analyze inventory performance of purchased items.

Material Requirements Planning (MRP)—This module involves the planning of material requirements generated in the inventory control and management module. This part of the system also allows the manual input of requirements to handle one-time purchase requirements when no established need or requirement exists within the system. The MRP module generates automatic purchase requisitions and passes that information to the material release system. This step is necessary before generating material releases because an item may not have an outstanding blanket purchase order with a supplier. In other words, no supplier may yet exist on file for that item. The proper personnel must have visibility to exception items so they can establish a purchase order.

Material Releases—This step involves the physical generation and forwarding of material releases to suppliers (either electronically or by mail/fax). A material requirement does not reach this stage unless it has an assigned purchase order. The material release in a non-electronic environment is a paper-generated document sent directly through the mail or faxed to suppliers. In an electronic environment, the supplier receives the release electronically from the purchaser, either through an EDI system or via the Internet. Both types of systems rely upon this module to generate the actual material requirement. The difference lies in how the two environments transmit the release.

Request For Quotation Processing—Within most large companies, the routine reordering of items with established purchase orders is the responsibility of a materials group not directly connected to purchasing. The request for quotation module is the direct responsibility of purchasing. When a user generates a material request with no current supplier, it is often the responsibility of purchasing to identify potential suppliers. One method to accomplish this is to generate requests for quotes (RFQs). An RFQ is a request to submit a proposal based on a set of specifications provided by a buyer. This module assists in identifying qualified suppliers to receive RFQ requests. The module automatically generates, issues, and tracks the progress of the RFQs throughout the system. Again, this may be done either electronically or manually.

Supplier Selection Assistance—Firms are placing an increasing emphasis on supplier selection because of the contribution the supply makes to strategic performance objectives. The supplier selection assistance module uses a basic set of mathematical algorithms to assist a buyer when evaluating different supply and cost scenarios.

Purchase Order Issuance—This module supports the generation of purchase orders, which involves the automatic assignment of purchase order numbers for selected items along with the transfer of purchase order information to the proper database(s). This module provides purchasing with visibility to current purchase orders on file.

Supplier Performance Measurement And Control—This module provides visibility to open-item status, and measures and analyzes supplier performance. The module provides updated information about the progress of a material release as it moves through the ordering cycle. The key features of this module include automatic inquiry of item status, monitoring of order due dates, and supplier performance analysis. Buyers must have current information about the status of material releases. The module should have the capability to monitor planned receipts against due dates, provide immediate visibility to past-due items, and flag those items likely to become past due. The system should generate summary reports of supplier performance compared against predetermined performance criteria. Criteria can include due-date compliance, quality ratings, price variances, quantity discrepancies, and total transportation charges.

Receiving And Inspection—This module updates system records upon receipt of an item. Most systems hold a received item in a protected state (unavailable for use) until all inbound processing is complete. Sophisticated systems are able to do this via a barcode reader that automatically transmits all necessary information into the database. This processing includes tasks such as inspection (if required), material transfer, or stock keeping.

Management And Reporting Capabilities—A well-designed ERP supply chain module can generate timely management reports, providing visibility to the entire materials process.

ERP and Data Warehouses

In many organizations, data were stored and processed in mainframe computers. Organizations are now moving toward multi-tiered systems of personal computer (PC) servers. In making this transition, many organizations are utilizing a "data warehouse." A data warehouse provides a means to store data from disparate systems in a way that provides the organization's decision-makers a quick and easy single point of access.

Data collected by the operations of the ERP system is continuously transferred to the data warehouses to enable "data mining." This allows users to go into the database, extract information they need, and manipulate it so as to discover patterns, cases, etc. for decision-making. For example, users might need customer and supplier profiles, usage of parts, products, inventory, and specific rules and exceptions to standard purchase requisitions.

Systems come with a variety of "canned reports." Some systems allow report generation via "On-line Analytical Processing" (OLAP), meaning that users can generate these reports on-line from any remote location. Another capability of a well-designed system is that the frequency of data reporting and system updating can match a user's operational needs. A system that operates in a real-time environment provides decision-makers with current data. Real-time updating means that all data files that include a specific address are automatically updated within the system.

The type of transaction often determines the type of system updating that occurs. For example, a firm requiring immediate visibility of current inventory levels (such as a distribution center processing orders throughout the day) would utilize real-time updating. Other types of transactions may require daily or periodic updating of system records. The type of transaction updating must match the need for the data. Material expediters, for example, require the most current data and status reports of inbound receipts whereas inventory analysts may only require weekly or monthly reports of inventory activity. The appropriate reporting frequency is determined by the rate of inventory turnover. If turnover is rapid, the user requires frequent reports and on-line computer terminal visibility. If not, then less frequent reporting may be acceptable.

Customer Relationship Management

One rapidly changing area that addresses the need for both internal and external integration of information systems is Customer Relationship Management (CRM). CRM is based on the premise that in order to get closer to your customers, you need to develop a relationship with them. CRM is the process of creating relationships with customers through increased integration and communication of customer requirements throughout the supplying company in order to create value for the customer. CRM is in fact an integrated sales, marketing, and service strategy that has significant SCM implications. Currently, between 400 to 600 software vendors claim to provide some aspect of CRM.

CRM promotes a totally new way of viewing the customer from an integrated perspective. Organizations interface with customers in a variety of ways; through Web-based transactions, phone calls, personal sales calls, faxes, and a variety of other media. However, information on customers' requirements communicated through these different media is only rarely collected and systematically organized. The promise of CRM is for organizations to be able to systematically organize customer data to better understand and serve the customer. CRM organizations are well positioned to "suggest" the best product-service bundle to the customer that meets his or her needs thereby generating additional sales. A good example of such an approach is seen in the Amazon.com Website. Once you purchase a book or CD in a particular area (e.g., mystery novel or jazz recording), you will be presented with other products in those categories that Amazon sells on your next visit to the site.

Although many software vendors claim that their software will provide "instant" CRM, few companies have effectively deployed a true CRM system. This is because of the difficulty of defining and operationalizing customer relationships. In an interpersonal relationship, two people mutually influence each other's behavior over a long period. Relationships have a number of characteristics:

- Relationships develop over time
- Not all relationships become commitments

- Relationships are bi-directional (involve interactions between parties)
- Successful relationships require mutual benefits

To develop customer relationships, firms must begin by understanding and classifying their customers. Examples of customer classifications (or "market segments") may include:

- Demographic segmentation
- Product end-use
- Buying situation (bargain hunters, one-time transaction, repeat customer, etc.)
- Customer benefits obtained from your company
- Customer buying behavior (erratic, brand-conscious, price-driven, etc.)
- Customer decision-making style (analytical, cost-driven, etc.)

Indeed, as shown in Figure 3–4, not all customers are created equal; nor should they be treated equally. Tier 4 customers are infrequent buyers, comprise 65 percent of the customer base, and are relatively easy to serve but represent 3 percent of total sales. The strategy with Tier 4 customers is to grow or aggregate volume to grow business.[10] Tier 3 customers are costly to serve (45 percent of costs), yet represent only 7 percent of revenues. Companies should consider ways to reduce costs, or in some cases, drop these customers. Tier 1 and 2 customers are only 11 percent of the customer base, yet comprise 90 percent of sales revenues. Strategies for keeping these customers include improving customer service, increasing customer loyalty, and developing closer relationships with these customers. CRM promises to better serve these

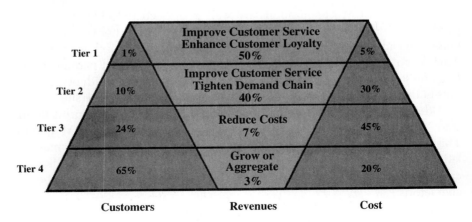

Figure 3–4   Not All Customers Are Equal

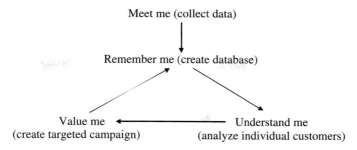

Figure 3–5   CRM Data Acquisition

customers by using relationships to grow revenues. CRM systems allow sales people to access integrated information allowing them to provide a higher level of customer service, and to introduce more repeatable sales processes and procedures to create value. Some of these processes and procedures may span areas such as product and service information, communication, channels for product/service delivery, and pricing. This requires that the company maintain a database capable of recording customer preferences. The system must be capable of collecting data from a variety of media (phone, Web, fax, mail, etc.) to address the individual customer. As such, the system should have the ability to gather and remember the response of an individual customer, as well as address that individual again in a way that takes into account his or her unique response.

Figure 3-5 illustrates how this interaction takes place.[11] Data are collected regarding product preferences, buying behavior, channel preferences, etc. The data can be analyzed in an aggregate manner to identify which "clusters" of customers to target with specific ad campaigns. Once this database is in place, the company can readily "recall" how the customer would like the product or service to be delivered the next time the customer interacts with the sales organization.

No single software technology exists that enables firms to fully achieve this level of customer integration. In fact, CRM is likely to involve a number of different technologies, including:

- Customer databases
- ERP systems
- Financial systems
- Call center technology
- E-mail
- Web technology, extranets, the Internets, intranets

- Sales force automation
- Artificial intelligence
- Data mining

Recent research on Customer Information System (CIS) capabilities in B2B service firms and their relationship to profitability found that improved customer information management did not directly correspond to reporting of growth in net income and sales.[12] However, CIS capabilities (the ability to gather quality data, store it, move it, and share it in the organization) were related to "Marketing Performance" measures such as lifetime customer value, retention and "share of wallet." Although there is no accepted universal measure of relationship strength, these indicators can be seen as a surrogate for a strong relationship. Whether such marketing technologies as sales force automation systems, call center technology and analytical tools are associated with these relationship indicators remains to be seen.

It is clear that customer relationships develop with interactions over time. Trends in technology and communications have made possible the use of the Internet to help manage the marketing process. The technology trends are large-scale databases, the "engine" that drives the Web, and the widespread adoption of Web browsers, not to mention the Internet itself. These technologies make it possible to collect and manage data on customers, communicate with them, and design products for them in a way that marketers only dreamed of in the past.

The standard model of marketing communication always contained a feedback loop. Now, on a large scale, we can incorporate that feedback quickly and specifically into the marketing process. Interactive Marketing incorporates these elements of database and Internet technology (the ability to address the customer specifically, remember what the customer said, and then provide a response that takes into account what was said). When you have many customers, remembering what the customer said is much easier when you can store that information in a database. This type of personalization refers to a unique communication and customization of a product. Both routes are available to an organization if it has customer information and the underlying capabilities to deliver.

B2B marketers have been interactive with their customers for a long time, with sales representatives as the main form of promotion and customer contact. All types of firms now have the potential to adopt this method of marketing and research suggesting that ultimately all firms should engage in personalization and customization.[13]

When Your Web Site is Not Aligned With Your Business Strategies

Organizations must examine their communications and interaction with customers in the context of their overall business unit, marketing and SCM strategies. This is especially important when one considers Web-based marketing. Look at your company's Web sites to see if they are consistent with basic positioning (low-cost vs. differentiation) and segmentation (broad vs. focused) strategies. Wal-Mart historically has pursued a low-cost strategy and has focused on inventory control and supply chain management systems to ensure that it delivers "Everyday Low Prices." Wal-Mart's Web site development history has been to try to secure a competency from the outside because it did not have the competency within the firm. Its competencies were in technologies focused on lowering costs and exchanging information with its suppliers, not on electronic interfaces with its ultimate consumer. Three Web development companies later, and a redesign that completely shut down the site before the Christmas 2000 season, Wal-Mart's site is now consistent with its basic positioning strategy and segmentation choice. The site is simple, so that its market segment, which is perhaps not used to ordering over the Internet, may easily navigate the site.

From the differentiation point of view, look at Target's site. It can be argued that Target pursues a "both" strategy (expect more, pay less), with differentiation being its major emphasis. Target creates a store atmosphere that is less cluttered than Wal-Mart and relies on its ability to deliver fashionable items in the housewares and women's fashion areas to attract its customer base. Target's customers are typically more affluent and spend more per visit than typical Wal-Mart customers. Target already has emphasized technologies on the consumer end of the supply chain with its in-store gift registry systems, the use of the Internet to facilitate that system, and other on-line ordering capabilities. These technologies are consistent with Target's overall strategy. However, Target bought a direct marketing fulfillment company as part of its Web strategy because it did not have the internal capabilities to fulfill orders.

We can also look at some publishing sites in this context. Each of the sites for CNN, USA Today, and the Wall Street Journal has a different appearance and portrays the unique differentiation position of the underlying medium. From a marketing communications point of view, each site effectively reinforces the brand image. The Wall Street Journal site is the only on-line media site that has successfully charged a subscription fee. This fee has allowed the Journal to reinforce the uniqueness of the underlying product, protect its brand, and earn revenue.

As CRM and Web-based technologies continue to unfold, we will witness a higher level of customer integration. However, these technologies must be linked to a business strategy that targets the right customers and be linked to a supply chain system that can produce new products and fulfill orders according to key customers' expectations. Few things are more damaging to customer relationships than unfulfilled promises, resulting from a poorly performing supply chain.

Decision Support Systems

By the early 1970s, the demand for all types of information systems started to accelerate. The increased capabilities and reduced costs justified computerized support for an increased number of non-routine applications. At that time, the discipline of decision support systems (DSS) was initiated. The basic objective of a DSS is to provide computerized support to complex non-routine and partially structured decisions.

At first, the cost of building a DSS prohibited its widespread use. However, the availability of low-cost personal computers around 1980 changed this situation. PCs allowed a person with limited programming ability to build useful DSS applications (e.g., spreadsheets with built-in macros). Analysts, managers, and others began building their own decision support systems.[14]

Given the complexity of supply chains, development of DSS to assist decision-makers in the design and operation of integrated supply chains is becoming increasingly common. These DSS help identify opportunities for improvements across the supply chain, far beyond what even the most experienced manager can provide through intuitive insight. DSS allow people to examine relationships and performance across the supply chain, including suppliers, manufacturing plants, distribution centers, transportation options, product demand, relationships among product families, and a host of other factors to optimize supply chain performance.

Effective supply chain DSS requires large amounts of both static and dynamic information from member organizations. The static information includes production rates and capabilities for all supply chain entities, bills of material, routings, and facility preference. The dynamic information includes forecasts, orders, and current deliveries. Using all of this information to solve, for example, a quick-response scheduling problem across the supply chain is virtually impossible with a single technology. However, all the data can be readily obtained from existing information systems through structured query language (SQL) calls to various databases or to the supply chain data warehouse if one exists.

Specific technologies that may be utilized for an effective supply chain management DSS include:

1. **SQL Interface.** Efficient databases are required to handle the vast amount of forecast, order, inventory, process, and product information. The DSS must serve as a data concentrator and have an SQL interface for direct links to common relational databases or data warehouses.

2. **Expert System Rules.** Once the data have been gathered and a schedule produced, the scheduler interprets the schedule and determines its validity. Expert systems technology can capture some of the scheduler's expertise. The expert system can apply and test the validity of production rules of thumb, analyze the schedule, and recommend policy changes that yield cost savings.

3. **Scheduling Algorithms.** The scheduling tool should be able to develop a schedule based on the information in its database. The process of generating the schedule involves determining what should be made, when, how much, and on what production units. The scheduling tool should contain algorithms based in traditional operations research algorithms, including capacity balancing, materials explosion, sequencing, lot sizing, just-in-time scheduling, and material flow adjustment.

4. **Linear Programming Capabilities.** The software tool should be able to formulate any linear, nonlinear, or mixed-integer model. Direct links should be available to the best commercially available optimizers. Special algorithms and approaches are needed for large-scale nonlinear problems and decision-making under risk and uncertainty.

5. **Blocked Scheduling.** Blocked operations defy most algorithmic approaches, especially when transitions involve significant sequence-dependent setup costs and losses. Examples of blocked operations that are particularly difficult include chemical reactors, plastics extruders, paper machines, continuous blenders, packaging lines, printing presses, and some flexible manufacturing processes. A combination of linear programming and expert system rules is particularly effective.

6. **Multi-Site/Multi-Stage Scheduling.** Multi-plant and multi-stage processes are encountered routinely. Linear programming can allocate production across plants and optimally distribute products to warehouses and demand centers. The information required includes raw material availability and costs, transportation costs, inventory storage costs, and plant capacity and capabilities for all supply chain entities. Multi-stage processes can be handled within the bill-of-material structure, which provides for different recipes and routings for making a product at each distinct stage of production.

7. **Graphical User Interface.** A powerful graphical user interface (GUI) is needed to provide facilities for the on-line creation of custom

windows and dialog boxes, pull-down menus, presentation graphics, and hypertext help. These capabilities enable new applications to be built in a matter of days and user interfaces to be constructed quickly and easily.

8. **User Definable Database.** Every scheduling application has unique attributes that need to be defined in the form of large matrices, bills of materials, product flows, and so on. The database should be user-definable and take an object-oriented approach. Extensive data manipulation capabilities should be provided via set and matrix algebra, a macro language, and an integrated expert system shell that operates directly on the database.

9. **Available-to-Promise.** In today's customer-driven business environment, customers want a quicker response to their inquiries as to whether a product or capacity is available-to-promise. Soon customers will want this response time to shrink to near zero. As global competition increases, more companies will move to such scheduling practices and bring their customers into their production processes.

10. **Demand Management.** Demand management is the operational management of demand information for planning purposes. In every supply chain there are operations that need to be planned based on predicted demand. The specific operations, including production of intermediates, purchase of raw materials, and production of finished goods are a function of asset flexibility and market lead times. The issue is not just forecasts but how to generate forecasts, manage them, reconcile new information with the forecasts, and constantly keep them up to date.[15]

Summary

The sharing of information among supply chain members is a fundamental requirement for effective supply chain management. At the ultimate level of integration, decision-makers at all levels within the supply chain member organizations receive the information they need, in the desired format, when they need it, regardless of where within the supply chain this information originates. Providing decision-makers within the supply chain the "right" information, in the necessary format, and in a timely manner is a major challenge. Before initiating supply chain systems that link external customers and suppliers, internal systems must contain the information required for the key decision-makers in all relevant functional areas. The information systems and the technologies utilized in these systems represent one of the fundamental elements that link the organizations of a supply chain. The range of technologies available to support supply chain management efforts is vast and ever changing. Unfortunately, there is not a single "right" IT solution for supply chain management. Organizations need to explore various options to arrive at a solution that provides the functionality required for their specific supply chain management initiative. Toward this end, benchmarking other organizations involved in integrated supply chain management efforts to identify "best practices" is essential.

Supply chain management initiatives are unlikely to succeed without the appropriate information systems and the technology required to support them. Given this situation, information systems and technology decisions cannot be taken lightly. These important decisions should be made by a cross-functional, inter-organizational management group that has been afforded the time and resources required to develop a supply chain information systems strategy, implement the strategy, and oversee its ongoing performance.

Endnotes

[1] F. L. Dubois and E. Carmel, "Information Technology and Leadtime Management in International Manufacturing Operations," *Global Information Systems and Technology: Focus on the Organization and its Functional Areas*, P. Candace Deans and Kirk R. Karwan, ed. (London: Idea Group Publishing, 1994), pp. 279–293.

[2] Donald J. Bowersox and David J. Closs, *Logistical Management: The Integrated Supply Chain Process* (New York: McGraw Hill, 1996).

[3] Robert M. Monczka, Ernest L. Nichols, Jr., and Robert B. Handfield, "Information systems, Technology, Procurement and Supply Chain Management: A View to the Future," NAPM International Conference, Anaheim, CA, 1995.

[4] Ibid.

[5] Ernest L. Nichols Jr. and Robert M. Monczka, "Value of Supplier Performance Measurement," working paper from the Global Procurement and Supply Chain Benchmarking Initiative at Michigan State University, 1997.

[6] Marianne Broadbent and Peter Weill, "Management by Maxim: How Business and IT Managers Can Create Infrastructures," *Sloan Management Review*, Spring 1997, p. 77.

[7] Dubois and Carmel, 1994.

[8] Emily Nelson and Evan Ramstad, "Hershey's Biggest Dud Has Turned Out to be New Computer System," *Wall Street Journal*, October 29, 1999, p. A1, and Shelly Branch, "Hershey Net Sinks by 19%; Snafus Linger," *Wall Street Journal*, October 26, 1999, p. A3.

[9]Dan Wecker, Lecture, Michigan State University, The Eli Broad Graduate School of Management, November, 1998.

[10]Debra Zahay and Robert Handfield, "Back to the Basics: How to Create Value from Technology," Working paper, North Carolina State University, College of Management, 2001.

[11]Debra Zahay and Abbie Griffin, "Electronic Marketing Metrics," Working paper, North Carolina State University, 2001.

[12]Ibid.

[13]Don Peppers and Martha Rogers, "Enterprise One to One: Tools for Competing in the Interactive Age," (New York: Currency Doubleday 1997).

[14]Efraim Turban, Ephraim McLean, and James Wetherbe, *Information Technology for Management: Improving Quality and Productivity* (New York: John Wiley, 1996), pp. 41–42.

[15]Adapted from Bernd H. Flickinger and Thomas E. Baker, "Supply Chain Management in the 1990s," *APICS-The Performance Advantage*, February 1995, pp. 24-28.

4

The Financial Impacts of SCM—Finding the "Sweet Spot"

IBM's Turnaround

From 1991 to 1998, the world's largest information systems manufacturer, International Business Machines (IBM), underwent a radical restructuring that has affected every area of its business, especially its supply chain. Between 1991 and 1995, the company's primary business, manufacturing computer hardware and peripherals, suffered intensely. During this period, the company lost *15 billion dollars!* (That's a lot of money, even for IBM.) Moreover, the company became so big that it forgot the two major concepts that had made it successful: customer focus and technology leadership.

Enter Louis Gerstner, the new CEO. Gerstner previously led R. J. Reynolds in the food industry, and understood the importance of managing the supply chain with a customer focus. The first task he set for himself was to completely re-focus the company, from a *computer manufacturer* to a *customer solutions provider*. As a solutions provider, the "new" IBM would work to create integrated hardware and software solutions for customers, and would purchase whatever products it needed to meet customers' needs. In some cases, this might even mean purchasing and installing a competitor's product, if that product was better able to meet the customer's requirements. For instance, perhaps a customer needed a network system to ensure that all of its salespeople were interconnected while on the road, so that they could dial in on their modems and upload their orders to a central system at the end of the day. IBM would purchase the network hardware, provide the appropriate software, install it, and in some cases, train the users.

This was a radical departure from what IBM had done in the past, and had profound implications for its future. First, it required IBM to take a hard look at many of its "traditional core" businesses, such as mainframes and mini-computers, and realize that it was no longer the world leader in these areas. Furthermore, these businesses were not profitable since many customers were moving away from these technologies. In some cases, IBM "spun off" businesses to companies such as Solectron, a contract manufacturer. It also meant that IBM would be outsourcing many of the supply chain processes and products that it had created internally in the past. Almost every major process in IBM's supply chain was a candidate for possible outsourcing; manufacturing, assembly, sourcing, software development, testing, and other areas.

After the dust cleared, IBM was a new company. In the past, it purchased only 30 percent of its cost of goods outside the company. Today, it purchases 70 percent from external sources. Consequently, supply chain management became much more important from an executive perspective. The changes at IBM are working, as the company went from losses totaling $15 billion between 1991 and 1995 to a net profit of $17 billion between 1995 and 1998. Quite a turn-around! Even so, IBM continues to outsource parts of its business. Most recently, it spun off the entire manufacturing arm for its personal computer division to a contract manufacturer. Although such outsourcing decisions are difficult, IBM continues to strive to remain well positioned in its supply chain, in order to withstand the competitive environment of the new millennium.

As discussed in the first chapter, the first step in creating a high performing value system is developing an in-depth understanding of an organization's position in the supply chain. By employing supply chain mapping methodologies, a business can create a map of first-, second-, and third-tier customers and suppliers with associated information flows, cycle times, inventory positioning, demand requirements, and emerging technology road maps for new products.

Once you have defined your supply chain, the next step is to determine your organization's internal competencies and those of other supply chain member organizations in an effort to identify which organization is best positioned to perform a specific activity. This process is often referred to as the "insourcing/outsourcing analysis." Insourcing/outsourcing decisions are among the most challenging faced in SCM. If your organization is on the "receiving end" of an outsourcing decision from a major customer that increases business, it is viewed favorably. But, if you happen to be employed in the division of the organization that was just outsourced, you may not view the decision in the same manner. Supply chain wide insourcing/outsourcing analysis are required if supply chain member organizations are to fully leverage their competencies to best meet the needs of the end customer.

This discussion is often lost in debates over existing capabilities and future strategic advantages. Managers often fail to recognize the distinction between a "capability" and a "competence." The insourcing/outsourcing decision is a search for your organization's "sweet spot" in the supply chain, that spot where the organization can make the greatest contribution to overall supply chain success as well as its own.

Where is the "sweet spot"? It depends on a range of factors and must be determined by the organization through a systematic assessment process. Furthermore, the "sweet spot" can change depending on the changing position of an organization relative to that of other supply chain member organizations in terms of costs, technology, productive capacities, and other factors (see Table 4–1).

Unfortunately, "sweet spot" decisions are often made based on financial return alone, without regard to the strategic importance or the organization's areas of core competence. Supply chain managers must take a comprehensive and long-term perspective when faced with insourcing/outsourcing decisions. The dangers of outsourcing before fully evaluating the resource requirements can be dangerous.

To create value systems, companies should have a basic understanding of the performance metrics for supply chain member organizations based on technology, potential for growth, and profitability. This means that the performance of key suppliers in terms of quality, delivery lead-time, on-time delivery, and technology should be described in financial terms that directly relate to bottom-line impact. A detailed market risk analysis should be performed with potential customers to assess the extent of patent loss exposure, price exposure, raw material and capital investment risk, demand risk and other relevant factors that can quickly turn a promising market opportunity into a major financial loss. It also means that key players should be aligned with an organization's internal strategies in order to exploit their expertise and knowledge in creating value. Finally, collaborative sharing of forecasting and demand information can help plan long-term capacity planning, inventory planning, and human resource requirements. In some cases, this may involve making some tough decisions, especially with respect to how one defines the

Table 4–1   Optimal mix of insourcing/outsourcing decisions for each component market that maximizes profit and minimizes risk

"Sweet Spot" Definition	Evaluation Criteria
Financial performance	• Anticipation of greatest profit • ROI
Critical nature of component	• Re-substitute components available that are superior to SBU's quality/performance • Will substitute negatively impact performance of network? • Are there multiple supply sources? • Is there a supply shortage or anticipated shortage?
Core competence & Competitive advantage	• Technology leadership • Alignment to corporate mission and vision • Competitive advantage analysis tool based on resources and capabilities

core competencies that have been in place in the company for some period of time. In this chapter, we present some of the financial realities of supply chains and address how companies can discover the financial "sweet spot" within their supply chain. This way, they can produce the highest returns given their intellectual and physical assets.

Insourcing/Outsourcing: A Controversial Issue

One of the most complex and important decisions facing businesses today is whether to produce/manage a component, assembly, process or service internally (insourcing) or whether to purchase the component, assembly, process, or service from an external supplier (outsourcing). While the insourcing/outsourcing decision has typically focused on whether to "make or buy" manufactured items, it is now being applied to virtually all business activities; including manufacturing, assembly, sales, human resources, design engineering, purchasing, information systems and a wide range of other activities.

Insourcing/outsourcing (make-or-buy) decisions have always been controversial. American workers are increasingly concerned that their employers are outsourcing manufacturing jobs to suppliers in developing countries with lower wage rates. In recent years, these issues have erupted: members of the United Auto Workers union have gone on strike to fight the increased outsourcing of components by companies to non-union manufacturers.

Outsourcing is also problematic as organizations expand their global operations to developing countries. In January 2000, one of the authors participated in an executive seminar involving a joint venture between a major U.S. automotive manufacturer and a Chinese automotive manufacturer. As part of this initiative, the partners were successfully co-producing vehicles for the Chinese domestic market in a factory in Shanghai. All the parts were being shipped from North American suppliers. As part of the joint venture, the Chinese company required the U.S. enterprise to provide executive training on modern management methods, in anticipation of the reduction of trade barriers. However, many of the Chinese managers believed that more open trade would increase their sales. They failed to understand that it would also bring on greater domestic competition in terms of quality, cost, price, and technology. The Shanghai seminar was intended to make these managers aware of the need for increased competition, especially within their own supply chain. At this time, the Chinese manufacturer was highly vertically integrated—it owned many of its own steel mills, parts fabrication facilities, component assembly operations, etc. This structure is similar to the U.S. company's structure in the early 1980's. In this seminar, the Chinese managers were shown the implications of failing to drive competition within the supply base. It was pointed out that the U.S. manufacturer suffered financially when they were highly vertically integrated. However, Chinese managers were reluctant to acknowledge this fact, and indicated that this would be difficult as there was not a large base of qualified suppliers in China to foster adequate competition. However, by relating the U.S. company's experience in divesting itself of component manufacturers and promoting greater competition in the supply base, the Chinese managers began to understand the positive aspects of competition within the supply base and recognize that awarding business on the basis of quality, service, technology, and price was critical.

Because of the importance of insourcing/outsourcing to organizational competitiveness, a number of factors must be systematically considered. These factors include a firm's competency and specific costs, quality, delivery, technology, responsiveness, capacity, and desire for continuous improvement.

Cross-functional teams are increasingly being used to make insourcing/outsourcing decisions. In most cases, these teams are made up of key representatives from marketing, logistics, manufacturing, engineering, finance, supply management, and other areas. Managers must bring a wide variety of knowledge and technical skills to bear on the insourcing/outsourcing decision ranging from long-term corporate and business strategies to in-depth cost analysis. In order to provide the most beneficial outcome to their organizations, managers must have a structured process in place that effectively considers full implications of insourcing versus outsourcing.

Recent benchmarking studies have found that organizations often make important insourcing/outsourcing decisions without fully understanding all the implications. A "quick and dirty" approach to this decision can have devastating results, including the loss of a core competence or the outsourcing of an activity to a supplier or customer that cannot meet customer performance requirements. In this chapter, we provide a formal process derived from the "best practices" of leading organizations that can be applied to insourcing /outsourcing analysis.

Initiating the Insourcing/Outsourcing Decision

Insourcing/outsourcing decisions are challenging for several reasons. The long-term strategic effects of the decision, as well as the shorter-term tactical effects must be considered using both objective and subjective criteria. In most cases, managers within a single function cannot make this decision. All aspects of the decision must be considered and therefore will require input from multiple functions.

The best insourcing/outsourcing position, or "sweet spot," is characterized as the optimal mix of insourcing/outsourcing decisions for each product/service, a mix that maximizes profit margin and minimizes company risk. Companies should complete a detailed mapping of the product/service supply chain and conduct frequent evaluations of internal operations and the external environment using a product/service Strengths, Weaknesses, Opportunities and Threats (SWOT) Analysis. By applying the SWOT methodology to each product/service market and integrating the outsourcing/insourcing outcomes into the supply chain structure, strategic positioning may be optimized and external threats may be identified.

In the initial research stages, a company should perform a business situation analysis of the firm's current market position. This should be done frequently, as conditions can change quickly. In the telecommunications market, for example, the economic downturn has caused many customers to pull orders from optical suppliers leading to both dramatic increases in inventory levels and excess capacity throughout the supply chain. It is now more important than ever for companies such as Nortel Networks to concentrate resources in areas that will give the highest return and deliver the most value to their customers.

Continuing with this example, each major product/service that goes into an optical network is viewed as a separate market. Identification of the best position, or "sweet spot," requires consideration of a number of factors. By constructing a detailed map of the product/service supply chain, firms gain valuable insight into the dynamics of the market for the item. How material moves, where inventory is kept, how various organizations in the chain communicate, and how scheduling and forecasting is handled are just a few of the areas to be studied. A map of their supply chain allows managers to identify potential weak links in the supply chain and to address those areas before problems occur.

By using a Market SWOT Analysis Worksheet, managers can make insourcing/outsourcing recommendations for a product/service based on the company's current and future position relative to the market. The possible recommendations resulting from this analysis are outsource, partnership, insource, or backward integration. The SWOT analysis should not be considered the final judgment or decision on what the company should do with the product or service. Further analysis should be performed to determine the proper course of action for the product/service. Additional issues to be addressed are insource/outsource costs, acquisition costs, or partnership fit. If partnership or outsourcing is recommended, the company should then consider the type of purchasing strategy that matches the product/service market.

Insourcing/outsourcing decisions are initiated for a number of reasons. Several of these reasons are briefly discussed in this section.

New Product Development

Insourcing/outsourcing decisions are often initiated during the new product development cycle. Because the product, service, subassemblies, or components have not yet been designed, minimal information may be available to guide the team in its decision-making. The item under consideration may represent technologies or processes unfamiliar to the company. In such cases, an outsource decision may be reached initially, unless the parts or technology under appraisal are considered core competencies. However, the analysis team should carefully consider the stability of the technology in question, the possible duration of the product life cycle, and the availability of reliable sources.

Strategy Development

An insourcing/outsourcing decision may also be driven by the strategy development process. A change in direction by top-level executives may require a change in sourcing patterns. For example, companies such as Spring, Union Pacific, Tenneco, Anheuser-Busch, and ITT have divested non-core businesses and are choosing to divest many product and process technologies formerly provided within those units.[1] In the 1990's, Jack Welch, CEO of General Electric, implemented a radical policy of divesting any business unit that was not at the top of its industry (even though many of these units were profitable at the time). Today, GE boasts record profits in the industries in which they chose to remain.

Poor Internal or External Performance

Insourcing/outsourcing decisions also result from the failure of current suppliers/distributors to satisfy the business unit's requirements. For example, if a supplier demonstrates an inability or unwillingness to manufacture a particular part or provide a key service, or shows an unwillingness to improve at the rate required, then the purchasing firm must decide whether to produce the item in-house or to develop another capable external source. Likewise, if internal manufacturing cannot meet the targeted performance levels, then the firm must either outsource with a capable supplier or invest the time and resources required to improve internal capabilities.

Changing Demand Patterns

Significant shifts in the marketplace stemming from changes in market economics caused by technological innovation often require a review. If demand decreases dramatically, production may need to shift from internal to external sources, better utilizing the buying firm's physical assets and intellectual capital. Certain types of suppliers specialize in lower-volume production. Likewise, if demand increases, then the firm might consider insourcing the part or component to realize economies of scale or scope. The firm might also utilize an external supplier in addition to its internal capabilities to meet this increased demand.

Shifting Technology Life Cycles

Changes in the technology contained in or used to produce a particular item may also trigger an insourcing/outsourcing analysis. The technology life cycle from a users perspective refers to the time from introduction to the point in time that it is no longer viable (i.e., replaced by a new and improved technology). An example here is the PC microprocessor: the Pentium was replaced by the Pentium II, the Pentium III by the Pentium IV, and so on. If the rate of technological change is relatively slow then the technology will have a long life. In such cases, there is some reasonable assurance that investment in capital equipment to produce or utilize that technology will have a longer payback period. On the other hand, if the technology is changing rapidly, outsourcing effectively shifts the risk to a source that specializes in this technology and is better able to manage new developments and the inherent risks.

Understanding Your Core Competence

In assessing trends in markets and technologies that affect the insourcing/outsourcing decision, managers must have a clear understanding of the key strategies of the business unit, functions, and supply chain member organizations. Some key questions that should be addressed include:

- What are the current and future strategies for the business unit?
- What are the current and future functional strategies within the organization?
- What is the current structure of the organization's supply chain?
- What will the organization's supply chain look like five or ten years from now?
- What are the current and future strategies of key supply chain member organizations?
- How will the supply chain contribute to the goals of the strategic business unit?
- What technologies are most critical to the supply chain in both the short- and the long-term?

A senior cross-functional team should address these issues with input from key supply chain member organizations. It is the responsibility of the team to make certain that the strategies are aligned. It is difficult to build an effective strategy if every entity has its own independent plan. Unfortunately, this situation occurs all too frequently. For instance, in one organization interviewed, the purchasing area was attempting to develop an alliance with a supplier possessing a key technology, while the marketing area was working with major customers to convince them to adopt a completely different technology! These situations are not only problematic, but also very costly. An insourcing/outsourcing team that employs representatives of different functions can help avoid these problems.

Core Competence

In their *Harvard Business Review* article, Pralahad and Hamel define core competence as "the collective learning in the organization, especially how to coordinate diverse production skills and integrate multiple streams of technologies."[2] A manager responsible for making an insourcing/outsourcing decision must develop a true sense of what the core competence of the organization is and whether the product or service under insourcing/outsourcing consideration is an integral part of that core competence. A key product or service that is closely interrelated with the firm's core competence would more likely be reflected in a favorable insourcing (make) decision, rather than an outsourcing (buy) decision. If a firm errs and mistakenly outsources a core competence, it may lose its competitive advantage.

How should a team decide whether a supply chain process is a core competence or not? The team making this decision must be careful not to confuse the concept of core competence with an organizational capability. An organization may be capable of providing a given product, service, or technology; however, a capability is not necessarily a core competence. A capability is *also* a core competence when the following three conditions are met:

1. The capability is valued by the customer.
2. The capability can be applied across multiple business units or products.
3. The capability is unique and cannot be easily imitated by competitors.

If all three conditions hold, there is a good chance that the product/process/ service under consideration is indeed a core competence.

In the 1980s, the Chrysler Corporation made a poor business decision based on its failure to consider the third condition listed. In examining the front-wheel drive technology being developed within their business units, Chrysler executives decided that the capability was indeed valued by the customer, and could be applied across multiple vehicles in different business units. However, executives neglected to consider that front-wheel drive technology was also well-developed within many of their competitors; hence, it was not a true core competence, and could not provide a competitive advantage.

On the other hand, an example of an effective outsourcing decision is found in the case of a mountain bike manufacturer that was interested in producing bicycles with titanium frames. Titanium, because it is light and strong, has many advantages over aluminum and alloy frames. However, the material has properties that make it extremely difficult to work with and the bicycle producer did not have the equipment or the workforce skills required to produce the frames. It had, in effect, a lack of capability. The manufacturer performed an insourcing/outsourcing analysis and found a former arms manufacturer in Russia that possessed excellent skills in working with titanium. With the arms market in Russia severely depressed, the arms producer was looking for new business. This match proved to be an excellent one and the bicycle manufacturer now outsources all of its titanium frames to the Russian company. The supplier clearly has a core competency in the titanium production process that the buyers use to their advantage.

As an organization begins to identify technologies and activities that are core to the business versus those that should be outsourced, a picture of the organization's current core competencies, as well as its future competencies, will emerge. Growth in the number of successful global firms has forced North American companies to dramatically improve overall competitiveness by concentrating on core competencies.[3] A core competence refers to a skill, process, or resource that distinguishes a company from other firms. In a competitive market, a core competence is a firm's strategic ability to build a dominant set of technologies and/or skills that enable it to adapt to quickly changing marketplace opportunities.

Core competencies often provide global competitors with an advantage in cost, technology, flexibility, or overall capability. Insourcing/outsourcing decisions are strategic in nature because they determine where a firm allocates its resources. These decisions reflect where management believes the company possesses a strong core competence. However, many firms have locked themselves into a "make" (insourcing) position through years of traditional thinking that, "we have always made this item, and we are not about to stop now!" The opening vignette illustrated how IBM considered mainframe computer manufacturing a core competence for many years even though this did not provide a competitive advantage. It took several years of significant financial losses and a change of leadership to shake this illusion and turn the organization around. The concept of core competence can have dramatic implications. If a firm's traditional capabilities are not "world class," it should consider getting out of the business. In the computer networking industry, major companies such as Nortel, Lucent, IBM, Hewlett Packard, Cisco, and Intel have recognized that their core competence lies in developing new technologies and providing end customer solutions. Thus, they are outsourcing "traditional" activities such as manufacturing printed circuit boards and PC assembly to third-party "contract manufacturers." In many cases, the contract manufacturers are purchasing the facilities from these outsourcing organizations. General Electric, on the other hand, has recognized that low-cost manufacturing is its primary core competence.

Technological Maturity

A final insourcing/outsourcing consideration involves an analysis of process technology. Welch and Nayak, in their Strategic Sourcing Model[4] (shown in Figure 4–1), outline a three-way analysis of how the firm perceives its process capabilities in relationship to its competition (low, tenable, or superior); the stage or maturity of the process involved (evolving/embryonic, growth, or

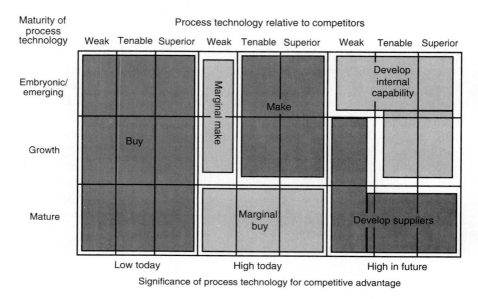

Figure 4–1 Insourcing/Outsourcing Model

mature); and the significance of the process technology for competitive advantage (low today, high today, or high in the future).

There are several possible outcomes within this framework. If the competitive advantage provided by a technology is low, then a "buy" decision allows the firm to leverage its own capabilities by focusing resources on high value-added activities. A "marginal buy" situation involves mature technologies that provide significant competitive advantage, yet are better developed in other industries. If licensing the technology is economically feasible, and the firm has demonstrated its ability to integrate and assimilate externally developed technologies, then it should purchase the technology.

In cases where a technology provides significant competitive advantage, but is not yet mature, firms should seek to internalize the technology that may then become a future core competency. For example, Honda's core products are internal combustion engines and power trains. Similarly, if the firm perceives that a technology may provide a future advantage but is still in an emerging or embryonic stage, that technology should be nurtured through research and development. This strategic sourcing model allows the analyst to consider more than just the cost/price dimension of insourcing/outsourcing in determining whether to insource or outsource a given product or service.

Understanding the Market

To conduct a thorough "sweet spot" analysis, a business should conduct a market analysis to identify the current market conditions within the firm's supply chain, as well as within competing supply chains.

Specific Market Research Objectives

The insourcing/outsourcing team should address the following questions:

1. What is the total size of the market and its forecasted growth?
2. What are the specific niches within the broader market?
3. What is your share of each market?
4. What is your growth rate in each market compared to your competitors?
5. What is the current structure of the supply chain (members, material flows, information flows)?
6. What criteria effectively evaluate products/business processes in terms of your insourcing/outsourcing decision? What parameters will be relevant for this evaluation?

The team also should perform the following tasks:

1. Evaluate the available suppliers/distributors/service providers for the product/business process based on chosen criteria.
2. Perform a Strengths, Weaknesses, Opportunities, and Threats analysis for each critical product/business process.
3. If outsourced, formulate a purchasing strategy based on the supply market that matches the product/service market.
4. Formulate recommendations based on the above analysis.

Assessing Costs

One of the most common pitfalls of long-term technology investment is including only variable costs associated with insourcing, applying the assumption that fixed costs associated with unused capacity will occur regardless of whether we insource or outsource. However, the latter assumption ignores the fact that *all* costs, fixed and variable, appear on a financial statement. To be truly competitive in the long term, the insourcing/outsourcing decision must compare like components: fully burdened insourcing costs versus the supplier's costs. By only considering variable costs, an organization risks its long-term survival. If it fails to meet industry expectations on rates of return and margins, the business may suffer from the "death spiral" of reduced margins, deteriorating stock prices, and an inability to re-invest in the business. To prevent this from happening, an insourcing/outsourcing team must take steps not to perpetuate bad decisions made in the past and take a hard look at the total cost implications of insourcing versus outsourcing.

Insourcing Versus Outsourcing— Advantages/Disadvantages[5]

After considering all these criteria, managers must carefully consider the capabilities within the organization compared to the alternatives in the market. In doing so, the team must paint a complete picture of the advantages and disadvantages of the insourcing/outsourcing decision, and weigh these factors against one another. A summary of these elements is discussed in this section, and is shown in Table 4–2.

Insourcing Advantages

There are a number of advantages to vertically integrating (insourcing) a product or service. When deciding whether to insource, the team should consider the degree of control the buyer wishes to exert over the transfer of technology. If the team desires a high degree of control so that proprietary designs or processes can be protected from unauthorized use, then they may prefer vertical integration over outsourcing. A vertically integrated firm increases its visibility over each step of the process by having more of the factors of production under its control. A dedicated facility also can result in lower per unit costs when economies of scale or scope can be realized. Insourcing also may allow a firm to spread its fixed costs over larger volumes.

Insourcing Disadvantages

The disadvantages of insourcing relate to the level of investment typically required when the insourcing decision is made. A high level of investment is required when a new plant and equipment are purchased. The firm must ensure that adequate volume is present to justify purchasing the plant and equipment required to manufacture the product internally. If a firm invests in dedicated plant and equipment that cannot be utilized for other types of products, the risk associated with the insourcing alternative increases. A good example is the semiconductor industry. In 1995, at least a dozen new semiconductor plants were under construction in the U.S., including three owned

Table 4-2 Advantages/Disadvantages of Insourcing and Outsourcing

Insourcing		Outsourcing	
Advantages	**Disadvantages**	**Advantages**	**Disadvantages**
• Higher degree of control over inputs	• Requires high volumes	• Greater flexibility supplier	• Possibility of choosing wrong control over process
• Increases visibility over the process	• High investment	• Lower investment risk	• Loss of control over process
• Economies of scale/ scope uses integration	• Dedicated equipment has limited	• Improved cash flow	• Potential for guardbanding
	• Problems with supply chain	• Lower potential labor costs shortages	• Long lead-times/capacity
			• "Hollowing out" of the corporation

by Intel and two owned by Motorola. The average cost of a chip fabrication plant was at that time approximately $1.5 billion, but was expected to rise to $3 billion by 1999. The life of process equipment is often as short as six months. Plant expansions are made on the premise that investment in new capacity can produce rapid market-share gains. On the risk side, however, analysts worry that the chip business may fluctuate in future years and that the increasing cost of wafer-fabrication plants could soar beyond the reach of all but a few companies.[6]

Another disadvantage to insourcing occurs when a firm tries to change or alter the product in accordance with market needs or demand. Matching demand to requirements in the various parts of the supply chain is an intricate process. It is often easier to switch suppliers than to alter internal processes.

Outsourcing Advantages

A major advantage of outsourcing is that it allows the buying firm a greater degree of flexibility. As market demand levels change, the firm can more easily respond with changes in its product or service offerings. Because specific assets require lower levels of investment, it is easier for the firm to make changes in its own production resources. Also, the buyer's investment risk is minimal, as the supplier assumes the uncertainty inherent in plant and equipment investment. Ideally, both the buying and the supplying firms should concentrate on their own distinct core competencies while outsourcing those products and services that are not considered areas of expertise. Also, outsourcing allows for improved cash flow because it requires less investment in plant and equipment. For example, by using contract manufacturers, Dell Computer supports $3 billion in annual revenues with only $60 million in fixed assets.[7]

A firm may achieve reductions in labor costs by transferring production to an outsource location that pays lower wages or has higher efficiencies, resulting in lower per-unit manufacturing costs. As the high cost of providing retirement and medical benefits continues to escalate, many firms are avoiding hiring full-time personnel whenever possible.

The bulk of outsourcing to achieve labor savings today appears to be going to China. China's admission to the World Trade Organization in November 2001 has increased its appeal for outsourcing labor by locking in lower duties for products it exports. Japanese management consultant Kenichi Ohmae compares China's emergence as a manufacturing colossus to Japan's spectacular postwar industrial boom, the rise of America's economy in the early 1900s, or even the dawn of the Industrial Revolution in Britain.[8] Companies currently producing in China include General Motors,

Motorola, Solectron, Dell, Ford, Daimler Chrysler, Toshiba, Sony, Matsushita, Canon, and many others.

Outsourcing Disadvantages

Conversely, a company assumes a great risk if it chooses the wrong supplier to provide the product or service being outsourced. The supplier's capabilities may have been misstated, the process technology may be obsolete, or the supplier's performance may not meet the buying firm's expectations or requirements. In one case, a manufacturer trusted a supplier to develop a component based on the supplier's claim that it had mastered the required process technology. By the time the buying company realized that the supplier was incapable of producing the product, the market for the final product had already been captured by a competitor.

There is also a loss of control. The buying firm may perceive that it has lost the ability to effectively monitor and regulate the quality, availability, confidentiality, or performance of the goods or services being bought because they are no longer under the firm's direct supervision. This may lead to concerns over product and service performance. The buying firm may have to institute costly safeguards to prevent poor performance by changing specifications, increasing inspection activities, or conducting periodic audits to ensure that the supplying firm is meeting expectations.

One company that has experienced outsourcing problems is Apple Computer. When demand for a new line of Macintosh computers increased dramatically during the 1990s, the company incurred an order backlog of more than $1 billion. The company was unable to obtain timely deliveries of critical parts, including modems and custom chips, and was not able to capitalize on the demand for its products. These parts shortages occurred because many components were custom-designed and outsourced from a single supplier. Because managers failed to accurately predict the growth in sales (the actual increase was 25 percent, while the predicted increase was 15 percent), the company alienated customers who were not willing to wait for new products. This situation was especially damaging because many customers made the switch to PCs using Microsoft Windows operating system instead of waiting for Macintosh. In this situation, outsourcing and partnering provided technological benefits, but resulted in a serious capacity shortfall.[9]

A final disadvantage of outsourcing is the potential for losing key skills and technology, which may weaken a company's future competitive position. The phenomena of North American firms outsourcing their manufacturing to low-cost suppliers who later became global competitors has been described as the "hollowing out of the corporation." Indeed, some would argue that many U.S. firms are now only "shells" that no longer produce anything, but simply act as distribution and sales networks. Although there is some truth to this statement, the outsourcing decision has to be balanced with the need to remain competitive and to outsource those tasks over which the firm no longer has a competitive advantage.

In many ways, the insourcing/outsourcing decision is one of the most difficult decisions that an individual organization and their respective supply chains must make in moving toward an integrated value system. The following three case examples provide insights from different companies who have experienced the effects of an insourcing/outsourcing decision: Solectron, Owens-Corning, and Cummins Engine.

Solectron: Thriving in an Outsourcing Environment

Solectron was founded in 1977 as the "Solar Energy Company," and originally manufactured solar energy products. Today, it is a worldwide provider of electronics manufacturing services to original equipment manufacturers (OEMs). The company provides customized, integrated manufacturing services that span all three stages of the product life cycle, including pre-manufacturing, manufacturing, and post-manufacturing. These services are integrated to the point that Solectron is now responsible for all supply chain processes associated with sourcing parts, manufacturing, and distribution of electronics and systems for almost every major OEM customer in the industry. Its list of Fortune 500 customers span the telecommunication, networking, computer systems, peripherals, semiconductors, consumer electronics, industrial equipment, medical electronics, avionics, and automotive electronics industries.

Solectron's growth has been exponential in the last decade. The reason for this growth has been attributed to Solectron's commitment to establishing long-term partnerships with customers and suppliers, supported by consistent quality, responsiveness, continuous improvement, and technological leadership. In deploying this strategy, Solectron has essentially created a new market, and thereby developed a new way of managing their customer and supply base, through an evolving *total business strategy* known as contract manufacturing. This has often involved acquiring manufacturing units of customer companies that they view as non-core to their business, and in many cases unprofitable. Solectron's key task is to make these operations profitable.

Solectron acquired several new divisions in recent years as a result of outsourcing of manufacturing plants by key customers such as IBM, Hewlett

Packard, Nortel Networks, Cisco, and others. Each acquisition was analyzed thoroughly, and was ultimately approved based on the following criteria:

- A chance to create new or expand existing customer and supplier relationships

- Adding unique capabilities to Solectron's value chain, such as design for manufacturability or order fulfillment

- Creating a presence in a new attractive market

- Adding capable people to the company and integrating them into the core business

- Potential for adding value to the supply chain via lower labor costs achieved by Solectron's global supply chain

One of the most important shifts in Solectron's strategies is the recognition that the nature of value has changed. In the past, customer's simply outsourced their manufacturing capabilities to Solectron. This evolved to including procurement of components, then to distribution of products to customers. Increasingly, Solectron is being asked to manage an ever increasing portion of their customers' supply chain, including supply base management and relationships, supplier development, design and supplier integration into new product development, manufacturing, distribution, order fulfillment, and even after-market service. The next time you purchase a "brand name" PC there is a good chance that no employees from the company ever came in contact with that machine!

Another good example of the delicate balance between insourcing and outsourcing of supply chain processes is Owens Corning's outsourcing of energy procurement to Enron, described in the following case.

Owens Corning's Outsourcing of Energy Procurement

Owens Corning is a global leader in building materials and composites systems, with 135 manufacturing facilities and more than 180 distribution centers in over 30 countries. Owens Corning was weathering perhaps the roughest period of its 60-plus-year history. The $705 million net income loss ($13.16 loss per share) the company posted on its 1998 income statement was largely attributable to a $1.4 billion provision for litigation claims pertaining to manufacture and sale of asbestos, the cancer-causing, fire-resistant material that the company stopped making in 1972. The 1998 loss came on the heels of a $284 million loss registered in 1996, also a result of asbestos litigation payouts. Though Owens Corning claims to have the asbestos matter under control via the National Settlement Program, an initiative designed to resolve claims over the next decade, massive payouts will continue for some time.

In response to the uncertainties facing Owens Corning over the next ten years, the CEO initiated a vigorous restructuring and refocusing effort. Among other goals, the CEO wanted operating costs eventually reduced by $175 million per year. Given that Owens Corning's fiberglass making and composites operations are extremely energy intensive, their global buyers of electricity and natural gas are under pressure to control costs. As the CEO put it, "As an energy-intensive industry, we are . . . targeting a substantial improvement in energy productivity." Given that Owens Corning's operating processes do not result in a by-product that can be recycled as an energy input for on-site generation, energy cost reductions at Owens Corning must come via price and cost reductions related to energy purchases.

Restructuring at Owens Corning

Owens Corning's manufacturing and composites operations are very energy intensive; expenditures entail $100 million per year for electricity and $40 million per year for gas. This total represents nearly 20 percent of global operating costs for 1997. U.S. electricity restructuring initiatives have provided energy buyers with new opportunities to drive down energy costs. Owens Corning has U.S. operations in some 20 states, most of which are restructuring, or have restructured, their gas and electricity markets.

Energy cost management at Owens Corning is a two-pronged effort. First, global buyers are responsible for getting energy to plant meters as efficiently as possible and at the lowest total cost. Second floor-level plant managers are responsible for monitoring energy expenditures, explaining variances, and managing individual loads efficiently.

Owens Corning's overall energy purchasing strategy involves participating in "intervention groups" that work at a legal and policy level to influence electricity restructuring policies currently being formulated in most states. These groups work with state utility regulators to insure that rates are reduced and that true retail competition is realized in the deregulated environment. In states where deregulation is in place or is pending, Owens Corning leverages its total spending with the supplier.

For Owens Corning, price is the primary metric used to evaluate potential electricity suppliers as it spends close to $1 million a month on electricity at some facilities. A second key supplier metric is *reliability*. Owens Corning's glass melting plants run around the clock; outages are extremely costly. However, since reliability is more a function of nonderegulated transmission systems than energy generation, the company has less leverage in this arena for forcing compliance and performance.

Owens Corning's strategy for reducing energy costs down remains uniform across the globe. "Regulators may vary from country to country, but our strategy does not," as one executive noted. Owens Corning has, however, been able to ramp up its leverage in the area of new ("greenfield") facilities. One criterion Owens Corning uses to decide where to locate new facilities is the energy rates they will be charged by the resident utility provider. In short, Owens Corning can insure an acceptable rate from a utility by simply threatening to build or buy its factory elsewhere.

Owens Corning tends to enter into long-term electricity contracts, given that 1) long-term agreements are often dictated by the current regulatory environment and 2) electricity prices are perceived as relatively volatile in the short term. Thus, locking in long-term electricity rates provides a hedge against uncertainty.

Owens Corning—Enron Joint Venture

No initiative underscored Owens Corning's commitment to driving down energy costs more than its joint venture with Enron Corporation of Houston. At the time, Enron was viewed as a powerful and growing energy company that was on the forefront of energy trading in a market that was rapidly becoming deregulated. However, recent events point to the potential dangers of outsourcing a major supply chain process to a third-party supplier with hidden liabilities.

In September 1999, Enron Energy Services, a subsidiary of Enron Corporation, and Owens Corning announced a $1 billion, ten-year outsourcing agreement for total energy management services at 20 of Owens Corning's major U.S. manufacturing facilities. The two corporations jointly implemented an energy savings program designed to decrease energy consumption and lower costs for Owens Corning. Through the agreement, Enron was to supply or manage energy commodity requirements including electricity and natural gas. The total spend on commodity over the life of the deal was projected to be $100 million annually. Owens Corning retained the ability to get bids and buy directly and independently if Enron was unable to meet certain costs and other parameters. The challenge for Owens Corning's energy buyers was to keep this "optional" spend, plus the spend at plants not covered by the Enron deal, below $40 million in order to drive total costs below the current $140 million level and meet restructuring targets. Owens Corning also wanted to mitigate risks of price volatility using Enron's expertise in managing large commodity portfolios.

A mantra chanted by supply chain managers is that their firms must "do more with less." The value proposition put forward by Enron was a form of risk assumption: for a sizable fee, Enron would own and manage a large share of Owens Corning's asset base, which had ballooned more than 50 percent over the last three years. Secondly, Owens Corning executives believed that synergies created by Owens Corning's expertise in insulation and energy conservation, and Enron's knowledge of energy management, would almost certainly drive Owens Corning's energy costs down dramatically. And as the second millennium brought more fallout from asbestos litigation, certainty was something that Owens Corning desperately sought. Unfortunately, Enron was anything but a certainty.

A major fallout occurred in late 2001, when Enron filed for Chapter 11 bankruptcy proceedings, owing to its off-balance sheet debts allocated to "partner" firms owned by the company. This has caused a serious disruption to the Owens Corning / Enron relationship and Owens Corning has had to pull out of the agreement. The problems arising from this situation point to the importance of conducting a thorough supplier financial analysis prior to engaging in a significant outsourcing venture. However, in fairness to Owens Corning, given its accounting practices, Enron's finances appeared sound when the agreement was implemented. Although Enron is seeking to recover via restructuring and a possible buy-out, the prospects are not good. Without a solid case for proceeding forward, Owens Corning may very well be left in the dark.

How can companies avoid this situation from recurring? By identifying a contingency plan for an outsourced commodity or service, this situation can be avoided. One senior manager noted, "I don't ever believe in completely outsourcing a process. It's always a good idea to maintain some level of capacity/capability internally—just in case the suppliers selected are not able to perform. This also provides you with some knowledge of cost issues that are important in understanding cost drivers in future negotiations."

The Cummins Engine Case

A detailed case study of the insourcing/outsourcing experiences of the Cummins Engine Company, published in the *Harvard Business Review*, outlined many of the various factors that a firm needs to consider during a typical insource/outsource decision-making situation.[10] A diagram of the process used in reaching this decision is shown in Figure 4–2.

As part of a routine competitive analysis, Cummins Engine determined that several competing manufacturing companies within the mature, capital-intensive heavy equipment industry, including John Deere, Navistar, and J. I. Case, all seemed to utilize conflicting sourcing practices that tended to fragment the potential competitive advantages generated through strategic sourcing. The insourcing/outsourcing decisions of these companies were frequently made using such simplistic criteria as volume or level of difficulty to produce a part or component. The firms tended to keep production in-house for high-volume items and items that were relatively easy to make. Most companies had no explicit analytical framework for distinguishing their essential core components from commodity-like items.

Insourcing/Outsourcing Process

When conducting insourcing/outsourcing analyses, Cummins Engine performed several critical tasks. The first was to determine the appropriate level of abstraction, i.e., the proper unit of analysis. For example, owing to the sheer number of individual components in most final products, it would be nearly impossible to make a sound insourcing/outsourcing decision on each component. Therefore, it was important to aggregate, or combine, the level of analysis moving from the individual component or sub-assembly level all the way up to the assembly or complete system level. For example, managers considered a backhoe loader from the systems perspective, treating it as a system made up of a variety of assemblies and sub-assemblies (the drive train,

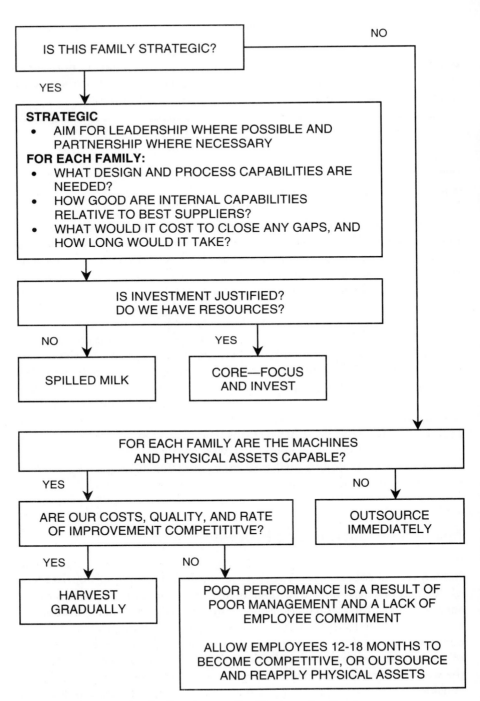

Figure 4–2 Cummins Engine—Insourcing/Outsourcing Process

chassis, cab, engine, and so forth). If one imagines the backhoe loader's engine as a subsystem, one can break down the engine further into a series of complex assemblies and sub-assemblies; e.g., fuel delivery system. This level of abstraction can be further redefined in terms of individual parts and components: pistons, rings, pins, and sleeves. A firm should analyze each level of abstraction and decide the appropriate level to use in determining its critical manufacturing requirements.

Firms facing the strategic insourcing/outsourcing decision must painstakingly evaluate the entire hierarchy of components, sub-assemblies, assemblies, subsystems, and systems for each of its major product lines to determine which subsystems and assemblies are essential to it's competitive position. This analysis should include future anticipated product generations as well. The character of the insourcing/outsourcing decision will vary widely among firms and among industries because of the variation in perceptions of core competencies, goals, and objectives. In addition to the identification and consideration of core competencies that will provide direction to the insource/outsource decision, the firm must also evaluate its competitive priorities in terms of overall business strategies. The nature of the overall business strategy should dictate broad guidelines affecting how to conduct the insourcing/outsourcing analyses.

The Decision

The internal insourcing/outsourcing analysis at Cummins Engine revealed that in order to meet emissions standards, the backhoe required a more advanced piston design. The implication was that Cummins needed to invest heavily to upgrade capabilities in this area. Since pistons are a key part of the engine assembly, an emotionally charged debate occurred over whether to insource or outsource the part. This debate lasted over three years. Many felt that Cummins should not surrender control of this highly critical component to a supplier. The debate was settled after management organized an interdisciplinary team to develop and implement an appropriate piston sourcing strategy. The team first identified the critical technologies and capabilities that would be required to specify, design, and manufacture pistons for heavy equipment engines. They visited leading piston manufacturers and performed a benchmarking analysis to measure Cummins' internal capabilities against those of the supply base. Their findings indicated that Cummins' internal capabilities in piston technology were inferior to at least two of the suppliers considered to be world-class competitors. These two piston suppliers were also aggressive innovators, and invested more than 20 times as much as Cummins did in product and process research and development. In addition, higher volumes produced by the suppliers allowed much quicker progression along the learning curve, thereby accelerating cost reductions. Given this apparent competitive disadvantage, Cummins made the difficult decision to outsource pistons to suppliers.

If a firm's insourcing analysis indicates a competitive disadvantage in the manufacture of key subsystems compared with a supplier, then management must decide whether to commit scarce resources to "play catch-up" or whether to outsource. Playing catch-up can be an expensive proposition that may adversely impact a firm's financial viability or restrict its ability to invest in other areas of the business. In pursuing the catch-up strategy, the firm must decide if it will seek competence in existing technologies or will attempt to "leapfrog" the competition through the use of a new technology. The choice of a wrong technology development strategy will consume scarce resources with little or no payback in terms of developing a competitive advantage.

Implementation

Once the firm has committed to outsourcing a key subsystem, it should attempt to develop or enhance its competence in other critical subsystems, particularly if the technology involved is relatively new or not readily available outside the firm. Another alternative to the total outsourcing of key subassemblies is to develop a long-term partnering relationship with a highly capable supplier (J. I. Case has done this in its engine joint venture with Cummins). This arrangement allows a higher level of management control over the supply base while limiting the investment risk of plant and equipment. That risk is shared with the supplier, allowing the buying firm to become more flexible to changing demands in the marketplace.

A company like Cummins can gain effective control over the performance of outsourced components by overseeing design and manufacturing activities and keeping current on "architectural knowledge." Architectural knowledge is "the intimately detailed and specialized power of translation required to capture customer requirements and reproduce them in the language of subsystem performance specifications." This body of knowledge is based on the interactions that occur between a customer's requirements and specifications and the manufacturer's capabilities. Architectural knowledge is developed over numerous exchanges of information between members of the two firms as a relationship develops. It is the extent of this architectural knowledge that defines the products' distinctiveness in the eyes of the customer. When highly capable suppliers of subsystems are available, it is not absolutely necessary for the using company to design and manufacture the sub-assembly in-house, but it is imperative that the firm demonstrate its capability to specify and regulate the performance of the subsystem in terms of customer needs. One method of preserving this capability is for the buying firm's engineers to work closely with the supplying firm's engineers in order to:

· Analyze product designs and review component performance

· Evaluate and substantiate the supplier's manufacturing process capabilities

· Oversee component testing technology and procedures

Likewise, the supplier must commit to providing on-site engineering support, design support, joint problem solving, and expert advice.

The grouping of individual parts and components into families of similar parts is another task within the insourcing/outsourcing process, and moves the insourcing/outsourcing decision into a higher level of abstraction. Instead of determining whether a firm should insource or outsource a particular part number, the decision shifts to whether it is cost-effective to continue to invest in the capacity or capability to manufacture each family of items. Managers must still analyze these families to identify if they are strategic in nature. Strategic component families differ from commodity component families in that with the former there tend to be few available suppliers and the likelihood of paying significant premiums is high. The guiding principle in these situations is to achieve product leadership wherever possible and strategic partnering with capable suppliers when necessary.

In order to facilitate this process, Cummins developed a three-tier classification "traffic light" scheme for separating commodity part families into different categories based on common process characteristics, manufacturing processes, materials, volume, and so on.

The green classification indicates that internal manufacturing is competitive with at least a 15 percent cost advantage over outsourcing. For these part and component families, internal manufacturing processes are highly capable, and the rate of performance improvement is high. The middle-range or yellow classification symbolizes those parts or families that are marginally competitive with about a 15 percent cost disadvantage compared to suppliers. Internal manufacturing capability is moderately high, but there is a need for improvement. For parts families in the red category, internal sourcing is at a clear cost disadvantage, with cost penalties exceeding 15 percent. In addition, moving part families from the yellow zone to the green zone requires significant cooperation from the firm's employees because they must upgrade their work skills and utilize more efficient techniques. In the red zone, upgrading internal manufacturing capabilities may require prohibitive levels of investment to make sufficient cost performance improvement to justify insourcing the item.

When outsourcing large numbers of parts that were formerly made in-house, the organization must upgrade its supply base management practices, including supplier selection and qualification, performance measurement, and supply-base optimization processes. Volume discounts can be leveraged through the use of higher volumes provided by fewer, more capable suppliers.

Even today, Cummins Engine is pushing the boundaries of its core competencies to explore radical new data mining technologies. Years ago, it began building electronic components into its engines to gather information about performance, pollution control, and other diagnostic data. Only recently, the manufacturer has begun experimenting with collecting and mining that valuable data.[11] For example, Cummins found that one customer's trucks were idling three times as long as trucks at other companies, leading to more wear and tear on the engine, higher fuel consumption, and more pollution. This represents an important new competency that is being "insourced" and invested in for the future. "We're trying to do things we never thought of before," says Ron Temple, Vice President of electronics technology at Cummins. "That's what data mining can do—show new relationships." In the end, this competency could help Cummins Engine achieve a new type of competency that will provide better customer service and a competitive advantage.

Summary

Finding the "sweet spot" via the insourcing/outsourcing decision process described is important to the economic success of a firm. The decision determines the firm's economic boundaries and its competitive character. Firms have historically conducted the insourcing/outsourcing decision process without a true strategic perspective. Typically, decisions were based on the purely economic issues of price, quality, and volumes. Several key factors will increasingly influence future "sweet spot" decisions. Purchasing, operations, and technology managers will need to work together closely to identify activities in which the firm has a distinctive competence and those activities best performed by external sources. Managers must obtain clear insights into the relative long- and short-term economics associated with insourcing/outsourcing decisions, particularly from a total cost position. Finally, firms must conduct more accurate assessments of those technologies that are crucial to future success.

Endnotes

[1]"The Whirlwind Breaking Up Companies," *Business Week*, August 14, 1995, p. 31.

[2]C. K. Pralahad and Gary Hamel, "The Core Competence of the Corporation," *Harvard Business Review* (May-June 1990), pp. 79–91.

[3]Ibid., p. 82.

[4]James A. Welch and P. Ranganath Nayak, "Strategic Sourcing: A Progressive Approach to the Make-Buy Decision," *Academy of Management Executives* 6, no. 1 (1992), pp. 23–31.

[5]Based on *Purchasing and Supply Chain Management, 2nd ed.*, Robert Monczka, Robert Trent, and Robert Handfield, Southwestern College Publishing, 2001.

[6]"The Great Silicon Rush of '95," *Business Week*, October 2, 1995, pp. 134–136.

[7]Shawn Tully, "You'll Never Guess Who Really Makes . . ." Fortune, October 3, 1994, p. 124.

[8]Chandler, Clay, "A Factory to the World", *Washington Post Foreign Service*, November 25, 2001, p. A01.

[9]"Is Spindler a Survivor?" *Business Week*, October 2, 1995, p. 62.

[10]Ravi Venkatesan, "Strategic Sourcing: To Make or Not to Make," *Harvard Business Review* (November-December 1992), pp. 98–107.

[11]Rick Whiting and Bruce Caldwell, "Data capture grows wider," *InformationWeek*, June 14, 1999.

5

Creating Collaboration and Trust in the Supply Chain

A Supplier's Perspective of Supplier Development[1]

Plastic Engineering, a small privately owned supplier located in Warwickshire, England, provides plastic injected parts to the automotive industry. A key customer, Standard Products, uses Plastic Engineering's parts to produce seat latches for a seat manufacturer. These latches eventually end up in a Ford-UK product. In 1997, Standard Products was pushing Plastic Engineering to improve their production process by creating a manufacturing cell. Standard products wanted a large number of latches produced, and realized that this would work better with just-in-time production and daily deliveries of approximately 4,000 units per day. When Standard Products representatives visited the plant, they found Plastic Engineering had quality problems and more material than necessary. To help Plastic Engineering achieve the sought-after performance improvements, Standard Products deployed a supplier development approach known as a Kaizen Breakthrough. A Kaizen Breakthrough is a focused approach to process improvement, based on studying the process, collecting data, and making changes to the process with the goal of reducing costs.

Mike Hart, manufacturing director of Plastics Engineering, describes what happened next, "Standard Products appointed team leaders who helped us to do it. They sent over six people at their expense that stayed for a week and showed us step-by-step how to create a manufacturing cell. At first, things went very badly, and we produced many bad parts. Eventually, the cell started working very well.

"In implementing the Kaizen Breakthrough, we first explained to everyone what was going on, and guaranteed to them that there would be *no job losses* as a result of their cooperation. This was a critical success factor. Next, two people came in and had a meeting with our people. A team leader from our facility was appointed. In this case, it was Paul Collins, a young special projects production supervisor who was well respected in the shop. He then chose people that he thought would be suitable from the shop floor.

"The whole process took one week, and involved relatively simple concepts. We began with problem-solving sheets and process maps, then studied the process and went about changing it. Afterward, the group made a presentation to the managing director and the manufacturing director. What was unique about it was that they pushed the changes through to a time scale they set. At the end of the day, it was their success that was being celebrated, not ours.

"Afterward, photographs were used to document the exercise and the group went around describing it to other suppliers in the Standard Products Supplier Association. What also happened as a result of this was that we recognized that we had only touched the tip of the rest of the factory. We then went about breaking the factory down into manageable segments that could be examined. We took different people from each segment to a Standard Products factory so that they could see what was expected of them. This was very important, as many people thought the whole idea was stupid initially. We are now in the process of implementing our fourth Kaizen Breakthrough team. There has even been some internal competition created between the teams!

"A side effect of the entire process has been that our successes have been brought to the attention of various boards which make decisions on the group of companies that we are a part of. We have caught their attention, and they are finally listening to what some of us at the bottom have been proposing. As a result of our participation, we are now helping Standard Products to develop new products, and they are continuing to help us on our production line. They realized they needed good suppliers and weren't happy with their current ones. We were low volume, but had great potential. Both parties ended up winners."

"The key success factor in the case of Standard Products was that they supplied us with something that we didn't have, rather than the other way around. Other companies tell you to improve, and then give you a list of consultants to call up. Another important factor was that cost reductions were shared—in an equitable manner on a product-by-product basis. They are also very honest with us. When we go to meetings, they begin with a good news / bad news approach. With many of our other customers, we don't really know where we stand."

In developing a high-performing value system, organizations are continually faced with the challenge of managing the "people" part of the equation. Relationship management affects all areas of the supply chain and has a dramatic impact on performance. In many cases, the information systems and technology required for the supply chain management effort are available and can be implemented within a relatively short time period. Inventory and transportation management systems are also quite well understood and can be implemented readily. A number of supply chain initiatives fail, however, as a result of poor communication of expectations and the resulting behaviors. Managers often assume that the personal relationships within and between organizations in a supply chain will fall into place once the technical systems are established. However, managing relationships among the various organizations is often the most difficult part of the SCM initiative. Moreover, the single most important ingredient for successful SCM may well be trusting relationships among partners in the supply chain, where each party in the chain has confidence in the other members' capabilities and actions. Without positive interpersonal relationships, the other systems cannot function effectively. One supply chain manager expressed this feeling succinctly:

> *Supply chain management is one of the most emotional experiences I've ever witnessed. There have been so many mythologies that have developed over the years, people blaming other people for their problems, based on some incident that may or may not have occurred sometime in the past. Once you get everyone together into the same room, you begin to realize the number of false perceptions that exist. People are still very reluctant to let someone else make decisions within their area. It becomes especially tricky when you show people how "sub-optimizing" their functional area can "optimize" the entire supply chain.—Materials management vice president, Fortune 500 manufacturer*

This manager's experience is not unique to his company. Almost every individual interviewed by the authors involved in a SCM initiative emphasized the critical nature of developing and maintaining good relationships with the customers and suppliers in the chain. In deploying the integrated supply chain, developing trust is required. In discussing the importance of relationships in SCM, trust building is emphasized as an ongoing process that must be continually managed. In short, trust takes time to develop but can disappear very quickly if abused.

In the early stages of supply chain development, organizations often eliminate suppliers or customers that are clearly unsuitable. After these firms are eliminated, organizations may concentrate on supply chain members who are most willing to contribute the time and effort required to create a strong relationship. Firms may consider developing a special type of supply chain relationship with these organizations, such that confidential information is shared, assets are invested in joint projects, and significant joint improvement initiatives are pursued. These types of inter-organizational relationships sometimes lead to strategic alliances. Strategic alliances allow firms to improve efficiency and effectiveness by eliminating waste and duplication in the supply chain. However, many firms lack the experience required to develop, implement, and maintain supply chain alliances. This chapter discusses a process that organizations can use to improve supply chain relationships, which can lead to the development of successful strategic supply chain alliances.

In this chapter, we:

- Discuss the "roots" of supply chain relationship development
- Develop a conceptual model of how supply chain alliance relationships are created
- Identify factors to consider when in selecting an alliance partner
- Discuss the different types of trust that exist in such relationships
- Discuss the key practices for developing trust in supply chain relationships

Roots of Supply Chain Relationship Management

The economist G. B. Richardson made the following observation about supply chain relationships:

> We must not imagine that reality exhibits a sharp line of distinction. What confronts us is a continuum passing through transactions, such as those on organized commodity markets, where the cooperative element is minimal, through intermediate areas in which there

are linkages of traditional connection and good will, and finally to those complex and interlocking clusters, groups, and alliances which . . . represent cooperation fully and formally developed.[2]

At the beginning of the twentieth century, inter-organizational transactions were often the domain of marketing and distribution personnel. Because material specifications were much more standardized at that time, cost was the primary differentiator in purchase decisions. Inter-organizational alliances or partnerships between buyers and sellers were generally not present among early twentieth-century organizations. Instead, vertical integration was often used to eliminate supply uncertainty.

The first truly "long-term" inter-organizational relationships evolved in Japan. During the post-World War II years, Japanese manufacturing organizations became regulated by the Ministry for International Trade, and subsequently established an integration scheme known as the keiretsu, which was characterized by informal but strict cooperation among members.[3] Since then, several factors have driven North American managers to consider alternative forms of relational governance. These factors included: 1) the globalization of the world economy; 2) the evolution of the World Wide Web and new forms of B2B e-commerce solutions; and 3) increasing requirements for customer responsiveness.

Globalization—The effectiveness of the Japanese keiretsu and the globalization of the world economy dramatically changed the business climate and these changes led many U.S. firms to embrace new types of inter-organizational relationships during the 1980s. Initially, most of these were equity-based. Increasingly, however, the rise of global competition and the fast pace of technological change convinced many firms that neither vertical integration, open market bargaining, nor equity sharing were effective mechanisms for tackling supply uncertainty and poor material quality. Managers today realize that an alternative form of supply chain relationship is required for suppliers to respond more quickly to global supply chain customers.

Information Technology—The emergence of the personal computer, optical fiber networks, the explosion of the Internet and the World Wide Web, and the cost and availability of information resources allow easy linkage and eliminate many information-related time delays in supply chain networks. Increasingly, organizations are moving toward a concept known as *electronic commerce,* where transactions are completed via a variety of electronic media, including the Internet. These technologies are critical supply chain "enablers." However, before these technologies can provide their full benefits, supply chain member organizations must establish relationships characterized by a willingness to share and receive information and collaborate to improve performance.

Increased Customer Responsiveness—As organizations began to consider their key core competencies, they began to outsource those activities considered non-core. Partnering occurred as firms sought to take advantage of market opportunities through a synergistic combination of strategic core competencies. This typically led to a reduction in the number of suppliers utilized for a particular part or service as buyers identified those suppliers with the greatest potential for partnering through a process known as *supply base optimization*. In general, firms were constrained in their reduction efforts by minimum capacity requirements (lower limit) and the number of suppliers with which it is feasible for them to communicate and share resources (upper limit). Conversely, suppliers limit the number of customers they do business with to focus only on their "preferred" customers. A requirement for supplier/customer optimization is that supply chain participants have a solid mutual understanding of the underlying business processes and capabilities of their selected supply chain partners.

While supply-base optimization represented an opportunity for those suppliers remaining after the reductions, it also resulted in a new breed of customer that demands increased responsiveness to a dynamic set of requirements. In these new value systems, buying firms are purchasing not only their suppliers' products or services, but also their suppliers' systems and capabilities, which in turn requires high levels of coordination. Second, buying firms in such relationships provide more than just financial compensation to their suppliers. Buyers share information with their suppliers. They also provide suppliers with guarantees of future volumes, prices, resources, and creativity that may be tied to suppliers' cost reduction and quality improvement efforts. Mutual interdependence, close organizational cooperation, increased levels of trust, and a strong tendency toward information sharing characterize such relationships.

Despite the strong drivers for closer supply chain relationships, the managerial processes and success of these relationships is fraught with pitfalls. An excellent illustration of the difficulty of maintaining integrated supplier-customer relationships is Office Max and Ryder Integrated Logistics.[4] In this case, Office Max sued Ryder Integrated Logistics in the amount of $21.4 million for breach of contract after 21 months of a seven-year contract that was initially described as a "strategic alliance." Ryder Integrated Logistics counter-sued Office Max for $75 million. It is becoming clear that a delicate balance between formal (economic and legal) and informal (social and psychological) factors is necessary to sustain long-term inter-organizational relationships. Managers require a blueprint for action that considers this balance and results in improved supply chain responsiveness. However, North American managers do not necessarily have to re-invent the wheel. In this regard, borrowing a page from Japanese supply chain relationships may be instructive.

NEC's Purchasing Policy[5]

Nippon Electric Company (NEC) of Japan has a long history of focusing on supply chain management as a key competitive strategy. Part of this focus is inherent in the Japanese business culture. The level of trust between buying companies and their suppliers has always been very high, and business is typically conducted on the basis of verbal agreements. Only rarely are written contracts used. Companies also feel comfortable being the major customer for a supplier. It is not uncommon for suppliers to have ninety percent of their sales with a single customer. Suppliers are also comfortable with this situation, feeling that as long as they continue to meet cost and quality requirements, the business will continue.

An important component of NEC's strategy is the emphasis on *ringi*, or "management by consensus." All decisions are made via cross-functional teams of multiple individuals. This process is inherent to Japanese culture. Issues are discussed exhaustively in both formal and informal settings before a decision is reached. However, Japanese executives are quick to point out that this process takes much longer than a more autocratic approach, which can be a problem when product development cycles must be reduced.

Evidence of the history of NEC's strategy of long-term relationships can be found in the company's purchasing policy manual, dated from 1977. The following excerpts provide insights into the evolution of this company's outlook on relationships with key suppliers initiated more than two decades ago:

Cultivation of Cooperative Companies

Based on the principles of mutual trust, coexistence, and co-prosperity and on the standpoints that subcontractors in particular are independent enterprises and are an extension of the production lines of the Company, a network of cooperative companies shall be consolidated as follows:

- Rate and evaluate centering on subcontractor suppliers and select eligible cooperative companies for guidance and cultivation.
- Positively counsel and guide the physical structure and management of the cooperative companies to improve their physical constitutions and to strengthen their management foundations and cooperate with them in promoting the formation of cooperative associations and in pursuing joint operations.

Business Accomplishment Criteria

Those engaged in purchasing business shall, fully realizing that their business is totally aimed at accomplishing the profit plans of the Company and that purchasing activities are important to create enterprise profits, positively and enthusiastically perform purchasing preparatory activities and overall purchasing functions, including make-or-buy problems, to strive to attain advantageous purchasing.

- To always maintain close relationships with the manufacturing, technical, and sales departments to understand their trends in advance, and to strive to acquire the needed information and knowledge.
- To investigate and study price, a demand, and supply trends in the purchase market and suppliers of new and substitute products to promote advantageous purchasing and to positively counsel and assist related departments and sections.
- To perform creative purchasing by introducing and utilizing new information regarding purchasing techniques and design and processing technologies without being prejudiced by traditional customs and practices.
- To positively counsel and assist to attain the business goals of the divisions and to do their utmost to attain the goals even when the requirements are difficult to accomplish by fully respecting their views and wishes.

Honda's Supplier Relationships[6]

Another Japanese company that emphasizes the development of trust as a central part of its purchasing strategy is Honda. Honda was established in 1948 in Hamamatsu, Japan, as a manufacturer of war surplus generators attached to bicycles, thus creating a crude form of motorcycle. The company thus began very modestly, but by 1954 had adopted the following objectives:

- International viewpoint
- Products of the highest efficiency
- Reasonable price for customer satisfaction

Initially, Honda was not allowed to produce cars but early on Mr. Honda began to lobby government officials to allow automobile production. Honda entered the automobile market in 1964. Mr. Honda received the permit after camping out at the key official's office for several weeks. However, upon getting the permit, Honda found that few existing automotive suppliers were willing to provide parts to the company. Thus, the few motorcyle parts suppliers who were finally convinced to supply the company with new automotive components became instrumental to Honda and close ties have been maintained with those early suppliers through today.

Since eighty percent of the value of Honda's products comes from suppliers, purchasing holds a very strong position in the organization. Eighty percent of items are single sourced with one set of dies (but dual competition by platform.) An example of this strategy is as follows: Supplier A produces steering wheels for Civics, and Supplier B produces steering wheels for the Accord. Either supplier can make either part, but each is a single source for a given platform. When a new model is introduced, both suppliers may bid on the extra volume, with the supplier delivering the best historical price and performance likely to get the business.

Honda's central objective is to manufacture throughout the world: "You must build where you sell, and buy where you build." Thus, Honda seeks to develop local suppliers worldwide. Today, Honda is the largest exporter of cars in the U.S.

Honda Supplier Support

The Honda supplier support infrastructure is vast. Eleven thousand employees work in Honda's Ohio operations, of which 1,000 work with suppliers. Currently, 310 people work in purchasing of whom 50 are engineers working exclusively with suppliers.

A key part of the supplier support and development function is to ensure that everyone within the supplier organization and within Honda understands the company philosophy. Tier One suppliers are expected to be self-reliant and responsible for working with their suppliers. Top management support is absolutely necessary within each supplier.

The premise of mutual dependability is another cornerstone of this program. Honda can be up to 50 percent of a supplier's business, but in general, Honda does not require a set percent of business from suppliers. Honda routinely sends out "How are we doing?" surveys to suppliers. The results are summarized and passed out to department heads. Honda does not use formal contracts for suppliers; it uses a purchases and sales agreement with boiler-plate terms only. No costs, volumes, or lengths of time are ever used in their agreements.

What Makes Alliances Different from Other Relationships?

As Figure 5–1 shows, organizations in a supply chain typically have multiple types of relationships. For example, Suppliers A and C both supply B, who in turn is a supplier to D. Supplier E may also supply another division within its own company, as well as supplying D. Finally, both D and E may in turn supply another customer F.

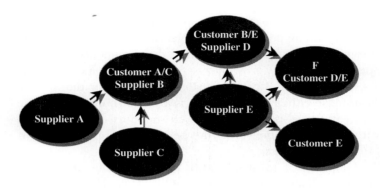

Figure 5-1   The Supply Chain: An Open System of Organizations

This tangled web of relationships may result in all sorts of interesting scenarios. For example, E is a supplier to D, yet also competes with D for business with F. As on-going mergers and acquisitions in industry occur, this web
of relationships can become even more complex.

Nevertheless, the strategic alliances that occur represent a major change
in the way companies do business. In creating integrated supply chains,
companies must re-think how they view their customers and suppliers. They
must concentrate not just on maximizing their own profits, but also on how
to maximize the success of all organizations in the supply chain. Strategic
priorities must consider other key alliance partners that contribute value for
the end customer. Tactical and operational plans should be continuously
shared and coordinated. Instead of encouraging companies to hold their information close, trust-building processes promote the sharing of all forms of
information possible that will allow supply chain members to make better
decisions. Whereas traditional accounting, measurement, and reward systems tend to focus on individual organizations, a unified set of supply chain
performance metrics should be utilized as well. Finally, instead of "pushing
products" into the supply channel, thereby creating excess inventories and
inefficient use of resources, consultative sales processes and "pull" systems
should be utilized.

When organizations in a supply chain focus on these goals, they may discover the need to re-design the entire structure of their supply chains. As
shown in Figure 5-2, a "collage" of potential strategic alliances emerges in
our fictional supply chain. For example, Customer B may decide to award all
of its business to supplier A, who has a better performance record, and

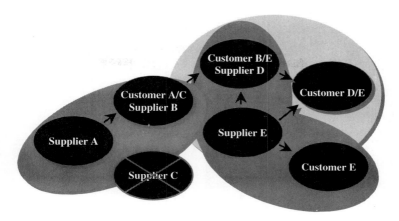

Figure 5-2   Needed: A "New" Approach

"optimize" its supply base. Companies D and E may form an alliance, thereby eliminating a number of non-value-adding activities that previously existed between them. Finally, D, E, and F may form an alliance to better share information and create synergies where possible, with D and E sharing the business according to certain pre-specified agreements.

In fact, strategic alliances can occur in any number of different markets and with different combinations of suppliers and customers. As shown in Figure 5–3, alliance configurations can vary significantly. A typical supplier-customer alliance involves a single supplier and a single customer. A good example is the relationship between Procter & Gamble and Wal-Mart, who have worked together to establish long-term EDI linkages, shared forecasts, and pricing agreements. Alliances also can develop between two horizontal suppliers in an industry, such as the relationship between Dell and Microsoft. These organizations collaborate to ensure that the technology roadmap for Dell's computers (in terms of memory, speed, etc.) will be aligned with Microsoft's requirements for its software. Finally, a vertical supplier-supplier alliance may involve multiple parties, such as transportation providers who must coordinate their efforts for multi-modal shipments. For example, trucking companies, must work with railroads and ocean freighters to ensure proper timing of deliveries for multi-modal transshipments.

All of this sounds reasonable. However, how does one initiate a strategic alliance? And under what conditions should they occur? These issues are addressed in the next section.

- Supplier-customer alliance
  - P&G, Wal-Mart
- Horizontal supplier-supplier alliance
  - Dell, Microsoft
- Vertical supplier-supplier alliance
  - Multi-modal transportation, e.g., OTR, RR

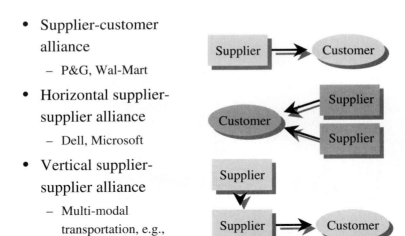

Figure 5–3 The Supply Chain: Opportunities for Alliances

A Conceptual Model of Alliance Development[7]

Figure 5–4 shows how organizations typically establish and develop supply chain alliances. The general model has a number of vertical and horizontal components. The vertical components are:

- Process component: outlines the stages of alliance development and shows the steps required to form, implement, and maintain an alliance.
- Strategic component: examines how strategic expectations and evaluations of alliance effectiveness evolve as an alliance develops.
- Operational component: positions the development of search and selection criteria and operating standards for managing an alliance.

Horizontal stages occur within each vertical stage. At each stage (as we go from top to bottom), managers must consider the strategic and operational issues that coincide with the following horizontal stages of development:

- Level One—Alliance conceptualization: Begins when a firm determines a collaborative arrangement has appeal and provides a potential beneficial alternative to the current arrangement. This level involves significant joint planning to determine the ideal strategic alliance and to project a realistic type of alliance.

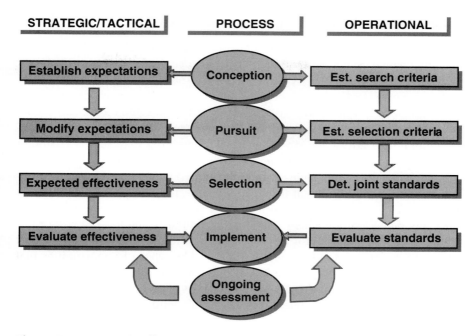

Figure 5–4   Strategic Alliance Conceptual Process

- Level Two—Alliance pursuance: The decision to form an alliance is finalized, and the firm establishes the strategic and operational considerations to be used for selection of the alliance partner.
- Level Three—Alliance selection: Managers determine the strategic and operational expectations for the arrangement through meetings with the alliance partner and the relationship is solidified.
- Level Four—Alliance implementation/continuity: The firm creates a feedback mechanism to continually administer and assess performance to determine if the alliance will be sustained, modified, or terminated. Should a conflict occur, the firm might need to explore different types of conflict resolution mechanisms.

Let's proceed through the alliance creation process shown in Figure 5–4 and discuss each of the elements. The first two stages focus on initialization of the alliance by the "initiating firm." The last two stages correspond to both parties, because the alliance partner has now joined the relationship. Alliances may begin with a single firm, but later extend to other firms in the supply chain. In each case, the same series of stages occurs, although the situation is complicated by the fact that two or more initiating firms are involved in the process.

Level One: Alliance Conceptualization

Many companies first consider forming an alliance when they realize that significant change is needed to improve performance. The entrance of new global competitors, industry consolidation, alternative distribution, retail formats, or major technological change may trigger this realization. In some cases, quality problems may cause organizations to redefine their core competence and decide to outsource those processes considered non-critical to create competitive advantage. In other cases, marketing may seek a customer and identify a need that can be met through an alliance relationship.

Any change initiative begins with awareness of a problem. However, problem awareness is not enough to induce change; managers must also be convinced that the possibility for an improved system exists. As we will discuss later, any type of supply chain relationship contains some level of risk or uncertainty, so the potential for improvement due to a change in strategy must appear to be large enough to justify the risk. The types of opportunities that initiating firms expect to receive in forming alliances often vary based on the type of channel relationship involved. The types of channel relationships are: Manufacturer/Material Supplier alliances, Manufacturer/Distributor alliances, and Manufacturer/Service Supplier alliances.

The decision to develop an alliance with a supply chain member organization is typically driven by the expectation of performance improvements in the areas shown in Table 5–1. This decision is also driven by the belief that forming an alliance will provide better results than those associated with a traditional adversarial relationship. Managers in such companies believe that a closer supply chain relationship provides the best opportunity for achieving

Table 5–1   Different Types of Alliance Goals

	Manufacturer Perspective	**Material Supplier Perspective**
Alliance Goals	• Improve inbound operations • Reduce costs • Reduce inventory • Improve quality • Reduce lead time • Stabilize supply and price • Increase utilization of supplier's technology and expertise • Shorter concept to market product development	• Increase sales volume • Increase customer loyalty • Provide value-added service • Increase switching costs • Reduce costs

Table 5–1   Different Types of Alliance Goals (*Continued*)

	Manufacturer Perspective	**Distributor Perspective**
Alliance Goals	• Increase sales volume • Increased availability • Increased freshness • Reduced damage • New product innovation • Lower inventory costs • Less damage • Invoicing accuracy • Improved pricing/promotions • Improved customer service • Improved order commitment	• Increased profitability • Reduced inventory • Increased turns • Fresher product • Reduced delivery cost • Tailored product • Configuration • Improved consumer value
	Manufacturer Perspective	**Service Supplier Perspective**
Alliance Goals	• Improve coordination between transportation operations and product supply • Reduce carrier base • Breakthrough reductions in cost • Breakthrough improvements in service • Improve warehousing and distribution labor productivity and space utilization • Maintain flexibility in product supply • Achieve consolidation benefits • Build support for industry-wide supply chain initiatives	• Increase market share growth in key accounts • Manage operational variability • Provide value-added service • Increase profitability • Develop closer relationships with industry leaders • Satisfy manufacturer customers • Ensure future competitive positioning

Source: J.M. Schmitz, R. Frankel, and D.J. Frayer, "ECR Alliances: A Best Practice Model," Joint Industry Project on Efficient Consumer Response, 1995.

their strategic goals. The ECR Alliance study previously cited also found that the most typical barriers to alliance conceptualization were the initiating firms' fear of change. Moreover, the creation of an alliance requires a new mindset toward approaching supply chain members that must be adopted. However, successful companies acknowledged that these fears existed and went about resolving them through internal training programs that explained the new types of work practices and their impact on job responsibilities. Alliances were driven by different initiating parties. In some cases, the buying company drove the movement toward an alliance, whereas in other cases the supplying company drove it based on marketing strategy.

Level Two: Alliance Pursuit

During alliance pursuance, initiating firms clarify and define their new strategies, then decide to pursue an alliance. This frequently involves a search for detailed information concerning the intended change as well as a detailed evaluation of potential partners. The initial goals established earlier are reviewed and secondary goals are created to refine the initial goals and identify the potential degree of achievement. For example, if an initial goal was inventory reduction, the secondary goal might be refined to include the specific order of magnitude such as inventory reduction of at least 20 percent.

These secondary goals help to identify the strategic and operational characteristics that the selected firm should possess to qualify as a potential alliance partner. For example, if the secondary goal was to improve quality to a specific level, selection criteria could require material suppliers to have a formalized quality control system and be ISO 9000 registered. This process of defining the selection criteria allows the initiating firm to reduce the number of firms to be considered for alliance partners.

The ECR Alliance study also found that the most successful alliances occurred when the relationship was developed around materials, products, or services that are strategically important to both partners. Once a potential partner was selected, the initiating firm determined whether the other firm wished to become an alliance partner. Both partners must perceive the potential for significant benefits from forming an alliance. Because the development of such relationships requires a substantial amount of time and resources, the potential benefits of forming an alliance must exceed the costs.

The initiating firm typically enters an agreement based on numerous expectations about the potential for benefits; a time frame for achieving them; a history of behavior with the other companies in the supply chain that determines the trustworthiness of the organization; and a set of perceptions about the trustworthiness of the other parties. Initially, these expectations and perceived risks are communicated with the other parties. Alignment occurs. The term "alignment" is important because it implies that the sets of mutual benefits projected are congruent for both parties. Each party enters into the supply chain relationship assuming that every other party has certain responsibilities and duties that they will carry out in the future. This stage of the relationship is critical because it determines the criteria by which the relationship will be deemed successful.

In evaluating a partner for possible alliance development, organizations often will perform a detailed assessment of the supplier/customer. In a buyer—supplier alliance, the buyer is purchasing not only the supplier's products and services but its capabilities as well. Within the integrated supply chain, trust must be developed not only between a single alliance, or link within the supply chain, but also among multiple partners located across the supply chain. Moreover, initiating firms must be able to trust not only their supplier, but also their supplier's suppliers! In turn, a supplier cannot simply trust a manufacturer, but also must trust the manufacturer's customers, who will dictate demand volumes, pricing, and other requirements. Managing multiple relationships within a supply chain is a challenging task. Thus, the selection of the supply chain partner often requires an in-depth evaluation of multiple criteria to identify the long-term potential for an alliance relationship. Some of the criteria that a company may use to assess the potential for integrating a partner into a supply chain include, but are not limited to, the following:

- Company profile information
- Management capability
- Personnel capabilities
- Cost structure
- Total quality management philosophy and programs
- Process and technological capability
- Environmental regulation compliance
- Financial capability/stability
- Production scheduling and control systems
- Information systems capability
- Supplier sourcing strategies, policies, and techniques
- Long-term relationship potential

Although obtaining this information on potential alliance partners requires a considerable amount of time, this is time well spent. Information obtained during the evaluation stage to determine the potential for a successful match and can identify potential problems in the supply chain relationship early in the process.

Level Three: Alliance Selection

Having thoroughly evaluated a supply chain partner using the selection criteria described above, the initiating firm can narrow the search to a single finalist who is most closely aligned with the initiating firm and appears to provide the greatest potential alliance success. Upon approaching this final partner, both firms must establish that they are truly committed to forming an alliance. This commitment can be communicated through verbal agreement or with a formal written agreement. Agreements may vary substantially in terms of duration, content, and level of detail.

In addition to signing an agreement, both partners must specify several criteria for managing the relationship and the processes that will be used to resolve any foreseeable problems. Factors to be considered include:

- How to manage the length of the relationship and under what conditions the alliance should be terminated.
- How to manage power imbalances when one party has more power than the other.
- How to address managerial imbalances when alliance partners fail to provide the same number of key contacts within each of their organizations.
- How to manage conflict when one supply chain member is engaged in behavior that benefits their organization at the expense of the other partner.
- How to jointly allocate costs required to develop and manage the alliance and the resulting benefits.
- How to develop a suitable match between the parties, based on management styles and corporate cultures. Building trust is an important part of this stage of the process and is discussed in the next section in further detail.

Although the potential alliance partners may not establish specific detailed expectations in all of these areas, how the alliance will be managed to achieve its goals is critical. This understanding enables partners to consider any potential problems that may limit the alliance's effectiveness. For example, partners must establish how potential power imbalances and managerial imbalances will be overcome, knowing full well that one partner may be devoting a greater share of time and effort to the alliance. Although such situations cannot always be changed, potential partners should recognize that the situation exists and must manage it within the context of the relationship.

In addition to these agreements on strategic effectiveness, the parties must agree on a number of specific joint operating standards. These operating standards refer to the details of doing business on a day-to-day basis. Some of the questions that must be answered at this stage of the relationship development process include:

- What procedures will enable each alliance partner to know exactly what its roles and responsibilities are, in order to reduce duplication of effort and establish accountability? This includes procedures for unexpected events, emergency procedures, and well-defined procedures that eliminate any questions or misunderstandings regarding each partner's roles and responsibilities.

- How will the partners measure, specify, and quantify operational performance? These measures must be tracked to improve operational activities and must include frequent joint appraisal to solve any problems as they arise.
- What type of information will be shared and how frequently will information transfer occur? This refers to the day-to-day requirements necessary for each party to adhere to the operating standards. The amount of information shared will often depend on the level of trust between the two parties.
- How responsive will each partner be to special requests from the other party and how can performance be improved through technology adoption? Responsiveness refers to the speed of interaction between parties and the ability to handle problems quickly and accurately. This means that the partner is taking corrective action to ensure that the problem is solved and will not happen again. Technology adoption refers to the willingness of the supply chain partner to adopt specific technologies that enable quicker response and improved performance. This includes EDI, Internet, and Extranet connections. Although it is taken for granted that such technologies will be employed, the extent of this electronic connectivity must be clearly established.

Although investment in physical resources (e.g., equipment) and human resources (e.g., training and dedicated personnel) is not always necessary in an alliance, it is important that partners discuss the need for such investments at this stage in the process. If a significant level of investment is required to proceed, the partners should agree on the financial commitment of each party.

Level Four: Alliance Implementation and On-Going Assessment

Once the initial agreement is reached, resources are committed, and the alliance is "kicked off." Ideally, each party then begins to commit the promised resources and to open up communications.

After a certain period of time, the parties either meet or fail to meet performance expectations. In cases where results meet or exceed expectations, everyone is satisfied. The level of trust between the parties increases because the parties have met their stated commitments. However, this is not always the case. Perhaps projected purchase volumes are not met or parties are unable to meet specified performance expectations for some reason. The test of a truly successful supply chain relationship is, therefore, not whether it always succeeds but how the partners manage the relationship when problems occur. When the relationship is not managed well, the relationship dissolves, and parties write off the whole experience as a loss. In such cases, the parties are unlikely to enter into such a relationship in the near future.

The key to successfully deploying supply chain alliances is through joint problem solving, which occurs when each party trusts that the other party is committed to making the relationship work. Through a process of examination of the problem, realignment of priorities, and continuous measurement of performance and activities over time, the relationship will continue and the supply chain alliances will not only grow but also will provide unanticipated benefits. For this to occur, however, key alliance contacts must visit each partner's facilities to meet face-to-face and develop a better understanding of the partner's operations. These visits allow the partners to manage changes within the relationship and facilitate the development of personal relationships between key contacts. If this process is unsuccessful, partners may try a variety of other methods of conflict resolution, such as mediation, arbitration, or the use of an ombudsman. (Filing a lawsuit only rarely results in a satisfactory financial outcome.)

As mentioned earlier, the ECR Alliance study found that a major barrier to implementation of successful alliances is the inability to abandon traditional strategic and operational practices. This includes the fear of organizational and personal change, incompatible systems, and, in some cases, the inability to secure the required resources committed to in the early stages of alliance confirmation.

The authors of the study found that successful partners used a continual feedback mechanism to ensure that the relationship was successful. Following initial implementation, alliance partners evaluated the strategic aspects of the alliance by comparing perceived and expected effectiveness, and also evaluated the operational aspects by determining each partner's adherence to predetermined operating standards. Both parties in the relationship formally assessed these comparisons.

If the comparisons reflect a positive evaluation of strategic and operational dimensions, it is likely the alliance will be sustained in its current form. If sustained, the partners:

- Perform ongoing assessments of perceived alliance effectiveness and adherence to operating standards.
- Revise strategic goals and operating standards based on competitive conditions and changing needs.

- View the alliance as a permanent system that continually moves between assessment (to evaluate strategic effectiveness and operating standards) and administration.
- Agree to sustain the alliance "as is" until (1) the alliance needs to be modified or (2) the alliance needs to be terminated because it has outlived its strategic effectiveness and/or failed to meet operating standards.

If, however, the comparisons reveal a negative or neutral evaluation of strategic and operational dimensions, the alliance likely will be modified. If modified, the partners determine what changes are required and implement them. Next, the partners assess the new changes. If the modifications are successful, the new assessment will determine whether the alliance is sustainable, and continuous administration and assessment will occur. If the modifications are unsuccessful, further modifications or termination of the alliance will result.

If the evaluation of strategic and operational dimensions is extremely negative, the partners will likely agree to terminate the alliance. Termination does not always indicate performance failure, but may be due to a change in one or both partners' strategic goals. In other cases, the goals may simply have been achieved, and there is no longer a need to continue the alliance. This is particularly true in dynamic industries with very short technological and product life cycles.

In the next section, we discuss an important attribute of supply chain relationships that occurs as an alliance relationship matures and is sustained: trust. We discuss how trust develops between supply chain partners and how it can be maintained and increased over time

Developing a Trusting Relationship with Supply Chain Partners

Trust is not something that simply happens. Trust is developed when a company's performance history and the reliability of its supply chain linkages can be demonstrated. If another party does not perceive your supply base or customers as reliable, then a strong convincing factor is an "open book" policy of past performance data.

Trust is not easily measured or identified. For instance, what specific criteria do *you* use in trusting someone? The elements of trust vary considerably depending on the situation. You may trust someone out of loyalty, or because he or she has always come through for you, or simply because you get a good feeling about his or her integrity, even though you haven't known the individual very long. In fact, any of these feelings is important in assessing trust. The numerous studies carried out on the types of actions and behaviors that lead to trusting relationships between individuals have enabled researchers to develop a "taxonomy" of types of trust.[8] If we are to understand how organizations learn to trust one another in a supply chain, we must first understand how individuals come to trust *each other*, in both the short-term and the long-term. Once we understand how trust develops, we can begin to understand the types of actions that can lead to a trusting relationship, resulting in the important benefits achieved through supply chain integration.

In this section, we describe the major types of trust and how they are developed, and illustrate each type with a supply chain example. In addition, we provide several of rules of thumb that supply chain managers can employ in their efforts to develop greater levels of trust with their supply chain partners.[9] In other words, we will consider how people can become trustworthy in the eyes of their customers and suppliers and thereby increase confidence that their joint goals and objectives can be achieved.

Reliability

This element of trust depends on the prior contact that one individual has experienced with another over time. If someone has acted in a consistent and predictable manner over an extended period, that person is likely to be considered reliable by the other party. However, reliability is also often based on the integrity or honesty of the other party. Integrity refers to the extent to which a person repeatedly acts according to a moral code or standard. If a person consistently follows this code, even in unusual situations, he or she is perceived as being reliable; therefore, trust in that individual is likely to increase.

It is important to note that a supplier or customer who applies coercion or stress to get a partner to act reliably will not improve the relationship. For instance, if a supply chain partner forces a supplier into a supply chain relationship, then the supplier is less likely to act reliably. On the other hand, if the supplier promises on-time delivery but repeatedly fails to follow through, the partner will be unlikely to trust that supplier. A rule of thumb for managers in helping to improve the level of trust in the relationship is:

Rule of Thumb 1: Follow through on your commitments and act predictably.

Parties in a supply chain who repeatedly say what they do and do what they say are more likely to instill confidence because they can be relied on to act predictably. A lack of congruence between words and action can lead to a deterioration of the relationship. For this reason, many managers seeking to create an integrated supply chain will first approach those suppliers who have consistently demonstrated on-time delivery, quality, and responded promptly to correct problems. These suppliers have shown that they are able to meet performance expectations reliably. Very often, the primary contacts in the buying company and the supply company have established a personal relationship that tells them that the other person will keep his or her word and act with integrity according to a mutually defined set of standards. This is an important point to remember: If you cannot follow through on a commitment, it is better to say so up-front. Admitting this is far better than making a commitment that you cannot keep.

Competence

Competence is one person's perception of the ability of another person to meet commitments. This form of trust is somewhat different than reliability. Competence-based trust can be broken down into three key areas.[10] The first area, specific competence, is trust in the other person's specific functional area. For example, a buyer purchasing a transmission system from a supplier trusts that the supplier can answer any relevant question he or she might have about the transmission system. The second area is interpersonal competence, which is the ability of a person to work with others. This refers to an individual's "people skills," including the abilities to listen effectively to another person, to negotiate effectively, to communicate and make a presentation, to reach a consensus with a group, and related skills necessary when dealing with others on a day-to-day basis. In managing a supplier or customer, these skills are especially important, as the majority of communication in the early stages of supply chain integration occur at face-to-face meetings.

The third area of competence involves business sense, which refers to an individual's experience, wisdom, and common sense.[11] This may also occur in specific technological or functional areas. For instance, if you are collaborating with an engineer in the supplier's organization who has worked for many years with a given technology and who understands the intricate details of his or her organization's product, you are more likely to trust that engineer's opinion when you ask him or her about a problem you are having with the product. Competence-based trust is therefore a powerful integrating mechanism between two parties in a supply chain.

Rule of Thumb 2: Make certain that your organization and your supply chain partner have assigned competent, knowledgeable, and experienced people to manage the alliance relationship.

This rule of thumb is especially important when you are working with a new supplier or customer. In some cases, companies will conduct a thorough evaluation of their partner prior to entering into a relationship. This can help support the decision to integrate the partner into the supply chain and will mitigate problems that may occur after significant resources have been invested in developing the relationship. If a supplier or customer is unwilling to commit experienced and knowledgeable people to the relationship, one should approach that firm with caution, as this may indicate that it is not fully committed to a supply chain alliance, and you may be better off looking for a different partner. Alternatively, discussions with top managers at the partner company may help them understand the need for such a person in developing the relationship.

Affect-Based Trust ("Goodwill")

This dimension of trust is difficult to define because it refers to the emotional investment that develops between individuals who trust one another. The importance of interpersonal relationships is vital to developing trust between organizations. Authors describe the shift to affect-based trust as the movement from an economically based reliance on contracts to a psychological reliance on developing and building the relationship between two parties.[12]

Affect-based trust can be broken down into two elements. The first, openness with the other party, describes a situation when each party feels that it can share problems or information with the other party. For instance, a supplier who provides information on internal costs or a buyer who provides information on future forecasts. Second, affect-based trust requires benevolence, which refers to the assumption by one party of an acknowledged or accepted duty to protect the rights and interests of the other party. Moreover, this type of trust can best be described as a faith in the moral integrity or goodwill of others, which is produced through repeated personal interactions. Over time, this leads to a certain bond between the individuals, defined by mutual norms, sentiments, and friendship:

Rule of Thumb 3: In selecting the primary interface with your supply chain partner, choose an individual who has extensive knowledge of the technology or function, good people skills, and good character.

Although this rule of thumb may seem obvious, it emphasizes the need for skilled people of good character. Supply chain managers who do not possess all of these skills may need to go through different types of technical or managerial training before being appointed full-time to a supply chain alliance position. Because supply chain relationships will undoubtedly be tested by conflict, it is important to get people involved who can manage these conflicts through controlled interactions with supply chain partners, supplemented by the knowledge required to solve technical problems. Inappropriate behaviors such as arguing, ignoring the problem, or glossing over it can harm the relationship and result in deterioration in supply chain performance. The perception of fairness regarding the manner that an organization deals with problems can influence behavior and help resolve problems. In addition, the supplier must feel that the representative from your company is involved in core activities and can elicit a response if necessary from other members of your organization. For instance, if the supply chain partner requires additional forecasting information but the liaison claims, "My boss won't let me release it," the supplier or customer may feel that it cannot trust this individual to look out for its needs. By appointing the best people to supply chain liaison positions, organizations can help ensure that they are maintaining a positive relationship with alliance partners.

Vulnerability

It has been said that trust cannot exist without some kind of vulnerability, and that trust involves adhering to commitments to others or to a stated course of action even if the probability of failure is greater than the probability of success.[13] Moreover, vulnerability suggests that some form of risk is present in committing to a supply chain partner, a risk that goes beyond the common types of uncertainties that accompany any supply chain situation. Vulnerability projects a feeling of being exposed in addition to uncertainty or risk. There is also a difference between risk-taking action and vulnerability. For instance, if one goes to work without an umbrella, then one is assuming the risk that it may rain. However, if one goes to work and asks an associate to bring an umbrella for him or her to use, then one is depending on that individual and is therefore vulnerable to that person's reliability and possibly forgetting the umbrella.

Within a supply chain situation, three types of vulnerability arise. The first, *adverse selection*, involves the inability to evaluate accurately the quality of the assets the other partner brings to the relationship. For instance, it may be difficult to assess whether a supplier's production system is capable of meeting your requirements. The second form of vulnerability is *moral hazard*, which refers to the inability to evaluate the assets committed when a relationship exists. If a supplier promises to increase the capacity of its system to meet your future requirements and you have no way of auditing it to ensure that it is actually investing in this capacity then a moral hazard exists. Finally, an *asymmetric investment* occurs when one partner commits more to the relationship than the other. For example, if a supplier has invested in an information system that links directly into your production plan, yet your company has failed to upgrade its computer systems to the level required to support the supplier's system, then a condition of asymmetric investment exists. Any one or a combination of the three types of vulnerability may be present when a supplier and customer enter into a supply chain relationship. Unfortunately, there is no such thing as a vulnerability-free integrated supply chain. Whenever parties rely on one another, vulnerability is present.

Rule of Thumb 4: The perception of vulnerability needs to be carefully managed by supply partners through information sharing, which helps assure the other partner that its interests are being protected.

It is not surprising that supply chain partners are less likely to commit to trusting behavior unless there is some type of risk involved. In such situations, trust can exist without action but trusting behavior involves actions based on trust. When there is no risk involved at all, the commitment to the supply chain may dwindle. In turn, this suggests that managers should not "roll over" and give suppliers or customers everything they ask for but should have an active role in maintaining the interests of their own organization. For instance, if a supplier asks for a price increase without providing sufficient justification, the buying company should not simply trust that the supplier is providing it with accurate information but should ask for supporting documentation and refuse to accept an increase without proof. This tells the supplier that it is still vulnerable to a market-based attitude on the part of the buyer.

Loyalty

Loyalty occurs after a period of reliable performance when one party develops a certain degree of faith in the other party. This leads one party to believe that the other party is not only reliable but will perform well in extraordinary situations, when it really counts. This goes back to the old adage, "You find out who your true friends are when you're in trouble." One can only be certain that someone cares when a situation makes it possible for that person not to care.[14] This often occurs through strong interpersonal bonds. For instance, if your organization suddenly gets a rush order from a major customer that requires material not currently in stock, you may need your supplier to expedite the material on overnight delivery. To do so, the supplier may need to schedule an extra work shift in order to meet the delivery window. A supplier who does this demonstrates loyalty to your organization.

Rule of Thumb 5: Show genuine responsiveness to your partner's needs and demand the same of your partner. Be willing to go the "extra mile" if necessary.

When one partner works to meet the other partner's needs, the relationship will continue to grow; the other party will also feel indebted as those needs are fulfilled. On the other hand, organizations should not fall into the habit of consistently requiring extraordinary support because the supplier or customer may fail to see the benefits of doing business with such an organization that does not respond in kind. This form of trust typically develops over several years. A partner's predictable actions, complemented by willingness to help the other party in a bind, will most often lead to a deeper sense of trust by a partner and a greater commitment to the future of the relationship.

By now, it is obvious that trust is a multidimensional concept. It is also obvious that trust occurs through the actions of both parties within the supply chain. Companies who are initiating a supply chain relationship can get the relationship off to a good start by:

- Employing a decision-making process that results in a high level of perceived fairness and equity.
- Becoming involved in a broad variety of activities with the supply chain partner.
- Increasing the level of competence within the organization, especially for individuals who will act as the key liaison with partners in the supply chain.

However, in developing supply chain relationships, a number of specific practices and technologies can be employed to develop and maintain strong relationships with supply chain partners. The following cases illustrate these concepts.

The Strategic Alliance Between Whirlpool Corporation and Inland Steel

Faced with intense competition, increasing expectations from customers, reduced product life cycles, and localized geographic markets, Whirlpool Corporation, a leading global manufacturer of household appliances, realized that its need to achieve a competitive advantage from sourcing and supply chain management efforts was greater than ever. Part of the strategy to achieve this advantage involved pursuing an alliance with a key steel supplier.

Steel is a major component of all the company's finished products such as washing machines, dishwashers, and refrigerators. The purchasing managers at Whirlpool faced a number of questions with regard to their purchasing strategy:

- What do we need to do to be competitive?

- Who is best suited to be the primary steel supplier?

- What do we need to know, and how do we get the information required to answer the question above, especially with regard to our organizational culture, technological roadmap, and where both organizations are moving in the long term?

- How do we establish and implement a strategic alliance in terms of confidentiality agreements, dispute mechanisms, negotiation strategies, and other issues?

- How do we evaluate the supplier to ensure that this alliance continues, with regard to continuous performance, goal achievement, and commitment?

- If we do not meet our objectives, do we change the situation or simply terminate the agreement?

Whirlpool realized it needed to reduce the number of steel suppliers it used and identify a qualified supplier with a common desire to enter into a long-term alliance. Whirlpool's organizational goals were to leverage the selected supplier's technical capabilities through early supplier design involvement, day-to-day redesign support, and process improvement. At the same time, top executives realized that in order to obtain these benefits, the supplier partner must perceive value in the relationship as well.

While all of this was occurring in 1984 at Whirlpool, the management team at Inland Steel was considering a different set of questions. Four vice presidents of marketing at Inland Steel, an integrated steel producer, were reviewing their market strategies and recent changes in their strategic alliances. They had decided to reduce their customer base, and were forming a new management plan. This was part of Inland's Customer Relationship Management (CRM) strategy, which entailed reducing their customer base in order to serve only preferred customers who would yield the highest long-term profitability. This strategy was a direct result of Inland Steel's total quality management program, which dictates that to delight the customer, one must identify and focus on key markets. A major component of this market strategy was to approach key customers with the idea of entering into long-term agreements. In doing so, Inland Steel realized that the best opportunity for reducing costs was to become involved early in new product design with key customers. However, to achieve this objective, the vice presidents determined that significant capital investment would be required to update Inland Steel's facilities with state-of-the-art steel processing technology. In some cases, this involved some degree of risk, as aligning capital investments with specific customers could shut out new business with other potential customers. However, the management team agreed that the only way to succeed in the current market structure was to reduce costs through early involvement in customer new product designs and to back this up with capital investments in design capabilities and new facilities.

Meanwhile, Whirlpool executives were mulling over whether Inland Steel was the right supplier with whom to form an alliance. Whirlpool Corporation had used Inland Steel as a supplier for several years, but also used many different steel suppliers during this period. The strategy of developing a formal buyer-supplier partnership was relatively new. As these two companies explored the idea, it became obvious that a complementary common strategic vision existed between the two companies, which could help make such a partnership a reality. This common vision was based on the fact that the Whirlpool Corporation needed to sustain a competitive advantage and support its direct customer relationships, while Inland needed to manage the transition inherent in a customer-focused market strategy. Thus, Whirlpool Corporation sought to work with Inland Steel to realize reduced costs vis-à-vis the competition, and Inland sought to obtain a major share of Whirlpool's steel contract. While this initial concept seemed straightforward, it required almost seven years to become reality.

The vision was initiated by first understanding that reducing cost did not simply mean lowering the price paid per ton of steel but rather to take cost out of the business processes. Linkages throughout every step of the value chain, not just between purchasing and sales, had to be established. The end goal became to maximize profitability at both companies while not relying on explicit formulas and equations formalized in contract form. Along the way, the companies encountered a number of obstacles. However, as the vice president of purchasing at Whirlpool Corporation described the process, "Neither of us let these problems get in the way of cost reduction efforts, which in the long run far exceeded the changes in market steel prices."

Overcoming obstacles in the relationship required a seamless organization and the elimination of levels of bureaucracy. Personnel in each firm had to be able to communicate directly with their counterparts in the other firm, all the way to the chief executive officer. The underlying foundation of the relationship was challenged many times during the early years. "The reason why this relationship works," says the vice president of marketing at Inland Steel, "is that Whirlpool Corporation created an environment that allowed questions to be laid out on the table every time a new issue came up."

A Road Map to Trust

The following is a timeline of the development of the strategic relationship between Whirlpool Corporation and Inland Steel. In 1984, Inland Steel began to share its market strategy and management vision with Whirlpool. The sharing was unique because the supplier (Inland Steel) took the initiative when pursuing the strategic alliance. By 1986, Whirlpool had reduced its steel supply base from eleven steel suppliers to seven, and Inland had invested more than $1 billion in new capital equipment. This investment was specifically designed for Whirlpool's steel requirements in the appliance industry that could not be used in Inland Steel's other major market, the automobile industry. Inland Steel needed to be granted access to Whirlpool's engineering personnel to identify the different ways that Whirlpool was using steel and convert these into process specifications. At this point, Inland was assured that it would receive a larger volume of Whirlpool's orders. One of the most important of Whirlpool's later actions was following through on that commitment.

In 1988 and 1989, the alliance was reevaluated by Whirlpool Corporation and Inland's orders from Whirlpool increased by 30 percent. Simultaneously, Inland began the first of their joint cost-reduction projects, which sought to eliminate cost from the business processes. By 1990, Whirlpool reduced its number of steel suppliers to four. The companies held a joint leadership meeting to bring discussion of the alliance to top management's attention and to formally develop a supplier council. The companies also developed a long-range vision, which was deemed critical to the success of the partnership.

The alliance further solidified in 1993. By this time, Inland Steel had established resources at its technical center dedicated to the needs of Whirlpool. In 1994, Whirlpool increased its orders to Inland Steel by another 15 percent, bringing Whirlpool's total volume of steel purchased from Inland to approximately 80 percent of total requirements. At this point, the two companies were sharing joint strategies, and Whirlpool's organizational restructuring was developed around the Inland Steel relationship. Purchasing management was actively involved in top-level strategic planning. To date, the strategic relationship between Whirlpool Corporation and Inland Steel is in place and producing benefits that a traditional buyer-supplier relationship could not have produced.

Issues and Concerns

In the course of developing greater trust between the two organizations, the companies had to address a number of issues. First, different employee practices between the two companies often led to conflict. This conflict was reduced in part by promoting greater cross-organizational interaction and understanding, such as having a purchasing manager work at the supplier's plant. The sharing of cost data was also problematic but this happened in segments to target specific cost drivers in different areas of the business process. In the long run, by focusing on quality improvements and reject-rate reduction, hourly labor costs became almost a non-issue. Even though Whirlpool had several CEOs during this period, the relationship between the companies remained intact because of the level of trust that had developed over time. The relationship was no longer just between people, but between organizations.

Inland Steel also was concerned that a single-sourcing policy might cause it to lose touch with the market, and was concerned with confidentiality of information. At the same time, Whirlpool was concerned about the risks of relying on only one supplier. However, these concerns were overcome by the belief that both companies would be low-cost producers in the long-term because of the relationship.

Mechanisms to Support the Relationship

Executive management at both companies recommended that organizations considering partnerships need to think early about how they will deal with issues such as those just mentioned. Although there is no one right answer, there are different approaches to these issues that must be tailored to the situation. For example, significant organizational realignment between Inland Steel and Whirlpool was needed so that people could work closely with their counterparts in the other firm.

The creation of a supplier council also was instrumental to the relationship. This approach permitted the sharing of strategies and tactics so that the parties became aware of each other's activities. Senior management discussion, both structured periodic meetings and informal conversations, also helped promote greater trust. Quarterly performance reviews by Whirlpool helped Inland understand how well they were meeting performance expectations. Engineers from Inland were also co-located at Whirlpool's product development center that created additional informal avenues for communication.

The underlying outcome for both Whirlpool and Inland is that the relationship became viewed as a covenant. In the words of one Inland Steel executive, "A covenant implies a promise that is enduring and provides a way to manage expectations. The single most important tenet of the relationship is the need to satisfy the end consumer who purchases the finished appliance. By focusing on this covenant, the relationship should survive and prosper over the long term."

Challenges to Managing Supply Chain Relationships

As we noted earlier, trust is a very fragile element binding organizations in a supply chain. Clearly, the concept of collaboration and joint competitiveness is often more appealing than going it alone. However, as demands on supply chains continue to escalate, the relationships between organizations will be tested. In any supply chain structure, a number of risks exist that must be managed between participating companies. Several of these challenges are discussed in this section.

Confidentiality

In order to function effectively, companies in a supply chain will need to know more about one another than ever before. To manage the flow of information and materials, organizations will need to share both strategic-level information (regarding corporate and business unit strategies, process investments, market intelligence, etc.), as well as operational-level information (number of orders, promotions, forecasts, pricing, etc.). For example, knowing when a competitor will be advertising in newspapers can be considered a strategic advantage (albeit, a short-term one). Suppliers and customers who leak such information about their supply chain members to competitors are potentially reducing the impact of the promotion. However, demand generation strategies such as promotions are useless unless the required products can be provided. This requires that all supply chain partners have advance notice in order to prepare their own organizations for the pending increase in demand.

A manufacturer of durable goods interviewed encountered this double-edged sword. A retail promotion for a new product was very successful and exceeded all expectations. In fact, demand for the product was so high that its manufacturing function was unable to produce enough units to meet the retailers' requirements. Retailers became extremely upset about the manufacturer's inability to meet demand for the product. Upon further investigation, it was discovered that the bottleneck resource was a small Asian supplier of a relatively easy-to-produce part. The part had been sourced from this supplier based on its low costs and on the assumption that its production was sufficient to meet forecasted demand (i.e., as long as demand remained stable). However, because the supplier had not been informed of the upcoming promotion, it simply did not have enough capacity to produce the part. As a result, the company decided to begin internal manufacture of the part, which further delayed shipment of the product.

Individuals in the supply chain who make major decisions, such as product volume, mix, capacity, and shipping dates, are constrained by the information available to them and attempt to make rational decisions in light of this information. Such information is often highly confidential and, if revealed to competitors, could undermine major strategic marketing and product strategies. As companies become more and more dependent on their supply chain members, they will have to find new and innovative ways to manage the risks associated with sharing proprietary and sensitive information with supply chain members.

Research and Development

As supply chain partners work more closely together, sharing new-product information will become increasingly important. Moreover, suppliers will bring with them proprietary technologies to be used in their customers' products, whereas customers may also jointly develop new products with suppliers and share with them their new-product configurations and architectures. Control over technology will continue to be a major issue. Supply chain partners will have to reach an understanding regarding ownership and control of technology and to determine an appropriate division of return on investment for the technology.

In the computer industry, technology ownership is becoming increasingly important as manufacturers and suppliers collaborate in building new products that often have product life cycles of less than six months. In one major company, all of the technology ownership issues are decided early in the relationship. Suppliers are required to sign a standard contractual agreement prior to the start of all design work with the buying company. This contract outlines the general nature of the relationship between the parties and establishes a protocol for issues such as nondisclosure of confidential information and patent rights for inventions related to the design activity. Such a contract is required before any business takes place with a supplier and serves to define underlying expectations for the future relationship.

Technology ownership and splitting market share will become even more important because of the increasing trend toward consumer direct marketing driven by technologies such as the World Wide Web. It is estimated that by 2007, more than 20 percent of product sales will be directly from manufacturer to consumers, thereby eliminating distributors and retailers. As this trend unfolds, there will undoubtedly be conflicts regarding market access, market share, and risk/cost/benefit sharing between the parties involved.

Increased Service Expectations

Most companies today are focusing primarily on the elements of a business transaction that take place at a single point in the supply chain. However, future challenges will involve how to manage both the pre-transaction and post-transaction elements. Because of increasing customer expectations, companies must find ways to determine customer needs, even before customers identify them! Such information might be developed by reviewing customers' preferred configurations and product designs, which leads to improved planning of processes prior to the actual transaction. Post-transaction service also will become increasingly critical for supply chain members. After the transaction has occurred, companies in a supply chain will need to identify methods of guaranteeing that customers will return to them for future business. Companies must find innovative ways to provide ongoing service to customers so that they can offer integrative solutions to their problems.

Leverage

Power bases in supply chains have shifted from manufacturers in the early 1980s to large retailers such as Home Depot and Wal-Mart in the 1990s. As companies continue to merge and acquire one another, power bases will continue to shift in the supply chain. However, the specter of too much control residing with a single supply chain member is a constant concern to organizations. How can a less powerful supply chain member achieve a competitive advantage in the face of this power imbalance? The use of reverse auctions is also creating a feeling of powerlessness and anger in the supplier community.

Mass Customization

The leverage issue will become even more complex when companies begin to "partition" their markets. In the future, organizations may participate in a collage of different supply chains, with each one focusing on a specific segment of end customers. Customers will continue to demand increasingly mass-customized products. This means that although aggregate demand forecasts may remain relatively stable, the number of different products will continue to increase resulting in a fragmented array of customer options. Furthermore, the forecasts for the product mix, demand at different locations, and volumes required will become increasingly difficult to develop and manage. Inventories may accumulate at one location, whereas another is starved for product and is turning away unhappy customers. How are companies to organize themselves to manage mass-customized markets in an integrated supply chain environment?

Shared Responsibility

As supply chain structures begin to evolve, increasing investments in information systems and technology will be required to integrate supply chain organizations. The payoff on such investments is not always evident, yet managers are constantly evaluated on detailed financial measures, which in turn drive analysts' responses on Wall Street. Lately, one of the most closely monitored ratios has been a company's return on managed capital and economic value added, which measures the return achieved given a company's existing level of debt and asset base. To justify supply chain investments, managers will need to determine who takes on the risk of the investment and who is entitled to the reward if and when it pays off. There will be no easy solutions in determining these financial arrangements. Such inter-organizational issues will continue to challenge supply chain managers.

Summary

This chapter has presented a general framework for managing supply chain relationships. The concepts proposed are by design broad and general. There is a very good reason for this: every supply chain relationship is unique and carries its own set of benefits, challenges, and potential conflicts. Companies who enter into close relationships with supply chain members must be aware that managing such relationships requires a great deal of time, effort, and resources. Just as in a marriage, parties to a supply chain relationship must be prepared to spend a great deal of time communicating, improving the relationship, and resolving conflicts as they occur. It is for this reason that we stated early in the chapter that supply chain inter-organizational relationships are one of the most difficult elements of the supply chain to manage. The processes described in this chapter can help managers select the right partners in the first place and conduct business in a manner that will foster trust within the relationship. Although these concepts appear to be straightforward, they are not always easy to apply. However, we believe they constitute a good set of ground rules for implementation of the other strategies described in this text.

Endnotes

[1]Daniel Krause, and Robert Handfield, *Developing a World-Class Supply Base*, Center for Advanced Purchasing Studies, Tempe, AZ: National Association of Purchasing Management, 1999.

[2]G.B. Richardson, "The Organization of Industry," *Economic Journal*, September 1972, pp. 883-896.

[3]T. Nishiguchi, *Strategic Industrial Sourcing: The Japanese Advantage*, New York: Oxford University Press, Inc., 1994.

[4]Robert Mottley, "Messy Divorce," *American Shipper*, 45, 1998, pp. 22-26.

[5]Adopted from *New Product Development: Strategies for Supplier Integration*. R. Monczka, R. Handfield, D. Frayer, G. Ragatz, and T. Scannell, ASQ Press, Milwaukee, WI, 1999.

[6]Adopted from Daniel Krause, and Robert Handfield, *Developing a World Class Supply Base*, Center for Advanced Purchasing Studies, Tempe, AZ: National Association of Purchasing Management, 1999.

[7]J. M. Schmitz, R. Frankel, and D. J. Frayer, "ECR Alliances: A Best Practice Model," Grocery Manufacturers Association, Washington, DC, 1995.

[8]R. M. Kramer and T. R. Tyler, *Trust in Organizations: Frontiers of Theory and Research*, Berkeley, CA: Sage Publications, 1995.

[9]For more information, see the following: Christian Bechtel, "The Development of Trust in Strategic Supplier Alliances," Ph.D. dissertation, The Eli Broad Graduate School of Management, Michigan State University, East Lansing, MI, 1998; R. M. Kramer and T. R. Tyler, *Trust in Organizations: Frontiers of Theory and Research,* Berkeley, CA: Sage Publications, 1995, M. Deutsch, "Trust and Suspicion," *Journal of Conflict Resolution* 2 (1958), pp. 265–279.

[10]Kramer and Tyler, 1995.

[11]D. Gambetta, "Can We Trust Trust?" in *Trust: Making and Breaking Cooperative Relations*, ed. D. Gambetta. Cambridge, MA: Basil Blackwell, 1988.

[12]D. McAllister, "Affect- and Cognition-based Trust as Foundations for Interpersonal Cooperation in Organizations," *Academy of Management Journal* 38 (1995), pp. 10–36. P. Ring and A. Van de Ven, "Developmental Processes of Cooperative Interorganizational Relationships," *Academy of Management Review* 19 (1994), pp. 18–40.

[13]Deutsch, "Trust and Suspicion," 1958.

[14]Kramer and Tyler, 1995.

6

Customer/Supplier Integration into New Product Development

Bob Lutz Shares His Strongly Held Beliefs at General Motors[1]

Focus groups? Over-used and unreliable. Design? Undervalued and "corporate criteria-ed to death." Content? Not at the expense of profit or shareholder value. So says Robert Lutz, freshly anointed product czar at General Motors, in a widely circulated memo entitled "Strongly Held Beliefs."

The memo, which was leaked almost immediately to the media, created such a buzz throughout the world's biggest car company that CEO Richard Wagoner felt compelled to issue a statement saying in essence, "Go, Bob, Go." Lutz, Wagoner said, was hired to challenge the status quo and that's what his memo does.

More than a half-decade of committee-laden "brand management" looks to be taking it on the chin at General Motors as Lutz pressures the corporation to develop more exciting products in less time and at lower cost.

Lutz, who declares his motto to be "often wrong, but seldom in doubt" assailed excessive democracy and "consensus building" as counterproductive and hailed the virtues of tension and conflict in the workplace.

He certainly generated some of the latter. Reaction to the memo, predictably, varies depending on its implications for the recipient. The memo is
shown below.

MEMORANDUM

From: Robert A. Lutz

Strongly Held Beliefs

1. The best corporate culture is the one that produces, over time, the best
results for shareholders.

Happy, contented employees, and an environment where nobody argues or
disagrees, and everyone compromises because the other person has goals,
too, is usually not the culture that produces great shareholder value. A
performance-driven culture is often a difficult place to work, and it certainly
isn't "democratic." Democracy and excessive consensus building slow the
process and result in lowest-common-denominator decisions. As Larry
Bossidy, former CEO of Allied Signal, so aptly said: "Tension and conflict
are necessary ingredients of a successful organization."

2. Product portfolio creation is partly disciplined planning, but partly spontaneous, inspired all-new thinking.

A good planning process can be an excellent baseline tool, a means of generating solid data. But it cannot robotically create a good future portfolio.
It will generate bunts, singles, walks, and the occasional double. But triples
and homeruns come from people who say, "Hey, I've got an idea!! Listen to
this!" Steven Spielberg does not research in moviegoer needs segments.
Needs-segment analysis can find a "small minivan" niche. It can't find a PT
Cruiser, or a new BMW Mini, or an H2!

3. There are no significant unfilled "Consumer Needs" in the U.S. car and
truck market (except in the commercial arena). There are "consumer turn-
ons" that research alone won't find.

4. The Vehicle Line Executives (VLEs) must be the tough gatekeepers on
program cost, content, and investment levels.

After (and maybe before) contract, requests for "priceable" content (it
never works out that way, anyway) or "volume-improving" content can no
longer be honored without offset. The VLE needs a program contingency, to
be reserved for last–minute fixes or enhancements, (and maybe I need one,
too). But the VLEs must evolve into often-unpopular "benevolent dictators"
when it comes to protecting their cost position. It must be inviolable. Programs that miss their cost targets cannot be tolerated.

5. Much of today's content is useless in terms of triggering purchase decisions.

Most customers want a vehicle of new, fresh exciting appearance, with a
rich, value-transmitting interior. They want a great powertrain, superb dynamics, and, obviously, safety and quality. But the thought that huge advances in voice recognition, or screen technology, or multi-function displays
or ever-trickier consoles, or embroidered floormats, etc. will somehow over-
ride other deficiencies (or, worse yet, "averageness") is wrong. What focus

groups say they would "really like in their next car" is not reliable, because they are, in the research, not really paying for it. ("Talking car" and all-digital instrument panels received high "want" ratings in their day.) The vehicles that are succeeding today (Honda, Toyota, Audi, VW) are not highly contented, or if they are, they charge for the option packs. A "base" Camry is really base!

6. Design's Role Needs to be Greater.

As one of you said to me the other day, Design is being "corporate-criteria-ed" to death. By the time the myriad research-driven "best-in-class" package, the carryover architecture, the manufacturing wants, the non-stone chip rocker placement, the carryover sunroof module, and on and on, are loaded in, and the whole thing is given to Design with the words, "Here, wrap this for us," the ship sailing toward that dreaded destination, "Lackluster," has already left the dock.

7. Complexity-reduction is a noble goal, but it is not an overriding corporate goal.

Standardizing options for the sake of simplifying the BOM, engineering and releasing effort, pricing, dealer stocks, etc. is very worthwhile. But it can be counterproductive if it reduces vehicle margins, i.e., the net revenue loss is greater than the demonstrated savings in the enabling disciplines.

A good rule of thumb is that, in the case of an option with a significant cost, where the freestanding "take" is less than 70-75%, the incorporation as standard will cost money. If "priced for," then a large proportion of customers are being asked to pay for something they don't really want. If it's "eaten" and not priced, we are reducing margins without enhancing value to those who don't care for the option.

My experience is that options running at 25-40% should remain options (perhaps grouped into packages); options running at over 75% should be incorporated as standard. The area between 40-75% requires judgment in each individual case, and a good dialog between affected parties.

8. We all need to question things that inhibit our drive for exceptional, "turn-on" products.

Edicts and criteria do some good; they create consistency and order, and they help someone achieve a goal that he or she feels is important. But many of our criteria are internally focused and prevent us from doing high-appeal, exciting, dramatically new products. A salesman cannot say to the customer, "It takes a bit of getting used to, I admit, but did you know that it satisfies 100 percent of GM's internal criteria?"

We don't want anarchy, but we do need more of a "Who says?" attitude. The focus has to be on the customer.

9. It's better to have manufacturing lose ground in the Harbour Report, building high net-margin vehicles with many more hours, than being best in the world building low-hour vehicles that we take a loss on.

10. We need to recognize that everything is a tradeoff, that we can't maximize the performance of any one function to the detriment of overall profit maximization. The same goes for every discipline: A gorgeous vehicle that

disappoints in quality will fail. A car incorporating every conceivable new safety technology makes no contribution to safety if it becomes unaffordable to the customer or we can't afford to build it. A vehicle with a single-minded focus on "absence of things-gone-wrong" will fail miserably if it is dull, unexciting, a dog to drive, and ugly. Even if it's the best ever found by J. D. Power!

11. Remember the Bob Lutz motto: "Often wrong, but seldom in doubt."

None of us is infallible, and we all make errors. Remember baseball, where a batting average of .400 is unheard of! But pushing and arguing for what you believe to be the right course (while recognizing you just might be wrong, therefore, still willing to listen) is the key to moving forward. Errors of commission are less damaging to us than errors of omission. In our business, taking no risk is to accept the certainty of long-term failure. (Even Aztek, in this sense, is noble!)

Changes to the New Product Development Process

The reality in many markets today is that 40 percent or more of revenues come from new products introduced in the prior year. Thus, unless supply chain participants can create a continuous stream of innovative products, customers will take their business elsewhere. In the late 1980s and early 1990s, many Western organizations began re-evaluating and re-engineering their new product development processes. The combination of speed to market pressures and the need for product innovation forced many firms to experiment with new ways of bringing new products to market. For example, American automakers recognized that Japanese automakers were consistently able to design and build a new automobile in less than 30 months. Until very recently, the "Big Three" automotive manufacturers required from 48 to 60 months to accomplish the same task. Japanese automakers were consistently "leapfrogging" their American and European counterparts and in so doing, achieving a significant technological and marketing advantage in terms of quality, design, and performance. One common strategy that emerged during this time was to view new product development as more of a rugby game than a relay race, stressing the importance of getting the functional areas together early and frequently in bringing the product to market. The implications for manufacturing were significant. No longer was the manufacturing function notified after the product design was complete; instead, it would become involved throughout the process.

In the long run, competitiveness is the result of an ability to nurture and develop, at a lower cost and faster than competitors, the core competencies that result in unanticipated, innovative products. Core competencies include a firm's collective learning, especially its ability to coordinate diverse production skills and integrate multiple streams of technology.[2] Firms must focus on those activities in which they have a learning and technological performance advantage. For example, 3M develops product lines around adhesives, while Honda considers their engine design and production a core competence.

As manufacturers focus more on their areas of competence and technical expertise, they must rely more on external suppliers to support non-core requirements. This is especially true in new product development. Firms are relying increasingly on suppliers for early design, concurrent engineering, and other product development support. To remain competitive, firms must receive competitive performance advantages from their suppliers that match or exceed the advantages provided by the suppliers of their global competitors. Firms are recognizing the strategic performance potential that collaborative relationships with suppliers can provide. They need a proactive approach to supplier integration into new product development; characterized by the formation of strategic alliances with core technology suppliers, open information sharing, co-location of supplier design personnel, and joint future technology planning. This approach must include strategies and tactics that directly promote supplier inputs into the new product development process. This practice suggests that a firm's strong commitment to internal technological development is not always necessary for competitive success. Successful technology acquisition or co-development is another means to achieve a sustainable competitive advantage. Some firms have been particularly successful borrowing innovative product and process ideas developed externally and applying them to better serve their market segments. In such cases, the borrowed technology could have been available for a long time. Among the most notable examples of this approach are seen in Japanese automotive and electronics firms that have competed very successfully in the world marketplace using many borrowed technologies. Other firms may not have adequate research and development (R&D) resources to allow much internal product or process development; such a firm must rely more heavily on external acquisition of innovative ideas to remain competitive. Thus, successfully acquiring and implementing a specific technology may well lead to a competitive advantage.

In this chapter, we review a number of important developments in new product development that have significant implications for value system creation, and present the key implementation issues involving supplier—customer integration into new product development, based on the results of a recent National Science Foundation study. Supplier development is then explored in the final section.

Supplier Integration Into New Product Development

Although there is increasing evidence that involving suppliers in the new product development cycle is important, there also is evidence that not all such efforts are successful. Moreover, successful supplier integration is dependent on a large number of variables. Supplier integration considerations include tier structure, degree of responsibility for design, specific responsibilities in the requirement setting process, timing of supplier involvement in the process, inter-company communication, intellectual property agreements, supplier membership on the project team, and alignment of organizational objectives with regard to outcomes. While the benefits of supplier integration appear to be obvious, the results of a recent study show that successful supplier integration projects have special common characteristics.[3] Specifically, successful supplier integration initiatives result in a *major change to the new product development process*. Furthermore, to be successful the new process must be formally adopted by multiple functions within the organization. The most important activities in the new development process are understanding the focal suppliers' capabilities and design expertise, conducting a technology risk assessment, and weighing the risks against the probability of success. Key questions that must be addressed are presented in the following sections and include:

1. Which suppliers should be involved?
2. Is the supplier able to meet our requirements?
3. Is the supplier's technology roadmap aligned with our technology roadmap?
4. Given the level of technical complexity, to what extent should the supplier be involved in the project?
5. When should the supplier become involved in the project?

Supplier Integration Approaches

The possible forms of supplier integration can be framed within the context of the "generic" new product development process shown in Figure 6–1.[4] The new product development process is a series of interdependent, often overlapping stages during which a new product (or process or service) is brought from the idea stage to readiness for full-scale production or service delivery. As the product concept moves through these stages, the idea is refined and evaluated for business and technical feasibility, the initial design is established, prototyping and testing are done, the design is finalized, and preparations for

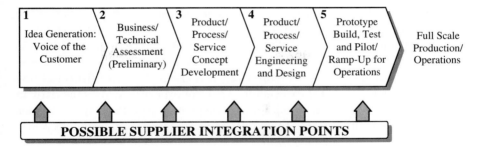

Figure 6–1   New Product Development Process

full-scale operations (tooling, layout, personnel, equipment, etc.) are completed. During this process, issues relating to cost, performance, timing, quality, and others, which result in tradeoffs and changes in the design are
addressed. The design may be modified numerous times before it is finalized.

In the first stage (idea generation), designers and marketing personnel
consider the need for the product, and typically tap potential customers for
ideas and input on what such a product/process/service might do, how much
it might cost, etc. Potential technologies also may be assessed at this point, especially if an existing supplier possesses an exciting new technology. In the
second stage, the team may perform a business assessment of the product,
and also identify the technical solutions to the customer's requirements. In
the third stage, the product/process/service concept is effectively conceived,
with performance specifications "frozen." In the case of product development, a preliminary prototype model may be created to define the concept.
Next, the actual development process begins: designers from both the supplying and buying organizations create design specifications. Tools such as
Quality Function Deployment (QFD) may be used to develop technical specifications that address customer requirements. They create a working prototype that enables testing and verification of existing production systems.
Finally, the product enters full-scale production.

Outside suppliers provide materials and services that comprise a majority
of the cost of many new products. In addition, suppliers may provide innovative product or process technologies critical to the development effort. The
supplier may have better information or greater expertise regarding these
technologies than the buying company design personnel. Supplier input
and/or active involvement of suppliers may be sought at any point in the development process.

While the concept and design engineering phases of new product development incur a relatively small portion of the total product development costs,

these two activities often commit or "lock in" as much as 80 percent of the total cost of the product. Decisions made early in the design process have a significant impact on the resulting product quality, cycle time, and cost. As the development process continues, making design changes becomes increasingly difficult and costly (see Figure 6–2). It is crucial then, for firms to bring to bear as much product, process, and technical expertise as possible early in the development process. In addition, companies whose development plans are well aligned with those of their key suppliers can shorten overall development time.

The degree of supplier integration in new product development can range from having no supplier involvement to a "Black Box" approach, where the supplier provides its own design without the involvement of the buying organization. In between are the "White Box" and the "Gray Box" stages. A "White Box" occurs when the supplier is brought in on an ad hoc basis, and acts as a consultant to the buyer's new product development team. This is largely an informal meeting, occurring only as needed. The "Gray Box" approach is more formal: joint development activities such as joint design, prototype manufacture, and testing occurs between the buyer

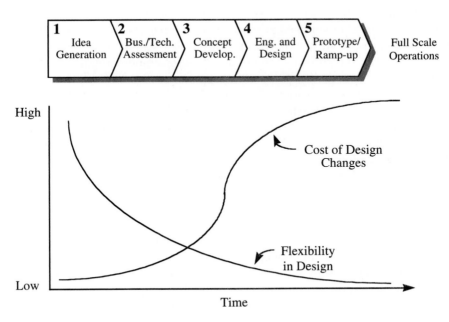

Figure 6–2   Design Flexibility and Cost of Design Changes

and supplier. In the "Black Box" approach, the supplier is formally empowered to design the component based on the buyer's performance specifications. In this type of approach, a high degree of trust typically exists between buyer and supplier, as the buyer relies on the supplier to design and manufacture an entire subassembly or module that will "fit" into their primary new product or service.

BMW's Global Integration in New Product Development[5]

BMW is initiating a project to improve the CAx collaborative processes it shares with its global suppliers. CAx refers to any type of computer-aided design (CAD), engineering, or manufacturing data used to develop and produce vehicle parts, process tools, or equipment. This data includes the following: 3-D digital models, geometric and process quality data, 2-D drawings, or product management system data. Collaborative engineering, as defined at BMW, is simply working simultaneously on synchronous CAx data with suppliers. Virtual simulation and a digital mock-up process also help shorten the development timeline and reduce material use in prototyping. These models have been developed extensively in Germany, and BMW is implementing this technology on a global basis with its key suppliers. Because co-location is not possible given the wide array of technology centers within the supply base, using digital technology will enable BMW's entire supply base to be "on the same page" throughout the new product creation and development stages, on a real-time basis, regardless of location.

Supplier Integration Into New Product Development Process Model

Based on a detailed analysis of multiple company case studies that were conducted as part of a major research project funded by the National Science Foundation,[6] a process model of supplier integration into new product development was created (Figure 6–3). This model is a compilation of supplier integration process "best practices." Additional insights into company practices at various stages of the model are also provided in this section.

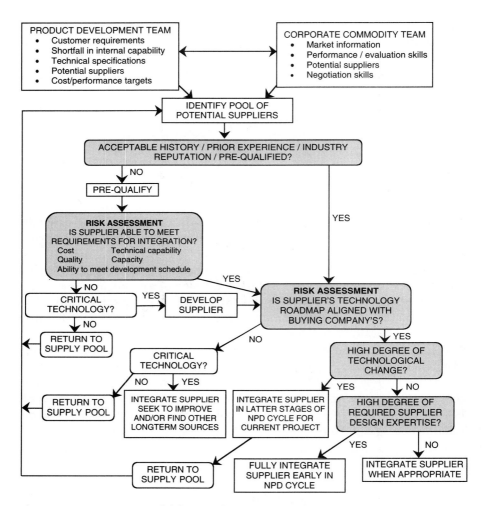

Figure 6–3   Process Model for Reaching Consensus on Suppliers to Integrate into New Product Development Project

Identifying Desired Supplier Capabilities and Potential Suppliers

All the companies that participated in this research indicated that the design and manufacturing process is being subjected to a much more thorough analysis than in the past. An important initial decision in this process involves a formal statement on the level of insourcing/outsourcing that will occur in core technology development. In order to reach consensus on difficult insourcing/

outsourcing decisions, successful organizations have developed a formal process for defining the level and types of product/process technologies to be outsourced. Whenever possible, companies are approaching the insourcing/ outsourcing decision from a systems perspective, and are asking suppliers to increase their responsibility for the level of integration. This was observed across a variety of products and processes; including chemical molecules, computer components, installation and maintenance of new processes, and automobiles.

The decision-making process begins with an assessment of strategic core competencies in product and process design and manufacturing. At this level, the analysis involves decisions regarding core technologies, system integration, and return on investment for resource allocations leading to internal technology development. In general, companies trended toward outsourcing commodity-like items, and focusing internal efforts on value-added processes such as system integration. In all of the companies, this decision was made at higher levels in the organization, and involved a strategic vision regarding the organization's future markets and technology roadmap over the next ten to twenty years.

Once consensus is reached, executives formalize the insourcing/outsourcing technology strategy and communicate it to the divisions, who are then responsible for establishing current and future new product requirements. The process of cascading the decision to the next organizational decision-making level is achieved through a variety of means. One of the prevailing organizational structures used to interpret and deploy technology strategies is the advanced technology group. These groups are typically located centrally, and are tasked with identifying major new subsystem and component technologies required in new products. Another approach involves integrating suppliers into process development and start-up. Some companies use institutionalized "platform teams," responsible for new product development with suppliers on a permanent basis. Finally, other organizations employ a letter of intent that formally specifies the nature of the relationship. At this stage product development teams are typically making the decisions, guided by the executive core competence vision.

The final insourcing/outsourcing decision-making hierarchy occurs at the component level, where decisions are typically made jointly by the product development and purchasing commodity team. Purchasing is responsible at this level for identifying leading suppliers within a commodity class and sharing this information with the commodity team.

After completing this initial stage of the strategic process, teams should have identified a vision statement regarding the company's internal core competencies, established a set of requirements for success in current and future new products, and have a general idea of the technology needs within these product groups. In addition, the company should have a general idea of the specific roles and responsibilities it requires of suppliers selected for new product development. New product/commodity teams should seek to formally specify these objectives in as much detail as possible. These objectives become the primary criteria used in supplier selection, negotiation, alignment, and relationship management.

A number of case examples illustrate this process. At NEC, a major manufacturer of fax machines in Japan, the primary metric used to drive all supplier integration projects is target cost. A target cost for a fax machine is first developed based on marketing's input, and is broken down into different categories of parts based on historical costs. This target cost is submitted to suppliers. Suppliers share their cost data with engineers, and provide information on labor, overhead, and material costs. To achieve the target cost, changes in processes and materials are discussed first, avoiding the topic of profit margins. If the supplier still cannot meet the target cost, the company initiates negotiation of profit margins based on volume considerations.

Other considerations that may influence the decision to integrate suppliers include a lack of internal design capability and the need to develop a non-core technology. For example, Intel relies extensively on its suppliers to deliver state-of-the-art process technology that it cannot develop internally. The key strategy within Intel involves holding suppliers responsible for delivering, installing, servicing, and maintaining machine tools. Suppliers are responsible for process ramp-up and equipment maintenance. While the company is also involved in supplier integration into new product development, process integration represents a unique application in a non-traditional area. Suppliers are first fully responsible for the maintenance of these machine tools; the maintenance tasks are then gradually turned over to internal people. Each supplier is responsible for a single process, which is performed identically at multiple Intel facilities around the world. Intel demands the exact replication of processes across its facilities: this principle is emphasized throughout its business strategies. The principle refers to the fact that any time a specification or task is transferred between functions or suppliers, the other party is responsible for exactly reproducing the requirements.

In another case, Dupont considered portions of molecules as building blocks in assessing supplier competence. The company's strategy was to accelerate the rate of new product development by focusing on fewer compounds annually, and to integrate suppliers who have proven capabilities and can perform multiple steps in the intermediate production process. Instead of asking suppliers to only supply basic elements, the suppliers make the intermediate molecules with the final molecules in mind. This involved showing suppliers "the big picture" (not just a small piece of the process), posing the question more broadly, and getting the supplier to perform a greater share of the process. Supplier integration was facilitated by broader confidentiality agreements covering more issues as the supplier gained access to more pieces of the molecular puzzle. In some cases, Dupont even licensed parts of molecules from university research centers! The strategy driving this integration process was to push it increasingly higher up the compound chain, becoming more of an "assembler" of the final compound or molecule.

Supplier Risk Assessment

Once the new product commodity team has reached consensus on the key objectives for integrating suppliers, a set of specific performance measures related to customers' needs and requirements should be used to identify potential supplier capabilities and drive the subsequent selection. Cost, quality, and delivery are, of course, relevant, but evaluating suppliers for potential integration into new product development should involve criteria beyond those used to evaluate ordinary material/service suppliers. Based on the experience of the companies studied, the following elements are likely to be important factors in considering new or existing suppliers for integration:

- **Targets:** Is the supplier capable of achieving the required targets regarding cost, quality, and product performance/function (e.g., weight, size, speed, etc.)?
- **Timing:** Will the supplier be able to meet the product development schedule?
- **Ramp-up:** Will the supplier be able to increase capacity and production fast enough to meet volume production requirements?
- **Innovation and Technology:** Does the supplier have the required engineering expertise and physical facilities to develop an adequate design, manufacture it, and solve problems when they occur?
- **Training:** Do the supplier's key personnel have the required training to initiate and successfully operate required processes?

All of the above criteria must be tied into the evaluation/measurement system, in order to develop a comprehensive risk assessment that answers the following questions:

- What is the likelihood that this supplier can bring the product to market?
- How does this risk compare to other potential suppliers?
- At what point are we willing to reverse this decision if we proceed, and what are the criteria/measures for doing so?
- What is the contingency plan in the event the supplier fails to perform?

It is no longer enough that a supplier be able to design and manufacture a prototype or start-up small volume production. Because of the intense competition and short product life cycles in many industries such as computer electronics, suppliers must also be able to meet product introduction deadlines and ramp-up their production volumes very quickly. Several of the companies studied assessed these criteria through a variety of means.

A good example is provided by a new product/commodity team from a computer manufacturer and a European supplier, who was selected after ten suppliers presented their design for a new project. The commodity team evaluated all presentations. During the course of the selected supplier's presentation, the team found that it could satisfy its requirements with an "off-the-shelf" chip set from this supplier. The team also visited selected supplier facilities, and the supplier deployed a dedicated engineering team over the course of the project. The commodity team also worked in parallel with other new product/commodity teams on the product development group. A key element in the structure of the teams in this company is that it is not a 100 percent engineering-led process, even though engineering has traditionally dominated decisions. The new vision is to retain a core set of knowledge to respond to end customer needs, and develop more interfaces with suppliers to identify which technologies can meet these requirements. The company cannot afford to be shut out of a new technology, so the group must constantly transfer knowledge from a variety of sources, including customer requirements, aftermarket (where new technologies often show up first), trade shows, competitive assessments, and alliances.

For another computer manufacturer, the supplier's capacity and flexibility are critical issues, and the team examines the type of agreements the supplier has with their contract manufacturers and how they affect the supplier's ability to increase output quickly. In this case, the supplier must have to the ability to increase productive capacity in the following manner:

- 25 percent in 4 weeks
- 50 percent in 8 weeks
- 100 percent in 12 weeks

A computer peripherals manufacturer faces the problem of having a very limited number of potential suppliers of several key components worldwide. However, because of the small number of suppliers, the company has done business with most of them, and recognizes their capabilities. Supplier selection is based primarily on the supplier's capability to design and manufacture the product in large volumes to performance specifications within the required time.

At another computer company, in the first stage of the new product development process (definition and planning), material support involves selection of technology appropriate to product requirements. Once this is complete, corporate materials can identify a potential list of suppliers. If the supplier is new to the company, the supplier will first perform a self-assessment survey. Then the new product/commodity team conducts a comprehensive assessment of the supplier's capabilities and arrives at a performance score.

When the supplier's capabilities are not at desired levels, the new product/commodity team has two options. If the technology is not critical to the product's functioning, a different supplier may be investigated. However, if limited numbers of suppliers are available and the technology is critical to the product, the company may undertake a more detailed technical assessment of the supplier in order to develop and improve the suppliers' capabilities early in the product development process.

Several companies in the study carried out detailed assessments of the supplier's technical capabilities prior to selecting them for a new product development project. In most cases, both formal and informal approaches were required to develop a reliable assessment. A typical approach would start with a standard survey augmented by informal evaluations by the buying company's engineers based on face-to-face discussions with the supplier's technical personnel.

A good example of how this decision is made involved a component supplier who made lead frames and over-molding for a semiconductor manufacturer. Although the company had the capability to manufacture these parts internally, they chose to team up with the supplier to produce them after the new product/commodity team (engineering, design, quality, marketing, and procurement) made an insourcing/outsourcing decision. The team decided to outsource because the internal process could not meet the customer's quality requirements (0-6 parts per million). The supplier was selected after the new product/commodity team reviewed the supplier's product, process, and control plans. Next, the team was expanded to include the supplier, to determine if it could meet the customer's requirements. Once the supplier's capability was established, it became a full-time member of the team.

In another case, an oil and chemical company's new product/commodity team evaluates suppliers involved early in its development efforts using a number of criteria in a "Total Cost of Ownership" model that considers:

- Reputation for meeting requirements
- Cost/availability of raw materials
- Difficulty of the process matched against the supplier's capability
- Waste generated in the supplier's process
- Number of steps required of the supplier
- Environmental compliance
- Technical competence

The choice of supplier is made by the whole team. Following the recommendation, the company audits the supplier's facilities for contamination, environmental compliance, quality, technical capability, and cost.

Assessing the Supplier's Technology Roadmap

Even after the new product/commodity team has carried out a detailed performance assessment prior to selection of a supplier, it must carry out a second type of assessment. This second assessment ensures the short-term and long-term alignment of the objectives and the technology plans of the buying company and the supplier. To obtain maximum strategic benefit from the integration of the supplier, companies must share objectives and have complementary future technology plans. This is commonly described in terms of a convergence of the partners' technology roadmaps (see Figure 6–4), which describe the performance, cost, and technology characteristics of future products each company plans to develop and introduce over some specified time horizon.

The specific approaches companies use to assess and achieve alignment of technology roadmaps with suppliers vary considerably. Regardless of the approach, sharing information is a critical element of the process. A second important element is providing some incentive or motivation for suppliers to work toward technology alignment with the buying company.

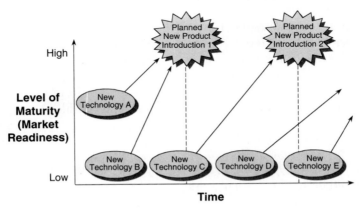

Figure 6–4   Managing Product and Technology Development

As organizations seek to improve the technological capabilities of their supply base, they will need to first build stronger relationships with suppliers, which involves sharing future product plans and alignment of technology roadmaps. In turn, suppliers may need to alter their technological plans to more closely align them with those of major customers. As this exchange of information takes place, industry standards may be influenced. This will not only require an intimate understanding of current suppliers' capabilities, but also a commitment and willingness to trust the other party.

At the same time, buying companies must maintain a competitive edge, and must be aware of potential new suppliers and technologies. Organizations may need to create separate groups responsible for advanced technology development and expertise. These groups will need to continuously monitor competitors' products, processes, and supply bases, and to suggest modifications to current sourcing strategies. In some cases, joint technology development with suppliers may yield substantive results, providing that appropriate targets can be set. Companies must conduct this activity on a global basis, scouring the world for the best suppliers. This study showed that geographical proximity was one of the least important factors influencing the choice of supplier for integration.

Many companies attempt to manage and obtain the best technologies for application by developing a "bookshelf" of current and emerging technologies and suppliers of those technologies. These companies monitor the development of new technologies and, for those that appear to have promising applications, manage their introduction in new product applications so as to balance the benefits of "first mover" status with the risks of utilizing new technology. The objective is to maintain a selection of promising and accessible technologies and suppliers on the "bookshelf," ready for the company to use in a new product application.

At one company studied, an engineer in the buying company initiated the company's most successful supplier integration project. The engineer recognized synergies between the capabilities of his company and a supplier and began talking informally with a counterpart in the supplier company. This led to a high-level meeting between executives from the two companies. At this meeting, supplier executives shared technology plans and roadmaps, and identified common research streams in a very broad category of materials. A "top four" list of projects was targeted directly to future product needs. This relationship has now solidified, with the two companies meeting periodically to share their technology roadmaps and update their project list.

A different type of technology roadmap sharing is done by one electronics company that isn't sure where needed technology developments are most likely to occur. In some cases, internal development groups will share early information about future technology roadmaps. For instance, in one commodity, the manager has established a technology roadmap with performance curves and expected targets by date. The target area is shared with multiple suppliers. Suppliers are told that if they can't hit the target by a specified date, they won't get the business. This concept varies somewhat from conventional early involvement wisdom. Due to the volatility of this industry, the company does not have the time or the need to form alliances and go through an early involvement program. Rather, the company's strategy is to make sure the technology is available by openly sharing technology roadmaps with any qualified supplier, and to move its business when necessary to take advantage of performance at the target price.

Assessing the Rate of Technological Change

Assuming that the buying company can establish that the supplier's technology roadmap is aligned with its own, another important factor it must consider is the rate of change in product technology. The current rate of technological change is challenging many companies' capabilities, and they are seeking the help of suppliers with the development and application of critical but non-core technologies in their new products. For instance, the product life cycle of some products such as personal computers is less than three months. One computer manufacturer in the U.S. mentioned that the need to quickly bring new products to market is the single most important reason for integrating suppliers. Because of this need, this manufacturer skips the prototype stage and goes directly from development to full production!

Although supplier integration is useful for managing the quick pace of technological change, it also represents a double-edged sword. If a particular technology is changing rapidly, then involving the supplier early has potential pitfalls: the buying company may become "locked into" a particular design or technology, release the product, and discover that the technology has become obsolete or has been replaced by a technology with improved performance characteristics.

Timing of Supplier Integration

Companies should consider two major factors when deciding when to integrate the supplier into the product development process: the rate of change of the technology, and the level of supplier expertise in the given technology. Generally speaking, if the technology is undergoing a significant amount of technological change, it should be delayed in the product development cycle. On the other hand, if a supplier's design expertise is significant and its technology experts can provide insights instrumental to crafting the new product, that supplier should be included earlier in the process (see Figure 6–5).[6]

Field studies suggest that certain types of suppliers are more likely to be integrated earlier. For instance, at a Japanese computer manufacturer, the extent of interaction between product development engineers and suppliers appears to depend on the volatility of the commodity technology. Suppliers of critical non-standard commodities are involved much earlier in the product development initiative. These suppliers have regular, face-to-face discussions with engineers. On the other hand, suppliers of non-critical, standard items are not integrated until the final stages of the development cycle, and communication appears to occur more frequently by means of information systems (i.e., CAD is used with non-critical items such as PCBs, keyboards, and chassis). In general, face-to-face discussions are quicker, and information can be exchanged more effectively. However, because suppliers are located within a day's travel to the operating divisions, co-location is often unnecessary.

At a U.S. electronics manufacturer, the supplier's level of involvement may vary. To get a good quote, the supplier must be brought in early and sit in on the customer negotiation meeting. This company typically relies on suppliers for their process technology, not their product technology: suppliers are involved in bringing in new processes that are not internal areas of expertise. Suppliers often understand the total design, and how they can influence the design, earlier than internal personnel. In this case, the functional specifications are defined, and suppliers work with the company to jointly ensure they are met.

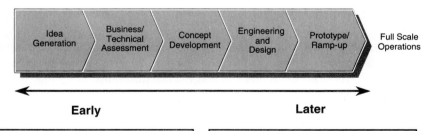

Figure 6–5   Integrate Suppliers at Different Stages

The Future of Supplier Integration

The companies in this study had a median of six years' experience integrating suppliers into new product development. They expect to increase their use of supplier integration in the future, and to involve suppliers earlier in the development process than they do now. Respondents were asked to characterize the success of the specific supplier integration effort, as well as the success of the overall development project in which the supplier was involved. On average, the respondents considered both the supplier integration effort and the overall development project to have been fairly successful.

Not surprisingly, results also indicated large variation in companies' level of satisfaction with their supplier integration efforts. In fact, only 20 percent of respondents agreed with the statement "We are currently satisfied with the results of our supplier integration efforts." More than 45 percent disagreed with the above statement. Despite these mixed results, respondents are committed to supplier integration for the future and their expectations are that supplier integration will continue to be important. This is indicated by the fact that more than 70 percent of respondents agreed "Expectations about the results to be achieved from supplier integration will increase significantly." Together, these results seem to indicate that many companies realize the importance of supplier integration, but have not yet perfected the process to successfully implement it.

Developing Suppliers' Capabilities[7]

In the early stages of new product development, a new product/commodity team may visit suppliers and find that they will have problems meeting performance expectations. It is definitely better to discover such problems *before* the product enters into the full production cycle. To deal with this issue, many companies are employing a strategy called supplier development. Leading organizations do not simply tell the supplier to improve, but are increasingly adopting a hands-on approach to improvement. This often involves working directly with the supplier to identify and resolve problems. Help may come in the form of process engineering support, financial support, or even support from within the supplier community itself. The following cases provide examples of how organizations implemented these approaches.

Process Engineering Support

One U.S. automotive company has used a group of 15-16 process specialists in supplier development for many years. These individuals specialize in areas such as castings and machining, and are typically in a "reactive" mode: they respond to quality or delivery issues when a problem is recognized. For instance, if a supplier is experiencing persistent process problems and the normal set of contacts cannot resolve it, then the process specialists become involved. In such cases, these individuals have the requisite skill set to watch a supplier's production line, talk to the supplier's production people, and subsequently understand the problem. They then work with the supplier to determine the root cause of the problem and potential solutions. This process may require several days and repeat visits. After the problem is resolved, they move on to another supplier, and often travel all over the world "fighting fires." Until recently, nearly 90 percent of the company's supplier development efforts were reactive in nature, and the remainder proactive. One of the company's objectives is to reverse this ratio.

Financial and Facility Support

Financial distress has been a common problem in the Asia Pacific supply base within recent years. A manager from a Korean electronics firm, Samsung, noted that most Small Manufacturing Enterprises (SMEs) in Korea are deficient in manpower capability, technology, and financial resources. The latter two are the primary focus of the company's improvement efforts. The company supports financial and technology initiatives by performing facility layout projects for suppliers, as it has expertise in the area. In the financial resource area, the company is able to assist by lending money at lower interest rates than financial institutions and waiving collateral requirements. Suppliers also may initiate supplier development assistance from the company by making a formal request. The electronics firm also employs specialists who assist suppliers in improving competency in areas such as supplier management and purchasing.

Another Korean company, Lucky Goldstar, emphasizes education as a key part of its supplier development program. The company also provides collateral for supplier's improvement projects, allowing the supplier to borrow funds at reduced rates for new equipment. The firm also helps suppliers purchase raw materials, and leverage steel prices from steel manufacturers.

Hyundai has begun to improve suppliers' technology and capacity through the creation of a Supplier Industrial Complex. This facility allows suppliers to work together in supplier clusters. This five-acre complex was purchased to help suppliers develop their own facilities, rent-free. The company envisions a joint plant, with joint painting and tooling facilities, to be shared by all suppliers in the complex. Currently, this concept is limited to domestic Korean suppliers, but may be extended internationally in the future.

Supplier Associations

Many organizations also are developing supplier support systems within their supply base, in order to concurrently improve the entire supply base. One of the largest such support systems is run by Toyota with operations in the U.S., which has formed a supplier association (*kyoryoku kai*) to support its objectives through its supplier members. In effect, the objectives are linked back to the company's internal policy deployment (*hoshin*) process, which ultimately dictates the real goals. These associations facilitate supplier development, by creating peer pressure with other suppliers in the tier, essentially creating a "shame factor" for low-performing suppliers.

This company has four supplier associations: three are regional and one is made up exclusively of tooling suppliers. First-tier supplier companies and the OEM buying company lead these associations. The association's strategy board generally consists of eight suppliers, whose membership rotates annually. This group defines what is to happen within the association. The primary meetings occur about twice a year, and include the presidents of all the supplier members. Together, the strategy board and the primary meetings constitute an extension of the *hoshin* process beyond the walls of the buying company. At a lower level, the parts and commodity groups meet approximately ten times per year to discuss evolving trends, technologies and new product requirements. However, the majority of the work occurs in the process group meetings. These groups are divided into three focus teams: Cost, Quality, and a group whose topic of emphasis varies every year according to Toyota and supply base needs. Possible topics for this group include automation, environmental issues, and cycle time reduction among others. Each of these groups meets approximately ten times per year. Although supplier associations were originally instituted in Japan, companies around the world are now using them.

Summary

Companies must recognize that supplier involvement in new product development can have both positive and negative impacts on technology risk and uncertainty. Organizations need to capitalize on the positive aspects of supplier involvement recognizing:

- The supplier may have greater experience or expertise with the technology and, as a result, may have better information about where the technology can be successfully applied.
- Some (or all) of the technological risk may be taken on by the supplier.
- The buying firm may have some ability to influence the direction of the supplier's R&D efforts in order to match developing technologies with the buying firm's technology strategy.

If a closer relationship between the buying company and the supplier develops as a result of supplier involvement, the supplier may be more willing to share information about its new/emerging technologies with the buying company. The buying organization may also provide various types of supplier development assistance to help motivate this information exchange.
However, organizations also need to recognize that:

- Involvement with a supplier may tend to lock the buying company into the supplier's technologies. This makes initial selection of the supplier a more critical issue, as the buying company needs to anticipate whether the supplier will remain a technology leader.
- A supplier with an "inside track" may not have as much incentive to innovate, slowing the pace of technological advancement. The buying company must find ways to ensure it is getting the supplier's best efforts.

In the next chapter, we discuss another benefit of supplier integration that is evident: significant reductions in cost across the value system.

Endnotes

[1] Appeared in Autoweek Online on October 12, 2001.

[2] C. K. Pralahad and Gary Hamel, "The Core Competence of the Corporation," *Harvard Business Review* (May-June 1990): pp. 79–91.

[3] Robert Handfield, Gary Ragatz, Robert Monczka, and Kenneth Peterson, "Involving Suppliers in New Product Development," *California Management Review*, vol. 42, no. 1, Fall 1999, pp. 59-82.

[4] R. Monczka, R. Handfield, D. Frayer, G. Ragatz, and T. Scannell, *New Product Development: Strategies for Supplier Integration.* ASQ Press, Milwaukee, WI, 1999.

[5] Presentation made by Rob McDarris (BMW) at the Southern Automotive Manufacturing Conference & Exhibition, Palmetto Expo Center, Greenville, SC, April 8-10, 2002.

[6] R. Monczka, R. Handfield, D. Frayer, G. Ragatz, and T. Scannell, *New Product Development: Strategies for Supplier Integration.* ASQ Press, Milwaukee, WI, 1999. Figures 6–1 to 6–5 are adapted from this text.

[7] Adopted from Daniel Krause, and Robert Handfield, *Developing a World Class Supply Base*, Center for Advanced Purchasing Studies, Tempe, AZ, National Association of Purchasing Management, 1999.

7

Strategic Cost Management in a Global Supply Chain

Strategic Cost Management—A Chemical Company Example[1]

Several years ago, a large multinational chemical company began developing corporate-level long-term alliance agreements with selected process equipment suppliers. The primary goal of this process was to reduce the supply base and future investment costs by identifying and selecting suppliers who would become common to all 18 business units. The long-term vision included realizing greater supplier integration in the design of new facilities and equipment.

Because this company historically accounts for less than 20 percent of a typical equipment supplier's volume, relying on fewer suppliers was expected to provide greater purchasing leverage. In addition, the company expected its alliance agreements to create benefits beyond those available from simple leveraged purchase agreements or traditional long-term agreements. For most equipment applications, the rate of technological change is stable, making long-term agreements with fewer suppliers a viable strategy.

Business units within this company are highly independent. The key to executing successful corporate-level sourcing agreements requires the following: 1) including business unit participation when crafting the agreements; and

2) showing how the agreements would benefit individual business units. The corporate staff helps individual buying locations to source equipment, while encouraging those locations to use alliance suppliers. Currently, business units must provide justification when selecting a non-alliance supplier for an item covered by a corporate alliance agreement. The company currently has 60 formal equipment agreements, 40 of which focus on cost reduction. For example, the company relies on one firm for all its copying equipment needs. This agreement features a per page copy rate, simplified billing, and monthly preventive maintenance on each machine without machine or service costs. Alliance suppliers represent 40 percent of total equipment purchases. This is significant given that 35 percent of a project's cost is engineered equipment. Furthermore, a key performance measure is a capital productivity ratio, defined as (dollars of sales)/(dollars of investment). This ratio receives attention at the highest corporate levels. Achieving the target for this measure requires efficient investment and completing projects in the most productive manner. Capital equipment supplier alliances are important because they affect the denominator of the investment ratio. These agreements are also important because the physical equipment itself may not be as important as the engineering process involved in securing the equipment. External design support is becoming increasingly important because a great deal of experience has left the company through early retirements and staff reductions.

All alliance agreements are with U.S. firms, with one-third of the agreements specifying a single source. Relying on multiple sources can be the result of (1) a single supplier being unable to provide national support, (2) a single supplier's inability to provide the entire range of items within an equipment commodity, or (3) historical capacity constraints within the commodity. Some agreements, for example, have five suppliers supporting a particular equipment commodity. If an equipment item or commodity is non-strategic, then a single supplier usually receives the contract. The company is currently reviewing and modifying each agreement to meet continuing or evolving needs.

Each negotiated agreement contains re-opener clauses for poor performance. The company can re-open agreements for poor service, poor quality, or noncompetitive price/cost. Furthermore, the company uses several approaches to ensure the competitiveness of its alliance agreements. The company:

· Identifies price trends within across commodity groups by tracking the Producer Price Index (PPI) and then compares those to price trends within the alliance agreements

- Relies on selective market bidding to test the equipment market
- Uses third-party price benchmarking
- Develops internal cost models based on experience and price trends and compares these with the actual price behavior within the agreements

Negotiated contracts are usually structured around a life cycle cost. The maintenance cost of a pump, for example, may be greater than the cost of the pump. Creating total cost life cycle models can be difficult when life cycle data does not exist. Furthermore, price is a complex issue due to the difficulty of comparing equipment features and options between companies. A strong internal reluctance to shift from unit price to total cost still exists because price is still the most visible indicator available. Alliance agreements are not that different structurally from standard agreements. The alliance agreements differ from a typical agreement in that (1) suppliers receive larger volumes in return for a lower price, (2) the agreements clearly establish the framework for removing costs within the relationship, and (3) the buying company usually requests preferential warranty or service. In return, the alliance agreements specify that suppliers will receive an agreed-upon portion of the buying company's total volume.

This vignette highlights the importance of carefully crafting supplier alliance agreements. These agreements are critical because *they provide the basis and foundation for pursuing early supplier design involvement and support* and establishing precedence for on-going strategic cost reductions. Ignoring the important relationship between these agreements and early supplier design involvement would result in a disconnect between SCM planning and results.

The Financial Impacts of Supply Chain Management: Rolling Up the Numbers

Many managers complain that senior executives do not understand the importance of supply chain management. At SCM educational seminars, the authors often hear, "I wish my boss were here to listen to this." There is no question that SCM can have a dramatic impact on profitability and cost; however, managers often fail to communicate this. Moreover, managers must be able to make a business case for improvements to the supply chain by translating supply chain improvements into financial terms that enable senior executives to understand and support such initiatives.

If you were to look at the financial statements of an average organization, how much would you guess the company spends on goods and services? In manufacturing, the figure is astonishingly high: the average manufacturer spends approximately 56 cents out of every dollar of revenues on purchased materials. For some industries this figure can be even higher.

When this much of a firm's revenue is spent on materials as well as services, improving supply chain performance represents a major opportunity to increase profitability. Consider the following financial information for Lowe's, a leading firm in the home improvements retailing sector. Table 7–1 shows earnings for the company for the quarter ending January 1999, as well as key balance statement figures.

From the figures, we can see that the pre-tax profit margin for Lowe's is ($168,253/$2,915,664) = 5.8 percent. This means that every dollar of sales generates a little less than 6 cents in pre-tax profit. Furthermore, the return on assets (ROA) is ($168,253/$6,344,651) = 2.7 percent. What can Lowe's do to improve these figures?

Note that every dollar saved in purchased materials increases pre-tax profit by a dollar. According to these figures, Lowe's would have to generate about $17 in sales to make the same improvement to the bottom line that saving one dollar in purchasing costs would have. This **profit leverage effect** is particularly important for low margin businesses, such as retailing. Also note that if Lowe's were able to cut its merchandise costs, this would not only affect profits, but would also reduce the amount of money tied up in inventory. The impact would be a higher ROA figure. To illustrate these points, let's see what would happen if Lowe's were able to cut merchandise costs by just 3 percent (Table 7–2).

Pre-tax profits would increase 37 percent, and the new pre-tax profit margin for Lowe's would be ($231,143/$2,915,664) = 7.9 percent. Lowe's would

Table 7–1   Selected Financial Data for Lowe's Company (all figures in $000s)

Earnings & Expenses	
Sales	$2,915,664
Merchandise costs	$2,096,331
Pre-tax earning	$168,253
Selected balance sheet items	
Merchandise inventory	$2,104,845
Total assets	$6,344,651

Source: Bozarth and Handfield, Operations and Supply Chain Management, Prentice Hall, forthcoming, 2003.

Table 7–2   Impact of 3% Cost Savings

Earnings & Expenses	
Sales	$2,915,664
Merchandise costs	$2,096,331
minus 3% savings:	− $62,890
	$2,033,441
Pre-tax earnings	$168,253
plus 3% savings:	+ $62,890
	$231,143
Selected balance sheet items	
Merchandise inventory	$2,104,845
minus 3% savings:	$62,890
	$2,041,955
Total assets	$6,344,651
minus 3% savings:	− $62,890
	$6,281,761

Source: Bozarth and Handfield, *Operations and Supply Chain Management*, Prentice Hall, forthcoming, 2003.

have to increase sales by ($62,890/5.8 percent) = $1.1 *billion* to have the same impact! In addition, the new ROA is ($231,143/$6,281,761) = 3.7 percent.

Clearly, there is a significant benefit to investing in SCM activities that have an impact on cost. Many opportunities exist to achieve dramatic cost savings far greater than the three percent figure used in the previous example. However, such initiatives require vision. More importantly, they require that managers in different parts of the supply chain work together to break down the intra- and inter-organizational barriers and achieve such savings. Breaking down barriers is a challenge; many organizations still operate in a functional cost-center manner, whereby managers focus on reducing costs associated with their own internal function. This approach significantly reduces the effectiveness of strategic cost management efforts that span the supply chain.

To combat this problem, some organizations have begun to develop internal supply chain "consulting" groups. These groups have a directive to work in a cross-functional manner across the organization to promote and conduct joint cost-savings projects. These groups are supported by a "percentage" of the savings they are able to generate with the remainder of the cost savings being shared by the different functions or business units. These cost savings may go toward the strategic business unit (SBU) or functional cost reduction goals set by the corporate executive team. In fact, the success of such programs at companies like Shell Corporation and GlaxoSmithKline has led many of the business functions in these organizations to depend on supply chain managers to achieve annual cost savings.

Strategic Cost Management Initiatives Across the Supply Chain

Increasingly, managers are considering the implications of cost management from a total supply chain perspective. In the past, many companies focused their efforts on internal cost management initiatives. Today, organizations are expanding the scope of these cost-reduction initiatives to include both upstream (supplier) and downstream (customer) members of their supply chains.

Such a change requires a fundamental shift in thinking by both managers and employees. This shift may take several years to be fully realized due to the pervasive "price-based" thinking that is ingrained in traditional corporate culture. Figure 7–1 presents a variety of different strategic cost management approaches. Most companies are undertaking initiatives that focus on internal cost-reduction efforts that span one or two functional groups in the organization, for the simple reason that these types of efforts typically require less

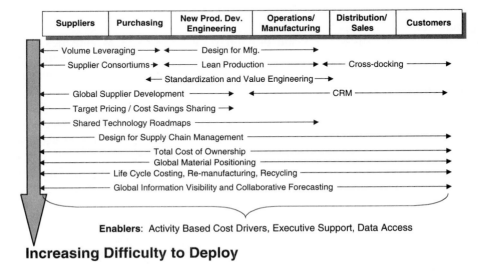

Figure 7–1   Strategic Cost Management

effort and coordination. Examples of some of these cost reduction strategies include purchase volume leveraging with suppliers, supplier consortiums, design for manufacturability, value engineering, standardization, lean production, and cross-docking. However, a new generation of cost management initiatives is also evolving that includes both upstream and downstream members of the supply chain. Such initiatives include direct involvement of three or more supply chain functions or partners working together to identify cost reduction process improvements. Examples include global supplier development, customer relationship management, target pricing, cost savings sharing, sharing technology roadmaps, and engineering change controls. The final set of initiatives involves those requiring multiple parties to collaborate. These parties might include customers, suppliers, and multiple internal business functions. Examples include total cost of ownership, global material positioning and supply chain re-design, life cycle costing, global information visibility, and collaborative forecasting. Such initiatives are only beginning to evolve among supply chain members, as they are often complex and difficult to implement. To be successful, strategic cost management approaches rely on a system of cost driver identification, executive support, and access to reliable cost data. Availability and access to reliable cost data are often the greatest barriers encountered in supply-chain cost reduction initiatives.

Strategic cost management approaches will vary according to the stage of the product life cycle. In the initial concept and development stage, organizations often will act proactively to establish cost targets. Target costing/target pricing is a technique developed originally in Japanese organizations in the 1980s to combat the inflation of the yen against other currencies. Target pricing, quality function deployment, and technology sharing are all effective approaches for cost reduction used at this stage. As a product or service enters the design and launch stages, supplier integration, standardization, value engineering, and design for manufacturing can increase the use standard parts and techniques, leverage volumes, and create opportunities for cost savings. During the product or service launch, organizations will adopt more traditional cost-reduction approaches including competitive bidding, negotiation, value analysis, volume leveraging, service contracts focusing on savings, and linking longer-term pricing to extended contracts. As a product reaches its end of life, organizations cannot ignore the potential value of environmental initiatives to remanufacture, recycle, or refurbish products that are becoming obsolete. For instance, print cartridge manufacturers such as Hewlett-Packard and Xerox have developed innovative technologies that allow customers to recycle laser toner cartridges that are subsequently refurbished and used again, eliminating landfill costs.

Major cost-reduction opportunities can be realized when supply chain managers are involved early in the new-product/service development cycle. When sourcing and materials decisions are made early, the full effects of a sourcing decision over the product's life can be considered. When supply chain managers are involved later in the product development cycle, cost reduction options are constrained because the major decisions regarding designs, types of materials, choice of suppliers, packaging, and distribution options already have been made. A manager at General Motors described this situation as follows: "In the past, we allowed engineering to determine the specifications, the materials, and the supplier. In fact, the supplier had already produced the first prototype! That's when they decided to call in purchasing to develop the contract. How much leverage do you have in convincing the supplier to reduce costs when the supplier already knows they are guaranteed the business, and they have already sunk money into a fixed design and tooling for the product?"[2]

When prioritizing efforts to reduce costs, companies often apply a structured framework depending on the value of the material/service to the company. In general, low-value generic items for which a competitive market exists should emphasize total delivered price. There is no need to spend time conducting a detailed cost analysis for these items. Products and services that are high value where a competitive market exists can be sourced through traditional bidding approaches. Unique products present a different challenge: companies must strive to reduce costs for products that have few suppliers, yet that are still low value. Examples include suppliers of unique fasteners, specialty papers, and specialty maintenance, repair, and operating (MRO) items. For such items, purchasers should focus on achieving lowest delivered cost. The primary focus of cost reduction initiatives should be on critical high-value products and services. Managers should commit time to exploring opportunities for value analysis/engineering, cost-savings sharing, joint identification of cost drivers, and customer—supplier integration early in the product development cycle for these items.

The remainder of this chapter presents a number of the initiatives, identified in Figure 7–3, for managing costs across the supply chain. We will begin by addressing opportunities to harvest the low-hanging fruit—that is, endeavors that require less effort to implement and generally have a quick payback. Later, we will discuss more complex initiatives.

Volume Leveraging and Cross Docking: Harvesting the Low-Hanging Fruit

Understanding your total purchase expenditure, classifying expenditure by commodity families, and consolidating requirements to leverage purchase volume is a simple yet effective cost reduction strategy. However, it is surprising that many organizations do not fully utilize it.

Leveraging is a straightforward strategy that follows directly from an organization's commodity strategy development process. A commodity is a general category or family of purchased items or services. Purchasing strategies are developed and implemented for items or services that are part of the same family, category, or classification. Examples of key commodity classifications across different industries include body side moldings (automotive), microprocessors (computer), steel (metalworking), cotton (apparel), wood (pulp and paper), and petroleum products (chemicals). Organizations often use commodity teams composed of personnel from operations, product design, process engineering, marketing, finance, and purchasing to make sourcing strategy decisions. The personnel involved should be very familiar with the commodity being evaluated. For instance, if the team is tasked with purchasing network computer servers, then users from information systems should be included. If the team purchases vehicles and vehicle parts, then maintenance managers familiar with these commodities should be consulted. In general, the more important the commodity, the greater the level of cross-functional involvement required for the sourcing decision. Together, the commodity team develops a commodity strategy that provides the specific details and outlines the actions to follow in managing the commodity.

The primary objective of a commodity strategy is to fully understand the purchase requirement relative to the business unit's objectives. This is often achieved through a strategy segmentation tool known as *portfolio analysis* (shown in Figure 7–2). The premise of portfolio analysis is that purchases can be classified into one of four categories or quadrants based on item value and the number of capable suppliers. Unique purchase strategies are associated with each quadrant and are described in the following section.

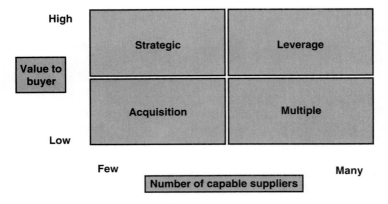

Figure 7–2   Portfolio Analysis Approach

Acquisition Quadrant—Acquisition items typically have few capable suppliers within a region and are of lower value. Many suppliers might conceivably be able to supply the item. However, the cost to search and compare supply alternatives often outweighs the value of the item. Generally, these items represent relatively low total dollar amounts, but may consume a disproportionate amount of time to acquire. Many acquisition items have standardized quality and technology requirements, and the "switching costs" of moving from one supplier to another supplier are low. The focus when acquiring these items should be on removing the effort and cost of transactions required to obtain these items. Typical items found in this category include office supplies, MRO items, tools, and other items that users often need on short notice. Proven purchasing strategies for acquisition items include the use of procurement cards, direct ordering systems through the Internet, and other automated transaction systems. Supply chain professionals do not want to focus their attention here. The value that supply chain managers contribute in this category is in assuring users that they can efficiently obtain these lower value goods and services.

Multiple Quadrant—The value of purchases in this quadrant is still relatively low, but a greater number of suppliers are capable of providing the product or service. The technology characterizing these items is standard and widely available. Switching costs are relatively low, but because more suppliers are available, supply chain managers should focus on price analysis as the primary tool for reducing costs. Price analysis effectively means shopping around for the best deal by sending out requests for bids or quotations to suppliers and accepting the most competitive bid price. Historically, almost all purchases were selected according to low price. Bidding can be an effective strategy when conditions involve a standard item with many available sources of supply. Such items might include vehicle tires, office furniture, steel castings and sheeting, and printers. Value in this quadrant is defined by achieving the lowest possible price assuming that delivery and quality are acceptable.

Leverage Quadrant—Items in this quadrant have a large number of capable suppliers with a medium to high annual dollar spend. Furthermore, the item or service is often used across the entire organization and purchased from multiple suppliers. By combining the requirements of different units, purchasing can effectively negotiate a better deal with a select few suppliers. Consolidating purchases and reducing the supply base can yield immediate and significant cost reductions. Suppliers can offer lower prices in part because their costs decrease with higher volumes as fixed costs are allocated over larger volumes. Variable costs may also decline owing to improved productivity over a higher volume of product. It is important for supply chain managers to ensure that remaining suppliers can handle additional business volumes and that the quality of the product or service is not adversely affected.

Strategic Quadrant—The fourth quadrant includes items that are critical to the buying organization's success and few suppliers are capable of supplying the good or service. Such items may be unique or customized, or may simply represent a high-dollar item. Because of the small number of suppliers, switching between suppliers may be difficult. Items in this quadrant may involve technology that is unproven or in development. Examples include computer microprocessors, pharmaceuticals, new chemical compounds, and aircraft engines. Supply chain managers should focus on developing close relationships with such suppliers to insure adequate supply and provide a basis for greater supply chain collaboration.

Cross Docking

Integration of distribution and transportation processes is the underlying principle in cross-docking. Cross-docking is a relatively simple concept. It is a process that takes place at the distribution center and covers any method for processing shipments that avoids putting the product into storage before sending it on to retail stores or other outlets. Instead, the distributor simply moves it from the receiving dock to the shipping dock, or holds it in a temporary staging area before moving it to the outbound dock.[3]

Cross-docking is similar to employing a break bulk facility in that it encompasses full trailer loads of product arriving from multiple manufacturers. As product is received it is sorted by store location. Product is then literally moved across the dock to be loaded into the trailer destined for the appropriate customer location. The trailer is released for transport to the retail store once it has been filled with mixed product from multiple manufacturers.[4]

Cross-docking provides a quick means for moving individual containers or pallet loads directly from the receiving area to the shipping area within a distribution center.[5] However, the implications of cross-docking go beyond the arrival of merchandise to the dock door. It involves moving merchandise from the manufacturer to the ultimate consumer in the shortest period of time. There are three possible levels of cross-docking: simple, intermediate, and complex.

With simple cross-docking, the supplier provides normal pallet loads. The distributor sets product aside next to the shipping dock and picks it out later to send to stores. This requires no pre-distribution, assistance, or investment in technology. Minimal coordination from the supplier and the knowledge that the product will be shipped within a day or two are all that is required. In this process, goods are received and transferred immediately to a "hot" order processing area on or near the shipping dock. Products are then picked out later to send to stores. Product storage, replenishment modes and order picker's travel time can all be greatly reduced by picking high-volume items on the shipping dock, resulting in lower warehousing costs.

Intermediate cross-docking involves equipping the warehouse with an automatic material handling system, so that the supplier does not need to segregate products by customer. This system handles segregation. Since the warehouse can apply labels upon request, pre-distribution does not occur until the shipment arrives at the warehouse. In this situation, coordination and communication are necessary, but at a lower level of integration than in complex cross-docking. Complex cross-docking, in its most sophisticated form, can require a substantial amount of coordination and support system integration among distributor, supplier, and customer. The supplier is responsible for preparing store-specific, multi-SKU pallets or full-case loads, and for making sure they get onto the shipping dock on time to get on the right outgoing truck. Often, pre-distribution of the product before the supplier ships it is imperative.

A good example of such a system is a Meijer distribution center.[6] Meijer operates cross-dock facilities called Retail Support Centers (RSCs) that can ship supplier-to-RSC-to-store, or supplier-to-warehouse-to-RSC-to-store. When product enters the RSC, information on what is on the truck has already been received through an advance shipping notice. Product is then automatically bar-coded and loaded onto a conveyor system. Laser scanners read the bar code and direct the product to store outbound trucks using a combination of mechanical and flow conveyors.

Cross-docking eliminates the intermediate put away, transfer, and retrieval steps found in traditional warehousing. Some of the primary benefits include the reduction of time, labor, storage space requirements, inventory, and costs related to handling inventory. Companies can take advantage of savings derived from buying in large quantities, while fulfilling customer needs for fast service through shorter order cycle time.

The economic benefits of cross-docking include full trailer movements from manufacturers to warehouses and from warehouses to retailers. Maximizing load dock facilities from fully loaded vehicles is made possible by better scheduling and a steady flow of products. Other benefits of cross-docking include higher inventory turns and a lower chance of damage through product handling. Slower-moving products can also be moved faster by receiving orders in sufficient time to prepare store-specific SKU's.

Cross-docking, along with electronic collaboration, functions before and after the merchandise passes through the warehouse. This results in a win-

win situation; suppliers ship only what is required and only in the requested amounts, are paid quickly, and are able to increase their inventory turns. Distributors handle the merchandise as little as possible, minimizing inventory costs and labor requirements.

In implementing a cross-dock operation, several issues need to be addressed. First, with the exception of simple cross-docking, investments in information sharing and in processing capabilities are required. Ideally, a company should establish continuous contact across the supply chain from the point of sale, distribution centers, manufacturers, and suppliers so as to ensure that orders after they arrive, are consolidated and shipped within the shortest amount of time. This requires a high level of information sharing along the supply chain, maximizing visibility, planning, and coordination. For example, distributors and retailers should work together to coordinate case-labeling responsibilities. If the distributor has an automatic sorting system, the supplier should be responsible for labeling, so inbound loads can simply be placed on conveyors. If product is to be manually sorted, distributors should produce labels and apply them as product is sorted in store order. The most efficient forms of cross-docking generally require order selection by the supplier, which may in fact increase the supplier's labor costs. Even if these incremental costs are passed on, however, total distribution costs will still be less than without cross-docking.

Cross-docking works best with products that have short replenishment lead-times, fairly heavy demand, and relatively predictable volumes and flows. It also should be targeted for products with potential cost benefits associated with consolidating large quantities to one location, which are then distributed locally in small quantities (e.g., items that are "slow movers"). Unfortunately, this is unsuitable for items with a limited shelf life, or products that require a great deal of serial number tracking. Many make-to-order products fall into this latter category.

Promotional products are among the items most commonly associated with cross-docking. These products are ideal because they are shipped in large quantities for sale during precise periods that have been scheduled in advance. For instance, some supermarkets cross-dock fast-moving products that are not shipped directly from suppliers to individual stores.[7] Slower-moving items that are delivered to distribution centers on store-bound assortment pallets are also suitable for cross-docking. Logistical economies are improved because less warehouse space and lower inventory levels are required and transportation costs are reduced.

Because of the relatively short lead-times associated with local sources of supply, suppliers that can ship from local points are better candidates than geographically distant suppliers. Retailers and wholesalers stand to gain the most from cross-docking because large volumes of goods are typically ordered in predictable quantities from a specified set of suppliers at regular time intervals. Cross-docking is feasible only when the overall pipeline benefits outweigh the added supplier costs. In addition, it is essential to ensure that costs of implementation are not merely transferred on to the supplier.

A poorly planned cross-docking operation can make maintaining consistent and reliable customer service difficult. Because there is no safety stock inventory, cross-docking requires a thorough understanding of the flows from supplier to manufacturer and from distribution to customer, and how they interrelate. As much information as possible is required about the receiving locations, including hours of operation, labor, number of dock doors, special requirements, etc. Transportation capacity also must be carefully monitored.

For cross-docking to work, suppliers, manufacturers, and distributors must coordinate production and shipping schedules, plan needs and available quantities accurately, and forecast timing of shipments. Many industry insiders believe the primary challenge to effectively increasing cross-docking is schedule complexity. Organizations also must overcome the range of issues that occur when internal functions, suppliers, or customers resist change by convincing them of the real cost benefits of cross-docking.

Design for Supply Chain Management

Supply chain members will increasingly need to improve coordination not just in the area of demand replenishment, but also in the joint development of new products. By joining forces and sharing design information and technology, significant synergies can be achieved to create new products that can quickly capture market share. An equally important benefit of this collaboration is the increased standardization and simplification of product designs that can lead to a "design for supply chain management" approach. This approach is likely to become more frequently used in the future.

"Design for supply chain management" extends the concept of "design for manufacturability," which refers to the process of simplifying product designs to allow easier manufacture and assembly, to the broader scope of the entire flow of material across all of the different supply chain entities. A product structure defines the component modules or elements required to make a product or family of products. It influences both production and distribution processes for a number of reasons. First, production flexibility and responsiveness is improved when components are interchangeable, and distribution complexity is minimized when standard components reduce inventory requirements.

An important attribute associated with a product's design is the actual complexity of the design with respect to the number of standard parts and components that go into the final product. Such attributes can have a significant impact on manufacturing and supply chain performance. For example, simulation studies have found that product structures with fewer end items, more intermediate items, and fewer levels in the bill of materials are associated with lower inventories and higher customer service.[8] Several firms have found that reducing the number of parts in a product helped avoid quality problems later in manufacturing, which also led to lower direct labor and overhead costs associated with receiving, scheduling, purchasing, storing, and moving parts throughout the supply chain.[9]

Design complexity affects performance both in the new product development cycle and throughout the demand fulfillment cycle. By effectively reducing design complexity in the initial product development stage, firms experience fewer engineering change notices (ECNs), fewer quality problems, and fewer new processes. This can result in shorter lead-times and reduced obsolete inventory costs throughout the supply. For instance, John Deere & Company used multifunctional design teams consisting of product and manufacturing engineers, marketing, manufacturing management, and outside suppliers to reduce the number of parts by 30 percent and the number of operations by 45 percent, resulting in lead-time reductions of 75 percent in their product lines.[10] Design complexity is reduced through the increased use of existing and standard components, integrating suppliers early in the product development process, reducing the number of options for the product, simplifying the assembly process, instituting design reviews, and developing an understanding of existing manufacturing capabilities by design teams. Value engineering activities also can be built into the design process with the objective of reducing the cost and complexity of a product while retaining the original functional specifications. Value engineering includes creating a catalog of internally produced parts, reviewing the catalog while the design is still in a formative stage, and providing a cost function for parts. In so doing, existing parts are used more often and part proliferation is avoided.

In recent years, technology has enabled companies to offer innovative solutions to the dilemma of mass-producing standard items that are easier to manage from a supply chain perspective but which still can be customized to the purchaser's specific needs. For instance, in the electronics industry, field programmable gate array (FPGA) integrated circuits can be mass-produced, yet configured by distributors in the field to a customer's specific application. This avoids having to produce an application-specific integrated circuit (ASIC), which would cost much more because of the small batch run. New research in product technology will continue to drive design for supply chain improvements across industries.

As product designs become more complex and more difficult to manufacture, the number of possible options and configurations of the product generally increases, as does the number of nonstandard parts. On the other hand, allowing fewer options and more standard parts results in products that are less complex and more adaptable to changes in product mix and volume, leading to more predictable planning and forecasting throughout the supply chain.[11]

In many industries, complexity is a difficult property to manage and, in fact, may be a function of several external factors. To help manage the proliferation of possible product combinations, organizations have to modularize their products at lower levels in the bill of materials. A product family can be designed as a product group with standardized components that can be assembled into a broader range of final products. The vast number of possible combinations can effectively create "mushroom products"—a reference to the fact that few components "mushroom" into many possible end combinations.[12] Components can be held in inventory and assembled into final products after the order arrives. This stage of production at the last possible moment is an application of postponement and can be performed at the factory or at any point within the distribution channel. Product structure can compress the time between order and shipment because part of the production process has been undertaken in advance of actual orders.

A good example is Philips Consumer Electronics which uses diversity planning in product development. When the company centralized production of television sets within Europe, establishing common components became a major challenge because of the differences in broadcast systems within the European countries, as well as with U.S. standards. The solution was to over design a standard integrated circuit to encompass all standards, even though only one is actually used in a given model. The standard component enables leveraging of purchases for cost savings, and allows production of more than one model on the same production line, which simplifies scheduling and increases flexibility.[13] In this situation, the company's utilization of a key component within the end product may be more costly than the country-specific model, but results in a lower total cost when viewed from an integrated supply chain perspective.

Another related factor affecting product complexity is whether a dominant design has evolved over time. In newly developing markets, a number of product designs frequently are competing to become the industry standard.[14]

Nowhere is this more important than in industries with short product life cycles. For instance, one company we visited has product life cycles ranging from six months to two years. Thus, manufacturers face a "typical" engineering challenge when developing products, as they must meet customers' requirements for higher performance (e.g., speed and capacity) while consuming the same or less energy and space than existing products with improved quality and short development times. This must be done while maintaining market-driven cost targets. The basic technology of these products has not changed dramatically since they were first introduced nearly forty years ago. However, the more demanding performance requirements have driven technological improvements in the materials, components, and subassemblies used within these products. The most significant technological advances have been made and will continue to be made in the components and subassemblies that create functionality for the basic technology. In seeking to develop products that are easier to manage from a supply chain perspective, supply chain partners with this company have pushed for product standards. Customers, manufacturers, and suppliers have formed an industry group that meets every quarter to review proposals and share opinions on emerging product standards. More than 250 companies are involved in this effort. Two acceptable industry standards have largely been adopted for major product platforms through these efforts.

This industry collaboration benefits all parties involved. Customers may better manage new product introductions as the standards help them plan their product designs. Suppliers can identify technology requirements early on, which allows them to invest in the capabilities and capacity requirements needed to meet challenging project goals. Furthermore, suppliers may influence or develop standards that are relevant to their products and processes.

Another important consideration in designing products for the supply chain is to consider how the product will be transported and handled across multiple supply chain channels.[15] A greater number of shipments are now taking place via inter-modal transportation, which may combine shipping, air, trucking, or rail. Products are increasingly being stored in "containers," which allows easier storage on carriers and facilitates movement between different modes. Design decisions can have a major impact on the ease with which products can be stored, assembled, shipped, broken down, and delivered to customers. Transportation experts should play a role early in the design cycle to improve decision-making. Designing products requires adopting a supply chain perspective that includes the entire chain of action required to move the product to customers, including the various stages of transportation and handling through distribution centers. Some of the critical design elements that need to be addressed include the following:

- **Transportation and Handling:** The characteristics of the product that make it transportable, with ease of handling and stowability.
- **Packaging:** The degree of protection needed to protect the product from damage and climatic conditions, dimensional considerations to fit unitized loads such as warehouse pallets, and labeling identification for automated barcode scanning.
- **Monetary density:** This is the monetary value per unit of weight such as dollars per kilogram and is normally inherent in the nature of the product. It determines the mode of transport and the costs of storage. High-value products are less sensitive to transport rates but are more sensitive to inventory holding costs.
- **Physical Density:** This is the ratio of cubic volume to weight. The ratio determines the costs of transportation and storage. Products with high volume-to-weight ratios are costly both to transport and store. Such products are best produced closer to the user locations in order to reduce transportation and storage costs.

Product design affects the costs of shipping and handling. One company producing and shipping an electronic production system incurred high transportation costs because they failed in the design stage to consider whether it could be shipped as a disassembled unit with less damage and at lower transportation cost. Another company shipped products that were too large for the conveyor sorting system of the customer's preferred carrier. While such details may seem minor at the design stage, they become significant later when the product begins moving through the different supply chain channels.[16]

A good example of design for supply chain is IKEA, an international furniture retailer.[17] Its furniture has high physical density and low damage potential, making it easier to ship. IKEA sells furniture that customers assemble themselves and specifically designs its products for ease of shipping and handling by both carriers and the final customer. Products are shipped as complete kits, to be held on store shelves and carried home by customers for final assembly. The cost savings come from both labor in final assembly and more efficient shipping through higher physical density and less damage in transit.

Another excellent example of design for SCM is seen in Hewlett Packard.[18] This computer peripherals manufacturer produces printers for worldwide distribution at its Vancouver division, which used to make all models of their printers and then ship them to their distribution centers (DCs). The printers have a few country-specific components, such as the power supply and owner's manual. The U.S. factory produced to meet demand forecasts, but by the time the printers reached regional distribution centers, demand had changed, and the DCs had no ability to respond to changing international demand patterns. This resulted in inventory imbalances with simultaneous inventory stockpiles and backlogs.

A project team studied the problem and analyzed the potential savings realized if the distribution center performed the final localization step (customized the printer for the local country) instead of the factories. This concept is known as "demand for localization." This required input from engineering, manufacturing, and distribution. Engineering had to redesign the product so that the power supply module could be plugged in externally instead of being internal to the product. Buy-in from manufacturing was imperative because the tasks performed by the factories and DCs would change. Distribution also had to support the change, because it would now be responsible for performing final localization operations and ensuring quality. As a result of the change, both cost and service was improved, and HP now designs all of its new products to be localized at the DCs.

Total Cost of Ownership[19]

Total cost of ownership requires managers to identify and measure costs beyond the standard unit price, transportation, and tooling when evaluating any type of supply or distribution channel. Formally, total cost of ownership is defined as the sum of all expenses and costs associated with the purchase and use of equipment, materials, and services. To use a total cost approach, a firm must define and measure an item's major cost components across the supply chain.

Most large firms base purchase decisions and evaluate suppliers on cost elements beyond unit price, transportation, and tooling. Research indicates, however, that companies differ widely about what cost components to include in a total cost analysis. An inverse relationship exists between the complexity of a cost component and its use in a total cost analysis system. For example, unit price data is low on complexity of data collection and is typically included. On the other hand, firms categorize field-failure data as highly complex and difficult to identify and therefore use this data less frequently. Field failures are still a cost, however, affecting the total cost of ownership.

Problems with total cost analysis are typically related to a lack of accurate cost data. Furthermore, an exact definition of total cost requirements can vary widely—even within the same company. Traditional accounting methods simply do not focus on quantifying the costs associated with a total cost activity system. The implementation of enterprise resource planning (ERP) systems increases, the ability of organizations to capture total cost elements. Also, the emerging data warehouse systems being deployed by companies allow users to efficiently extract and compile cost data.

Total cost data comes from a number of different areas within the supply chain. Activities as diverse as finance, accounting, quality assurance, manufacturing, receiving and inspection, and purchasing all contribute cost information. Coordinating the collection of data from diverse organizational functions can be difficult, particularly with a manual data collection system. Purchasing plays a critical role in total cost analysis. It is the logical function to manage a total cost system because of its close interaction with functions inside and outside the firm, and the importance of total cost data in the sourcing process.

Developing a Total Cost System

Companies developing a total cost of ownership measurement system should utilize a structured approach. An overview of such an approach is presented in this section.

1. **Identify Total Cost Items to Evaluate.** Not all purchase items require total cost measurement. Typically, 20 percent of purchased items contribute 80 percent of total costs. The best total cost candidates include those items having the highest dollar impact on the purchasing budget. Problem items contributing high nonperformance costs are another logical choice. Families of similar items are also good candidates. Similar items from the same supplier can be grouped into a composite index of total cost.

2. **Map Processes and Identify Affected Functions or Activities and Associated Costs.** Certain functions or activities are affected when a supplier does not meet its performance standards. In order to understand this, the total cost team should identify the actual steps in a process when an order is transmitted. That is, they must follow an item as it is shipped from the supplier, inspected, put into inventory, used in the internal process, and delivered to the customer. In mapping this sequence of events, total cost measurement requires departments or functions to record the time and resources committed to the normal activity, as well as any secondary activity devoted to resolving any problems.

3. **Identify Scope of the Model and Cost Elements**. Once the team understands the process of material flowing through the supply chain, it should focus on the major costs associated with the process. At this point, the team should check to ensure that the scope of the model is not too broad, that it is relevant, and that the elements are controllable.

4. **Identify Performance Criteria, Collect Data, and Establish Model.** This step establishes the categories and criteria used to compare actual-versus-anticipated supplier performance. A company also can include other performance areas and parameters unique to its operating requirements. The relevant equations that link these performance criteria to actual cost dollars also are important. This step requires the establishment of a structured measurement and recording system to monitor the total cost of an item or family of items. Larger and more complex systems will require a computerized system to collect data and generate total cost reports.

5. **Document Model and Use It!** Total cost data allows performance comparisons between suppliers and alternative distribution channels. It is not enough to say Supplier A had a total cost of $10,000 whereas Supplier B had a total cost of $15,000. This does not compare the relative efficiency (as measured by the total cost to the purchase cost) of the two suppliers. The development of a standardized ratio or index supports direct comparisons or supplier ranking based on total cost. A standardized index allows comparisons of overall performance between suppliers. The index relates total cost to contract purchase price:

$$\text{Total Cost Index} = (\text{Purchase Price} + \text{Nonconformance Costs}) / \text{Purchase Price}$$

The index allows a comparison of one supplier's total cost performance index against another supplier's regardless of the actual dollar values. If Supplier A has an index rating of 1.3 and Supplier B has a rating of 1.1, then Supplier B is clearly the lower-cost supplier. For every $1 paid to Supplier A for purchased material, the total cost of doing business with that supplier is $1.30. Total cost measurement identifies alternative supply chains with the potential to provide the lowest total cost. Tracking and identifying performance criteria and the costs of nonperformance require time and effort to identify the items.

Applications of Total Cost of Ownership Data

Total cost of ownership measurement is increasingly important as supply chain managers strive to select the lowest total cost sources of supply and distribution (not the lowest price). Total cost of ownership applies not only to items sourced from external suppliers, but also to internally manufactured items. Companies implement total cost systems to realize very specific benefits.[20] A total cost of ownership approach allows a firm to:

- Select supply sources and distribution channels based on total cost considerations.
- Improve supplier and distributor performance by identifying areas of nonperformance with responsibility for corrective action.
- Clearly define performance expectations and communicate those expectations to supply chain partners. Total cost systems should have a feedback mechanism that provides both positive and negative supplier feedback.
- Increase supply chain partner accountability and control. Total cost requires supply chain managers to develop an awareness of non-price factors that are under the control of suppliers and distributors that contribute to total cost.
- Select preferred suppliers/distributors based on performance merit. The practice of developing partnerships with partners over an extended period of time requires comprehensive performance data. Total cost data allows a firm to rank supply chain participants and select the top performers.
- Introduce measurement discipline throughout the organization by relying upon an equitable and consistent evaluation tool.

Total cost measurement information can be used in a number of areas. The data provides the ability to quantify and communicate areas of nonperformance to concentrate performance improvement efforts. Total cost information is also used during negotiations to identify areas requiring contractual performance improvement. The information also assists in the overall supplier selection process by providing historical performance data and a means to rank supplier/distributor performance, which is especially useful if a firm is reducing its supply base. Finally, a structured approach to total cost may allow a buying company to recoup nonperformance costs through charge-backs to non-performing participants. In the future, we will likely see many more innovative applications of total cost data.

Elements of Total Cost

To use the total cost approach, the major costs of the product or service being managed must be identified, defined, and measured. When employed effectively, the concept of total supply chain cost is a powerful driver of strategy, as the following case illustrates.

Solectron's Total Supply Chain Cost Model[21]

Solectron is a worldwide provider of electronics manufacturing services to original equipment manufacturers (OEMs). The company provides customized, integrated manufacturing services that span all three stages of the product life cycle, including pre-manufacturing, manufacturing, and post-manufacturing. These services are integrated to the point where Solectron is now responsible for all supply chain processes associated with sourcing parts, producing, and distributing electronics and systems for almost every major OEM in the telecommunication, networking, computer systems, peripherals, semiconductors, consumer electronics, industrial equipment, medical electronics, avionics, and automotive electronics industries.

One of the major drivers underlying Solectron's competitive strategy is its *Total Supply Chain Cost Model*. Steve Ng, formerly Solectron's senior vice president and chief materials officer, discussed four major challenges associated with deploying SCM strategies at Solectron:

1. Where is the value created in the supply chain and who controls the value? Further, if one controls the value, where should one invest next to improve value?
2. How can we get the attention of our customers' executive management so that they understand our SCM strategy? Unless the customer understands the benefits of the strategy and its execution, it is very difficult to execute it down the line.
3. The U.S. environment is still operating in a "partnership" mode. The next major challenge will involve cross-enterprise decision-making in which decisions are made to optimize value across all organizations in the supply chain. Although Japanese *keiretsus* have operated in this mode to some extent, U.S. companies are very unfamiliar with this type of competitive environment.
4. How can we simplify our supply chain strategy and capture it in a quantitative model so that all supply chain decisions flow down from this model?

The *Total Supply Chain Cost* model developed by Solectron addresses the last challenge. The model continues to evolve, but is used as a basis for making future supply chain decisions. Table 7–3 presents the key elements of the model. The model expands decision-making from a simple "buying price" perspective to one that emphasizes total supply chain cost improvements and joint competitive advantages as materials and information pass from the supplier, to Solectron, and on to the customer. This is reflected in the bottom-line selling price to the customer. Note that in Table 7–3, the speculation returns and speculation costs reflect the fact that growth margins can be increased through greater responsiveness, achieved by positioning inventory and capacity strategically throughout the supply chain.

This model helps Solectron understand: 1) customer requirements regarding what needs to be delivered; 2) the variables and constraints to doing so; 3) how to minimize excessive exposure to obsolescence due to engineering change orders; and 4) how to optimize direct material cost, cost of acquisition, and plant-to-plant and plant-to-volume flexibility. The model also can be used in "what if" analysis to help set customer expectations, especially with regard to product introduction, time-to-volume margins, and liability to exposure.

On the supply end, the structure helps to organize "Value Partnerships" with key strategic suppliers. Such partnerships will eliminate the need for negotiation and pricing because the *Total Supply Chain Cost Model* provides the basis for making their supply chain decisions. Maximizing return on assets and cash flow are the primary drivers underlying these relationships. Each supplier relationship should increase value, reduce cost, and remove uncertainties preventing the increase of market share.

The *Total Supply Chain Cost Model* acts as an important bridge between customers and suppliers. Customers often may make extraordinary demands that require major investments in capability (lead-time, cost, capacity, and inventory). Customer requirements are used as a baseline for creating innovative solutions by working backward with the supply management group. Solectron must be able to leverage its preferred suppliers to create solutions. They can then go to the customer and offer potential solutions by considering a different set of suppliers and technologies. The total cost model thus serves as the integrating mechanism for driving supply chain relationships backward and forward in the chain.

Table 7–3 Total Supply Chain Cost Model

Total supply chain cost =	Buying Price	
	+ Supplier perform-ance cost	• Supplier quality • Delivery performance
	+ Cost of acquisition	• Document control • Component engineering • Planning • Sourcing • Tactical buying • Freight/duty • Receiving • Internal quality assurance • Warehouse costs • Production control • Kitting/Kanban • Manufacturing accounting
	+ Out-of-sync planning	• Delays between MRP runs • Changes amplified by MRP ("bullwhip" effect)
	– Speculation returns (ability to meet up-side demands)	• Driver: profit margin
	+ Speculation cost	• Buffer cost (inventory, capacity) • Fulfillment speed requirement costs • Upside flexibility cost (e.g. +30% in a given week or month) • Excess inventory • Mark downed inventory
	+ Manufacturing cost	• Labor, materials, etc.
	+ Selling cost	• Sales, general and administrative expenses
	+ Distribution cost	• Transportation cost
	+ Profit	
	= Selling Price	

Global Logistics and Material Positioning

Trade is increasingly taking place within trading blocs such as the European Union, the North American Free Trade Area, and other regional groups. These blocs are established to promote regional development, while often presenting tariff and non-tariff barriers to imports from outside of the bloc. Global companies wishing to supply markets within these blocs may eventually have to establish production facilities inside the bloc if they wish to serve these markets with significant volume. The result accelerates a phenomenon already taking place that emphasizes the growth of intra-regional economies at the expense of trade from outside of these blocs.[22] Another important trend in this regard is that the bulk of international trade takes place in materials and intermediate components. Global corporations will ship semi-manufactured products between their own facilities or from suppliers to assembly plants and distribution. The trend toward global supply chains has been fueled by needs for centralized research and development, the development of homogeneous markets and global products, the need for economies of scale in specific industries, wage differentials between advanced countries and less-developed countries, and political efforts to maintain low tariff barriers. Global networks also have been aided by improved transportation and communication, the explosion of the Internet, and the development of organizational capacity to manage complex supply chains.

Unfortunately, the costs associated with managing the phenomenon of global expansion and trade are sometimes prohibitive. Creating a supplier and distribution network in multiple countries is a time-consuming and arduous task that can cost millions of dollars yet still result in failure. Furthermore, the complexities of international logistics add significantly to the total cost of doing business.

A number of important issues will have to be addressed with respect to global supply chains.

- What issues are critical to the successful integration of the global supply chain?
- In a global context, how does crossing international borders influence management decisions in the supply chain?
- How can management organize this process to serve the needs of global supply chain members?
- Is it even possible to manage total cost given a task of this size and scope?

Economic factors will have a major effect on how global supply chains are structured, including both technical separation in production and distribution in the production process and ownership of functions. A supply chain design will also be affected by risk, trade restrictions, and long lead-times. For instance, transportation systems required to manage supply chains in European markets are unique. The emergence of the European Union has led to an impending set of bottlenecks that will occur in the already strained transportation infrastructure. This structure is being challenged by the deregulation of the transport market and the liberalization on cabotage (i.e., carrying goods in domestic commerce by a foreign carrier). A number of other significant transportation barriers exist in Europe, including the problems associated with nationally owned rail networks, water transport, and the new types of transport operators that may emerge in the coming years. We may witness the emergence of pan-European companies, mega-carriers, subcontractors, and niche carriers, all seeking to fill different market needs within the European community. One of these is the German Post Office, which is seeking to expand its third-party logistic services on a global basis in order to compete with the likes of FedEx and United Parcel Service.

In other regions of the globe, the infrastructure presents significant challenges to organizations attempting to establish integrated supply chain structures. Emerging markets such as China, India, Latin America, Southeast Asia, Africa, and Central Europe have incredibly large numbers of consumers with rising spending power. A visitor to any of these countries will be bewildered by the number of global corporations attempting to form joint ventures, build plants and distribution centers, and establish channels in order to tap into these markets. However, the infrastructure within many of these countries is not adequately developed. Legal constraints prevent many common supply chain systems from being deployed. Shipments may be held in customs for interminable periods. Highway systems are inadequate in scope, and roads are often in poor repair. In other cases, transportation may be complicated owing to local adverse weather conditions. Telecommunication systems are often unreliable (although the proliferation of wireless networks is changing this situation quite rapidly). Governments can also shift hands quickly, resulting in constantly changing leaders with varying levels of support for Western corporations doing business in their country. Finally, rapidly fluctuating currency markets and economies can change a fair economic proposal into a major financial loss in a relatively short period. In the face of these problems, developing global networks of suppliers and distributors, managing global operations, and shipping to global customers becomes an increasingly complex process fraught with uncertainty and risk. Corporations will need to develop personnel with foreign language, negotiation, and problem-solving skills who are willing to be assigned to these areas. These individuals will be faced with an interminable set of challenging problems and will need to be flexible and skilled at developing key relationships with new supply chain members.

Global Supplier Development

Although the term "globalization" is commonly used by managers, "localization" is less often used. Managers are beginning to realize that establishing a distribution network or production facility may be insufficient as a long-term strategy for establishing a presence in an emerging market. Another difficult, yet necessary, challenge is to establish, to the fullest extent possible, a *localized supply base* to support local production and sales facilities.

There are three major reasons why establishing a local supply base is a critical component of international market expansion.

- First, the total cost to import products to emerging countries is often prohibitive. Managers have claimed that the cost of shipping heavy and bulky goods is often twice the value of the item itself. If one also considers the cost of warranty, field service, and other important factors, the costs continue to increase. From a cost standpoint, developing a local source may be the low-cost strategy.
- Second, in order to encourage technology transfer and increase employment levels, governments are increasingly enforcing domestic content laws that require that manufacturers purchase a significant percentage of their parts and components domestically. Senior management has begun to understand that "if the world is your market, then the world must be your supplier."
- Third, perhaps most obvious but often overlooked, is competition. In order to gain access to the lowest costs, cutting-edge technology and best capabilities, organizations must be global in their search for the best suppliers. By aligning technology roadmaps with leading-edge suppliers, designers can ensure that their products and services will truly be world-class, not just the best in the region.

Unfortunately, establishing a localized supply base in a new or emerging country is a significant undertaking. In some cases, local suppliers' production capabilities may be well below world-class levels, especially in the areas of production technology, engineering and design abilities, information systems, quality, and delivery capabilities. Poor logistics infrastructure may also complicate matters. In order to effectively meet these challenges, organizations are now recognizing that a key to success is the investment of resources in a team of specialists whose sole task is to identify new suppliers in a region, assess them, and improve their capabilities as quickly as possible. In cases where suppliers for a given commodity or service are not available in a region, a new source may be developed or an existing supplier operating in other locations may be persuaded to establish operations in the new region.

At first, this task seems daunting. How can you take a local supplier with limited capabilities and raise it to the level of a world-class competitor, while enjoying the benefits of low-cost inputs? Alternatively, how successful can you expect to be in asking a supplier that works successfully with your firm in one country to set up a new production facility in a market where it has never operated? Is it possible to develop suppliers in an area where none with the required capabilities exist? A recent study of automotive and electronics companies in Japan, Korea, the United Kingdom, and the United States interviewed hundreds of managers to gain insights on these questions.[23]

According to the survey, four important characteristics define companies that succeed in developing global supply networks to manage total supply chain costs:

- **Corporate Global Vision:** Does the organization create an effective global vision as a primary driver for investing resources and effort in seeking global suppliers and customers? Without an ideal vision of what the organization is attempting to accomplish, managers at different locations throughout the world have difficulty coordinating business unit strategies and functional goals. As organizations seek to expand their global operations, an effective vision serves as the primary force for developing and deploying a global supply base.
- **Management Structure and Systems:** Is the company effectively organized to promote coordination among the different global strategic business units? Best-in-class companies have invested in enabling structures and systems to deploy their global vision. These enablers include the following: 1) global commodity councils and reporting systems to facilitate communication among the different business units; 2) International procurement offices (IPOs) and sales offices with contacts in government agencies to promote sharing of expertise and knowledge regarding regional sourcing/sales opportunities; 3) improved total cost models for decision-making; and 4) global information systems capable of providing sourcing and demand information to global production and design sites.

- **Configuring the Global Supply Base:** Are sourcing and sales strategies developed to optimize the mix of local suppliers/distributors and transplant suppliers? As organizations set up production in new regions, they often discover that some mix of local and global suppliers is optimal. However, the mix may change as they gain experience with local suppliers.
- **Supplier Development:** Is the organization deploying resources to ensure that suppliers' capabilities are aligned with competitive and manufacturing strategies? Supplier development approaches varied in different regions according to the specific types of problems encountered. Approaches focused on either using process specialists to attack isolated technical problems or applying a full-scale intervention when systemic problems were traced to poor management practices within the supplier's organization.

Although developing a global supply chain strategy requires a fundamental shift in the way one thinks about doing business, one of the drivers for making decisions has to lie in understanding the total cost of ownership across the entire global supply chain. By understanding the cost drivers that underlie total cost, managers can implement strategies designed to reduce these costs. Furthermore, these total costs must be understood across the entire product life cycle; the drivers must be set in the new product development cycle and then managed over the life of the product, through to its disposal.

Target Pricing[24]

Competitive demands of the 1980s forced many companies to develop closer relationships with key suppliers and to pursue continuous performance improvement. Along with closer relationships has come an increased willingness to share cost information. Today, more companies are using target-based pricing to determine the relevant price they must achieve for their new product to succeed. Target pricing is then followed by cost-based pricing to drive continuous cost reductions throughout the product life cycle yet allow suppliers to benefit from suggested cost saving ideas. Combining these innovative strategic cost management approaches relies on a critical component: identifying and sharing cost information.

One of the last frontiers of information exchange between firms is the sharing of detailed cost data. Most North American supply firms have been reluctant to share this information. Some suppliers simply do not have a handle on their true cost structure. Other suppliers view cost data as proprietary information that provides insights into areas that the supplier wants kept confidential. A supplier may be reluctant to reveal how much it earns from a contract for fear of a price reduction demand. For whatever reason, the detailed sharing of cost data has been a step many North American suppliers have not yet been willing to take. Although these fears may be justified to some extent, target and cost-based pricing are increasingly being viewed as ways for both buying and selling parties to benefit from detailed cost information sharing.

Target Pricing Defined

Target pricing is an approach used in the initial stages of the new product development cycle to establish a contract price between a buyer and seller. Japanese manufacturers develop this approach in an effort to motivate engineers to select designs that could be produced at a low cost. These manufacturers came up with a simple concept to address cost: the cost of a new product is no longer an *outcome* of the product design process; rather, it is an *input* to the process. The challenge is to design a product with the required functionality and quality at a cost that provides a reasonable profit. In a new car, for example, the development team may work with marketing to determine the target price of the vehicle in its market segment. Using final price as a basis, the product is disaggregated into major systems, such as the engine and power train. Each major system has a target cost. At the component level (which represents a further disaggregation from the system level), the target cost is the price that a purchaser hopes to attain from a supplier (if the item is externally sourced).

The following contrasts traditional and market-based pricing. With target pricing, a product's allowable cost is strictly a function of what a market segment is willing to pay less the profit goals for the product.

Traditional Pricing: Product Cost + Profit = Selling Price

TARGET PRICING: SELLING PRICE–PROFIT = ALLOWABLE PRODUCT COST

Generally speaking, the supplier cannot always achieve the target cost upon first discussion. Moreover, the supplier's current price to provide a product or service today is probably greater than the target price set forth by the buying company. The difference between these two figures becomes the *strategic cost reduction objective.* Both parties work together, through such efforts as value engineering, quality function deployment, design for manufacturing/assembly, design for SCM, and standardization to reduce this gap. Setting product-level target costs that are too aggressive may result in unachievable item target costs. Setting too low a strategic cost reduction challenge leads to easily achieved target costs, but a loss of competitive position. In setting target prices and target costs, the new product development team should bear in mind the cardinal rule of target costing: *the target cost can never be violated.* Moreover, even if engineers find a way to improve the functionality of the product, they cannot make the improvement unless they can offset the additional cost.

Once a purchaser has established a target price with a supplier for the first year of a contract, additional cost reductions over the life of the product can be made through cost-based pricing.

Cost-Savings Sharing Defined

Cost-savings sharing differs from traditional market-based pricing in several ways. First, cost-savings sharing requires joint identification of the full cost to produce an item, which is not the case with market-based pricing. Second, profit is a function of the productive investment committed to the purchased item and a supplier's asset return requirements. Profit is not a direct function of cost. The cost-based approach provides a supplier with incentives to pursue continuous performance improvement to realize shared cost savings and invest in productive assets.

An important feature of cost-savings sharing is the financial incentives offered to a seller for performance improvements above and beyond the improvements agreed to in the contract. This differs from the traditional market-based pricing approach where one party (usually the purchaser) seeks to capture all cost savings resulting from a supplier's improvement effort. Traditional pricing practices have deterred cooperative efforts to make design, product, and process improvements. A cost-based pricing approach recognizes the need to provide financial incentives to a supplier.

Prerequisites for Successful Target and Cost-Based Pricing

For target pricing with cost-based pricing to work, joint agreement must exist on a supplier's full cost to produce an item. Identification of all costs provides the basis for establishing joint improvement targets. The total cost to produce an item includes labor, materials, other direct costs, any costs owing to start-up and production, and administrative, selling, and other related expenses.

Besides total cost components, the parties must jointly identify and agree upon product volumes, target product costs at various points in time, and project quantifiable productivity and quality improvements. Each firm also must agree on the asset base and return requirement at the supplier that determines an item's profit. The parties also must agree on the point in time when mutual sharing of cost savings takes place, as well as on the formula used to share the rewards. Mutual sharing of rewards usually occurs for savings above and beyond the performance improvement targets agreed to in the purchase contract, and for savings on any items incidental to joint performance improvement targets.

This approach requires a high degree of trust, information sharing, and joint problem solving. This process will fail if one firm takes advantage of the other or violates confidentiality agreements. The parties also must be willing to provide the resources necessary to resolve problems affecting overall success.

The ability to manage the risks associated with target pricing is another key prerequisite. A major risk area concerns volume variability. Because volume affects cost levels, both parties must carefully consider and manage the impact of changes from planned volume projections. Higher-than-projected volumes typically will result in a supplier achieving greater economies and lower per-unit costs. These lower costs are not the result, however, of a supplier's performance improvement. Conversely, lower-than-projected volumes may raise a supplier's average costs. Contractually, the parties must determine how to manage changes from the buying plan.

Cost-Based Pricing Applications

A cost-based approach to determining price is clearly not appropriate for most purchased items. Many items do not warrant cost analysis as the marketplace effectively determines price. Products that are readily available from multiple sources, standardized instead of customized, and heavily influenced by the market forces of supply and demand do not fit a profile appropriate for cost-based pricing.

What types of items are appropriate for a cost-based cooperative approach? A cost-based approach is feasible when the seller contributes high value-add to an item through direct or indirect labor and specialized expertise. This approach is particularly appropriate for complex items customized to specific requirements. Also, products requiring a conversion from raw material through value-added designs at a supplier are possible candidates. Examples of such items include a specially designed anti-lock brake system or an instrument panel for an automobile. These items require a high value-added conversion from raw materials into a semi-finished product. The supplier is also likely to contribute design and engineering support.

The "Greening" of the Supply Chain: Life Cycle Costing, Re-Manufacturing, and Recycling[25]

The roots of environmentalism can be traced to the period during the Second World War when severe material shortages occurred worldwide. As a result of these shortages, people were forced to become creative and reuse or recycle whatever materials they possessed. More recently, in response to heightened government regulation and increasing public awareness of the effects of industrial production on the environment, organizations are now undertaking massive initiatives to re-structure their supply chain processes and products in order to minimize their environmental impact. A number of manufacturing firms have already begun to develop environmentally friendly practices. Hewlett Packard has made "green" a top-level corporate mission, along with time-based competition and cost reduction, and has reduced releases of toxic chemicals 71 percent.[26] Dow Chemical and General Motors have established functions that are specifically responsible for waste and recycling management. Xerox has developed a feedback loop that includes the "reverse logistics" process involving the removal of old equipment from their customers' facilities, the removal of good parts from these old products, and the disposition of scrap parts into recycling efforts. International Paper is investing in large-scale ink-removal processes to tap into the emerging market for recycled paper.[27] These firms have come to realize that *recycling reduces energy requirements, reduces gaseous and solid pollutants, and conserves raw materials.*[28] In the process, environmentally friendly supply chain practices have also helped these companies to become more competitive and have had a positive impact on the "bottom line."

Within the context of these corporate initiatives, supply chain managers will play an increasingly important role in implementing environmentally friendly practices. There are several reasons why the supply chain is central to this issue. To begin with, supply chain managers are the primary agents of change in decisions regarding the procurement and disposition of materials and are responsible for the entire flow of materials throughout the supply chain. Design decisions, cost control, manufacturing planning and control, and supply-base strategy will have a major effect on the environmental performance of an organization.

To understand the impact of the supply chain, consider that the total cost of production is the sum of the costs of labor, materials, and overhead *minus* any return from the successful sale of surplus materials. Disposition of surplus materials is not only important to the environmental movement, but also to profit maximization. Such materials include: 1) scrap and waste; 2) surplus, obsolete, or damaged stock; and 3) surplus, obsolete, or damaged equipment. Supply chain managers who often hold diverse views on environmental issues (ranging from active environmentalists to those merely sympathetic to the cause or those who view it as a radical conspiracy against big business) frequently overlook this fact.

In integrating "green" approaches into SCM, two generic types of orientation are generally adopted by organizations: **Proactive** vs. **Reactive** supply chain approaches (see Table 7–4).[29]

Reactive approaches refer to policies aimed at meeting the minimum set of actions required to comply with government regulations or customer requirements on environmental concerns. This includes such actions as the proper disposal of toxic waste, meeting emissions requirements, meeting recycling content requirements,[30] and maintaining adequate facilities to meet EPA inspection criteria. In such cases, avoidance policies aspire to meet the minimum penalty associated with the failure to satisfy a set of "floors" dictated by customers and governments. Clearly, these "floors" vary across industries, but the strategic equivalent is the same across industries.

Reactive approaches often rely solely on public relations ploys as a means to address the public's environmental concerns. These activities often involve token "feel good" measures, such as recycling Styrofoam cups in the office, rather than a full-fledged commitment to zero emissions. In other cases, reactive strategies are "end-of-pipe" strategies in that they fail to address the source of the problem and merely attempt to minimize the effects of toxic elements in the air and water after they have already been produced. Such ploys are often considered as "add-ons" to corporate strategy, as opposed to a real commitment to improvement.

In contrast to reactive policies, proactive policies are maximization-oriented. They set about to reduce costs through waste reduction in a variety of programs designed to benefit both the environment and the firm's profits. With regard to the supply chain, four specific areas were identified as potential candidates for such programs.

1. Supplier selection and evaluation
2. Surplus and scrap disposition
3. Carrier selection and transportation of hazardous materials
4. Product design, packaging, and labeling

Table 7–4   Environmentally Friendly Supply Chain Practices

Materials Function	Proactive	Reactive
Supplier Selection and Evaluation	• Disclose and label material composition • Consider long-term costs of doing business with supplier • Reusable packaging and shipping materials • Use suppliers who can show evidence of sustainable and well-managed sources of raw materials • Require supplier participation on industry-wide environmental panels and organizations • Environmental risk assessment • Sustainable resource management	• Environmental issues not included as an evaluation criteria • Dispose of packaging materials • Sole reliance on EPA regulations
Surplus and Scrap Disposition	• Careful analysis of material impacts *prior* to use in new products • Reclaim hazardous materials	• "After the fact" remedial actions to solve environmental disposition problems • Dump hazardous waste, and use non-specialists to take care of the problem
Carrier Selection & Transportation of Hazardous Material	• Environmental audits of major carriers • Extra protection on rail cars and trucks • Reduction of dumping extra leftover hazardous material	• Relatively little attention paid to transportation selection, except when a spill occurs
Product Design, Packaging and Labeling	• "Cradle to grave" life cycle analysis of materials used at the design stage	• End-of-life strategies not part of design process

Table 7–4   Environmentally Friendly Supply Chain Practices (*Continued*)

Materials Function	Proactive	Reactive
Product Design, Packaging and Labeling	• Remanufacture • Recycle corrugated • Standardized, re-usable containers • Label plastic parts for later reuse	• Dump products at end of life • No recycling • Non-reusable containers • No plastic labeling

During visits with a number of firms, these different policies were dis-cussed with environmental engineers, purchasing, and logistics managers. The importance of each area varies by industry. However, in order to have a real impact on corporate environmental initiatives, supply chain managers must become aware of the opportunities for proactive versus reactive policies within each of these areas.

Green Supplier Evaluation and Selection Practices

A great deal of work documents the various criteria used in corporate sup-plier selection performance systems which generally assess quality, cost, service, and delivery.[31] However, many leading-edge companies are now con-sidering their supplier's environmental record as a key determinant of per-formance. Moreover, suppliers in such companies are being selected for their own environmentally friendly practices including their sources of raw materials as well as the methods by which they dispose of scrap and surplus, how they reduce surplus packaging, their actions to reduce fuel usage, and whether they are using environmentally friendly practices to lower their ma-terials costs.

Environmental considerations are very important in the office furniture in-dustry.[32] At Herman Miller, environmental concerns are integrated much more closely into supplier-selection strategies and material disposition. For instance, this company partners in order to solve problems and to manage waste streams. In this manner, companies set industry-wide standards that can leverage suppliers into changing their production methods.

Probably one of the most important supplier-selection initiatives at Herman Miller is in its wood procurement policies. In particular, nations with tropical forests are often developing countries that have allowed indiscriminate commercial logging. Clear-cutting practices have resulted in deforestation and the destruction of plants and wildlife inhabiting the rain forest. To prevent contributing to this problem, Herman Miller has made several sourcing decisions. To begin with, designers decided to eliminate rosewood from their patented lounge chair. Although tropical woods are still an important part of their product line, they now only purchase tropical woods from suppliers who can document their responsible forestry practices. This means that supply chain managers work with suppliers to develop and use management practices that consider environmental, economic, political, and social issues to ensure the long-term viability of the rain forest. They also work with organizations such as the Tropical Forest Foundation and the International Tropical Timber Organization and have participated in the renegotiation of the Tropical Timber Agreement.

Supplier evaluation is very important in the chemical industry. At Dow Corning of Midland, Michigan, a big part of SCM involves assessing the environmental policies of suppliers (primarily other major chemical companies). Some of the evaluation criteria that address environmental issues include:

- Are their costs out of line, signifying that they may have had to pay environmental cleanup fines in the past?
- Is the supplier in danger of being shut down by the government because of environmental violations?
- Are they a healthy company? What is their employee exposure and safety record?

A key element of evaluation involves understanding and assessing the environmental risk associated with the particular chemical being purchased. Environmental risk is assessed by analysis of the quality of the item. Different purity levels will result in different waste considerations. For example, limestone is low-risk, but titanium dioxide is high-risk. Dow looks for suppliers who are "green" according to industry standards.

Surplus and Scrap Disposition

Companies must increasingly find ways to reduce scrap and waste, and thereby send less material to landfill. This is increasingly important as the number of landfills continuously shrinks owing to the fact that people are protesting the opening of new landfills.

A good example of this is an automotive company's policies regarding procurement of indirect materials for the plant. If a process engineer or maintenance person elects to bring a new material into the plant, such as an adhesive or a paint, the engineer must first file a Material Safety Data Sheet (MSDS) with the plant's environmental engineer. The engineer serves as a contact person to ensure that the emissions standards are being met and must gain approval for the material from a Hazardous Materials Approval Committee. This committee is composed of a cross-functional team of employees that reviews any new hazardous materials, the fire marshal, and other employees working with regulatory reports that must be filed with the EPA and other regulatory agencies. If the composition of the material is unknown, process implementation is delayed until the suppliers disclose all ingredients of materials that require an MSDS. In cases where the supplier has refused to provide such information on the grounds that the material composition is proprietary, the company will refuse to introduce the new material into the plant until its environmental effects are fully known. The supplier will simply not be allowed to do business with the company under these conditions. In this regard, the plant environmental engineer plays a key role as a liaison and information support person to aid purchasing and plant employees who are encountering potentially hazardous environmental situations.

In the furniture industry, many companies are seeking to reduce scrap and hazardous waste disposal through a number of mechanisms. At one company, trained specialists handle waste. The company is very active in its relationships with any hazardous solids disposal contractors. Other hazardous liquids used in the manufacturing processes are reclaimed and scrap materials such as steel, cardboard, polyfoam, and fabric are recycled whenever possible.

Another company has sought to eliminate hazardous wastes at the design stage, and has worked closely with external sources to implement environmental initiatives. In the manufacturing area, the company has worked to be an industry leader in water-based transfer processes for coatings, and has sought to limit the amount of formaldehyde emitted by its adhesives. It also has worked on wood yield rates within its processes by employing computer-controlled cutting systems and computer-based cutting pattern systems. It also works diligently with state environmental and safety agencies, and has a high-level representative serving on the federal solid waste board and was active in the federal negotiations for both Title 5 and the Control Technique Guidelines.

Carrier Selection and Transportation of Hazardous Materials

The transportation of hazardous materials in the supply chain is an important factor to monitor. Dow Chemical considers environmental concerns an important feature of their supply chain.[33] As a member of the Chemical Manufacturers Association, Dow participates in the "Responsible Care" program initiative. Responsible Care involves a dedication to responsibility regarding the community's concerns about chemicals, including their manufacture, transportation, use, safe disposal, health and safety, prompt reporting, and counseling of customers.

Carrier selection is a critical consideration in the purchase of raw materials. Dow carefully analyzes its supplier's capabilities regarding distribution, safety, incidents, health records, and adherence to Responsible Care. Generally, only suppliers who are signatories to Responsible Care will be considered. Those who do not sign are viewed on an exception basis—will the supplier subscribe in the future? Another issue related to carrier selection is, who moves the product? Dow specifies sources and routings and then relies on the supplier to comply. The supplier will be allowed to move the product if it is considered safe. Otherwise Dow will control the product, and will arrange distribution. Dow has its own group of contract carriers to perform this function.

Dow Chemical is a leader in transportation safety and has designed special rail cars for carrying hazardous chemicals in order to prevent a spill. The cars have extra thick steel armor to prevent punctures from releasing toxic liquids and gases in the event of a derailment. In addition, special couplings have been designed to reduce the likelihood of puncturing the tanks. Finally, Dow designed a special tank that would reduce the amount of material left over in the tank after pumping it out. Normally, this leftover material would be thrown out when the tank was cleaned. In this manner, Dow helped to set the standard for railcars determined by the Chemical Manufacturers Association (CMA). Although these precautionary measures cost more, the cost of litigation, cleanup of a spill or accident, and loss of customer goodwill would likely far surpass the extra investment.

Product Design, Packaging, and Labeling

Companies that are truly "leading edge" in creating a "green" supply chain are using life-cycle analysis, which identifies all of the potential environmental effects of a given material in a product from "cradle to grave." While this requires significant effort to develop, it can measurably improve environmental performance for a product over the course of its life cycle. Many companies are now seeking ways to re-use and recycle products after they have reached the end of their useful life. This requires a number of innovative approaches, including closer cooperation with customers in the supply chain.

Herman Miller has created a database of environmental programs that are active at the firm. This database answers the sales force's environmentally oriented customer questions. In addition, the company produces and distributes numerous brochures, white papers, and videos regarding the handling of environmental issues. These actions are a function of the company's original founder, who had strong beliefs regarding the role of business in the community and believed that organizations should act as "good stewards" of the environment. These beliefs filtered down throughout the organization over the years and eventually were written into the company's mission statement. A separate, profitable division within the company now handles re-manufactured furniture. The company strips the furniture of metal, wood, and fabric and sends these materials to be processed. The used furniture is sent to the remanufacturing arm, which refurbishes the furniture and sells it in secondary markets. In addition, the company is recycling metal chair arms because it offers a new feature–adjustable chair arms. When customers buy these new arms, they can arrange for pick-up of the old arms by the dealer. This reverse logistics service has been well received by the company's customers and salespeople even claim that it has helped them win orders over their competitors.

Packaging is another important element to be managed in "greening" the supply chain. Corrugated packaging is being used more intensely, as it is easier to recycle. Standardized, re-usable shipping containers should also be favored over disposable ones; in fact, such containers can be used positively to signify JIT delivery between buyers and suppliers. For instance, the same furniture company mentioned previously uses molded plastic trays that accommodate a fixed number of parts that are easily stacked and then stretch wrapped. As pieces are removed, workers simply pile up the trays for return to the supplier. The packaging tray is lightweight and easy to handle and is composed of plastic material that would otherwise be destined for a landfill. These packages also help promote productivity; the labor content to handle the packaging has been reduced by 40 percent.

This same company now requires its suppliers to label the chemical composition of plastic items. Therefore, future recyclers will know the exact content of the different types of plastic found in the parts. This helps address one of the major problems associated with recycling plastic in that there are so many different variations that it becomes difficult to determine the appropriate recycling process. By documenting the material composition, future recycling efforts can be significantly improved.

These examples clearly illustrate the importance of integration of environmental considerations into supply chain decisions. All of the companies discussed here believe they have an obligation to the public to make environmentally responsible decisions throughout their supply chains. This goes beyond simply being a "good corporate citizen." Many companies also are finding that such policies are not only good for the environment, but that they are also good business decisions that generate cost savings and higher margins in many cases.[34]

Cost Management Enablers

To succeed with the strategic cost management approaches discussed in this chapter, managers must have ready access to reliable cost data and executive support. A discussion of these requirements follows.

Activity-Based Costing

Activity-based costing focuses on capturing the costs that the specific activities required during production. Each product's usage of specific activities during the manufacturing process serves as the basis of the product's cost. The allocation bases, or cost drivers, are direct measures of the activities performed during production.[35] The basis of the cost-allocation approach is that products do not directly consume resources—they consume activities during production. Each activity is associated with a cost that can be allocated directly to a product. An activity-based costing system provides an understanding of the overhead or indirect costs attributable to a specific item, controls and manages costs by understanding the events and activities that create costs, and includes all relevant costs in the decision-making process by accurately tracing costs to cost units.[36]

Activity-based costing is an effort to meet the requirements of product cost analysts and to overcome the inherent shortcomings of traditional cost accounting systems. There should be a direct relationship between purchasing's use of progressive cost techniques and the growth of innovative cost accounting systems.

One of the challenges of adapting traditional accounting systems to activity-based costing is the inability to accurately allocate factory overhead and indirect costs. Most cost accounting systems were designed to record aggregate inventory levels for the balance sheet and total cost of goods sold for the income statement but are inadequate for assigning expenses to products, services, and customers. In particular, most small suppliers have poor cost accounting systems that randomly assign indirect and support costs to customers in a non-rigorous manner. As such, buyers must beware of costs being assigned to their purchased product or service for which they should not be paying. This does not mean that purchasers should focus on all areas of cost. Rather, they should look for areas with large expenses in indirect and support resources where often there is a 25 to 100 percent opportunity for cost reduction. Also, purchasers should look for situations in which a large variety exists in products, customers, or processes, generally indicating a poor focus and poor allocation of costs. A good rule of thumb is to apply the Willie Sutton rule. Willie Sutton was a famous bank robber. When asked why he robbed banks, he replied "Because that's where the money is!" Similarly, companies should look for the money and apply activity-based costing to identify cost saving opportunities.

Executive Support: Making the Business Case

The process of aligning SCM goals with corporate objectives is especially important for success with strategic cost management efforts. Supply chain managers often face broad directives from corporate management, such as to reduce costs or improve quality. The strategy development process takes place on four levels:

- **Corporate Strategies:** These strategies are concerned with (1) the definition of businesses in which the corporation wishes to participate and (2) the acquisition and allocation of resources to these business units.
- **Business Unit Strategies:** Business unit strategies are concerned with (1) the scope or boundaries of each business and the links with corporate strategy and (2) the basis on which the business unit will achieve and maintain a competitive advantage within an industry.
- **Supply Chain Strategies:** Supply chain strategies, which are part of a level of strategy development called functional strategies, specify how purchasing/operations/logistics will (1) support the desired competitive business level strategy and (2) complement other functional strategies.
- **Commodity or Process Strategies:** These strategies specify how a group tasked with developing the strategy for the specific commodity

being purchased or process being managed will achieve goals that will support all higher-level strategies.

Companies that are successful in creating integrated value systems are able to do so because the strategy development process is *integrative*. This means that the strategy is drafted or has significant input from those people responsible for implementation. Integrative supply chain strategies occur when corporate strategic plans are effectively "cascaded" into specific supply chains and commodity/process goals through a series of iterative planning stages. Corporate strategy evolves from corporate objectives that effectively evolve from a corporate mission statement. The CEO, taking into consideration the organization's competitive strengths, business unit and functional capabilities, market objectives, competitive pressures, customer requirements, and economic trends, crafts corporate strategies. What distinguishes an integrative strategy development process is that business unit executives, as well as functional top management, provide direct input during the development of corporate strategy.

A major output of the strategy development process is a set of functional strategic objectives, including supply chain strategic objectives. As managers interact with other members within their business, as well as with corporate executives, a major set of strategic directives should begin to emerge. These strategic objectives may or may not provide detail concerning how they are to be achieved. However, the process is not yet complete. Unless supply chain executives can effectively translate broad-level objectives into specific supply chain level goals, these strategies will never be realized. Purchasing, operations, and logistics must couple each objective with a specific goal that it can measure and act upon. These specific goals become the initial steps for a detailed strategic cost formulation process. Remember, objectives drive goals, whether at the highest levels of an organization or at the functional or departmental level. Only when executive level support is obtained based on a solid business case can strategic cost management initiatives be approved.

The best way to do so is simple—provide for a quick payback! This often means approaching projects first that have potential for a "quick win"—that is, a sure probability of immediate cost savings. When executive management sees the benefits of such strategies, gaining support for other more complex and involved strategic cost management efforts is easier.

Endnotes

[1]R. Monczka, R. Handfield, D. Frayer, G. Ragatz, and T. Scannell, *New Product Development: Supplier Integration Strategies for Success*, Milwaukee, WI: ASQ Press, January 2000.

[2]Interview with Tom Faybus, General Motors, October 2001.

[3]"Cross-docking Takes Costs Out of the Pipeline," *Distribution* 92 (Sept. 1993), pp. 64-66.

[4]D. Bowersox and D.J. Closs, *Logistics Management: A Systems Integration of Physical Distribution, Manufacturing Support and Materials Procurement*, 4th edition, Michigan State University, 1994.

[5]E. Clyde, "Cross-Docking: A Proven Plan for Profit," *Material Handling Engineering* 47 (Nov. 1992), pp. 93-96.

[6]Jim Postma, Meijer's Distribution Systems, lecture, Michigan State University, April 4, 1994.

[7]"Cash on Delivery," Supermarket News, (August 30, 1993), pp. 17–21.

[8]L. Krajewski, B. King, L, Ritzman and D. Wong," Kanbon, MRP and Shaping the Manufacturing Environment," Management Science 33 (1987), pp. 39–57.

[9]R. Walleigh, "Product Design for Low-Cost Manufacturing," *Journal of Business Strategy*, 4, 1989, pp. 37-42.

[10]J. Kirik, "New Product Design at John Deere," *Proceedings of the 1989 American Production and Inventory Control Society Just-in-Time Conference*, Falls Church, Va.: APICS, 1989.

[11]Henry Stoll, "Design for Life-Cycle Manufacturing," *Managing the Design-Manufacturing Process*, ed. John E. Ettlie and Henry W. Stoll, New York: McGraw-Hill, 1990, pp. 79-113.

[12]H. Mather, "Design for Logistics (DFL) - The Next Challenge for Designers," *Production and Inventory Control* 25, 4th Quarter, 1992, pp. 7-10.

[13]J. Boorsma, "Diversity Planning," *Logistics News (Philips Consumer Electronics)*, 102, January 1991, p. 2.

[14]David Teece, "Profiting from Technological Innovation: Implications for Integration, Collaboration, Licensing and Public Policy," *Research Policy* 15 (1986), pp. 285-30.

[15]Phil B. Schary and Tage Skjott-Larsen, *Managing the Global Supply Chain*, Copenhagen: Handelshojskolens Forlag, 1995.

[16]Ibid.

[17]Ibid.

[18]Hau L. Lee and Corey Billington, "The Evolution of Supply chain management Models and Practice at Hewlett Packard," *Interfaces*, Vol. 25, No. 5, September-October 1995, pp. 42-63.

[19]Adopted from R. Monczka, R. Trent, and R. Handfield, *Purchasing and Supply Chain Management*, Cincinnati: Southwestern College Publishing, 2001.

[20]R. M. Monczka and S. J. Trecha, "Cost-based Supplier Performance Evaluation," *International Journal of Purchasing and Materials Management*, Spring 1988: p. 3. and Lisa Ellram, *Total Cost of Ownership*, Tempe, AZ: Center for Advanced Purchasing Studies, 1993.

[21]Adapted from *Introduction to Supply Chain Management*, Robert B. Handfield and Ernest L. Nichols, Jr., Prentice-Hall, 1998.

[22]Schary and Skjott-Larsen, 1995.

[23]Robert Handfield and Daniel Krause, "Think Globally, Source Locally," *Supply Chain Management Review*, Winter, 1999, pp. 36-49.

[24]Adopted from Monczka Trent and R. Handfield, 2001.

[25]Adapted from S. Melnyk and R. Handfield, "Greenspeak," *Purchasing Today*, July 1996, pp. 32-36.

[26]Faye Rice, "Who Scores Best on the Environment?" *Fortune*, July 26, 1993.

[27]"How Green is Green Paper?" *Business Week*, Nov 1, 1993, pp. 60-61.

[28]U.S. Environmental Protection Agency, *Report to Congress on Resource Recovery*, April 1973. See also *Phoenix Quarterly*, Institute of Scrap and Iron, Fall 1980, p. 10.

[29]Melnyk and Handfield, 1996.

[30]*Business Week*, Nov 1, 1993, pp. 60-61.

[31]Lisa Ellram, "The Supplier Selection Decision in Strategic Partnerships," *International Journal of Purchasing and Materials Management*, Fall 1990, pp. 8-14.

[32]See R. Handfield, S. Walton, L. Seegers, and S. Melnyk, "The Green Value Chain: Practices From the Furniture Industry," *Journal of Operations Management*, Vol. 15, No. 4, 1997, pp. 293–316.

[33]Melnyk and Handfield, 1996.

[34]M. Porter and C. van der Linde, 1995. "Green and competitive," *Harvard Business Review*, Vol. 73, No. 5, pp. 120-134.

[35]Robin Cooper, "ABC: A Need, Not an Option," *Accountancy* 106, No. 1165, September 1990, pp. 86–88.

[36]David Dugdale, "The Uses of Activity-Based Costing," *Management Accounting* 68, No. 9, October 1990, pp. 36–38.

8

Navigating the Business to Business (B2B) E-Commerce Landscape

A Magical Place Called GEPolymerland[1]

To the observers of the numerous B2B Web sites, GEPolymerland.com is a magical place. For one thing, it is one of the few that can be called *successful*. GEPolymerland.com is the online distribution site for GE's resins business. Sales made through the site in 2000 increased twelvefold from 1999 to $1.2 billion, or 25 percent of GE's total resins sales, which exceeded $3 billion in 2001. What is their secret? Advocates of the site credit its ease of use, good timing, and perhaps most of all, a strong underlying business model. Putting the operation online didn't require changing fundamental business relationships: the Web site was just a way to make the enterprise more efficient. Since 95 percent of online orders go straight into GEPolymerland's information management system without human intervention, the site cuts GE's transaction and inventory costs and speeds up orders. The GE division based in Huntersville, NC was created out of the distribution network of Borg-Warner Chemicals, a major resins maker acquired by GE in 1988. In 1997, Polymerland launched an e-commerce site. Chairman Jack Welch directed the division to combine its resins distribution networks with its resins businesses. To ensure the success of the effort and that customers used the site, GE made sure customers were involved in the planning.

"I volunteered to be a guinea pig to make suggestions from a buying stand-point," said Jim Dzwilewski, a purchasing manager for Shamban Corp., a maker of industrial plastic seals. He said GE "took some of my suggestions and put them into practice" (such as allowing customers to order a product by their internal part number rather than GE's). Another "old school" pur-chasing manager, Lee Zacharyasz of Milwaukee-based Techstar Manufactur-ing Corp., said it took him some time to get used to the online process. He said he made a lot of friends at Polymerland during 11 years of placing or-ders there and that the site's lack of human interaction at first took him "out of my normal comfort zone." "At this point, I'm so sold on the advantages, I wish everybody would do it," he said.

Customers access the site with a login name and password, and each ac-count is customized to the customer's specific needs. In the "order center" section of the site, customers can check product price and availability, track a shipment or review past invoices. They also can create purchase order tem-plates for products they order frequently. The site has extensive research and design tools that allow customers to access technical information on prod-uct characteristics such as strength, color, and malleability. Mr. Zacharyasz says he likes having all the information he needs at the touch of a button. He used to call GEPolymerland representatives three to five times a day inquir-ing about different orders. "Not that I don't want to talk to anybody there," he says, "but I have a lot of work to do!"

Using the Internet to buy and sell goods and services is one of the hottest trends in business today. The Internet is poised for unprecedented growth, especially with the introduction of new standards. Traditionally, unstable op-erations among trading partners have been among the biggest barriers to cre-ating an efficient and successful supply chain. The problem is often driven by process defects and a lack of knowledge about the supply chain. Effective SCM requires collaboration. The Internet provides a means to enhance com-munication and collaboration among trading partners so that business processes are streamlined and more effective. Companies that until recently viewed each other solely as competitors are enjoying the benefits of working together to develop a universal standard for business documents and transac-tions.

Up until this chapter in the book, we have *not* emphasized technology as the path for creation of high performing value systems. Instead, we have em-phasized that applying technology to a dysfunctional, fragmented set of busi-ness processes will only exacerbate the problems present in your supply chain.

However, when business processes have been mapped and relationships among key supply chain partners are understood, a full commitment to deploying B2B applications around the supply chain structure can provide a significant competitive advantage. Our research reveals that implementing B2B applications before fully understanding the nature of supply markets, customer needs, technology roadmaps, cost drivers, and internal business processes is a *major mistake*. Although the media is emphatic about jumping into this technology, believing it the right thing to do, there are sound reasons for not doing so. In short, baseline requirements must be developed before any type of Internet B2B application is deployed.

Although it is difficult to predict what evolving future systems will look like, one observation is clear: To successfully redesign your supply chain into an integrated value system, an organization must establish an effective understanding of the business processes and information standards that enable buyer-to-seller communication. It is easy for the average executive to become lost when navigating the ever-changing landscape of B2B standards, reverse auctions, electronic consortiums, private or public exchanges, and extensible markup languages. In this chapter, we review some of the emerging B2B technologies and present guidelines for managers seeking to link their organizations with supply chain partners via these technologies. Although we could not possibly cover all of the existing standards and evolving formats, we have chosen to describe some of the most prominent among these and discuss their suitability for various supply chain environments. We have also attempted to avoid as much jargon as possible. Nevertheless, the material may be difficult for many readers to comprehend. For this reason, readers who do not have a strong foundation in information technology may skip the latter part of the chapter.

In this chapter, we:

- Describe the evolution of the Internet
- Describe B2B technologies in brief
- Describe the origins of E-commerce: Electronic Data Interchange (EDI)
- Describe the evolving set of emerging auctions, hubs and exchanges
- Briefly introduce the standards for B2B communication
- Provide some of the salient features of the standards described
- Provide strategic recommendations for information managers seeking to derive standards for integrating their supply chain electronically
- Describe some of the technological shifts foreseen in the industry
- Describe emerging solutions for these technological shifts

The Evolution of the Internet

The Internet was first developed by the National Science Foundation as a means to link research scientists at different universities within the United States, and later, around the globe. Communicating via a single electronic medium, scientists could share research ideas and concepts quickly, facilitating innovation.

The development of HyperText Markup Language (HTML) enabled "point and click" graphics and text, forever changing the way business is conducted. Moreover, HTML became a universal standard, employed all over the world. A second major development was the technologies of "Web servers." In the early 1990's, a small company known as Cisco Systems began to develop servers specifically designed for Web users. This company is a clear leader in this area today. Web servers allow smaller companies and individuals to create and develop Web sites with a minimum investment. With the development of Web-based "browsers" such as Netscape, users could instantaneously communicate and seek information across multiple organizations worldwide. This has changed the way that people work (i.e., via e-mail, online catalogs, retailing, and information), learn (via on-line learning resources such as scmrc.ncsu.edu), as well as how they live and play (via Web chat rooms, sports networks, and on-line games).

As a result of this technology, the growth of the Internet has been explosive. Through all of this growth, one important lesson has emerged about the Internet: the marginal cost of bytes approaches zero. This means there is no limit to the amount of information that can be stored and transmitted via the Web.

Attributes of the Internet

Several attributes of the Internet make it markedly different from previous forms of B2B transactions.

Core Technology Architectures

One way of thinking about the Internet is as a large brain; like a brain, it consists of a network of electrical circuits that allows completely free flows across the network. One of the reasons the Internet grew so quickly was due to its inherent core technology design. Although in the early years the hardware was based exclusively on centralized mainframe computers located at large universities and research institutions, the Internet quickly evolved to a system of open distributed communication between smaller mini-computers or servers. These smaller computers were linked through a set of packet-switched communication protocols, which constituted the rules of the road for exchanging information in a format that could be readily interpreted by all. The development of HTML was a foundation for this protocol.

Software Standards

Many of the applications developed for today's Web rely on software such as HTML, Java, C++, Visual Basic, Perl, and others. However, many of the software applications used for years by companies rely on older software that does not always communicate well with current forms. Thus, the older technologies must be constantly upgraded to support the needs of a modern Web-based network. One of the primary software applications that enabled users to "surf" (navigate and search the Web for information) was the so-called "Killer apps." The Killer apps are World Wide Web browsers that enable users to search the entire network for information linked to keywords and search criteria. The first such browser was Netscape, but also include Microsoft Internet Explorer, Lycos, Yahoo, and others. Netscape is still the most common browser, although Yahoo is the site visited most by people seeking information on the Web. The Yahoo site gets an average of 30 million "hits" a day.

Lack of Central Control

Despite the growth of the Internet, no central "Webmaster" exists to control what information is passed along on the Web. Although the widespread acceptance of protocol exists, this lack of control means that growth is unabated. A downside of this phenomenon is the potential for misinformation to appear on the Web. Because every user owns his or her data, ensuring reliability and control is difficult. There are also security concerns; "hackers" who can gain access to information systems or create viruses that systematically attack Web sites and computer files via e-mail.

Who Pays for the Internet?

In its early years, the Internet was sponsored primarily by government and universities, who operated the mainframe computers that formed the network. The development of HTML and the point-and-click technology quickly attracted the interest of businesses willing to invest in this new communication form. Today, users can get onto most Web sites and access a wealth of information, virtually for free! To what extent, however, is the Internet really free? After all, *someone* has to pay for the servers and the cost of maintaining Web sites. Some Web sites provide users with free information, but charge for advertising. In 1997, revenues from sites of this type totaled approximately

$300 million. Other Web sites charge for information (an estimated $100 million in 1997). Such sites are usually protected by a "firewall," which means a user can only gain access to the site after paying a fee via credit card and providing a password.

The final site form is one that provides a product or service. Revenues for product sites were estimated at $500 million in 1997, but estimated at $2 to $4 billion in 1998 consumer sales. This included sales of personal computers, travel, books and music, flowers, food, and beverages. Despite these revenues, few "dot-coms" in the market were profitable as of the writing of this book. An additional problem is that of "cannibalism." By selling on the Web, companies may be stealing sales from their traditional retail outlets and making them less profitable. Nevertheless, the expectation of future profits has attracted many investors to dot-com company stocks.

Intranets and Extranets

One of the largest areas of growth in the Internet is the evolution of B2B transactions, as noted earlier. Most of this is occurring through the application of Internet technology (i.e., Web-based information, hypertext linkages, and browsers) to organizational applications known as Intranets and Extranets. Intranets are internet technologies for internal use within an organization's internal functions and business units. For example, Motorola University's Web site provides updates on classes, information, and texts available to internal users who wish to learn more about a specific topic or to upgrade their job skills. Extranets, on the other hand, are Internet technologies for controlled access external use. For instance, Federal Express has a purchasing Web site where suppliers can access their recent "supplier scorecard" rating or check invoice status. Extranets are especially well suited to SCM applications.

Advantages of the Internet

The Internet clearly provides a number of advantages over traditional buying channels. First, it is more convenient. Buyers can quickly access the Web and conduct a search to identify suppliers and determine the lowest price and best service available. This drives down prices in many retail and industrial sectors, since prices are now visible to all customers and the lowest price will almost always win customers' orders. In addition, a company selling on the Web does not have to worry about shelf space at its various retail outlets; stock can be kept at a central location and shipped to customers when required.

Another benefit of the Internet is that customers have faster access to new products and information, and can research products before purchasing them. Economies of scale are easier to obtain. Little working capital is needed and an online retailer usually gets paid before it has to pay its suppliers. A single Web site, once established, can cover the globe. It is also far easier for a successful Web site to branch into selling other products. Vast amounts of customer data can be collected far more readily on the Internet than from other channels. Everything can be recorded: not just transactions, but which Web pages a customer visits, how long he or she spends there, and what banner ads they access. This can produce a formidable array of data that makes possible both one-to-one marketing—directing sales at particular individuals—and "mass customization"—changing product specifications to match individual orders to the individual customer's preferences. In summary, the Internet allows reach (audience size), richness (service customization), and affiliation (response to customer's needs).

One of the evolving capabilities of the Internet is to communicate point-of-sale information from automated machines to centralized data accumulation storage sites, to enable mass-customization to occur at specific locations. One example of such an application is Reedy Creek Technologies,[2] which has the capability to extend supply chain information visibility to point of sale vending machines. For a very small monthly fee, the technology is able to track SKU sales information from soft drink and other vending machines. This information is transmitted to the vending company using either packet radio, cellular, Internet Service Provider, or Ethernet modes to a vending company database using email messaging over the Internet. This data can then be interfaced with the vending company's ERP system, analyzed for sales patterns, and used to create alerts regarding replenishment information, stock-outs, or machine breakdowns. This technology will provide significant benefits, allowing vending companies to customize machines located in different communities, after early detection of sales patterns for any given machine. In addition, the information will help to reduce costs, improve fill rates, reduce stock-outs at machines, and optimize vehicle routing schedules.

Disadvantages of the Internet

Some of the challenges or barriers to buying and selling on the Internet are also beginning to emerge. First, Web sites do not provide the social aspects of shopping or negotiating a contract, nor can they offer the same potential for impulse purchases that come from visits to a shopping center. E-Commerce cannot offer the instant gratification that today's consumers have come to expect. Many consumers like the convenience of "point and click" shopping but may be unwilling to wait several days to receive their items. Transportation costs also come into the equation. Consumers may not be willing to pay the higher additional cost associated with the shipment of small orders. Many Web retailers found that during the Christmas 1999 shopping period, they were unequipped logistically to deal with the rush of orders, and almost two-thirds of orders placed on the Web a month before Christmas 1999 on many sites did not reach their destination by Christmas day.

The B2B Technology Landscape

Technology has always driven change. No single era has brought so many new developments as the 20th century, especially in the last twenty years, with the ever-increasing integration of information systems. Although still in its infancy, the Internet has already changed how companies do business and created new opportunities in many fields.

The first group to take advantage of the Internet was retailers, using the Web as a means to reach a large customer base at very low costs. This led to the boom of e-commerce retailers at the end of the 1990's. Companies, as well as investors that drove stock-valuations of these companies up, soon realized that it was not enough to put up a flashy Web Page and offer goods over the Internet. The companies actually had to be able to deliver their products and services in a profitable manner. Furthermore, these companies that wanted to achieve larger margins by leaving out the costly middlemen realized that they also had to adopt their supply chain to the Internet in order to establish distribution services for this new market channel.

In response to the new evolving markets appearing on the Internet, a flurry of new technologies emerged to facilitate electronic commerce. We will begin by describing one of the predecessors to e-commerce as we know it today: EDI. We will then describe some of the newer technologies on the B2B landscape involving auctions and exchanges in more detail. In Chapter 9, we will discuss the newer forms of collaborative e-commerce, supply chain visibility systems, in greater detail.

EDI: The Technology That Started It All

EDI is not all that complex. Technically, it's a simple message format created in the 1970's by industry trade groups to reduce inefficient paper-based communications between trading partners. EDI is commonly transmitted over private networks—also called "value-added networks"—which are designed to provide better security and reliability than an open public network like the Internet. Despite the age of this technology, few companies have eliminated their EDI networks, even though the Internet systems are cheaper to use and more accessible to a wider group of suppliers and distributors.[3]

Why are companies choosing to maintain their old EDI systems? First, because they have spent a considerable amount of funds to implement these systems and aren't likely to abandon them soon. Second, a $250,000 tire order is not the same as a $25 book purchase. The Internet works well for consumer purchases, but doesn't always function as well for the complicated B2B transactions. Anyone who has had an order placed with a Web retailer "mysteriously disappear" is familiar with the uncertainty of ordering a critical item online. Value-added networks such as that run by Peregrine Systems are designed to eliminate such uncertainties. They provide the electronic equivalent of certified mail, and have a high degree of security. Many businesses prefer to use these private networks for sending sensitive business communications.

Early applications of EDI implemented from the 1980s-1990s helped to eliminate many of the steps involved in traditional information flows. The basic components of an EDI system include:

- A standard form (EDI standards)
- A translation capability (EDI software)
- A mail service (EDI network)

EDI standards include the basic rules of formatting and syntax agreed upon by network users. The formatting standards dictate whether specific documents can be communicated electronically, what information is included within these documents, what sequence the information should follow, what form of information should be used, and the meaning of individual pieces of information. Communication standards dictate what type of "electronic envelope" is to be used, the baud rate and protocol at which the message is sent, and what times of the day are acceptable for sending and receiving messages. Many companies early in the evolution of EDI adopted the American National Standard Institute's (ANSI) ACS X12 series of standards.

The second element of EDI is a translation capability. That is, the software translates company-specific database information into EDI standard format for transmission. The translator develops a document specification list that defines the content requirements for each transaction set. This list shows what lines of information (data segments or data elements) belong in each document and in what order they should appear. Not all data segments will necessarily be used in an EDI transaction. In addition, a segment directory specifies exactly what is to be included in each data segment through a data segment diagram that indicates all the elements that can be included, the sequencing, and whether each segment is mandatory, optional, or conditional.

Finally, a mail service is required to transmit the document. Documents are usually transmitted via a direct network or a third-party provider. A direct network is a link between computers via modems. This alternative works well when a limited number of trading partners are involved. However, when a firm has many trading partners, a third-party network avoids such traffic problems as maintaining open lines, time transactions, and maintaining security over the transmission. This kind of value-added network (VAN) serves as an intermediary "post office" for the partners. A "mailbox" for the sender and receiver also is maintained into which all electronic transmissions can be transferred simultaneously. The network then sorts each transmission into the appropriate mailbox. The trading partners check their mailboxes at agreed-upon times to retrieve the electronic transmission. A further advantage of VANs is that in the absence of industry-specific standards, EDI systems with incompatible formats may communicate.

An EDI transaction between buyer and seller ideally progresses in the following manner (see Figure 8–1). The computer in the buying company monitors the real-time inventory status of the item purchased using technologies such as bar-code scanners. When, according to a predefined reorder criterion, it is determined that there is a need to order more of the item, the application program notifies the translation software. An EDI purchase order is created and released against a pre-negotiated blanket contract, and the purchase order is sent to the supplier. The supplier's computer receives the order and the EDI software translates the order into the supplier's format. A functional acknowledgment, which indicates receipt of the order, is automatically generated and transmitted to the buyer.

Sometime later, depending on the purchase order data, a status request may be generated by the buyer and transmitted to the supplier. The supplier's computer automatically translates the status request, checks the status of the order, creates a status reply, and transmits it to the buyer's computer, which automatically updates its purchasing file.

When the original EDI purchase order is created, a number of additional electronic transactions may occur. Bridging software transmits the relevant

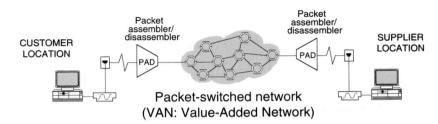

Data enter the packet-switched network one packet at a time.
Packets may take different physical paths within packet-switched networks.

Figure 8–1   EDI: A Packet-Switching Application for Supply Chain Transactions

data to the buyer's accounts payable application, to the buyer's receiving file, to the supplier's warehouse or factory file, and to the supplier's invoicing file. Once the order is filled from the supplier's warehouse or factory, a shipping notice is created and transmitted to the buyer. This shipping notice may require some manual data entry by the shipper. However, this is the first time in the process that manual entry is required.

Upon receipt of the goods, a shipping notice is electronically entered into the receiving file. Although additional data entry may be required, technology often eliminates this step as well. The receipt notice is transmitted through bridging software to the accounts payable application and to the supplier's invoicing application, whereupon an invoice is electronically generated and transmitted to the buyer. Once the buyer's computer receives the invoice, it is translated into the buyer's format and the invoice, receiving notice, and purchase order are electronically reconciled. A payment authorization is electronically created and transmitted to accounts payable, the receivables application is updated to indicate an open receivable, and payment is transmitted electronically from the buyer's bank to the supplier's bank. An electronic remittance notice is transmitted to the supplier, and upon receipt, this information is translated into accounts receivable and the buyer is given credit for payment. Within this process, there are only three instances of manual data entry. In traditional information flows, each step would require that paperwork be completed and filed by clerical staff. Thus, EDI allows fewer opportunities for errors, eliminates mailing or physical transmission delays, lowers clerical costs, and saves a great deal of time and paperwork.

Virtual Private Networks: The Next Generation

Despite the promise of greater diffusion of EDI via VANs, this approach to EDI requires significant investment by participating companies. The technology requires investment in EDI specific hardware and software. Because there are service fees associated with VANs, they may be more expensive to use than direct networks. Smaller suppliers in particular found investment in EDI technology difficult to justify and struggled with the demands buying companies placed on them to adopt various EDI systems. Finally, EDI was never considered an "interactive" mode of communication. Each time a transmission was sent, it implied that a "decision" had been made: an order for a fixed amount placed, a forecast of future demand fixed, a lead time for delivery specified, etc. There was never any means for the buying and supplying parties to reach a decision through joint, bi-lateral communication. In the last five years, however, a new technology has emerged that will change the world of B2B information systems: Internet EDI.

As Figure 8–2 shows, the Internet facilitates collaboration among parties in the supply chain through an online "virtual private network." Instead of having to invest a significant amount in dedicated EDI systems, a supplier can be connected to a large customer via Internet EDI simply by having a computer, a modem, and software. In other cases, a T1 line may be used to transmit higher volumes of data. (In fact, Ford has offered to connect its suppliers to the Internet for as little as $8 a month, which has improved communication with their supply base.) This system works as follows. Suppose a supplier wishes to notify a customer that it is shipping an order. First, a local Internet Service Provider (ISP) creates a Virtual Private Tunnel (VPT) using tunneling protocols. Some of the protocols include PPTP, L@F, and L2TP. Some of the protocols identified have been clustered around different industry groups. For example, many high-tech companies have adopted Rosettanet (http://www.rosettanet.org), while U.S. automotive companies are adopting protocols established by the Automotive Industry Action Group (http://www.aiag.org). Using this protocol, data is transferred over the Internet from the supplier to the customer's router at their headquarters. The router at headquarters then strips off the tunneling protocols and forwards transmission to the specified recipient. When the customer wishes to place an order with the supplier, the reverse process takes place.

Despite the guarantees that EDI standards generate the right data, EDI reliability problems do occur. One automotive supplier interviewed identified a number of problems with its EDI transactions with customers. The software in use in this particular supply chain has a different version installed for each participant, and in fact 25 different EDI versions are now being used in the

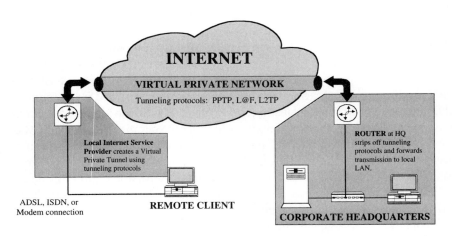

Figure 8–2   Internet EDI with Virtual Private Networks (VPNs)

OEM's supply chain. Unfortunately, the translation between these different versions is not seamless: data packets are switched resulting in EDI transmissions with incorrect, out-of-phase data. At one point, the supplier noted, "We had the same order, one sent by fax and the other by EDI, and the numbers did not match! Which one were we supposed to use?"

Another problem that exists within this automotive supply chain is that as the system was developed, all of the purchase orders were written by part number and location, meaning that suppliers might receive 16 different documents for a single shipment of different part families (not just one document containing the entire order). Furthermore, the EDI system only allowed users to download PDF files but did not allow the information to be downloaded into a spreadsheet to facilitate analysis. To overcome these barriers, the automotive OEM must drive a standard Web-based application through the chain to enable sub-tier suppliers (many of whom are not using EDI today) to become compliant to this standard that enables downloads of digital data.

As noted earlier, using EDI over the Internet with Virtual Private Networks (VPNs) is an important application, and provides numerous benefits. VPNs are typically much less expensive and present fewer standards problems but also typically require a common platform on both ends. The tunneling protocol used helps to address security concerns that users may have in employing the Internet for data transmission. However, the true benefits of the Internet go far beyond this. In fact, the Internet enables buyers and suppliers to achieve a level of collaboration that extends far beyond EDI technology as it was originally conceived. To truly understand how this collaboration takes place, we must delve into the details of the Internet's evolution and understand the properties of "Net-centrism."

Auctions, Hubs, and Exchanges[4]

The appeal of doing business on the Web is clear. By bringing together huge numbers of buyers and sellers and by automating transactions, Web markets expand the choices available to buyers, give sellers access to new customers, and reduce transaction costs for all participants. By extracting fees for transactions occurring within the B2B marketplaces, market makers can earn significant revenues. And because the marketplaces are made from software—not bricks and mortar—they can scale up with minimal investment, promising even more attractive margins as the markets grow. However, in order to make some sense of this burgeoning sector of the economy, we need to classify the different types of B2B marketplaces. Kaplan and Sawhney introduced the two-by-two matrix shown in Figure 8–3 as a means of classifying the B2B marketplaces.

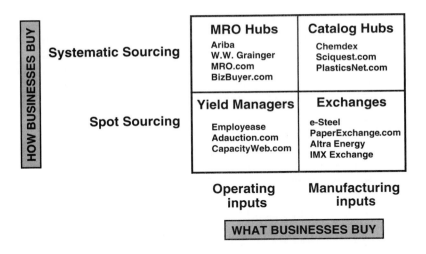

Source: Kaplan and Sawhney, Harvard Business Review, May-June 2000.

Figure 8–3   The B2B Matrix

As this exhibit shows, the authors first classify all purchases as either *manufacturing inputs* or *operating inputs*. Manufacturing inputs are the raw materials and components that go directly into a product or process. They are usually purchased from industry-specific (vertical) suppliers and distributors. They also tend to require specialized logistics and fulfillment mechanisms. Operating inputs, by contrast, are not parts of finished products. They include maintenance, repair, and operating (MRO) items, office supplies, and a wide range of other goods and services. Virtually every business needs these items. As a result, they are frequently purchased from horizontal suppliers, such as Staples and American Express that serve all industries. And they are much more likely to be shipped via parcel delivery firms such as FedEx or UPS.

The second distinction in the matrix is how products and services are bought. Companies can engage in either spot sourcing or systematic sourcing. Systematic sourcing involves negotiated contracts with qualified suppliers. Because contracts tend to be long-term, the buyers and sellers often develop close relationships. In spot sourcing, the buyer's goal is to fulfill an immediate need at the lowest possible cost. Commodity trading for items like oil, steel, and energy exemplifies this approach. Spot transactions rarely involve a long-term relationship with the supplier. In fact, the buyer often does not know whom he or she is buying from. Using these categories, we can now explore each of the quadrants of the matrix shown in Figure 8–3.

MRO Hubs are e-commerce providers of horizontal markets that enable systematic sourcing of operating inputs. Operating inputs tend to be low-value goods with relatively high transaction costs, so these e-hubs provide value largely by improving efficiencies in the purchasing process. Many of the best-known players in this arena, including W. W. Grainger, Ariba, and Commerce One, started out by licensing "buy-side" software for e-procurement to large companies which used the software on their own intranets. Now, instead of licensing their software to individual companies, e-hubs are hosting it on their own servers to provide an open market. These markets give buyers access to consolidated MRO catalogs from a wide array of suppliers. Newer entrants in this area include BizBuyer.com, MRO.com, PurchasingCenter.com, and ProcureNet. Because MRO hubs can use third-party logistics suppliers to deliver goods, they can dis-intermediate, or bypass, existing middlemen in the channel without having to replicate their fulfillment capabilities and assets.

Yield Managers create spot markets for common operating resources like manufacturing capacity, labor, and advertising, which allow companies to expand or contract their operations on short notice. This type of e-hub adds the most value in situations with high price and demand volatility, such as found in utilities markets, or with huge fixed-cost assets that cannot be liquidated or acquired quickly, such as manpower and manufacturing capacity. Examples of yield managers include Youtilities (for utilities), Employease, and eLance (for human resources), iMark.com (for capital equipment), CapacityWeb.com (for manufacturing capacity), and Adauction.com (for advertising).

Exchanges are close cousins of traditional commodity exchanges, and are essentially on-line exchanges that allow buyers and sellers to smooth out the peaks and valleys in demand and supply by rapidly exchanging commodities needed for production. The exchange maintains relationships with buyers and sellers, making it easy for them to conduct business without negotiating contracts or otherwise hashing out the terms of relationships. In fact, in many exchanges, the buyers and sellers never know each other's identities. Examples of exchanges include e-Steel (steel), Paper Exchange.com (paper), IMX Exchange (home mortgages), and Altra Energy (energy).

Catalog hubs automate the sourcing of non-commodity manufacturing inputs, creating value by reducing transaction costs. Like MRO hubs, catalog hubs bring together many suppliers at one easy-to-use Web site. The only difference is that catalog hubs are industry-specific. They can also be buyer-focused or seller-focused—that is, some catalog hubs essentially work as virtual distributors for suppliers; others work primarily as buyers in their negotiations with sellers. Examples of catalog hubs include PlasticsNet.com (in the plastics industry), Chemdex (initially in the specialty chemicals industry), and SciQuest.com (in the life-science industry). Because their products tend to be specialized, catalog hubs often work closely with distributors to ensure safe and reliable deliveries.

Aggregation or Matching, Neutral or Biased?

E-hubs create value with two fundamentally different mechanisms: *aggregation* and *matching*. E-hubs that use the aggregation mechanism bring together a large number of buyers and sellers under one virtual roof. They reduce transaction costs by providing one-stop shopping. PlasticsNet.com, for example, allows plastics processors to issue a single purchase order for hundreds of plastics products sourced from a diverse set of suppliers. The aggregation mechanism is static because prices are pre-negotiated. Adding another buyer benefits only the sellers, while adding another seller benefits only the buyers. The aggregation model works best when:

- The cost of processing a purchase order is high relative to the cost of the item procured.
- Products are specialized, not commodities.
- The number of individual products, or stock-keeping units (SKUs) is extremely large.
- The supplier universe is highly fragmented.
- Buyers are not sophisticated enough to understand dynamic pricing mechanisms.
- Purchasing is done through pre-negotiated contracts.
- A meta-catalog of products carried by a large number of suppliers can be created.

The matching mechanism is quite different; here the goal is to bring buyers and sellers together to negotiate prices on a dynamic and real-time basis. For example, Altra Energy makes a market in energy and electricity by allowing industry participants to list bids and asks on specific quantities of liquid fuels, natural gas, and electric power. The matching mechanism is required for spot sourcing situations, where prices are determined at the moment of purchase. The matching mechanisms can also take the form of an auction, as is the case with FreeMarkets.

In the matching mechanism, the roles of the players are fluid: buyers can be sellers, and vice-versa. Therefore, adding any new member to the e-hub increases the market's liquidity and thus benefits both buyers and sellers. While catalogs benefit only from the aggregation mechanism, exchanges benefit from both aggregation and matching. Therefore, successful exchanges will reap greater benefits from being first movers. In fact, it is possible that the first exchanges or yield managers to achieve a large-scale client base may take on natural monopoly characteristics. The matching mechanism works best when:

- Products are commodities or near-commodities and can be traded sight unseen.
- Trading volumes are massive relative to transaction costs. Buyers and sellers are sophisticated enough to deal with dynamic pricing.
- Companies use spot purchases to smooth the peaks and valleys of supply and demand.
- Third parties can conduct logistics and fulfillment, often without revealing the identities of the buyer or seller.
- Demand and prices are volatile.

Another final attribute of e-hubs to consider is whether they are neutral or biased. Neutral e-hubs are operated by independent third parties and do not favor buyers over sellers or vice-versa. But an e-hub can also be biased. When they favor sellers, biased e-hubs act as forward aggregators that amass supply and operate downstream in a supply chain or as forward auctioneers that host auctions for buyers. "Forward" in this sense means that the process follows the traditional supply chain model, with the supplier at the start and the buyer at the end. Ingram Micro, for example is a forward aggregator in the computer industry. Ingram Micro amasses products from multiple large suppliers such as Compaq, IBM, Cisco, and Microsoft, and carries out the distribution and order fulfillment function to resellers and buyers, as well as additional functions such as a call center, financing, and configuring products. Ingram Micro essentially aggregates selling power for small value-added resellers, providing them with virtual back-office functions and the benefits of economies of scale in purchasing. Biased e-hubs that favor buyers act as either reverse aggregators or reverse auctioneers. "Reverse" here means that the e-hubs attract a large number of buyers and then bargain with suppliers on their behalf. A reverse auctioneer, for example, hosts an auction where there are many sellers but just one buyer. Examples here include FreeMarkets, a reverse auctioneer serving Fortune 500 companies, and FOB.com, a reverse aggregator serving small buyers in chemical and other vertical markets.

Reverse Auctions

There is no question that the number of independent exchanges has declined of late—primarily because many businesses failed to consider that benefits must accrue for both parties in order for them to succeed! However, reverse auctions still hold promise in terms of exploring market pricing. A recent auction for a commodity group included several global suppliers (see Figure 8–4). The pricing behaviors that took place in this auction stunned the buying company executives who witnessed them. The price paid for the commodity was well below the group's expectation of market price. One executive who participated said, "It showed us just how little we really knew about what the market was doing." As the complex web of neutral, forward, and reverse aggregators begins to unfold, we will undoubtedly witness rapid changes in the evolving market structures on the Web.

A number of different technology features can be included in reverse auctions, including:

- Real time with countdown clock and instant feedback
- Overtime/automatic extensions
- Hosted, secure web-sites
- Bundling items into lots
- Reserve, starting and ceiling prices
- Bid decrements
- Multiple currencies and transformational bidding

It is a mistake to believe an organization can simply run a reverse auction without a great deal of preparation prior to the event. Some of the important things that must be completed prior to engaging a reverse auction include:

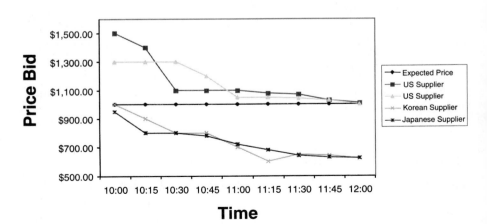

Figure 8–4   Exploit Vertical/Horizontal Exchanges Where Appropriate

— Determine where this item fits in your sourcing strategy. Specifically, appropriate items for a reverse auction
— Have a clear scope for requirements
— Have many qualified bidders available
— Must be a competitive market with excess capacity
— The buyer's business must be important to bidders
— Price is the key selection criteria
— Buyer is willing to award business based on the results of the auction

- Technology providers must be carefully researched before selection. The complexity of the various reverse auction software packages varies from a simple "do-it-yourself" auction that can be run from your own server, to one that includes complex "total cost of ownership" equations and currency conversions for supplier inputs. A myriad number of potential options and features can be included on different providers' software packages. Freemarkets is the current leader in terms of market share, a number of reverse auction providers are also available.
- User documentation must be developed carefully so everyone understands the rules of the auction. A specific set of rules for placing bids, evaluating bids, rules for "overtime," and other issues must be established. In addition, the user documentation should provide technical information on how to install the software at the bidders' and buyers' sites, computer requirements, and impact of actions taken at the keyboard on the outcome.
- Train bidders! This is a very important point. Many suppliers may not know how an auction works. One of the key points is to ensure that suppliers understand that they should *never bid below their cost of production*. Although this may seem obvious, suppliers may get excited during an auction and bid a price that they will later regret. This is not a good use of a reverse auction.
- Set up a call center and back-up plans for technical issues during bid events, in case things go wrong.
- Monitor and analyze the auction results afterwards. Debrief on the "lessons learned" for the next auction, and ensure this information is communicated to the right people.

Standards: The Basis for B2B Integration[5]

No one can deny that the Internet is changing the rules of business. In effect, a new network economy is emerging in which companies trade with suppliers and customers over the Internet in real time. However, ensuring a seamless, consistent customer experience requires real-time automation of business processes that span trading partners. Traditional ways of doing business, such as e-mail, fax, and voice mail, introduce delays and require data to be entered into information systems multiple times. Hence the need for dynamic B2B integration that can automate business processes across a diverse range of packaged and legacy applications and systems within the corporation and among supply chain partners. The ability to develop these B2B relationships and realize their potential value in the shortest possible time is critical to the long-term success of today's business. Indeed, no business can afford not to investigate how to efficiently automate business processes with trading partners, lest they fall behind their competitors.

At the same time, businesses are forging deeper relationships with their customers. Customers expect to be informed every step of the way from contact to completion of transaction, 365 days a year, 24 hours a day. Rather than adding the costly human resources that would traditionally be required to provide such service levels, companies now invite customers to interact directly with their information systems via automated e-mail systems, self-service Web sites and information portals. Customers expect their interaction not only to be real time, but also to be personalized, presenting information that represents their specific history with the company.

To meet these demands, businesses must be able to automate business processes that span the entire extended enterprise. In effect, they must be able to integrate their information systems and applications with those of their suppliers and customers—reliably, securely, and in real time. Not surprisingly, this need has led to a tremendous growth in B2B integration, as companies become e-businesses, responding to customer demands immediately and making changes to their business dynamically as market opportunities shift.

Although businesses have operated EDI networks to share data with partners for years, EDI has not become widespread because of its limited functionality, complexity, and high cost of operation. Today, with the widespread adoption of the Internet, newer technologies are enabling companies to more quickly accomplish the objectives of B2B integration. Open standards such as XML and HTTP can greatly reduce the speed and cost of implementation. This is important not only for obvious economic reasons, but because it encourages the so-called "network effect" whereby more partners and suppliers will adopt B2B integration technology, increasing the value to all partners. To establish e-commerce-based supply chain management, companies must adopt an effective means for B2B communication.

A comprehensive study performed by the Supply Chain Resource Consortium in April 2001 reveals that a number of consortiums and groups were formed to develop data exchange standards for deployment of B2B efforts.[6] A brief introduction to the many different standards is presented in this section. After reviewing these standards, we will discuss which of these appear to be emerging as the de facto standards.

Extensible Markup Language (XML)

XML base standards have evolved over the last several years and have functioned very well for horizontal industry groups (e.g., electronics, automotive, etc.). Many consortiums have tried to introduce a single standard that would work equally well with both horizontal (across industries) and vertical (within a single industry) groups, thus eliminating the use of multiple means of communication. But the vision of a single standard for B2B communications and collaboration over the Internet remains just that. Although XML appears to be the up-and-coming technology for creating communication standards for the Internet, the reality of using it exclusively remains distant.

RosettaNet

RosettaNet's global initiative is to adopt and deploy open and common business interfaces, enabling small and large buyers and sellers of computer technology to do electronic business more efficiently. This standard specifically deals with the business processes of the electronics, semiconductor manufacturing, and IT industries. More than 200 of the world's leading companies from these industries participate in RosettaNet's standards development, strategy, and implementation activities. RosettaNet is a vertical standard and is specific to the above-mentioned industries presented.

BizTalk

BizTalk is a Microsoft initiative. BizTalk seeks to provide the software and business communities with resources for learning about and using XML for Enterprise Application Integration (EAI) and B2B document exchange both within the enterprise and over the Internet.

Open Applications Group (OAG)

The Open Applications Group, Inc. is a non-profit industry consortium comprised of many of the most prominent stakeholders in the business software and components industry throughout the world. OAG currently has the largest number of business processes defined.

ebXML

The purpose of the joint ebXML initiative is to reach beyond traditional EDI by combining the two organizations (United Nations Center for Trade Facilitation and Electronic Business (UN/CEFACT) and Organization for the Advancement of Structured Information Standards (OASIS) strengths. For more than ten years, UN/CEFACT has successfully developed electronic data exchange tools, notably the EDIFACT standard for international trade, but its implementation has not reached the desired level amongst small and medium-sized enterprises. OASIS has emerged, as the leading world organization for applied XML technologies, but has not reached the level of interoperability that would make XML the preferred choice for B2B communication.

eCO Framework

Formulated by CommerceNet, the eCo Framework focuses on discovery. It is used to discover businesses that provide particular products and services. Once it finds these businesses, it figures out how to interact with their e-commerce system. The eCo Framework uses a seven-layer architectural model to describe e-commerce systems. It finds information at each of these layers by querying an associated type registry. A published interface exists for registries at each layer of the architectural model.

Industrial Data Framework (STEP)

ISO TC184 has produced the STEP standard, which specifies and uses the EXPRESS data definition language, which now has early and late bindings to XML. This framework is more concerned with the design phase of products and supply chain issues than with trading. It gives specifications to describe and transfer industrial data between the trading partners. The industrial data is typically comprised of the technical details of the products.

Java EC Framework

The Java Electronic Commerce Framework was developed by Sun Microsystems under the umbrella heading of Java Commerce. It aims to provide a complete infrastructure for Internet-based electronic commerce implemented in the Java programming language. The result is a set of Java tools and enabling technology. These include a client-side wallet in Java and a set of Commerce "JavaBeans."

The wallet is intended to be extendable to support different operations using a variety of value-transfer instruments and protocols. Key to the Java Wallet are "cassettes," or digitally signed containers (Java archive files) for

Commerce JavaBeans components. JavaBeans are modular bodies of Java code. Commerce JavaBeans components are re-usable components that implement specific on-line transaction protocols (e.g., credit-card payments, electronic checks). The Java Wallet is designed to automatically download and install cassettes specified by a particular transaction.

Object Management Group (OMG) Electronic Commerce Domain Specifications

This architecture and associated specifications are predicated on the use of objects to realize electronic commerce functions and whole systems. Several OMG specifications apply to special area markets or domains. Each specialty area represents the needs of an important computing market. The CORBA Electronic Commerce Domain architecture is comprised of specifications that relate to the OMG-compliant interfaces for distributed electronic commerce systems. Currently, there are four modules: Document, Community, Collaboration, and Document Object Model (DOM) mapping. The specifications detail modules, interfaces, and types. For each interface, details of attributes, operations, events, and additional semantics are provided.

The specifications also cover specific business objects that relate to the OMG-compliant interfaces for business object systems. Currently, two formal specifications are available: Task and Session, and Workflow. The Electronic Commerce Domain specifications build extensively on the Business Object Domain Task/Session specification. Task and Session defines business-level notions of people, places, and things through the types User, Resource, Task, and Workspace.

Open-EDI Reference Model (ISO 14662)

The Open-EDI Reference Model, ISO 14662 aims to lower the barriers of traditional EDI. These barriers are seen to stem from traditional EDI being based on detailed bilateral agreements, both business and technical, between business partners. Open-EDI is intended to alleviate these problems by introducing standard business scenarios and support services. The Open-EDI Reference Model is a framework for the integration of existing and future standards that enable the inter-working of organizations without prior agreement among the trading partners. The framework is generic in that Open-EDI applies to business transactions within and across sectors, involving one or more types of data or media. It is meant to be independent of specific implementations, business content, conventions, activities, and organizations. Open-EDI emphasizes the primacy of the business aspects rather than the system aspects of transactions. It also emphasizes the autonomy and flexibility of organizations to engage in electronic transactions with one another. While the general requirements for standards and standardization are set out in the framework, no individual standards are specified.

The Open-EDI Reference Model uses two views to describe the relevant aspects of business transactions. The Business Operational View (BOV) addresses the aspects of semantics of business data in business transactions and associated data interchanges, as well as the rules for business transactions. The Functional Service View (FSV) addresses the supporting services meeting the mechanistic needs of Open-EDI, with a focus on the Information Technology aspects: service capabilities, service interfaces, and protocols.

As an overall framework and reference, the Open-EDI Reference Model is not applicable for direct use. Although intended to be the reference model for a set of deployable standards, the development of such standards is not taking place. However, some of the concepts defined have been influential in subsequent development of e-commerce/e-business processes and specifications. These include the segregation of business/technical (functional) perspectives and requirements, scenarios, repositories, roles, and semantic components.

Spirit

The SPIRIT general-purpose computing platform defines software that supports a wide variety of application types. The general-purpose computing platform facilitates application portability, interoperability, and modularity. Agreement among Service Providers and IT suppliers on such a platform is required to meet Service Providers' needs for integrated systems and technology independence in a multi-vendor software environment.

The objective of SPIRIT was to provide a core set of specifications for use in each company's purchasing of software components for general-purpose computing platforms. The SPIRIT specifications are based on widely accepted industry standards. Participating companies expected to use the SPIRIT specifications as a basis for their own software procurement.

The intent of SPIRIT is to adopt and adapt specifications from other sources. The sources of adopted specifications include both standards bodies (e.g., ISO, ITU-T, IEEE, and others) and industry consortia (e.g., NMF, X/Open, and others). Adaptation is performed only as necessary to:

- Ensure consistency among specifications from diverse sources.
- Harmonize the use of certain specifications within specific usage scenarios.

- Remove ambiguities and/or inconsistencies within chosen specifications.
- Limit features and options for reasons of availability within specific time frames.
- Limit features and options for technical and/or business reasons.

Internet Open Trading Protocol (IOTP)

The Internet Open Trading Protocol covers the area of specification of a unifying framework for trading over the Internet. It is now maintained by Internet Engineering Task Force (IETF) Internet Open Trading Protocol (trade) Working Group. The objectives of IOTP are to:

- Enable development of interoperable products to support electronic commerce (any IOTP enabled consumer can "trade" with any IOTP-enabled merchant).
- Replicate the consumer's real-world experiences in the virtual world (e.g., provide invoices and receipts, linking delivery to the offer and payment).
- Provide a "universal shopping experience" (a consistent interface for all trading steps, irrespective of the identity of the trading parties).
- Encapsulate any Internet payment method that complements but does not replace available and emerging payment methods.

IOTP is based on a two-party operation (the low-cost trade model). Its architecture describes the various roles of the parties involved in Internet trade—consumer, merchant, value acquirer, deliverer, customer care provider—and the types of transactions that can occur between these parties. The IOTP specification, which is based on XML, sets out the content, format, and sequence of the messages that pass among the trading parties.

Open Buying on the Internet (OBI)

The objective of OBI is to provide a standard framework for secure and interoperable B2B Internet commerce with an initial focus on automating high-volume, low-dollar transactions between trading partners. The OBI architecture comprises four entities: Requisitioner, Buying Organization, Selling Organization, and Payment Authority. It involves the following interactions: Product selection, order placing and approval, order fulfillment, and payment. The OBI technical specifications focus on interoperability among trading partner systems, and particularly secure transmission of OBI objects to OBI-compliant trading partners over the Internet. OBI uses the X12 850 EDI standard for order formats. Transport is based on the Hypertext Transfer

Protocol (HTTP). Security service is provided by the Secure Sockets Layer (SSL) protocol. Digital signature syntax is provided by the PKCS #7 cryptography standard. Digital certificates are based on the X.509 V3 certificate syntax standard. It is now being updated to allow the use of XML-formatted data as an alternative to the American EDI format.

Universal Description, Discovery, and Integration (UDDI)

Technology and business leaders Microsoft, IBM, Ariba, and others have worked together to develop the UDDI specification—a sweeping initiative that creates a global, platform-independent, open framework to enable businesses to:

- Discover each other
- Define how they interact over the Internet
- Share information in a global registry that will more rapidly accelerate the global adoption of B2B e-commerce

The UDDI project takes advantage of the World-Wide Web Consortium (W3C) and IETF standards such as XML, HTTP, and Domain Name System (DNS) protocols. It also addresses cross-platform programming features by adopting early versions of the proposed Simple Object Access Protocol (SOAP) known as XML Protocol messaging specifications.

Open Financial Exchange (OFX)

Open Financial Exchange is a unified specification for the electronic exchange of financial data among financial institutions, business, and consumers via the Internet. Created by CheckFree, Intuit, and Microsoft in early 1997, Open Financial Exchange supports a wide range of financial activities, including consumer and small business banking; consumer and small business bill payment; bill presentment and investments, including stocks, bonds, and mutual funds. Other financial services, such as financial planning and insurance, will be incorporated into the specification in the future.

Open Financial Exchange, which supports transactional Web sites and personal financial software, streamlines the process financial institutions' need to connect to multiple customer interfaces, processors, and systems integrators. By simplifying the implementation of online financial services for financial institutions, Open Financial Exchange will help accelerate the adoption of online financial services by financial institutions and their customers.

The "Emerging" Standards

Based on an extensive analysis of these standards, the Supply Chain Resource Consortium study concluded that four have emerged as the front-runners in terms of adoption: RosettaNet, BizTalk, OAG, and ebXML. The nature of these standards is described next, and their suitability for application in different supply chain environments is discussed.

RosettaNet

RosettaNet is an XML-based vertical standard initiated by the companies in the IT industry, targeted solely for B2B supply chain integration. It has the potential of improved penetration into the electronic and semiconductor industry and hence *reduces diffusion* of other standards in the industry. The RosettaNet Implementation Framework (RNIF) is used to create Partner Interface Process (PIP) guidelines that define how computer systems will cooperatively execute e-business processes in the supply chain. There is a restriction on other standards using its framework. A set of Framework Signal Messages defined by RosettaNet must be used as in a specified format; no unapproved third-party content can be included in these messages. RosettaNet must approve the use of third-party messages. Third-party messages must be exchanged within the context of existing PIPs in RosettaNet. Adoption of RosettaNet requires substantial work by an organization in mapping business processes to conform to the standards, leading to a significant set-up cost. RosettaNet does not provide deployment specification, management specification, measurement specification, negotiation specification, or introspection specification.

A number of important features of Rosetta are noteworthy. RosettaNet has an Electronic Component Technical Dictionary (ECTD) which defines how product attributes will be listed for various product families. This is essentially a standardized taxonomy that defines the attribute-based characteristics that buyers and sellers may require for efficient e-commerce transactions. RosettaNet is not trying to define business transactions. Rather, it is trying to define the language used in those transactions. However, as one manager mentioned: "I think that RosettaNet has failed to leverage and build on the work that was done earlier in developing EDI standards."

RosettaNet provides an Automated Demand-Chain system based on standard product descriptions. This aids in reducing the number of incorrect orders and returns, and provides better tools for checking inventories, configuration, and compatibility. By making Extranets cheaper to implement using XML, RosettaNet can help suppliers cut costs and boost profits. Another efficiency to be gained from RosettaNet is in the area of reports. Manufacturers and distributors typically demand reports through their supply chain in proprietary formats on a weekly or monthly basis. The cost of generating multiple reports for multiple trading partners can be significant. As product definitions standardize, the reporting functions among trading partners will likely be streamlined.

BizTalk

The BizTalk Framework is designed to foster application integration and electronic commerce through data interchange standards based on XML. The BizTalk server provides a mechanism for converting and reformatting data from business applications to XML format. The data is mapped to their analogs in the other business applications utilizing the data. BizTalk does not have detailed integration scenarios and process definitions like OAG and RosettaNet. The set-up time is considerably less than the extensive OAG and RosettaNet standards.

A BizTalk Editor is provided to define the data elements for the system to write them to or read them from XML. A "mapper" links comparable elements between source and destination files for proper field translation. An application designer charts out the business process logic for the data to move through and the technological means for moving it from place to place.

The BizTalk Server has one major dependency: it runs on Windows 2000. A BizTalk Server is not needed to translate and wrap the data at each end. A server is needed only to speak the same language in the same way. The only server that matches that BizTalk Framework standard is from Microsoft.

Open Application Group (OAG)

OAG is an XML-based horizontal standard targeted for all industries. It focuses on developing implementable best-practice models for business software interoperability, and strives to achieve "plug-and-play" business software integration. OAG is not specific to SCM like RosettaNet, but can also be used in ERP and customer relationship management (CRM) applications. OAG has developed the largest set of business messages and integration scenarios for enterprise application integration and B2B integration.

In effect, OAG defines integration scenarios and suggests how messages are exchanged. It does not provide detailed process specifications and definitions as in RosettaNet. OAG does not have its own message transport framework, but strives to adopt existing technology where possible and will benefit from the use of RosettaNet (RNIF) and BizTalk framework as an implementation framework.

Another important function of OAG is that single business applications can be added without replacing the entire suite after the implementation of OAG. Customers will be able to select individual business applications from the best source without sacrificing integration and data sharing. The overall system cost of OAG is reduced dramatically because of the lowered cost of establishing and maintaining integration. Application vendors will spend less on technology infrastructure and focus more of their resources on the specific business applications they produce best. Application vendor sales cycles are reduced when users are faced with lower costs and time to integrate the application.

EbXML

EbXML is an XML-based horizontal standard. Its initiative is to research and identify the technical basis upon which the global implementation of XML can be standardized. EbXML will attempt to standardize the exchange of electronic business data in application-to-application, application-to-person, and person-to-application environments. The system is designed for electronic interoperability, allowing businesses to find each other, agree to become trading partners, and conduct business.

EbXML provides a transition path from accredited EDI standards to XML-based business standards. It includes a required registry to allow process owners to submit or update their mapping templates and support legacy information including historical EDI directories. The ebXML lexicon contains data and process definitions, including relationships and cross-references, expressed in business terminology and accessible by classification scheme. The lexicon bridges the specific business or industry language and the knowledge expressed by the ebXML business models in a more generalized, industry-neutral language.

Which Standard Should Be Adopted?

Criteria to Consider

The array of emerging standards, auctions, exchanges, and other formats available is overwhelming. Executives need to consider several issues in working with customers and suppliers to select a standard. Specifically, the following key issues should be evaluated carefully before deciding which B2B standard to adopt:

- **Control over an installed base of customers:** A standard should be supported by major companies in the industry to which that standard caters. RosettaNet, for example, is backed by major IT, semiconductor manufacturing, and electronic companies.

- **Simplified implementation:** The need for simplified implementation is a critical feature. XML can shorten the implementation time and offer a more flexible way to communicate, and the communication may be carried out over the Internet. The simplicity of XML also enables electronic communication even for small companies. The fact that BizTalk is a Microsoft solution indicates that it will be widely used and thus developed quickly. Even though there are solutions with better process support, we think such solutions will take a longer time to implement. This is a "plus" for BizTalk. RosettaNet is unlikely to have fast implementation as its primary feature, owing to its relative extensive process support. This may change in the future when there are reference implementations and a broader base of customers begin to adopt the standard. A disadvantage of the RosettaNet solution is that mapping the processes, looking for weaknesses, and then finding ways to improve the e-commerce business interfaces represents extensive work.

- **Improved flexibility:** A standard such as XML makes changing the design of the communication platform easier. One can more easily add a new actor or redirect the communication toward a new direction when one is not stuck in the specifications of EDIFACT. Standards like BizTalk and ebXML have flexible relationships providing more agile frameworks that support changes.

- **Set-up time and complexity:** By trying to define the processes, there is a risk that companies are locked into predefined business models and that the flexibility provided by XML is suppressed. In long-term relationships it will be necessary to adopt a standard that supports the business processes of both partners.

- **Intellectual property rights:** The traditional standard committees, like ebXML supporting X12-XML, have a substantial intellectual capital regarding business communication. We believe that these actors will be valuable members of new standardization efforts. Also critical is the considerable amount of experience of electronic communication within the member organizations of RosettaNet and BizTalk. Many of the actors in the standardization initiatives are members of several framework initiatives. An example is Microsoft, which is present in virtually every initiative, although with varying levels of involvement. This will probably reduce the differences in intellectual property among the different initiatives, making the character of the different solutions more similar.

- **Ability to innovate:** When trying to lead development, innovation is always important. Industry initiatives have a better possibility to innovate than initiatives driven by the standardization committees. Industry initiatives such as RosettaNet, with all their well-known members, hold out the possibility of achieving new solutions.

- **First-mover advantages:** We believe that the first XML-based standard, or framework, that will be fast to implement and relatively easy to use even for smaller companies will diffuse quickly. BizTalk/ebXML might have the potential to do this. On the other hand, older standards such as OAG have been in the market since 1995, and have been successfully implemented in companies like Ford Motor Corporation.
- **Experience:** OAG dates back to 1995; companies might adopt OAG based on its history of industry experience and results. For upcoming standards like BizTalk, the technology is still young and development moves fast. Companies might be less willing to invest in newer, less mature solutions.
- **Reputation and brand name:** If a standard has a good reputation, there will be less diffusion of other standards competing in the market, leading to broad adoption of the standard. Having major organizations participating in a framework initiative is important because it makes users believe in the project. Both BizTalk and RosettaNet have this credibility.
- **Backward compatibility:** When comparing the X12-XML feature of ebXML with BizTalk and RosettaNet, it is clear that ebXML goes furthest in its attempt to use the prior standard X12 as a foundation for the new framework. Both BizTalk and RosettaNet are clearly independent from traditional EDI.
- **Symmetric versus asymmetric standards:** The various standards and specifications can be grouped into two categories. In fact, these capabilities require tools that can be characterized as *symmetric* or *asymmetric e-business processes*. This criterion is perhaps one of the most important for executives to consider in selecting a B2B standard. The differences between symmetric and asymmetric business processes are discussed next.

Symmetric e-Business Processes

With symmetric e-business processes, each trading partner assumes an equal level of control over the relationship. Usually, the relationship is conducted using standard protocols. A large corporation would send a purchase order to the small supplier using the same technology as it would with it largest supplier.

The RosettaNet consortium has been building a symmetric e-business model that is being rapidly implemented. Symmetric e-business is message-based. As such, transactions are relatively easy to automate and back-end integration is always possible. Furthermore, this automation enables handling of tremendous volumes of e-business transactions. The most important benefit of symmetric e-business is that a company can deal with all of its trading partners in the same fashion. Automation of trading with one supplier means automation of trading with all suppliers. Symmetric e-business enables plug-and-play connectivity to e-business exchanges. This is a side effect of the inherent symmetry—an exchange can act like any other trading partner. As an example, a large manufacturer of computers could use RosettaNet e-business processes to completely automate the notification of trading partners and exchanges about a new product.

Partner Interface Processes (PIPs) originate as high-level business documents describing an important discrete flow of information between two companies to accomplish a business function such as a check on price and availability of a component. The RosettaNet consortium's objective in defining PIPs is to standardize business processes (i.e., the business-level flow of information over the Internet) in a manner that allows trading partners' computer systems to align those processes. Thus, RosettaNet standards allow the trading partners to communicate effectively and to function, when necessary, as a single virtual system. Currently, these processes are loosely defined at best. Only by aligning interchange processes can two disparate systems link internal processes. This is critical, since computers cannot interpolate steps in a process that is not well defined.

The second relevant feature of RosettaNet's work is its focus on the process's machine sensibility. Specifically, the information flow can be modeled easily and the message content, contained in an XML-based dialect, can be parsed with standard tools. This enables implementers to focus on more important and challenging endeavors: the back-end integration and the supporting application logic for specific complex processes.

RosettaNet focuses evenly on all phases of product development and commerce. PIPs create the ability to collaborate in real-time to aid in product design and manufacture. As a result, the benefits of e-business can extend beyond the operational efficiencies of streamlined procurement into the more dynamic product development and introduction stages of a product life cycle. Symmetric e-business has grown into a mature and powerful paradigm for business.

PIPs serve as a bridge across the Internet, connecting businesses' enterprise information systems. The clustering of PIPs creates a virtual cross-enterprise workflow in which trading partners can experience a unified process to accomplish a single goal. Graphical, intra-enterprise workflow applications are the focus of most leading-edge manufacturers today, but only the workflow applications that support inter-application and inter-company workflows are likely to survive.

The symmetric process also supports symmetric e-business through XML and RosettaNet. As a result, users can automate symmetric RosettaNet processes within current internal business processes. The power of e-business comes with process integration. This strategy provides external and internal workflow integration, blending external and internal workflows into a seamless e-business environment. For example, an organization could automatically initiate a PIP to notify distributors of a lifecycle change for a product from within a standard workflow triggered by a lifecycle change. The power of the strategy goes well beyond graphical workflow to deliver a full-featured e-business environment for collaborative product commerce, document and product lifecycle management, revision control, security, workflow, and back-end integration.

Asymmetric E-Business Processes

There is a limit, however, to the power of symmetric e-business, even with the recent work by RosettaNet. The message-based symmetric model does not perform well in complex processes; it breaks down when there is no clear next step in a process. Asymmetric e-business, on the other hand, includes any business conducted over the Internet in which the partners do not have equal control over the relationship. Usually, this takes the form of a Web site hosted by one of the trading partners; the host controls all content and all access rights. Web sites, such as business exchanges, provide a good example of the key characteristic of asymmetric e-business: Most marketplaces and exchanges currently offer only asymmetric e-business processes. This means that a user (or system) cannot automate interaction with a Web site. As a result, few marketplaces have seen much success within any vertical industry.

The asymmetric model allows manufacturers to exploit the Web to allow customers, partners, suppliers, and members of the extended organization to collaborate on design, manufacturing, and marketing throughout a product's lifecycle using asymmetric e-business technology. Web-based collaboration portals offer complete networks of product and process knowledge that can be leveraged as a strategic enterprise asset to drive innovation and expand revenue and market opportunities.

There are two key advantages to this model. First, the use is not inherently dependent on a defined set of trading partners; all they need is a Web browser to enable asymmetric e-business via an Internet exchange. Second, achieving powerful functionality is far easier via asymmetric models than via symmetric models. Building an asymmetric application is as simple as writing a Web application—something thousands of companies already have done. On the other hand, before the application can be built, symmetric model applications require a consensus on the process flow, the format of the exchanged data, and the exception handling routines.

Advantages of Symmetric and Asymmetric Standards

By re-examining the drivers for e-business previously discussed, one can see that the various requirements can only be met using a combination of symmetric and asymmetric models. The key advantages and disadvantages of asymmetric or symmetric model are shown in Table 8–1.

- **Access to internet resources:** Symmetric e-business enables companies to exploit marketplaces and exchanges from within mission-critical, automated processes.
- **Customer pressures:** Suppliers are likely to be pressured to provide both symmetric and asymmetric e-business tools. In the high-technology sector, suppliers are being asked to support RosettaNet as well as richer functionality in their corporate Web sites.

Table 8–1   Advantages and Disadvantages of Symmetric and Asymmetric e-Business Processes

Characteristic	Symmetric e-Business Process	Asymmetric e-Business Process
Model	Message-Based	API-Based
Example	RosettaNet	BizTalk
Back-end Integration	Common	Possible from Host Side Only
High Transaction Volume from One Business to Another	Strong	Weak
Process Automation	Easy	Difficult
Cost of Implementation	Medium to High	Low to Medium
Time to Implement	Longer	Shorter
Dependencies on Trading Partners	High	Low
Plug-and-Play with Other Partners	Automatic	Not Possible

- **Elimination of manual data entry:** The elimination of manual data entry will occur only with automated processes. As described above, only symmetric processes can be automated.
- **Collaborative design with partners:** Asymmetric e-business is far more powerful and flexible than symmetric e-business. As a result, collaborative design is best accomplished using a platform that supports asymmetric e-business. Thus an asymmetric business model is compatible and can be effectively used by the trading partners having different legacy systems.
- **Flexible, integrated build-to-order (BTO):** BTO needs to be supported through both symmetric and asymmetric e-business processes because it must support small-volume as well as large-volume customers looking for process automation.

Looking Forward: Emerging Technologies

Although the current B2B technology environment is complex, things are still changing! A number of emerging technologies will further alter the B2B landscape. Several of these technologies are discussed in this section.

Object-Oriented EDI

XML seems like a promising way to improve EDI, but the development is not likely to stop there. Object-Oriented EDI, or OO-EDI, is an often-mentioned way to develop EDI. OO-EDI is based on an object-oriented analysis technique, the Object Management Group's Unified Modeling Language (UML) to produce object models describing cross-enterprise business processes.

An actual comparison between XML and OO-EDI is potentially misleading: the two solutions are not mutually exclusive. XML is a tool for structured information transfer over the Internet. Combining XML and the logic of OO-EDI might take advantage of both techniques. The developers of OO-EDI claim that this solution will support the business processes in a way that no standard has done thus far.

Digital Cash

The use of the Web as an electronic marketplace is increasing, and is creating a need for a cash payment system that is scaleable and secure. Electronic cash is the electronic equivalent of real currency, and can be implemented using public-key cryptography, digital signatures, and blind signatures. In an electronic cash system, there is usually a bank, responsible for issuing currency; customers who have accounts at the bank and can withdraw and deposit currency; and merchants who will accept currency in exchange for goods or a service. Using digital cash, the cash flow in the supply chain can be made on a real-time basis. There can be instantaneous order placement and payment, virtually eliminating any delays.

Hybrid C++

Microsoft seems intent on giving Java a run for its money with its new C++ programming language. A hybrid of C++, Visual Basic and Delphi, this language will likely dethrone Visual Basic. The new language is designed for quicker e-commerce development than prior languages allowed. Unlike Java, it supports native COM API access. It also supports Internet services such as SOAP, XML, and the BizTalk framework.

C++'s language structure is similar to Java and includes automated garbage collection. The language uses Java-like simple thread synchronization and uses references instead of pointers. Features such as attributes and delegates have been added, simplifying and securing the code. The syntax is less complex, avoiding some current C++ pitfalls.

Ontology

The main purpose of ontology is to enable communication between computer systems in a way that is independent of the individual system technologies, information architectures, and application domain. An ontology is defined by a vocabulary of basic terms and a precise specification of what those terms mean. It provides a set of well-founded constructs that can be leveraged to build meaningful higher-level knowledge. The terms in an ontology are selected with great care, ensuring that the most basic foundational concepts and distinctions are defined and specified. Ontologies include richer relationships between terms. It is these rich relationships that enable the expression of domain-specific knowledge, without the need to include domain-specific terms. An ontology-based approach enables greater agility and flexibility in the business models possible and reduces the need for organizations to adopt common infrastructure and implement domain-specific standards. Spontaneous and organized commerce between trading partners will be more viable.

The UNSPSC Code

An emerging code developed by the United Nations will assign a code to every product that can be purchased, as well as geographical information. This could lead to the following scenario:

Suppose building contractor X wants to buy a bulldozer. First, he has to know the UNSPSC Code for bulldozers. Typically he will log on to the UNSPSC Code search site (http://www.b2nb.com.au/UNSPSCSearch.asp) and search for the item. The entry in the UNSPSC index for bulldozers is 22101510. The last two digits that designate the business function need not be specified, as this can be provided as additional information. As soon as a bulldozer is manufactured at the plant, it will be embedded with a smart-tag that contains all necessary information about the bulldozer that would facilitate the negotiations. Some information that would likely be needed for this would be:

- Geographical position
- Item description
- Manufacturer
- Price range (for automatic negotiations, a range of price should be provided)
- Capacity/quality specifications

The item is given an IP address conforming to the IPv6 specifications. The IP address of the bulldozer would probably look like this:

$$3FFE:1200:3028:FF01::43:08A2:05E6$$

The first six numbers show the home base's IP address in the hexadecimal format and the last two numbers are the UNSPSC code of the bulldozer in hexadecimal format. When the bulldozer is transported from one place to another, it will be given *care-of* addresses by the mobile nodes: this care-of address will be communicated to the home base. The home base will be attached to a database of all items and its location. While giving care-of addresses, the addressing rule can be specified such that it provides information about the geographical location of the item. This information, which is built in with the smart-tag, has to be constantly updated through a GPS system.

Now that contractor X has obtained the code for the required item, he can start the Package IP search engine in his computer (this can also be an online program) and give this code as the search key. This search engine is designed to find all the home bases, which has items having this UNSPSC code in their databases. The search engine will act as a client application, which will connect to the specified package IP ports of the home bases for posing the query. The home bases will check for the last two numbers of the IP addresses in their tables for matching purposes.

If a match is found, the home base will then return the IP address (care-of, if the item is not directly connected with the home base) to the search engine. Together with the IP address, the home base also will provide information on the quantity of items that are associated to that base and the locations of each item.

Once contractor X has obtained this information, he or she can decide which items are to be contacted, based on the location of the items as well as the quantity at each location. In this case, the quantity required is just one bulldozer, so the person makes the decision on the basis of proximity. Then he or she proceeds to contact the item directly for negotiations. This is done using technologies such as Agent Technology, Bidding/Auctions, etc.

Once the items are "short-listed" and communication is established, negotiation begins between the buyer and the seller. A negotiation framework will need to be established to:

- Identify or anticipate a purchase requirement
- Determine if negotiation is required
- Plan for the negotiation
- Conduct the negotiation
- Execute the agreement

Although this technology is not yet completely deployed, it promises to bring about a new era of web-based requests for quotation and negotiation that will be unparalleled.

Problems With Implementing Standards

A recent academic study of 20 organizations revealed that the reach and range of most systems is still limited to little more than simple transactions, and even that only across similar business units (see Figure 8–5).[7] When one looks at global reach across customers or suppliers, even with similar systems, little technology exists with proven capabilities.

Standards will clearly play a major role. They will be powerful forces for achieving considerably increased interoperability across B2B channels. The process of standardization, however, is a challenging one. To achieve significant benefits the ad-hoc B2B industry-led efforts will have to enter the mainstream and the full rigor of ISO or ANSI ratification. Businesses cannot wait for standards in order to take advantage of the global Internet infrastructure and the emergent B2B channels and collaborative commerce networks. Such standards, whether embodied in software or an online service, may be necessary but will never be strategic. Not all companies can afford to invest in such a capability by themselves; independent net markets have emerged to provide them with a shared marketplace infrastructure. Lastly, standards are always difficult to achieve through consensus, particularly in cross-industry initiatives, where companies cooperate and compete with one another. It is

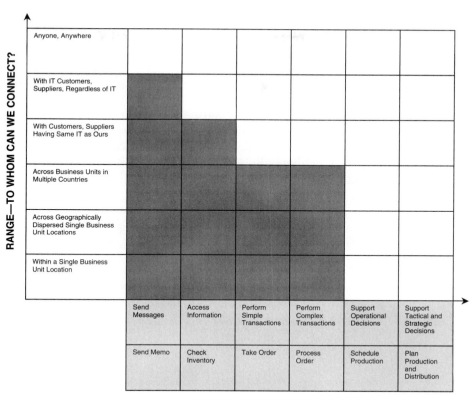

RANGE—WHAT CAN WE SHARE?

Figure 8–5   Actual Range/Reach of Current Systems
(Source: Broadbent, M., P. Weill, and D. St. Clair (1999), "The Implication of Information Technology Infrastructure for Business Process Redesign," *MIS Quarterly*, 23, pp. 159–182.

unsure whether any standard will be able to capture the richness, inventiveness, and complexity of a global B2B landscape that is developing in Internet time.

Endnotes

[1]Adapted from *The Wall Street Journal*, "Just One Word: Plastics," by Alex Frangos, E-commerce special section, May 21, 2001, p. R20

[2]Interview with Neal Davis, CEO of Reedy Creek Technologies, and Russell Thomas, Business Development Manager, TEC Program, North Carolina State University, December 11, 2001.

[3]Nick Wingfield, *Wall Street Journal*, "In the Beginning," e-commerce section, Monday, May 21, 2001, pp. R18.

[4]This section is based on an article by Steven Kaplan and Mohanbir Sawhney, "E-Hubs: The New B2B Marketplaces," *Harvard Business Review*, May-June, 2000, pp. 97-103.

[5]Based on a report developed by the following North Carolina State University students in the Supply Chain Resource Consortium http://scrc.ncsu.edu): Ajith Kumar Parlikad, Amit Heblikar, Anand Kosur, Karthik Gandlur, Manjiri Kaundinya, Rohit Razdan, Srinivas Balisetti, Uday Rao, under supervision of Professor Robert Handfield.

[6]Ibid.

[7]Broadbent, M., P. Weill, and D. St. Clair (1999), "The Implication of Information Technology Infrastructure for Business Process Redesign," *MIS Quarterly*, 23, pp. 159–182.

9

Creating Information Visibility

The Importance of Accurate Supply Chain Information

In the summer of 2000, with its order book overflowing but its assembly lines sputtering from lack of parts, Cisco Systems decided to crank up its supply line. It committed to buying components months before they were needed; it also lent the manufacturers who build most of their Internet switching gear $600 million interest-free to buy parts on Cisco's behalf. As it turned out, Cisco made a bad business decision. On Monday April 16, 2001, with both its sales and the value of its surplus components shrinking, Cisco announced that it would write off $2.5 billion of its bloated inventory. People were in shock. Cisco was the darling of Wall Street; it had enjoyed unprecedented growth and an associated rise in its stock value. CEO John Chambers said his company was the victim of a sudden, unanticipated economic chill. In November 2000, Cisco's orders were growing at a 70 percent annual clip. However, others claim that Mr. Chambers and other Cisco executives ignored or misread crucial warning signs and that their sales forecasts were too ambitious. They overestimated Cisco's backlog because of misleading information supplied by Cisco's internal order network and continued to expand aggressively even after business slowed at various Cisco divisions. After hiring more than 5,000 between November 2000 and March, 2001, they laid off more than 8,500 people in April 2001. Alex Mendez, an ex-Cisco executive who left in November 2000 to become a venture capitalist, claims that "Cisco always had a bit of trouble finding the brakes."

Like other high-tech companies, Cisco was caught unaware by the one-two punch of the broader slowdown and the subsequent retrenchment in the telecommunications sector. When Cisco's 600 top executives met for their annual retreat in May 2000, they planned on increasing revenue by 60 percent. One cloud loomed on the horizon: components for some products, particularly switches used in corporate computer networks, were in critically short supply and customers had to wait as long as 15 weeks compared to the normal one to three weeks. To aid this situation, Chambers and top aides devised a two-fold strategy to revitalize Cisco's supply chains: help contract manufacturers accumulate parts and commit to buying specific quantities of components from key suppliers. Contract manufacturers worried that this strategy involved setting overly aggressive expansion plans. For example, Solectron had warned Cisco that they appeared to be ordering more parts than needed. In October 2000, sales in the telecommunications industry grew less than 10 percent from the previous quarter. At this time, at least two Cisco suppliers began warning Cisco that shipments were slowing, or not meeting forecasts. By November 2000, Mr. Chambers said orders were "comfortably" more than 70 percent ahead. Furthermore, he emphasized that the latest downturn was an opportunity for Cisco to break away from rivals such as Nortel and Lucent Technologies. By December 2000, however, he had changed his tune. On December 15, 2000, Mr. Chambers gathered his top executives and asked "What happens if we're off by a billion or a billion and a half in quarterly sales?" Things got worse; sales to telecommunications carriers fell 40 percent in the next quarter. The speed of the sales decline was surprising. The root cause was then determined: facing two- and three-month waits for some popular Cisco products, some customers had been double- and triple-ordering, once from Cisco and then again from Cisco distributors. Once the product was shipped, customers canceled the duplicate orders. All of a sudden, their backlog vanished into thin air. Mr. Volpi, a Cisco executive, claims that without the misleading information, "we might have seen better and made better decisions."

Chambers outlook remains positive. "We will always err on the side of meeting customer expectations. The day we stop taking risks as a company is the day I would sell the stock." An expensive gamble indeed. Even after its write-off, Cisco reported inventories of $1.6 billion, up 33 percent from July.

Adapted from *The Wall Street Journal*, "Behind Cisco's Woes Are Some Wounds of Its Own Making," by Scott Thurm, p. A1, April 18, 2001.

Without the buy-in of supply chain members, asking them to react faster in response to real-time ordering systems is an exercise in futility. A supplier who receives an order via the Internet, prints it out, and puts it on a stack on their desk is not contributing to supply chain value. Instead, when information is shared across the supply chain and made available to all parties, such that demand requirements, capacity limitations, inventory positioning, and collaboration between partners is established through *a priori* agreements, then the power of the Internet can begin to be fully exploited. This means providing an Internet-accessible, real-time forum where buyers and their suppliers can communicate and share inventory and forecasting information, and allow for the effective dissemination of engineering change orders (ECOs) throughout the supply chain. The changes that must take place to truly exploit the potential of B2B e-commerce with supply chain partners are explored in this chapter. We begin by discussing the importance of information visibility in a supply chain to avoid the "bullwhip" effect.

The Importance of Information in Supply Chains: Avoiding the Sting of the "Bullwhip"

Lack of information or distorted information passed from one end of the supply chain to the other can create significant problems, including, but not limited to, excessive inventory investment, poor customer service, lost revenues, misguided capacity plans, ineffective transportation, and missed production schedules. These are not deliberate attempts to sabotage the performance of fellow supply chain members. Rather, distorted information throughout the supply chain is a common result of what logistics executives at Procter and Gamble (P&G) and other organizations have termed the *bullwhip effect*.

The Bullwhip Effect

In the 1990's, P&G, began to explore this phenomenon after a series of particularly erratic shifts in ordering up and down the supply chain for one of its most popular products, Pampers disposable diapers. After determining that it was highly unlikely that the infants and toddlers at the ultimate user level were creating extreme swings in demand for the product, the review team began to work back through the supply chain. It was found that distributors' orders showed far more demand variability than found at the retail stores themselves. Continuing through the supply chain, P&G's orders to its supplier, 3M, indicated the greatest variability of any of the supply chain linkages.[1] Four causes of this phenomenon were identified:

1. Demand forecast updating
2. Order batching
3. Price fluctuations
4. Rationing within the supply chain[2]

This bullwhip effect is certainly not unique to P&G or even to the consumer packaged-goods industry. Firms such as Hewlett-Packard in the computer industry and Bristol-Myers Squibb in the pharmaceutical field have experienced a similar phenomenon. Even moderate demand variability becomes magnified when viewed through the eyes of managers at each link in the supply chain. If each manager makes ordering and inventory decisions with an eye to the firm's own interest above those of the change, stockpiling may be simultaneously occurring at as many as seven or eight places across the supply chain. One study projected $30 billion in savings could result from streamlining the order information-sharing process in grocery industry supply chains alone.[3] Why do such disparities in information sharing exist?

Supply-Chain Organizational Dynamics

Several interorganizational dynamics come into play when addressing information sharing across the supply chain. Two issues in particular are risk and power. All enterprises participating in a supply chain management initiative accept a specific role to perform. They also share a common belief that they and all the other supply chain participants will be better off because of their collaborative efforts. Each member specializes in the function or area that best aligns with its competencies. Risk occurs when each firm must rely on other supply chain members, as well as its own efforts, to determine the success of the supply chain. Some supply chain members are more dependent on the success of the supply chain than others. Thus, members with the most at stake must take more active roles and assume greater responsibility for fostering cooperation, including the information-sharing efforts, throughout the supply chain.

Power within the supply chain is a central issue, one that in today's marketplace often centers on information sharing. Although not universal to all industries, there has been a general shift of power from manufacturers to retailers over the last two decades, which has resulted from a combination of factors. One is the trend toward consolidation at the retail level within the supply chain. Gone are the days of "Mom and Pop" grocery stores in every neighborhood or the locally owned, independent hardware store in each town. In the interest of capitalizing on the benefits of economies of scale, giant retail conglomerates operate as part of nationwide supply chains. In fact, relatively few of the thousands of retailers operating in the United States control the majority of dollars in this industry. Clearly, this consolidation impacts the entire supply chain. Fewer and fewer firms control access to consumer trading areas.

For several reasons, major retailers have risen to this position of prominence through technologies such as bar codes and scanners, size and sales volume, and most importantly, their position within the supply chain—right next to the final consumer. This combination of factors has put retailers in a very powerful position within the supply chain.

Wal-Mart's and P&G's experiences demonstrate how information sharing can be utilized for mutual advantage. Through state-of-the-art information systems, Wal-Mart shares point-of-sale (POS) information from its many retail outlets 3directly with P&G and other major suppliers. Rather than causing Wal-Mart to lose power within these partnerships, this willingness to share information provides the retailer with a competitive advantage by freeing its resources from many of the tasks associated with managing supplier's products. The product suppliers themselves become responsible for the sales and marketing of their products in the Wal-Mart stores through easy access to information on consumer buying patterns and transactions.[4]

As businesses and industry groups explore development of information visibility systems to support their supply chain management efforts, they will face several challenges. One impediment undoubtedly lies in developing a common language in terms of planning, format, and priority across several vastly different constituencies. A number of the technologies discussed in Chapter 8 are specifically focused on this key issue. Information-sharing requirements are well beyond those of a manufacturer and its distributor's need to process orders consistently. All relevant information ultimately must circulate to and among all organizations between the supply chain's point of origin and its point of consumption, such as ordering (i.e., orders for component parts, services, and finished products), inbound transportation, manufacturing, warehousing, inventory management, outbound transportation, sales, marketing, forecasts, and customer-service information.[5] Although no standard approach is being utilized in terms of technology or information, most business leaders agree that the greatest potential for information visibility lies in the power of the Internet as a data-sharing platform.

Several applications of the Internet to supply chain management problems have emerged in the last several years. The Internet facilitates collaboration between supply chain members to achieve better information visibility and decision-making. Although the number of such applications is growing daily, the focus of this chapter is on creating *information visibility* between original equipment manufacturers (OEM's) or large service providers (such as airlines) and their lower-tier suppliers. We begin by discussing the various elements of information visibility, and provide some examples that illustrate the power of information visibility in supply chains. Next, we highlight the results of a recent benchmarking study on information visibility carried out by the Supply Chain Resource Consortium and then discuss other applications of collaborative information visibility, such as collaborative forecasting and collaborative contracting. We conclude with a brief example of how one company successfully implemented a system to provide supply chain information visibility throughout its supply base.

Creating Information Visibility in Supply Chains[6]

What is Information Visibility?

Information visibility within the supply chain is the process of sharing critical data required to manage the flow of products, services, and information in real time between suppliers and customers. If information is available but cannot be accessed by the parties most able to react to a given situation, its value degrades exponentially. Increasing information visibility between supply chain participants can help all parties reach their overall goal of increased stockholder value through revenue growth, asset utilization, and cost reduction. To improve responsiveness across their supply chains, companies are exploring the use of collaborative models that share information across multiple tiers of participants in the supply chain: from their supplier's supplier to their customer's customer. These trading partners need to share forecasts, manage inventories, schedule labor, and optimize deliveries. In doing so, the partners reduce costs, improve productivity, and create greater value for the final customer in the chain. Software for Business Process Optimization (BPO) and Collaborative Planning, Forecasting and Replenishment (CPFR) are evolving to help companies collaboratively forecast and plan amongst partners, manage customer relations, and improve product life cycles and maintenance. Traditional supply chains are rapidly evolving into "dynamic trading networks"[7] comprised of groups of independent business units sharing planning and execution information to satisfy demand with an immediate, coordinated response.

Some of the considerations that must be addressed prior to implementing an information visibility system include the size of the supply base and customer base with which to share information, the criteria for implementation, the content of information shared and the technology used to share it. Clarifying these issues will help to ensure that all participants have access to the information required to effectively control the flow of materials, manage the level of inventory, fulfill service level agreements, and meet quality standards as agreed upon in the relationship performance metrics.

Dell's Information Visibility System: The Benchmark

Perhaps no other company has been more successful in implementing information visibility as a competitive strategy than Dell Computer. Dell has fulfilled its commitments to customers through the company's direct model, in which it holds only hours of inventory yet promises customers a lead-time of five days. Component suppliers who wish to do business with Dell have to hold some level of inventory, since their cycle times are typically much longer than Dell's.8 For example, if a supplier has a lead-time of 45 days and Dell is promising on-line customers a lead-time of five days from order placement to delivery, the supplier must have real-time information to meet Dell's strict demands. Dell has developed a business model that features a lean, build-to-order manufacturing operation. By utilizing the Web, Dell provides its supplier with forecasting information and receives information about the supplier's ability to meet the forecasts. Dell uses i2 Technologies products for demand-fulfillment operations and products from Agile Software for engineering-change-order and bill-of-materials management. Communication regarding engineering changes, component availability, capacity, and other data flows both ways between Dell and its suppliers, in addition to forecasting and inventory data. Dell is also able to review suppliers and place Web-based orders into their factories in hours. After outsourcing to third-party contract manufacturers, Dell executives realized that many of these manufacturers did not have adequate visibility of customer orders. This was a major driver in the initiative to increase visibility of orders. Dell's build-to-order web-based customer model has become the benchmark for other industries. Organizations such as General Motors, Ford, and General Electric are seeking to create "build-to-order" models using the Web as the platform for taking customer orders.

Benefits of Information Visibility

Information regarding forecasts, changes in production schedule levels and on-going supply chain performance metrics need to be conveyed by customers to suppliers on a regular basis. Information flows from suppliers to customers can include current order lead times, capacity levels, order status, and inventory levels. The benefits of having designated parties receive this information are numerous. Receiving and conveying the correct information will ensure that the suppliers are aware of what needs to be produced, while at the same time, the buying firm is sure that it is possible to receive ordered quantities on time, every time. The most important benefit of a visibility system is not that the system is able to correct a supply chain problem, but that it allows people to become aware of problems earlier, and thus take corrective action more quickly than they would otherwise. The benefits of information visibility include reduced lead times, improved constraint management, better decision-making, lower costs, and increased profits. Although problems such as shortages, changes in customer orders, engineering changes, obsolete inventory, and equipment failures can still occur with a visibility system in place, the effects of these problems are less than if the participants in the supply chain were not made aware until a later point in time. In other words, visibility systems may be able to turn a potential $500,000 problem into a $5,000 problem.

When implemented properly, a visibility solution results in the following additional benefits that promote improved supply chain performance:

- **Breaks organizational barriers:** Enables sharing of mission-critical information about business activities and interaction on a real-time basis across the supply chain.
- **Builds visibility into supply chain:** Provides people a real-time view of supply chain performance metrics.
- **Managing by metrics:** Aligns performance metrics with cross-organizational business processes and assigns ownership of processes and metrics to specific individuals.
- **Reduces process cycle times:** Allows supply chain members to respond to market or customer demand in hours or days, not weeks or months.
- **Encourages decision-making collaboration:** Facilitates the ability to make decisions collaboratively on the Internet, bringing relevant internal and external stakeholders into the process.
- **Reduces opportunity and problem resolution latency:** Measures and monitors supply chain activities iteratively, which allows people to quickly respond to events as they occur.

Conversely, the dangers of poor execution of supply chain processes include increased lead times, higher costs, and less informed decision-making. For example, in the semiconductor industry, a lack of visibility across the supply chain, coupled with inaccurate supply/demand forecasting, is hurting the industry's ability to deliver products promptly, efficiently spend capital, and properly manage inventory.[9]

I-Supply: A Visibility System that Works!

A visibility system that has gained popularity in the automotive industry in the last two years is I-Supply, a system developed by Supply Solutions of Detroit, Michigan. This system has largely been adopted by first-tier automotive suppliers, but is beginning to be adopted by automotive OEM's such as Daimler-Chrysler and GM, and is slowly migrating to other industries such as healthcare and high-tech. In November 2001, Covisint, the private exchange for GM, Ford, and Daimler Chrysler, selected I-Supply as it's primary vehicle for taking orders with first-tier suppliers. Software systems such as I-Supply are designed to attack the problem of extended lead times that exist in many industries (Figure 9–1). Lead times in the automotive industry, from the time an end-customer orders a vehicle through the different tiers of suppliers, can be more than 200 days with significant amounts of inventory held at each link of the supply chain (dealers, OEM's, Tier-1, Tier-2, and Tier-3 suppliers). I-Supply enables an OEM customer or Tier-1 supplier to provide downstream participants with real-time visibility of its production planning system via the Internet. Jeff

SCM Today: A Sequential, Push Structure

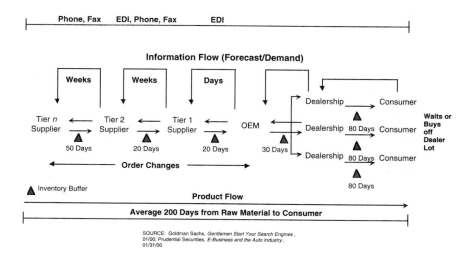

Figure 9–1 An Automotive Supply Chain

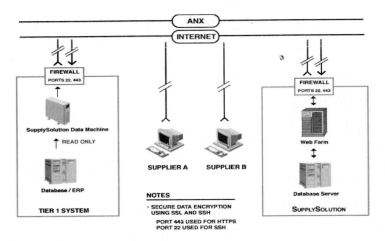

Figure 9–2 The "I-Get-It" Network System

Trimmer, former Director of Operations and Supply for Daimler Chrysler, described the success of the pilot program with Supply Solutions:

> For the first time we have a tool that potentially allows us to manage the complexity of our supply chain. Companies that use this tool to eliminate waste, reduce cycle time, and improve quality throughout their supply chains will not only satisfy their customers better and earn greater profits for themselves but will also see their supply chains earn greater profits as well.[10]

The key to the I-Supply system is the "I-get-it" network system. The heart of "I-get-it" (as shown in Figure 9–2) is a pizza-shaped box installed on the customer's ERP or MRP system. Every 15 minutes, the software installed in the box takes a "snapshot" of inventory and order status in a read-only format, which is then transmitted in a secure manner to the Supply Solutions Web site. Only authorized suppliers are allowed to access the Web site to obtain this information from their customers' system.

Once the software captures the data, it is displayed in a series of dashboard console screens that provide critical metrics on various aspects of supply chain performance. The dashboards of information to customers and suppliers are shown in Figures 9–3, 9–4, and 9–5. The first console (Figure 9–3) displays the item inventory status at the customer's location to the supplier responsible for replenishing this item. Naturally, such a console is not used for every item, but is reserved for critical items used directly in the product or service. Based on historical usage, forecasting and desired service levels, the customer inputs a

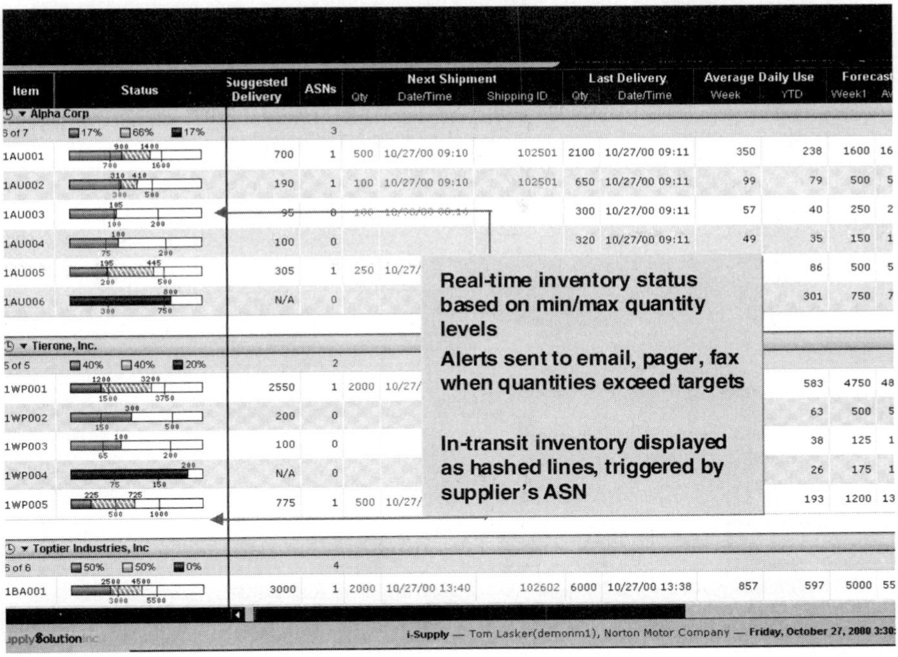

Item	Status			Suggested Delivery	ASNs	Next Shipment			Last Delivery		Average Daily Use		Forecast	
						Qty	Date/Time	Shipping ID	Qty	Date/Time	Week	YTD	Week1	Av
▼ Alpha Corp														
5 of 7	17%	66%	17%		3									
1AU001	980 1400 / 700 1600			700	1	500	10/27/00 09:10	102501	2100	10/27/00 09:11	350	238	1600	16
1AU002	210 410 / 200 500			190	1	100	10/27/00 09:10	102501	650	10/27/00 09:11	99	79	500	5
1AU003	195 / 100 500			95	0				300	10/27/00 09:11	57	40	250	2
1AU004	100 / 75 200			100	0				320	10/27/00 09:11	49	35	150	1
1AU005	195 445 / 200 500			305	1	250	10/27/						86	500	5
1AU006	800 / 300 750			N/A	0								301	750	7
▼ Tierone, Inc.														
5 of 5	40%	40%	20%		2									
1WP001	1200 3200 / 1500 3750			2550	1	2000	10/27/						583	4750	48
1WP002	300 / 150 500			200	0								63	500	5
1WP003	100 / 65 200			100	0								38	125	1
1WP004	200 / 75 150			N/A	0								26	175	1
1WP005	225 725 / 500 1000			775	1	500	10/27/						193	1200	13
▼ Toptier Industries, Inc														
5 of 6	50%	50%	0%		4									
1BA001	2500 4500 / 3000 5500			3000	1	2000	10/27/00 13:40	102602	6000	10/27/00 13:38	857	597	5000	55

Real-time inventory status based on min/max quantity levels

Alerts sent to email, pager, fax when quantities exceed targets

In-transit inventory displayed as hashed lines, triggered by supplier's ASN

Figure 9–3 Item Inventory Status at the Customer's Location

desired minimum and maximum level of inventory for each item to be held at its facility. The status of the inventory is displayed as a bar—which is color-coded as either green (level is between the minimum and maximum), red (shortage), or blue (over the max). Inventory in-transit from the supplier (triggered by an advance ship notice sent by the supplier to the customer) is displayed as a crosshatch, indicating that the replenishment will occur by the date and time shown. When inventory levels fall below the minimum or above the maximum, the key contact at the supplier is alerted, either by e-mail, pager, or fax. The alert lets the supplier know that a critical incident has occurred that needs attention immediately to avoid problems at the customer's operation. In addition, the average daily use is calculated and archived (Figure 9–4), and can be exported in digital format. Similarly, material forecasts are displayed and can also be exported to an EDI transmission or Excel spreadsheet. The most recent receipt of a shipment (pulled from the ERP system) is also displayed. Finally, the critical inventory tab (Figure 9–5) provides a summary of all items predicted to drop below established minimums or to reach zero levels within a user-defined time period. These values are calculated based on current inventory plus expected shipments minus projected usage. Critical inventory items are sorted in ascending order

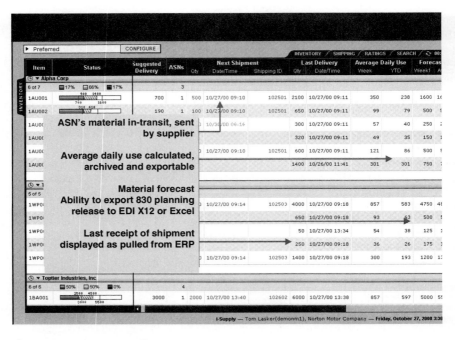

Figure 9-4 Average Daily Use

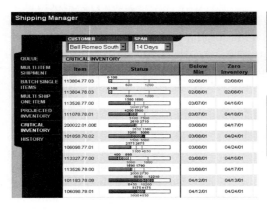

Figure 9-5 The Critical Inventory tab provides a summary of all items predicted to drop below established minimums or to reach zero levels within a user-defined period

according to the nearest projected dates in the "Below Min" column, providing a quick summary for the customer and supplier to identify which items are most likely to create problems in the near future.

One of the significant benefits provided by systems such as "I-Supply" is to enable vendor-managed arrangements to occur, without requiring the supplier to physically locate an individual in the customer's facility. Vendor-managed inventory (VMI) refers to an agreement whereby the supplier is responsible for managing inventory levels of their product at the customer's facility, and is already in use in many automotive and electronics companies. The system was originally pioneered by Bose, a manufacturer of high-fidelity speakers, and was originally called "JIT 2." Although initially resisted by suppliers due to the additional costs incurred as a result of providing personnel at the customer's location and holding inventory, VMI is becoming more commonplace when accompanied by an appropriate partnering agreement.

Honeywell has established VMI agreements with a number of critical suppliers, and spent a great deal of time identifying the supplier's benefits to help speed the rate of deployment. Honeywell emphasizes that suppliers are responsible for consignment inventory, direct floor stocking, and releases from a rolling forecast. In some cases, a full-time or part-time supplier representative at the facility not only manages inventories of items, but may also provide Honeywell associates with technical assistance on product-related quality or engineering issues that arise. In return, suppliers are rewarded with more business, the opportunity to be "designed-in" to new products being developed at Honeywell, stabilized production schedules that allow improved cost efficiencies, fewer transactions, quicker payments, lower selling expenses, assured sales, and earlier access to information.

A Fictional Example of Supply-Chain Information Visibility

A true supply chain visibility system should provide a clear and common view of events in a supply chain to all designated participants. Some of the key information that should be included:

- Present production rate (as percent of capacity)
- On-hand inventory

- Inventory in transit
- Advance ship notices
- Forecasts
- Damaged goods
- Actual vs. delivered amounts
- Real-time alerts
- Upcoming engineering changes

In addition, the system should have the following properties:

- A simplified approach to system installation should make it easy to install the system.
- A Web-based "Point and Click" graphic interface.
- A "wizard" to guide users in the systems operation.
- Ability to interface with legacy, MRP, and ERP systems.
- Cellular and mobile capabilities. Given that the system may generate alerts to participants of shortages, engineering changes or capacity problems, the system should be able to alert users via cell phones, pagers, faxes, or e-mail.
- Real-time updates. The system should be capable of updating inventory status on a real-time basis.
- Verification of information input to ensure accuracy. Wherever possible, the system should automate tasks, eliminating manual intervention.
- Alert notices for shortages, emergencies, bottlenecks, etc.

To illustrate the effect of a visibility system, let's consider a fictional example of a system with these properties in which a number of companies participate in a supply chain network. The companies in the example include Robots Inc. (a large OEM sponsoring the system), an application service provider (ASP), and several suppliers of Robot Inc. The system implementation involves defining "roles" for each of these parties, which in turn plays a part in associated levels of security and permissions. Different operations in implementing the system will require certain parties to be authorized for a particular role. For example, an access control list could specify which parties are allowed to edit a particular component in a Bill of Materials (BOM) or register for alerts.

Returning to our example, Robots Inc. wishes to provide an information visibility system that allows all suppliers in the supply chain to view orders. Robots Inc. contracts Application Service Provider (ASP) to deploy its product "SCView" and plays the role of sponsor and ultimate buyer. Thus, Robots Inc. has the ability to exercise the following system functionalities: Add Organization, Enter BOM, View Status, View Alerts, Create ECN, and Create Report (shown in Figure 9–6).

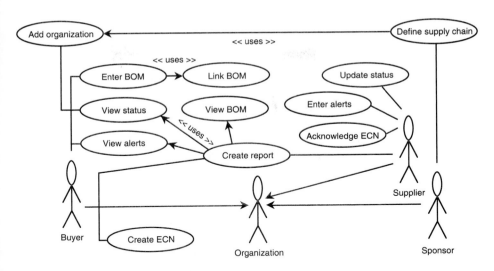

Figure 9–6 Supply Chain Visibility System

In this system, Robots Inc. is the ultimate buyer. Individual customers are not part of the information system, although end customer orders would be built into the ordering system via another system. Other companies in our example are Chassis Inc., Controls Inc., Gears and Motors Inc., and Wheels Inc. Robots Inc., in the role of buyer, will enter the BOM for a final end product (a robot). The BOM describes the different components that go into the product. In our example, this BOM will include a part line that has a number and description for a chassis. Robot Inc.'s BOM for the chassis includes all of the components that are provided by suppliers in the supply chain. First-tier suppliers, such as Chassis Inc., will also define the supply chain for their immediate suppliers. The system enables suppliers such as Chassis, Inc. to define the properties of their BOM, but also to trigger the following functionalities: Update Status, Enter Alerts, Acknowledge ECN, and Create Report (Figure 9–6). Examples of suppliers are Chassis Inc., Controls Inc., etc. as they play the role of suppliers of parts to Robots Inc. Notice that these organizations may also play the role of buyer (depending on where they are located in the supply network). In our example, Chassis Inc. plays the role of supplier of chassis to Robots Inc. Chassis Inc.'s BOM will be a breakdown of parts needed for its chassis. Robots Inc. is also the sponsoring organization, and in effect defines a supply chain to which all buyer roles and supplier roles will attach all entities such as BOMs, Alerts, Status, etc. The following scenario illustrates the functionality of the entire system and demonstrates how actions between members of the supply chain network take place.

Events in the Supply Chain

1. The Application Service Provider provides the software service SCView to organizations in multi-level supply chains.
2. Five organizations choose to participate in the SCView network, at three levels: ultimate buyer, first-level suppliers to the ultimate buyer (Tier-1 supplier), and second-level suppliers (Tier-2 suppliers).
3. The ultimate buyer, Robots Inc., sells a robot kit that consists of components in a pick list.
4. Robots Inc. provides a BOM to the ASP showing components and suppliers for production of the robot (note that in this case, Robots Inc. provides the kit packaging for the product):

Part Number	Qty	Description	Supplier
Doc-00001	1	Assembly and use instructions for the robot kit	Robots Inc.
Chas-00001	1	Mechanical parts of robot	Chassis Inc.
Sen-00001	2	Sensor package	Controls Inc.
Con-00001	1	Computer control module with interface kit	Controls Inc.
Pack-00001	1	Kit packaging	Robots Inc.

5. The representative from Robots Inc. enters this BOM information into the system.
6. The representative from Robots Inc. enters information for their suppliers and gives them permission to:
   - Enter BOMs
   - Enter suppliers
   - Enter alerts
   - Update status
   - Acknowledge ECNs
   - View reports

7. The suppliers and their information:

Supplier	Contact	E-mail	Supplier ID
Chassis Inc.	Bob M.	Bob@chassis.com	S-001
Sensors Inc.	Jim N.	Jim@sensors.com	S-002
Controls Inc.	Bill P.	Bill@controls.com	S-003

8. The representative from Chassis Inc. is notified that they are part of the software network. He receives information on how to access and use the Web site.

9. The representative from Chassis Inc. enters the following BOM:

Part Number	Qty	Description	Supplier
11-00001	1	Gear kit	Gears and Motors Inc.
11-00002	1	Plastic chassis	Chassis Inc.
11-00003	2	Main wheels	Wheels Inc.
11-00004	2	Secondary wheels	Wheels Inc.
11-00005	2	Electric motors	Gears and Motors Inc.

10. The representative from Controls Inc. is notified that they are part of the SCView network. He receives information on how to access and use the Web site.

11. The representative from Controls Inc. enters the following BOM:

Part Number	Qty	Description	Supplier
12-00001	2	Light sensors	Controls Inc.
12-00002	3	Touch sensors	Controls Inc.
13-00003	1	Control module	Controls Inc.
13-00004	1	Interface	Controls Inc.
13-00005	2	Installation hardware	Controls Inc.
13-00006	1	Control module documentation	Controls Inc.

12. The representative from Chassis Inc. enters information for their suppliers and gives them permission to:

- Enter BOMs
- Enter suppliers
- Enter alerts
- Update status

13. The suppliers and their information are:

Supplier	Contact	Email	Supplier ID
Wheels Inc.	Mary M.	mary@wheels.com	S-003
Gears and Motors Inc.	Sally N.	sally@gnm.com	S-004

14. There is no visibility into the supply chain beyond the organizations listed.

15. The quantities above establish the number of parts required as they propagate down the supply chain.

16. Robots Inc. makes an order for 1000 robots to be delivered by June 15, 2002. (We assume this order was previously negotiated under a blanket contract with suppliers outside of the system, and includes agreed on pricing, delivery cycle times, etc.).

17. Robots Inc. enters the order parameters into SCView Order:

Part Number	Qty	Description	Supplier	Delivery
Chas-00001	1000	Mechanical parts of robot	Chassis Inc.	06/15/2002
Sen-00001	2000	Sensor package	Controls Inc.	06/15/2002
Con-00001	1000	Computer control module with interface kit	Controls Inc.	06/15/2002

18. Representative from Chassis Inc. receives the order and does the following:
    - Calculates their part needs based on current inventory and allowances
    - Sends orders to their suppliers

19. Representative from Controls Inc. receives the order and does the following:
    - Calculates their part needs based on current inventory and failure rates
    - Does internal resource planning and allocation

20. Possible status of an order: No Status, Awaiting Shipment, Manufacturing, Shipped.

21. The default status for each organization is "No Status."

22. Representative from Robots Inc. updates status to "Awaiting Shipment" when order is made, 0 inventory.

23. Representative from Chassis Inc. updates status to "Manufacturing" and estimated ship date.

24. Representative from Chassis Inc. updates status to show plant running at 90 percent capacity this week, 0 inventory, 0 inventory in transit.

25. Representative from Controls Inc. finds that all items are in stock and processes the order immediately. Updates status to "Shipped," enters estimated in-transit time.

26. Representative from Controls Inc. has another order that is occupying plant capacity and has some inventory remaining. He then updates status to show plant running at 50 percent capacity this week, 1000 sensor packages and 250 control modules inventory, 2000 sensor packages and 1000 control modules in transit.

27. Representative from Robots Inc. views supply chain looking for status and alerts.

28. Representative from Gears and Motors Inc. updates status to "Awaiting Shipment" and enters an alert that their electric motor brush supplier lost a container in a hurricane in the Atlantic, delaying motor assembly for two weeks.

29. Representative from Robots Inc. receives e-mail on cell phone or pager containing notification of alerts in the supply chain.

30. Representative from Chassis Inc. receives e-mail on cell phone or pager containing notification of alerts in the supply chain.

31. Representative from Wheels Inc. checks status across the supply chain and decides to delay shipment of wheels for one week since Chassis Inc. will be delayed in shipping chassis.

32. Representative from Wheels Inc. updates status to "Inventory."

33. Representative from Wheels Inc. updates status to show plant at 95 percent capacity this week, 3500 Main wheels and 4500 Secondary wheels inventory, 0 inventory in transit.

34. Brushes arrive and Gears and Motors Inc. representative updates status to manufacturing and sets a second alert notifying that that brushes have arrived.

35. Representatives from Robots Inc., Chassis Inc., and Wheels Inc. receive e-mail notification that there are alerts in the supply chain.

36. Representative from Gears and Motors Inc. changes status to "Shipped."

37. Representative from Wheels Inc. changes status to "Shipped."

38. Representative from Chassis Inc. changes status to "Shipped."

39. Engineer at Robots Inc. changes wheel specification design.

40. Engineering change notice is communicated to Chassis Inc. and Wheels Inc. and scheduled to take place in two weeks.

The above scenario provides a sample set of the transactions that take place in a visibility system. A simple example showing actual quantities exchanged between participants in a supply chain (using different companies than the above scenario) is shown in Figure 9–7. This example assumes a

Acme Planning Data

			Company			Supplier		
Part Number	Qty	Supplier/Buyer	Needs	Order	Inventory	Plan Build	Plan Ship	Inventory
123	1	Best	200	200	25	200	200	50
345	2	Best	50	100	3	0	100	200

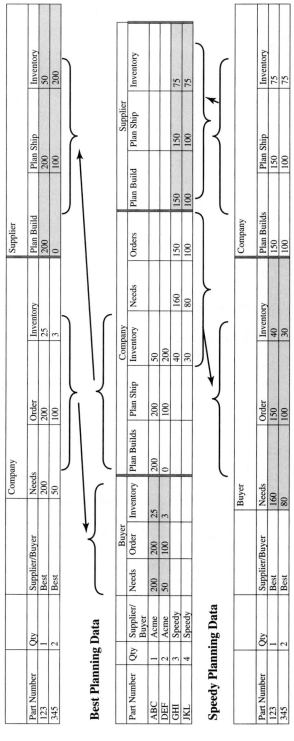

Best Planning Data

			Buyer			Company			Company			Supplier		
Part Number	Qty	Supplier/Buyer	Needs	Order	Inventory	Plan Builds	Plan Ship	Inventory	Orders	Needs	Inventory	Plan Build	Plan Ship	Inventory
ABC	1	Acme	200	200	25	200	200	50						
DEF	2	Acme	50	100	3	0	100	200						
GHI	3	Speedy							150	160	40	150	150	75
JKL	4	Speedy							100	80	30	100	100	75

Speedy Planning Data

			Buyer			Company		
Part Number	Qty	Supplier/Buyer	Needs	Order	Inventory	Plan Builds	Plan Ship	Inventory
123	1	Best	160	150	40	150	150	75
345	2	Best	80	100	30	100	100	75

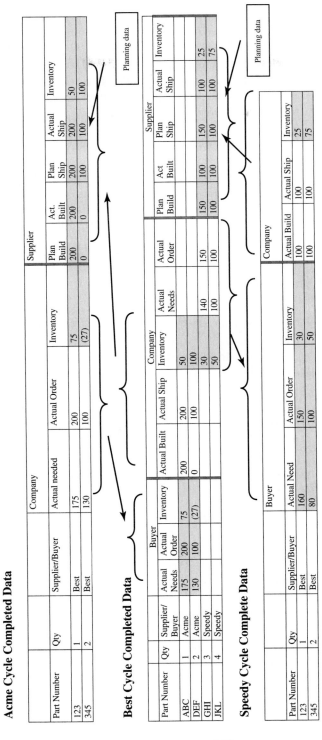

Figure 9–7 Example of Quantities Shipped in an Information Visibility-Enabled Supply Chain

three-company supply chain. Acme builds the final product, Best is a supplier to Acme and Speedy supplies to Best. The example shows the status of inventory and shortages before and after one planning cycle. This example effectively illustrates the importance of having all supply chain participants capable of understanding what orders and inventory levels are in the supply chain network.

Many leading companies, including Ford, Barnes & Noble, Hershey Foods, General Electric, Subaru, Eveready Battery, and the Swedish furniture retailer Ikea, have deployed various solutions to streamline supply chain operations.[11] The burst of user interest in supply chain visibility shows no sign of slowing. The ARC Advisory Group released a study estimating that the SCM software market will more than quadruple to $518 million by the end of 2005, growing at an annual rate of 33 percent.

Information Visibility System Best Practices[12]

The North Carolina State University Supply Chain Resource Consortium conducted a recent benchmarking study of information visibility best practices. The supply chains of various companies were examined through published literature and white papers on the Internet, in order to gain an understanding of effective practices in supply chain visibility. Development and deployment issues were also addressed. The benefits of supply chain visibility to these companies were identified and the methods and technology that enabled these benefits were outlined. The key results of this study are summarized in the following section.

Company Profiles

The six companies that participated in this study represented a variety of industries, including automotive, electronics contract manufacturing, computers, telecommunications, pharmaceuticals, and agricultural equipment. All the companies questioned operated on an international scale with multiple facilities worldwide, making information visibility across the entire supply chain difficult. In addition, the companies had multiple suppliers shipping to a limited number of receiving locations making the visibility of accurate information across the supply chain critical for planning and controlling materials. All of the companies had a high material spend ranging from $425 million to $80 billion annually. The companies had at least two suppliers for differentiated parts, and maintained between one and eight contacts per supplier depending on importance.

Insource or Outsource System Development?

All the companies had outsourced their SCM software systems. Outsourcing this type of system is common, given the investment required to develop a "homegrown" system. All companies used long-term system contracts incorporating clauses stipulating future upgrades and changes. Every company had a process in place for benchmarking and evaluating existing B2B supply chain software. Conducting a detailed industry analysis is absolutely necessary prior to committing to a system. All respondants compared their system to the systems of other companies, both in and out of their industry.

It is extremely costly and time consuming to develop an information sharing system in-house, which is why companies should look for existing systems that can be modified to address company specific requirements. Developing the software in-house is not a core competency for most companies; it not only ties up critical resources, but also diverts the company from its core activities. Today there are many different software packages for information sharing across the supply chain, such as I-Supply by Supply Solutions, Trade Matrix by i2, Visibility Solutions by Manugistics, and emerging solutions being developed by the major ERP providers such as SAP and Oracle. Most companies seeking to deploy information visibility solutions outsource software system and create a long-term relationship with an Application Service Provider (ASP).

All but one of the companies pilot tested their systems followed by parallel conversion and full system integration. The primary barriers to system implementation included lack of technical expertise and compatibility with suppliers, internal resistance, and the lack of standards in technology. In response to these problems, most of the companies have relied on strong top management support for the system early in the process. By far the biggest problem faced by companies is incompatible supplier systems. Many smaller suppliers rely on outdated legacy systems that are often not even networked within their own organizations. In some cases, organizations reduced their supply base to eliminate suppliers who were not prepared to invest in new compatible systems.

Most of the companies noted that their visibility system has proven to be reliable. However, all had nevertheless installed a backup system in the event of a system failure. Many of these systems operate independently of existing ERP systems, since data integration across multiple facilities with different legacy systems is a major constraint. In all the companies, most of the information was updated on a regular basis and the systems performed all expected tasks, including issuing warnings and alarms if a shortage was imminent. The companies were using RosettaNet, EDI, or XML as a communication platform.

What Information Should Be Shared?

For each category of information to be shared with suppliers, representatives from each of the benchmarked companies ranked the importance of the information on a 1 to 5 scale, with 5 being the most important. An average of the results is shown in Table 9–8.

The information deemed most critical to share with suppliers by the benchmarked companies included material releases, material requirements, inventory, order status, sales forecast, rejection of order and quality specifications. Non-critical information included material budgets, acknowledgment of order, payment, and manufacturing capacity. Identifying the information that should be shared is an important decision that has to be made very early in the development process. In not including the proper information, it becomes increasingly difficult and costly to add functionality as the system progresses through the development process. However, systems efforts can often grow to epic proportions if individual users are given unlimited opportunities to add customized requirements. This can result in the cost of the project exceeding the initial budget projections well before the system is implemented, leading, in some cases, to termination of the project. An electronics industry executive noted that the disadvantages of customizing visibility systems to meet every user requirement were system complexity and the associated expense. He noted that organizations are better served by deciding on a limited set of variables that are considered standard in a package, thereby obtaining 85 percent of the desired functionality without adding expensive customization.

Industry standards in the area of information sharing dictate sharing of the following information: maximum capacity, lead-times, forecasts, purchase orders (POs), blanket contracts, demand pull releases, PO change orders, advanced shipping notices, invoices and identification of bottlenecks. Because these represent only the major items that should be shared with suppliers, it is our recommendation to use these as a minimum starting point for deciding what information should be included in the visibility system.

The ability to track deliveries from suppliers needs to directly correlate with the importance of the supplier and their distance from the plant. If delivery lead-times are relatively short, then sharing shipping and delivery information is not a high priority. However, if suppliers are located around the globe sharing shipping and delivery information becomes extremely important.

Establishing performance measurements, such as on-time delivery and quantity discrepancies, is essential to any company. An information visibility system not only facilitates collecting performance measurements, but also allows sharing this information with suppliers. Communicating closely within this area makes both the supplier and the buyer aware of any existing problems and facilitates problem solving. Performance measurement is a critical element in creating a high-performing value system. Sharing performance measurement information and working with the suppliers on improvement initiatives is a much better approach than looking for new suppliers every time a problem occurs. Respondents indicated that the greatest benefits would come from sharing past due orders, planned receipts versus due dates, items likely to become past due, quantity discrepancies, and predetermined performance criteria versus outcomes. One can also share financial data, such as invoices and acknowledgement of payments over this system. This should result in cost savings and the ability to tie a supplier's financial data and responsiveness to their overall supplier rating.

Who Should Participate and What Information Should They Be Allowed to See?

One of the key concerns of a company about to implement information visibility software is the reach of the system into the supply chain network; should the system extend beyond Tier-One suppliers into Tier-Two and beyond? Managers in our study didn't think so. Managers generally responded that the importance of information sharing beyond Tier-One is negligible in maintaining an efficient and valuable information network. This is due to the fact that the suppliers, which represent the majority of a company's purchases, are in Tier-One. However, most of the companies did not dictate what information their Tier-One suppliers should share with their suppliers. Managers also noted that Tier-One suppliers should be proactive in sharing information with their Tier-Two suppliers, but that it was not the responsibility of an OEM to fund this effort. Some of the companies also experienced resistance from the suppliers due to the complexity of integration, lack of technical expertise, and the costs involved.

What Are The Required System Capabilities

Before a visibility system can be implemented, various systems need to be researched and benchmarked to find which system is best to support a particular supply chain. Benchmarking needs to be done inside the industry in question

Table 9–8 Ranking of Content Shared in Visibility Systems

Ranking of Shared Content Importance

Criteria	Telecom	Pharm	Auto	Elec	Elec	Agr. Equip.	Average
Material releases	5	5	5	5	5	5	5.0
Material requirements	5	5	5	5	5	4	4.8
Inventory	4	5				5	4.7
Order status	4	5			3	5	4.3
Advanced shipping notice	4	5	5	4	3	5	4.3
Sales forecasts	5	3	5			4	4.3
Quality specifications	1	5	5	5	5	5	4.3
Rejection of order	5	5			5	2	4.3
Quantity discrepancies	4	5	4	3	5	4	4.2
Shipment status	4	5	4	4	3	5	4.2
Invoices	1	5	5	4	4	5	4.0
Current inventory–supplier	3	5		4		4	4.0
Purchase orders	4	5	2	5	5	3	4.0
Rejection of delivery	4	5			3	4	4.0
Product specifications	1	5	4	4	5	5	4.0
Engineering changes	1	5	5	3	5	4	3.8
Scheduled receipts	1	5		4	5	4	3.8
Planned receipts vs. due dates	4	5		3	4	3	3.8
Transportation mode	3	5	4	3	4	3	3.7
Current inventory–your company	1	5	4			4	3.5
Payment order	1	5			4	4	3.5
Order acceptance	3	5			4	2	3.5
Past due orders	3	5	4	2	5	2	3.5
Shipping method	1	5	4	3	4	3	3.3
Acceptance of delivery	1	5				4	3.3
Predetermined performance criteria vs. outcome	1	5	3		4	3	3.2
Request for quotes	1	5	4	3	3	3	3.2
Tracking shipment	1	5	3	3		4	3.2
Manufacturing lead-times	2	1	3	3	5	4	3.0
Acknowledgment of payment	1	1	5		3	4	2.8
Manufacturing capacity	1	1	4	3	4	4	2.8
Order acknowledgement	2	5		2	3	2	2.8
Items likely to become past-due	5	1	3		2	3	2.8
Material budgets	1	1				3	1.7

as well as in other industries. The system should be easy to upgrade since today's business environment is constantly changing. It should also be user-friendly and operate in real-time.

The system should be able to create reports including, but not limited to, present production rate, inventory, inventory in transit, and bottlenecks in the system. It should include a warning system to provide an alert for events such as materials shortage, interruptions in production, and late shipments. On average, it will take anywhere from three months to a year before the system is fully implemented and operating efficiently.

System Implementation

The three main ways to implement a new system are the parallel, plunge, and pilot approaches. In a parallel approach, the two systems (old and new) are run in parallel, and the old system is gradually phased out. In the plunge approach, the new system is activated after testing. A pilot conversion is when the new system is first implemented on a limited scale and then expanded to the full operation. A pilot conversion proves the functionality of the system and demonstrates the feasibility of full-scale implementation. A pilot conversion will also be cheaper to correct if it is not up and running throughout the company. Most of our benchmarking companies carried out a pilot followed by a parallel conversion.

In order for the system to be implemented, company-wide support is needed. Systems implementation efforts are costly and time-consuming events. Top management support is mandatory. Internal support in implementing the new software system is crucial if any problems occur. Having support from managers providing updates on progress and regular meetings will help to facilitate the transition.

Most of the companies interviewed were very flexible and did not have to change suppliers because of their new system. The only technical barrier was that some suppliers lacked a Web browser. Compatibility with suppliers is a necessary condition for implementing a visibility system. The best solutions to an information sharing system today are Web-based, which means barriers such as cost and extremely advanced technology are slowly disappearing. An EDI system is not necessary when using a SCM software system. However, factors like the importance to the end product and volume of parts supplied should continue to be evaluated in addition to the basic system requirements when identifying which suppliers should be included in the system.

A recent study of a major airline's top 100 suppliers, completed by the Supply Chain Resource Consortium, revealed that suppliers generally fall into one of four categories when it comes to evaluating technical readiness for adopting a visibility system.[13] As presented in Figure 9–9, the results of the study found that suppliers can generally be classified as one of the following types:

- Early Adopters (14 percent of population)—most likely to adopt new visibility technologies
- Early Majority (35 percent of population)—likely to follow early adopters once they see that the system works
- Late Majority (27 percent of population)—may adopt the new technology, but very slowly
- Laggards (24 percent of population)—unlikely to adopt any new technology under most circumstances.

The results also suggest that assessing a supplier's learning orientation is a good way to identify potential partners for inclusion in a visibility system. Moreover, companies should pilot their systems with the early adopters and early majority, learn from these early pilots, and apply these lessons to the late majority and laggards in later phases. In some cases, laggards may need to be replaced by other suppliers, or business re-allocated to the early adopters/late majority.

What are the Internal Company Criteria Required for Functionality of the System?

The appropriate level of information visibility within the company depends on the needs of the company and the industry in which it operates. Once information visibility requirements have been determined, managers should evaluate different types of systems while focusing on the functionality of each system. Functionality is crucial to the success of any supply chain. Critical system functionality areas include inventory accuracy, forecasting accuracy, and production scheduling stability. Participating companies in the study deemed these functions to be extremely important. When sharing inventory information through a real-time system, accuracy of inventory levels reported is paramount. The system should be able to accurately share information on what is actually taking place in the supply chain. The following requirements are addressed in the systems used by our partner companies: addition of suppliers, creation of reports, enter/view status of materials, and enter/view alerts. Also, implementing a system that supports real-time access is a *must*.

Adopter Categorization on the Basis of Relative Time of Adoption of Innovations

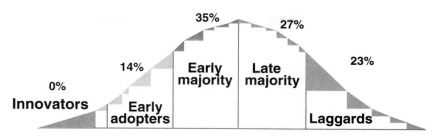

Time of adoption of innovations

Figure 9–9   Adoption of Visibility Systems (Zahay and Handfield, 2001)

Collaborative Planning, Forecasting, and Replenishment (CPFR)

CPFR is a set of guidelines established by the Voluntary Inter-industry Commerce Standards (VICS) Association (http://www.cpfr.org); implementing these guidelines changes the way supply chains work. Through effective information sharing across the supply chain and following the CPFR guidelines, organizations can lower costs and greatly improve customer service. Most companies do a reasonable job of forecasting aggregate annual demand for their products and services. However, it becomes extremely difficult, for example, to predict the correct amount of a specific product required at a particular store on the second "Monday" of a given month. The CPFR methodology focuses on improving this situation.

Of all of the promising applications that the Internet holds, collaborative forecasting is probably one of the most important. Why? The effect of poor forecasting at the customer level has a direct relationship to the bullwhip effect that occurs throughout the supply chain. This lesson was painfully learned in the telecommunications industry in early 2001 as this next case study illistrates.

How did executives in the telecom industry get their forecasts so wrong? In November of 2000, Merrill Lynch and Co. predicted that domestic equipment purchases by phone and data carriers would grow by 15 percent, to over $65 billion, in 2001. Now, the brokerage firm believes such purchases will fall 7 percent during 2002.[14]

Although Cisco is often referenced as the company that had the greatest shortfall, others also fell into the same trap. In 2000, Nortel Networks estimated that it would spend $1.9 billion to boost production and add 9,000 jobs to meet "explosive customer demand." Instead, Nortel cut over 30,000 jobs and lost $19 billion in the second quarter of 2001. What happened? The blame lies, in part, with the calculations used to predict future sales along with high inventory levels of telecommunications equipment. Even Nortel Chief Executive John Roth, in April 2001, chided his own company's demand forecasting methods after he chopped 2001 expectations. "As recently as October of last year, all the conversations I was having with my customers were, 'John, you haven't shipped me enough equipment yet, when are you going to get the volume up?'" Mr. Roth said "The people we did not talk to in our customers were the treasurers, who found out in January that they were having difficulty in raising the money to pay for the equipment."

Frederick Fromm, president of Oplink Communications, Inc., a Nortel supplier, says his company's forecasts over the last few years were based mainly on informal conversations with customers. "Quite openly, our forecast was that demand was exceeding our capacity, so let's build capacity as fast as we can." At the same time, many telecommunications companies had fewer experts available to forecast demand. David Loomis, an Illinois State University Professor, estimates that equipment makers and telecommunications carriers fired half of their forecasting employees over the last five years, chiefly for cost-cutting reasons. Clearly, such forecasting expertise seems necessary in an industry undergoing the turmoil of deregulation and lacking many of the government statistics and research methods used in other businesses. However, many telecommunication companies really had no formal forecasting process in place. They rely mainly on feedback from their sales forces and are influenced by the dozen or so research houses that regularly publish estimates. This time, however, as the parade of earnings warnings and restructurings by telecommunications equipment manufacturers illustrates, "You're basing guesses on guesses and that multiplies the ability to get it wrong," says Tim Stronge, research director at TeleGeography Inc., which publishes telecommunications statistics. And the future looks even more uncertain: "We're all riding this massive storm, and no one really knows where we're going," says John Ryan, of RHK, a telecommunications research firm.

Cisco has already taken steps to ensure that such a mistake doesn't occur again. Cisco is developing a new forecasting tool called eHub, which is designed to eliminate the need for human intervention. The system automates the flow of information between Cisco, its contract manufacturers, and its component suppliers. The key ingredient is a technology called a Partner Interface Process, or PIP. A PIP is a chunk of code that sits on the back end of a company's enterprise system and dictates the way it will exchange data and documents with other firms in the supply chain. When a demand forecast PIP is sent out, showing cumulative orders, that forecast goes not only to contract manufacturers but also to chipmakers such as Philips Semiconductors and Altera. "Before, when contract manufacturers such as Celestica, Flextronics, and Solectron all came to Philips at the same time and said they wanted 10,000 of a certain chip, that was a total of 30,000 chips," says one senior engineer. "Now, Philips can say, 'Hold on, I'm on eHub. I know that total aggregated demand is only 10,000."

Without a focused process for creating forecasts between partners in the supply chain, these types of errors are likely to occur again. A number of software packages claim to provide shared forecasts across the supply chain. These packages include various ERP (enterprise resource planning) and APS (advanced planning and scheduling) systems. But the drawback of these packages is that they tend to be internally focused. An ERP system does little to make information available across the extended supply chain. ERP alone is not an answer to effective real-time information sharing. Let us assume that information is available across the supply chain at a particular time, but that information is not current and circumstances have changed dramatically but have not been effectively communicated. The result is a mismatch among the participants in the supply chain, which typically leads to unwanted inventory or unwarranted stock outs. For this reason, collaborative planning and forecasting applications *must* be made on a real-time basis.

Single Forecast–Developed and Shared Across All Groups

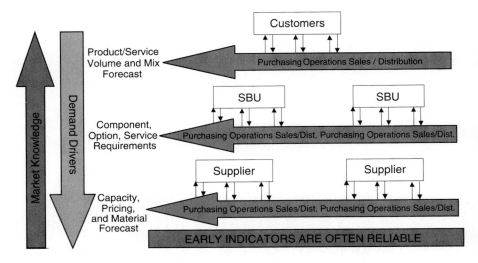

Figure 9–10   Single Forecast—Developed and Shared Across all Groups

It is a well-known fact that every forecast is always wrong. However, it is less well known that when forecasts are shared across multiple functions, strategic business units, and customer/supplier tiers, they are more useful (see Figure 9–10). Why? By identifying possible exceptions and allowing many different people to provide their perceptions of the situation, the end result is greater forecast accuracy.

Visibility of end customer option penetration and service requirements is often retained by OEMs, yet can dramatically reduce inventory costs and obsolescence in the supply chain. Suppliers can also be instrumental in providing critical capacity, material shortages, pricing, and market knowledge that can also benefit end customers. Research also exists to suggest that data collected in new product pilots during the first ten weeks is often very reliable. However, to get the full benefit from this information it must be shared across the supply chain.

Understanding the factors that drive demand is of paramount importance in demand planning. Most important is end demand and product mix. When measured at an aggregate level, there often appear to be few patterns, and a wide mix of Stock Keeping Units (SKUs) or customer requirements. Upon closer analysis, however, companies may be able to derive different underlying patterns of demand. A typical pattern often emerges, even across industries.

- Using the "80-20 rule," we typically find that a small number of products/SKUs/ service requirements constitute a very large proportion of the total volume of demand. In many cases, demand variations from month to month are not significant. In the automotive industry, for example, a significant proportion of automobile production volume goes to rental agencies such as Hertz, Alamo, Avis, and Enterprise. Demand from these outlets is relatively stable throughout the year.
- A larger proportion of SKUs (30 percent) exhibits a greater volatility–yet is still manageable. In our automotive example, a second category of business is for off-lease demand. Automobile companies know when an individual's lease is ending and can contact the individual ahead of time to determine if he/she is interested in another lease or purchase. Demand for these vehicles is seasonal, yet aggregate levels can be predicted through better customer management.
- The most volatile items are those that represent the least amount of volume, are the most difficult to forecast, yet are potentially profitable. Once you understand where this volatility lies, you can position capacity and upside/downside flexibility to be able to respond to these requirements if needed. If this demand is not profitable, the solution is even simpler: you don't need this business! In the automotive industry, the area showing the greatest volatility is for end customer demand at dealer lots, and especially in the build-to-order web-based channel, which is a small but growing segment. To fulfill customer demand for this segment, automobile companies need to be able to respond quickly to web-based orders by enabling suppliers to sense demand for these items throughout the supply chain.

The rise of the Internet led people to believe that information could be made available to all supply chain participants via company Web sites. Companies rushed to establish a Web presence that typically was presenting static information. The inability to have real-time information did not help any participant in the supply chain. Amazon.com has been successful in extending its ERP package to the consumer so that people can go on-line and order anytime they want. By extending the ERP solution, Amazon did get a sense of the customer demand, but most likely this information did not flow to all participants in the supply chain. If this had been the case Amazon.com would be able to give its customer's precise ship dates rather than the more general statement "normally ships within two to three days." To give information like "will reach you in two days at this time" requires collaboration among the various participants (suppliers, manufacturers, distributors, etc.) in the supply chain.

Collaboration is not about merely having a Web presence, and it does not entail ordering on-line. In fact CPFR is about all participants in a supply chain (suppliers/manufacturers/wholesalers/retailers/customers) sharing information real-time with information regarding inventory position, change in demand levels, upgraded forecasts, and other relevant information.

Collaboration is about synchronization of consumer trends and forecasting suggested orders. If all the participants in a particular supply chain discovered that a change in demand patterns was about to occur, they could take appropriate actions (slow down or ramp up supply) to minimize adverse effects was felt in the chain (see Figure 9–10). The requirements are that information is supplied real-time, global, in a secure manner, and simultaneously. Unfortunately, this is a tough requirement to fulfill. However, the CPFR methodology absolutely requires that the customer commit to being involved in developing the forecast from the outset. This, in turn, requires that a serious dialogue on the nature of demand occur between the customer and the supplier. If a supplier does not understand its customer, it will do a poor job in forecasting—this will have a ripple effect along the supply chain. Trust is a stumbling block that often needs to be overcome for CPFR to be successful. Companies are reluctant to open up their internal systems to their trading partners because they fear that sensitive company information will be shared beyond the trading partners. This hurdle can be overcome by having legal agreements among all involved.

Benefits of CPFR

The CPFR methodology has been very successful in a number of companies. Some of the organizations that piloted CPFR methodologies included:

- Wal-Mart and Sara Lee
- Nabisco and Wegmans
- Kimberly-Clark and K-Mart

Early results of CPFR pilot programs have been extremely encouraging. For instance, exchanging information such as forecast and replenishment data with supply partners allowed Wal-Mart to achieve significant improvements in fill rates and customer satisfaction. After 24 weeks in operation, the following results were achieved:

- Two percent improvement in retail store in-stock.
- A 14 percent reduction of in-store inventory while increasing sales 32 percent.

- An increase of 17 percent in retail turns on the pilot items.

Nabisco also achieved impressive results from its CPFR pilot from July 1998 through January 1999. These include:

- An increase in category sales by 13 percent compared to an eight percent decline for other retailers in the market.
- Sales increases for the Planters brand were especially dramatic at 53 percent as measured for 30 weeks ending January 17, 1999.
- The majority of the increases in retail sales were attributed to jointly developed business plans that leveraged enhanced category management strategies and increased category focus.
- Service level to stores increased from 93 percent to 97 percent.
- Days of inventory was reduced by 2.5 days (18 percent).

These results were achieved with minimal stress on the supply chain owing to CPFR. As can be seen from these results, the benefits from CPFR can be significant. The reason behind these results is really quite simple: sales increased for products because the products were simply on the shelf more often! In fact, other research in the grocery industry reveals that on average, many SKUs have a stockout rate of 15 percent on any given weekend, which results in lost sales. Anyone who has visited a grocery store on a Sunday evening has experienced this phenomenon!

Future Applications of CPFR

Companies may begin CPFR as a pilot with a single trading partner to demonstrate the value proposition. A number of food and consumer packaged goods companies have piloted and are in the process of implementing CPFR. CPFR certainly does not represent the end of supply chain redesign. Visionaries will drive the movement in new directions and will take advantage of state of the art technology. In the future, we may see "portals" that are able to identify and negotiate planned promotions, new product introductions, inventory policy changes, and store openings and closings. Such portals would enable companies to forecast demand, allocate demand to selected suppliers, calculate replenishment plans, authorize shipment, organize loads, select routes, and track shipments to delivery. Portals will be linked to different information sources, starting with consumer-surveys and range to weather forecasts and road conditions to select the best delivery routes. Today, this may sound somewhat futuristic, but the technologies are available and it is just a matter of time before organizations take advantage of them.

Collaborative Contract Management Visibility Systems

An emerging area critical to supply chain relationships is contract management. A team often negotiates contracts governing global commodity agreements, yet the participants in the supply chain often do not have visibility of these agreements. Nowhere is this more critical than in relationships in the high-tech industry between OEM manufacturers, contract manufacturers, and component suppliers. Participants must be able to understand and determine compliance to contracts, as well as the key visibility points and customer requirements. One company that is helping to make this work is Accordus, a start-up company that has developed a collaborative contract management system.

To illustrate the benefits of a collaborative contracting system, consider the following situation. Cisco makes a commitment to buy X dollars of components from various smaller suppliers at different specifications as presented in their statement of work. This commitment is based on a broad-level master agreement negotiated with a contract manufacturer. For example, the master agreement might contain the following information:

- Plus or minus 10 percent on forecast—90-10 percent risk split (Contract Manufacturer bears 10 percent risk)
- Turnaround time—notification of changes to contract within a time period
- Freeze dates to master production schedule and cost overruns on changes within freeze rates
- Liability issues—inventory held against forecast orders
- Negotiations with their own suppliers against their supplier's lead-times
- Commodities (low risk) versus designed-in components
- Price protection (against change orders—given percentage)

The broad master agreements generally only cover capacity requirements in sales dollars, but do not allocate capacity to specific product lines. The implications of these contract terms are far-reaching. In early 2001, Cisco wrote off $2.5 billion in inventory—this included only committed contracts to suppliers. However, interviews with industry executives suggest that another $5 billion in "deferred commitments" to contract manufacturers and other suppliers have not been reported. The downturn means that these parties must hold on to large amounts of inventory that are diminishing in value rapidly owing to technological obsolescence.[15]

Master agreements are used to establish broad-level issues—companies buy based on these agreements. Hedging and liability exists. Companies need to establish floors with their subcontractors—and therefore must have contracts in place to cover Cisco contracts. When the economic downturn hit the telecommunications companies, all of the master agreements were broken simultaneously. In addition, multiple master agreements may exist between OEM and contract manufacturers. OEMs may also have collaborative master agreements with many contract manufacturers. In addition, the engineering master agreement, which identifies design specifications, should be able to be moved and shared collaboratively to allow all parties access.

As part of the master agreements, a sub-agreement with particular parameters is tracked as a service level agreement (SLA) with a bill of materials. An SLA includes the:

- Bill of material (BOM)
- Price
- Forecast quantity
- Flexibility plus or minus percent within that price range
- Product level performance (testing, QA, etc.)
- Turnaround time—based on lead-times
- Supply base specifications (directed sourcing)
- On-time shipments, "dead on arrival," etc. definitions
- Engineering changes—transaction levels

Note that BOM's frequently change and are substituted over time. Eventually, a "gold" design occurs, which essentially means a frozen product. Subsequent changes become more expensive. Once launched, the design will change only in rare cases, if the change will improve the product; existing product will be transitioned and the change phased in.

Collaborative contract management approaches provide visibility of key contractual terms to all parties. The collaborative contract can be dynamically updated as the terms and conditions change. Over the course of a negotiation, these systems track changes to the contract, and the underlying reasons why. All key parties, including operations, purchasing, and finance, can obtain required information. This is a powerful tool for finance, as it allows the monitoring of the organization's exposure and liability within the supply chain. Contract manufacturers essentially "live and die" based on the "float" (e.g. difference between incoming revenue and outgoing payments) in their supply chain and must therefore control the degree of risk via their inventory hedges. While the balance sheet only tracks accounts payables and receivables, an organization's actual commitments extend to the master agreements, which do not appear on the books. By having access to contracts in place, organizations can better manage their liability, operations executives can manage exceptions and conflicts that occur owing to changes in terms, and purchasing can better manage compliance to global contracts. Collaborative contractual visibility is a function that is only beginning to emerge in current supply chain systems, but holds significant potential.

Deploying Information Visibility Systems: A Case Example

The following is a case example addressing the deployment of an information visibility system, as described by a large first-tier multi-plant global supplier to the automotive industry interviewed by the authors.

Motivation for Investment

We were looking for a tool that gets our company and its supply chain connected via the Internet. We needed to align our supply chain with a simple tool to get our feet wet, and start to prepare for the new automotive supply chain that will produce the 10-day car. Information will need to be shared quickly to establish a supply chain to support a one-piece flow. The initial tool is expected to provide the following functionality:

- Suppliers and our company will view the same information
- Inventory status, schedules, history of transactions displayed
- Reporting capability
- Alerts to exceptions
- Communicate replenishment triggers
- Supplier ratings
- Next generation for EDI
- Logistics information

Some of the benefits we hoped to achieve by implementing the system included:

- Increased customer satisfaction
- Supply chain flexibility
- Decreased inventory
- Decreased number of expediting activities
- Decreased production interruptions or changes
- Increased focus on collaboration and proactive activities

Implementation

The implementation process consisted of a series of stages. Several software vendors were initially reviewed. We chose to pilot with one, and then a second. The possibility of developing the software internally was also considered. The criteria that we used to select the vendor involved several issues. First, we were looking for a provider that wanted to have a relationship with us. We want to use our knowledge of supply chain management to improve the product to benefit us as well as other participants across the supply chain. As a result, cost is a major factor in determining the level of our relationship with our knowledge and their product. We always perform a pilot to let the provider and us test the product and its value proposition. Another key area for us to consider is the service level that is provided. We now look at Application Services Providers as a viable option to lessen the load of our internal IT staff. Finally, we decided to proceed with the pilot. We piloted six sites and about 50 suppliers. After a month, we added three other sites with the same suppliers. Our second pilot used the same plants with some new suppliers and some in common with the original pilot. Several criteria were used to select initial internal customer and supplier participants:

Internal:

- Some plants wanted to participate in the pilot, because they were interested in influencing the decision for the system, wanted to gain early benefits, and support the SCM initiative.
- Other plants were chosen because of our desire to have all customers covered, the plant needed improvements, and we wanted to have a few levels in the supply chain. We were not going to just pilot software. Our interest was in learning about the value of visibility, understand the business process gaps at the plants, and monitor many key performance indicators.

Suppliers:

- Suppliers who wanted to be involved did so in order to be on the front end to influence the business process
- We decided to use a cross section of suppliers (good and poor performers, complicated and simple products, multiple locations, varying shipment frequency, etc.)

Pilot Program

In our pilot, we implemented the system in two to four weeks, but it really takes a month or so to get the business processes adjusted and the users familiar with the software. The amount of training required varied at each location. We utilized centralized training sessions where it was applicable. Otherwise, we used site training sessions, and some one-on-one sessions. It was a requirement to have hands on training with all of the individual users in every situation. The outcome of doing so is that everyone in the organization saw the value of information visibility in its simplest form. We realized that a tool is only as good as the business process execution in the plant and the standardization and acceptance of the process across plants. We also learned that one replenishment method would not work in all situations. Rather, it is better to have several different methods that are executed the same way across the organization. We also recognized that there were entrenched manual processes (e.g., releases and ship schedules) in the suppliers' business processes that would be difficult to change.

Supplier Selection

We decided to implement the system across multiple tiers of suppliers in some cases. There are some commodities where information must be shared down the supply chain—fabrics, leather, electronics. Those are where we send more information down the chain and provide more information in general. We explicitly specified to our Tier-1 suppliers what information they would have to supply to their Tier-1 (our Tier-2) suppliers.

Determining the right person to receive the information at each company was tricky. We try to communicate at several levels when we want to make sure the message gets across. Not surprisingly, we encountered resistance across many of the different tiers of suppliers. Suppliers were comfortable with the way things have been done in the past and what we had told them to do they did without questioning. With the new technology, they have the responsibility to make decisions for their company, and that has not always been an easy transition.

Barriers and Solutions

We encountered many barriers along the way, but were able to overcome them. These barriers and solutions included:

- **Barrier:** Lack of technical expertise in suppliers. *Solution:* The pilot system was fairly simple, and we had the provider as well as our IT resources provide assistance.
- **Barrier:** Internal resistance. **Solution:** Internal resistance was addressed by saying that this is a pilot and that we want to learn about the software, but also want to determine where our business processes are out of line. In addition, participants were given the opportunity to have input into the system requirements up front.
- **Barrier:** Lack of internal resources. **Solution:** Lack of internal resources was addressed by trying to prove with the pilot that with this new business process, fewer resources would be required. However, this is a constant battle—lack of resources will be a huge issue if we look down the road at full implementation of the system.
- **Barrier:** Lack of top management support/understanding. **Solution:** We had to do several knowledge-sharing events with our leadership group and some one-on-one sessions as well. We also provide frequent updates on the status. This helps to keep executives up to speed on the progress and prevents problems from occurring.
- **Barrier:** Lack of standards in the technology. **Solution:** We do not use a common platform across the company. This was our biggest challenge. Different business processes are used across plant locations and within our plants. Training helped to solve this problem.

Lessons Learned

Several lessons learned from this pilot implementation included the following:

- Top-down support is absolutely critical. People will not participate initially unless they are told to do so.
- Involvement from all levels of the organization will also help people to participate (functional, business unit leadership, and plant leadership).
- Current systems transactions processes are not adequate—new ones need to be developed.
- Business process execution must be in place. Without a good business process that is executed in a consistent manner, the best system in the world will not solve your problems.

Conclusion

Clearly, implementing supply chain visibility systems is a major undertaking. These systems are expensive and quantifying the return on such investments is not as simple as one might think. Issues surrounding justification of system costs include identifying the assumptions on potential benefits, as well as the length of time required to achieve these benefits. In addition, companies must carefully define who the supply chain partners are they wish to share information with, the level of commitment of these parties to becoming part of the solution, and the benefits of visibility versus the costs of implementation. Clearly, not every member of a supply chain will become part of a visibility solution. Issues that also must be considered include the technology provider, the types of information to be provided, security of information flows, and alignment of information with existing business processes. Information visibility is clearly much more than a simple technology that can be purchased and installed. It requires true collaboration and understanding of all parties regarding their responsibilities, service level commitments, and contingency plans when things go wrong. Most importantly, it is clear that a major critical success factor involves having support from top management from the outset. By ensuring that these ingredients are in place before attempting to deploy information visibility systems, the likelihood of success for all parties increases significantly.

End Notes

[1] Hau L. Lee, V. Padmanabhan, and Seungjin Whang, "The Bullwhip Effect in Supply Chains," Sloan Management Review, Spring 1997, pp. 93–102.

[2] Ibid.

[3] Ibid.

[4] Ira Lewis and Alexander Talalayevsky, "Logistics and Information Technology: A Coordination Perspective," Journal of Business Logistics, 18, No. 1, (1997), pp. 141–157.

[5] Ibid.

[6] This section is based on a benchmarking report developed by the following associates of the Supply Chain Resource Consortium: Steven Edwards, Robert Handfield, Meenakshi Lakshman, Michel Dialo and a number of undergraduate supply chain management students at North Carolina State University.

[7] S.J. Cole, S.D. Woodring, H. Chun, and J. Gatoff, 'Dynamic Trading Networks', *The Forrester Report*, January 1999.

[8]Nicole Lewis, "Valuechain.Dell.Com Provides Pipeline to Info Exchange." Dell Portal Adds 'Value.' CMP Media Inc., 2001.

[9]Ibid.

[10]www.supplysolutions.com

[11]Supply-chain visibility boosts bottom line," *InfoWorld* 5/21/01, www. itworld.com

[12]This section is based on a benchmarking report developed by the following associates of the Supply Chain Resource Consortium: Steven Edwards, Robert Handfield, Meenakshi Lakshman, Michel Dialo and a number of SCM undergraduate students at North Carolina State University.

[13]Debra Zahay and Robert Handfield, "The Role of Learning in Adoption of B2B Technologies," working paper, North Carolina State University, March, 2002.

[14]Paul Kaihla, "Inside Ciscos $2 Billion Blunder," *Business 2.0*, March 2002, pp. 88-90.

[15]Based on interviews conducted by Robert Handfield with electronics industry executives, September, 2001.

10

Managing Change in the Supply Chain: Lessons from General Motors

Rick Calabra at GM Revisited

Rick Calabra[1] had spent some time with Mountainview, one of GM's key suppliers of electronic components.[2] Michael Mitchell, Mountainview's General Manager, described some current supply chain issues that his company needs to resolve with GM. Mountainview has increased its business with GM from $50 million in 1996, to $90 million in 2000, and is projected to reach $140 million by 2006. Of this amount in 2005, close to $60 million will be a directed source, which is a significant increase in the proportion of models. "Directed source" means that Mountainview will be supplying a first-tier supplier (such as an interior module assembler) that will insert the components, ship them to GM, and pay Mountainview directly. The first-tier supplier is required to use Mountainview, hence the term "directed source." Mountainview has no desire to build complete assemblies, but wishes to focus on components. However, they will consider producing subsystems.

One of the first opportunities for improvement discussed was in design standardization. Mitchell brought out a set of three components that are used on different GM platforms; they appear almost identical. Although Mountainview does not make the plastic outer knobs, it does produce the population of components, and they are all very different. The problem is that the differences between models are in some cases so minute that production

337

workers cannot tell them apart. In one case, the wrong set of knobs was shipped. When GM tested them, they worked once, but failed to work thereafter! Mountainview was able to ship the correct components the next day, but naturally hopes to prevent such problems. This situation illustrates an opportunity to standardize and reduce design complexity. However, if Mountainview were to work with the engineering center to introduce families of products into vehicles, a lot of complexity could be reduced thereby reducing the possibility of errors.

The second major issue is a bigger problem: re-designing GM's current supply chain for components supplied by Mountainview. The supply chain for this particular component is very complicated, as parts from Japan are shipped to Auburn Hills, then to multiple locations of a GM first-tier supplier, and then to different GM facilities. The network is made even more complex in some cases by a lack of EDI—where orders are still done by fax or phone. In the case of this program, components come from Japan, go to Alchem[3] in Mexico, then onto Mountainview, which ships to Moran[4] Plastics in Canada. Moran is not connected online, so all information is transmitted by fax. Schedule instability often causes problems in Japan, leading to premium freight charges (someone hand-carrying a part onto an airplane) and engineering obsolescence issues. In some cases, both EDI and fax are used, although the numbers on these transmissions do not always match up correctly.

The result of over-ordering is product obsolescence. In January of 1998, Moran had ordered enough components for 50,000 vehicles from Mountainview, but only built 38,000 for GM. This resulted in obsolete inventory, the cost of which was split among Moran, General Motors, and Mountainview. Although GM's final build schedule is fairly accurate (within 5 to 10 percent), it measures production at an aggregate, not at a component level. This is where problems occur, which in turn results in the "bullwhip" effect throughout the supply chain.

Furthermore, order information flows via EDI from GM to its first tier supplier, but via fax between the first tier and Moran and between Moran and Mountainview. Tier-2 and Tier-3 suppliers cannot access the GM Supply Power site and therefore are more susceptible to receiving inaccurate forecasts from their next higher tier supplier who usually builds a buffer into their requirement. Furthermore, shipment schedules may reach Tier-2 and Tier-3 suppliers late, giving them less time to plan and schedule production. Sometimes, due to poor planning, suppliers must make premium freight shipments.

Rick Calabra thought about the existing situation and commented that "This is more or less representative of many branches of our supply chain." What could be done to improve the situation? Calabra had attended a workshop on Collaborative Planning, Forecasting and Replenishment (CPFR) and wondered if it would work. Based on what he had read, Calabra noted that CPFR has been very successful on the retail side of the supply chain, but has had limited use between OEM manufacturers and suppliers to date.

Calabra also wondered what the role of vendor-managed inventories (VMIs) were in GM's supply chain redesign efforts. VMI involves having suppliers store parts, and in some cases, even assemble them onto vehicles! Union representatives wanted an active voice on this issue, which GM is now testing at their Gravatai, Brazil, plant where the Chevrolet Celta is produced. For the first time, the world's largest automaker is putting one of its suppliers on a vehicle assembly line. At GM's much-watched Blue Macaw project in south Brazil, Lear Corporation (one of the largest auto suppliers) has been assigned its own 8000-square-foot subassembly area within the GM facility, dressing out doors for the Celta. Not only do the 10 to 12 Lear employees install locks, windows, and other components in the doors, they also detach those doors after the car body leaves the paint shop and reattach the finished pieces as the vehicle nears completion on the assembly line. Furthermore, Lear is one of the 16 suppliers that have plants built adjacent to the GM's manufacturing plant. This project is unique in the car industry. If successful, the setup may be copied in future GM manufacturing operations.

In order to reduce the order-to-delivery (OTD) time, GM's Celta plant is also testing the use of co-designed modules, supplied from secondary suppliers. GM hopes to introduce the concept in their new Lansing Plant, which is scheduled to open for production in 2003. GM is pushing the use of the Internet for ordering vehicles in the Gravatai, Brazil, plant; it hopes to deliver the Celta within three days of an order. Calabra wondered how all of these new experiments in different parts of GM's supply chain would tie together. Trying new concepts at new plants is easy; implementing them throughout existing plants and other parts of the supply chain remains a challenge.

Managing Change in the Supply Chain

In most organizations, existing supply chains are fragmented; few managers truly understand the underlying business processes that take place with their major customers and suppliers. Supply chain redesign begins with a leader, such as Jack Welch at GE, Larry Bossidy at Allied Signal, or Louis Gerstner at IBM. These individuals recognized that in order to make a significant contribution to their organization's competitiveness, they needed to make major changes in their supply chains. They also realized that changes in the supply chain would require significant changes in the internal culture of the purchasing and logistics functions. In fact, many organizations realize that to redesign their supply chains, they must radically alter the perception of the purchasing and logistics functions as non-value-added functions. In this chapter, we look at the experiences of one company that underwent significant change in the early 1990s, and that is continuing to evolve in the 21st century: General Motors Corporation (GM).

Why GM? Isn't this a traditional automotive company? To the contrary, GM is one of the best examples of a radical culture change that has impacted the company's supply chain. The popular press is quick to use GM as a counterpoint in discussions on "innovative" management strategies demonstrated by Honda, Toyota, Daimler Chrysler, and other automotive competitors. However, relatively little press has been given to GM's accomplishments in becoming a global e-business supply chain leader. GM has made a commitment to becoming a leader in supply chain re-design and in the last five years has undergone a radical change in its global management structure.

Integrating GM's supply chain is no simple task. Moreover, GM is a huge organization that spans:

- 50 countries of operation
- 200 countries with GM presence
- 70 assembly plants
- 8.6 million vehicles
- $6 billion logistics spend
- $105 billion material purchase spend
- 72 product programs
- 20 vehicle lines
- 11,931 product suppliers
- 10,000+ dealers
- 69 transportation providers

In the words of Brad Ross, Executive-in-Charge of Order to Delivery (OTD) at GM:

> *When you have a company this large, this complex, and this global, it requires a mastery of the flow of materials and products across the enterprise from the suppliers to the ultimate customer. That's a simple definition of supply chain management. We need to manage the flow of information, cash, process/work—and certainly our*

products—expertly. If we do that, we demonstrate operational excellence.[5]

GM's strategy involves re-designing its supply chain to design, build, buy components, and deliver innovative new vehicles in ways never imagined. Led by its recent CEO, Richard Wagoner, GM has undergone a radical change throughout its management structure in the last five years. This chapter relates the genesis of a supply chain management strategy known within GM as OTD, and how this initiative started with a small group of people with a big idea. It emerged to become a full-fledged global operation charged with driving the revolution. This change was driven by a simple concept: satisfying the customer, with some aspects of product and service that are often overlooked.

The story of this change illustrates some important lessons for managers serious about redesigning their organizational supply chains. By examining the events that took place within the last decade at GM, several key "lessons learned" are readily apparent. We believe these lessons can be applied across industry or organizational environments, and are universal in nature. Why? Simply stated: Because the authors have witnessed the same problems in many different industries. In the following narrative, we will point out a number of "Critical Change Factors." *A Critical Change Factor (CCF) is defined as an element of change management that is required to truly enable an organization to redesign its supply chain.* In other words, CCFs represent the underlying changes during the process of supply chain re-design. Such changes increase the probability of success. These CCFs are key points that senior executives should address as they move forward with their supply chain redesign efforts. The story begins with one individual (who is no longer at GM): Jose Inaki Lopez.

Radical Change Management: The Lopez Era[6]

The emphasis on supply chain management at GM dates back to the early 1990s, when GM was in a financial crisis. In 1991, Jack Smith was appointed as the new CEO to lead the beleaguered company. Smith recognized that GM was in a crisis mode. Financial experts, in reviewing the company's history, agree that in early 1992, GM was in a dire financial situation. That such a large and powerful organization could be on the brink of collapse was a lesson in the dangers of promoting financial performance measures at the expense of customer satisfaction. It was a lesson that few GM managers are likely to ever forget.

Smith quickly realized that 70 percent of GM's expenses were in purchased goods, logistics, and services. If GM were to continue, purchasing cost savings would be a primary means of survival. Smith quickly made a decision to promote Jose Inaki Lopez as chief of GM's procurement operations for North America. Lopez had already built a solid track record at GM Europe, where he had achieved a turnaround in profitability and cost savings. Upon arriving in North America, Lopez introduced the World Wide Purchasing (WWP) process in order to achieve a series of significant cost savings throughout GM's supply base. This strategic decision, more than anything else, allowed GM to survive during this time in its history.

The choice of Lopez to lead the SCM change initiative at GM points out the first of our CCFs. Change must be initiated by a leader with credibility:

CCF 1: The change leader must have a demonstrated track record to gain credibility with executives and employees.

Lopez indeed had a string of successes in Europe, and was immediately recognized as someone who could create change. An observer to this event, Tom Putvin,[7] was a veteran purchasing person who worked within GM in several different divisions, including Buick, the Chevrolet Central Office, the Truck and Bus division, Powertrain, and later at the GM World Headquarters. During his time at GM, he noted that the purchasing activity across GM was the largest in the country, second only to the federal government. However, each of the divisions (Chevrolet, Buick, Pontiac, etc.) represented a separate entity, and did not work together to achieve economies of scale. Putvin's transfer in 1992 provided an opportunity to work at GM North American Headquarters and to be part of a new initiative described by Lopez as "World Wide Purchasing" (WWP).

Tom Putvin recalls the atmosphere at GM at the time that Lopez arrived:

> *In terms of perspective, I grew up in the organization where from a purchasing point of view everything was done separately. There was no coordination between the divisions (Buick, Chevrolet, Oldsmobile, and Pontiac). For instance, when I was at Buick in Flint, if we called up a supplier and requested parts from them, and they told us "we're running parts for Chevrolet"—we would say "Pull their job and make it for us!" In fact, the other divisions were the enemy! Operating units competed against one another for resources in the supply community—GM was effectively a set of independent organizations—Buick, Pontiac, Olds, and Chevy did not talk to one another.*

In the early 1990s, Lopez had developed his philosophy and WWP system in Germany and had been very successful in his approach to supply chain management. GM in North America was experiencing an extremely competitive market due to the Japanese automotive manufacturers. GM needed to cut costs in order to stay in business. Lopez arrived at North American Operations (NAO) with the idea of implementing the same supply chain model that had worked well in Europe, and was given full authority by the head of the company, Jack Smith, <u>to make it happen</u>. This points out our second CCF:

CCF 2: In order to achieve success, the Change Leader must create a sense of <u>urgency</u> within the organization. The Leader must make people understand what the effects of failure are if change does not occur.

Lopez had a very close relationship with Jack Smith, who was head of GM Europe when Lopez was rising through the ranks. Smith trusted Lopez because he knew his track record in Europe——the ability to transition from a process engineering orientation to a supply chain perspective, thereby saving large sums of money for the Opel organization in Europe. This brings up the third CCF:

CCF 3: The Change Leader must have the full support of the top senior executive in the company in order to truly re-design the supply chain. Without this support, the likelihood of success is very low. The Change Leader must also elevate the role of supply chain management to a senior level in the company, reporting directly to the Chief Executive Officer.

Lopez was able to bring about change quickly in a company that had a history of being very hierarchical. A company where it would seem to take forever to get things done. Lopez employed a metaphor that is still shared amongst managers within GM today: that of an elephant on a tether. Lopez related the story of an elephant at a circus that is tethered by a small chain to a stake in the ground. The elephant could easily tear it out and walk away—why doesn't he do so? Because these elephants have been conditioned to being tied to a stake from birth—when they were unable to break away. Thus, they cannot believe they can do it, when in fact, it can very easily be done. In order to succeed, people at GM must be re-conditioned to accept change, and embrace change! Only then can they tear up the stake and walk away from a confined position!

By creating an internal culture focused on driving improved internal integration among purchasing, engineering, logistics, and operations, Lopez helped turn around a company on the verge of collapse. In less than a year as head of GM's North American purchasing organization, Lopez established a different mindset and raised the importance of purchasing and supply chain management as a core contributor to GM's competitive success.

Changing the Purchasing Culture

Although stories of Lopez's somewhat eccentric management style abound, no one can deny his effectiveness in creating change. One of his major cultural impacts was changing the practice of awarding business solely on the basis of supplier relationships; instead, he mandated that business to suppliers be awarded on a competitive basis based on proven performance. In so doing, he drove 10 percent cost savings to the bottom line in his first year. Lopez's quick success brings us to our fourth CCF:

CCF 4: In bringing about change, the Change Leader should seek some "early wins" that can be quantified in dollars, and communicate these "hard numbers" to the rest of the organization. Early wins support the validity of the strategy throughout the company and sustain momentum for changing the culture. Through their success, the early adopters will convince others in the company to adopt principles of supply chain redesign.

In his quest for immediate quantifiable cost savings, Lopez insisted that *everything* at GM be sourced on a competitive basis. GM had progressed from a decentralized, slow-moving company, to one in which cost savings was a major initiative in all aspects of its business. With the competitive pressures brought about in the marketplace by the quality of the Japanese vehicles and the interest in what they were doing, the purchasing group realized that Toyota had fewer than 200 suppliers, while GM had more than 20,000! As a result of this benchmarking, GM began a major initiative to rationalize and reduce their supply base.

Internal Integration
of Supply Chain Functions

Internal integration of purchasing, engineering, operations, marketing, and sales is a prerequisite for solid supply chain management. Congruent with a change in the overall culture surrounding supply chain functions, leading companies have established matrix-based structures across product lines and commodity groups that enable supply chain functions to be truly global.

It is a little known fact that Lopez's enormous impact at GM was achieved in less than a year. Jack Smith, the CEO of GM, announced the appointment of Lopez as Vice President of World Wide Purchasing on April 24, 1992. Lopez left on March 15, 1993. During this brief tenure at GM, Lopez radically altered the perception of purchasing as a "non-value added" function within GM, especially with respect to its relationship to engineering. In a sense, he was one of the early pioneers that brought attention to the impact of supply chain management across all industries. Lopez was instrumental in changing the role of purchasing within GM. Before that time, an engineer working on a new platform might decide to work directly with a supplier's engineering team, and leave GM purchasing completely out of the picture. This reflected GM's engineering-oriented culture; engineers tended to look "down their nose" at purchasing staff, viewing them largely as "paper pushers" and not as people that could make a valuable contribution.

As a direct report to Jack Smith, Lopez changed this perception immediately. Lopez initiated a simple approach for awarding business, QSP. That is, business would be awarded to suppliers on the basis of Quality (Q), Service (S, including delivery), and Price (P). The QSP mantra was later extended by Harold Kutner to include T: Technology. GM no longer awarded business based on "engineering relationships" with suppliers—which was novel at the time—but is a recognized CCF in supply chain redesign:

> CCF 5: Performance metrics to track the success of supply chain redesign should focus on total cost (including cost of quality, delivery, inventory, service, and technology) and composed to internal and external customer value requirements.

Another major contribution of Lopez's legacy was the World Wide Purchasing (WWP) organizational matrix structure that focused on core commodity teams and platform teams. This structure ensured the integration of product and technology knowledge on a global basis. Platform teams would scan the globe for leading-edge technologies at the best quality, service, and price. A new group called Advanced Purchasing was also created to help identify and integrate suppliers into new products early in the product development process and provide insights into end customer requirements.

The structure of this organization is shown in Figure 10–1. Although the names have changed, the structure is largely similar to the initial structure established by Lopez in 1992. Note that each of the divisions now reports to a single executive in charge—including Order to Delivery (formerly known as Production Control and Logistics). An innovative feature of this structure is that commodity groups (chemical, metallic, electrical, etc.) have dedicated technical people scouring the world for the latest technologies and "blue sky" developments in these respective areas that can affect GM's product strategies. The new organizational structure points to another factor that is critical in establishing a successful supply chain redesign:

> CCF 6: A major re-organization is often required for successful implementation of supply chain redesign. The new organization must promote global cross-functional teaming and reduce duplication of resources across products and services.

One of the most important changes made to GM's supply chain organization was the creation of a global structure. GM embarked on a series of organizational structure strategies with automakers, distributors, and suppliers on six continents. Over the years, GM has made an effort to form partnerships on a global basis. In doing so, GM has realized that local conditions require a different set of operating procedures, and have been careful not to force its policies and procedures on its partners, with the exception of one set of criteria: QSTP. For instance, GM has worked closely with Shanghai Automotive (SAIC), one of its joint venture partners, in helping to build and sell Buick Regals in China. It is also helping to prepare SAIC managers for the realities of true open-market competition that will occur with China's entrance into the World Trade Organization (WTO), by providing training through General Motors University.

Because of its size and global scope, creating a truly global supply chain management infrastructure proved daunting. To begin with, a detailed supplier performance measurement system was developed to enable measurement of performance for any GM supplier in the world allowing a true "apples-to-apples" comparison for global commodity managers. Communication of supply chain management initiatives and updates on a global basis was accomplished through technology. Lopez initiated a weekly tradition that

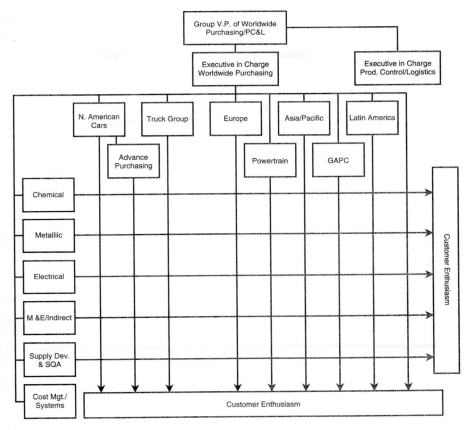

Figure 10–1   World Wide Purchasing Structure at General Motors (1999).

continues today: every Friday morning at 8 a.m. EST, purchasing executives from divisions all over the world conduct a global teleconference. Information shared includes updates to product development efforts, changes in market conditions, pricing updates, and other new developments. The dividends from this strategy were tremendous: GM remains as one of the strongest global brands across every continent:

CCF 7: A global structure is required to ensure clear communication and visibility of customer requirements, new technologies, and new sources of supply for successful supply chain re-design. This global structure should enable the organization to recognize and exploit regional differences and opportunities to improve end-customer value.

The GM structure allowed Marketing, Engineering, and Advance Purchasing to understand common customer requirements on vehicle platforms across the company. These customer needs can then be translated into engineering needs that go out 5 to 10 years or more into the future. It also identifies those suppliers that have the technology roadmaps to address these engineering requirements. The vision for Advance Purchasing was that it would "bundle" standardized specifications for purchasing inputs early in the new product development cycle across multiple platforms, thereby achieving significant cost savings. The result of this communication was a joint technology development plan with suppliers, which in some cases leads to a co-development activity. In a co-development activity, engineers from GM and supplier organizations work together on a variety of different technologies, with benefits shared based on negotiated agreements. This is a major departure from the old culture that existed at GM:

CCF 8: A smooth transition between product development, production, and order fulfillment is required for successful supply chain redesign.

The New Era of Order to Delivery: Drivers for Change

Harold Kutner took over as Executive VP of WWP and Logistics when Lopez left (after Rick Wagoner briefly held the position). Wagoner became the CEO of GM in 1998. Following GM's implementation of its World Wide

Purchasing strategy, executives began to recognize the important contribution made by supply chain partners to product design, sourcing, logistics, and overall supply chain strategies. Although Lopez had initiated the supply chain revolution, Wagoner and his team realized that supply chain management involved much more than improved coordination between purchasing, production, and order fulfillment. Moreover, three major trends were becoming apparent in GM's markets that were drivers of improved coordination not just internally, but externally with suppliers and customers.

1. The Internet. The Internet allowed more customers to have more knowledge than ever before regarding products and services they are considering purchasing. In a presentation, Brad Ross of GM noted that:

> *Recent data indicates 150 million people in the U.S. alone access the Internet on a regular basis. They spend 10 hours online each month, and that number is continuously growing. And from a transportation industry standpoint, we know that the majority of car buyers research their purchases on the Internet. GM's Buy-Power website allows a customer to research any GM product, configure their ideal vehicle and locate a dealer to complete the sales transaction. Currently, it is available in 40 countries, and importantly, we get an average of 2,000–4,000 dealer leads each day. This computer activity translates into savvy customers who are increasingly unwilling to compromise on their vehicle purchases. They have access to data that gives them the skinny on prices, quality, and the like. Armed with this information, they are quicker than ever before, as a group, to reward companies that give them the most value for their hard-earned dollars.*[8]

2. Competition. In the automotive industry, more new products are being brought to market every year. This year, GM alone will introduce 16 new products and three vehicle refreshes. Every company is fighting for every single percentage point of market share they can get. A recent deal announcement following the events of September 11 resulted in zero percent financing on new vehicles. In an interview, one manager noted that:[9]

> *The events of September 11, 2001 reinforce all the more why we need to take the waste out of all of the nodes of the supply chain. In a sense, supply chain management is more important now than it ever was. It reinforces the need for sharing more information with our supply chain partners. The information systems we are looking to put in place are not a cheap solution—and the solution is only as*

good as the proactive capabilities of our Tier 1 suppliers to be able to make use of that information and drive improvements down through the supply chain. Everyone is plowing new ground on this issue: but it all comes down to business value.

At the same time, all manufacturers are continuously improving their quality and continuing to reduce their costs, to the point where quality and cost will not be competitive differentiators anymore. It will all be about product features and the performance of the supply chain. Why? Because superior supply chain performance improves customer satisfaction, reduces costs and lead times, and subjects customers to fewer product trade-offs. Lastly, a steady stream of new integration strategies across manufacturers, suppliers, and non-traditional competitors is taking place. The insight to be drawn is that manufacturers are competing as entire supply chains. Perhaps the better description is "network—the customer fulfillment network." Savvy manufacturers will integrate across all of the entities in their supply chain or network to gain competitive advantage. So integration becomes a new strategic objective in the competitive arsenal.

3. Emerging technology impacting traditional business models. Entire new business models are being driven by technological innovation. This new technology means that real-time demand sensing and inventory visibility is possible. Automotive OEM's can instantaneously capture what's selling and what's not in the field and immediately share it with dealers, and can track vehicles from when they leave the plant to when they arrive at the dealership, regardless of shipping mode. They also have real-time process visibility across order management, manufacturing, distribution and logistics—including simultaneous communication to multiple tiers of suppliers. Why is that important? Imagine the power of all tiers of suppliers understanding GM's requirements in terms of required components and their needed delivery, well in advance, allowing proactive planning on the suppliers' part, and probably improvements in lead time and cost reduction for suppliers and their OEMs. Such technologies were idealized concepts only as recently as a few years ago.

The Customer in Control

Rick Wagoner and his executive team realized that an important theme was emerging from these changes: The customer is in control. It was no longer acceptable to simply push vehicles that are convenient for GM to build into the hands of unempowered customers. The new business models required that dealers and customers be in control. What does customer in control (CIC) mean? Brad Ross notes that:

For starters, it means that GM customers shouldn't be forced to compromise on their exact vehicle of choice. When a customer walks into a dealership, or explores our GM BuyPower website, they should be able to get exactly what they want. Too often, customers have made compromises versus what our sales information said they could have. That means that to some degree, that customer is going to be disappointed. At the same time, our data shows that we get less revenue from our product sales because customers tend to settle for less than they would have if they got their vehicle of choice. That's called "lose—lose." Customers also expect fast order fulfillment lead times, and they expect reliable delivery promises. And, with the advent of the Internet, they expect real-time order status. In the past, it could take two to three months for a customer to receive a vehicle they ordered—if they knew they could order one in the first place! Not only that, the dealer wouldn't be able to share just when that vehicle might be delivered. Why? Because they didn't know, and we didn't have the ability to tell them. Now, we track our lead times and delivery date reliability and improving both are a top priority. And we are seeing dramatic improvements. Bottom-line, we want to make it easy to do business with GM.[10]

GM's Response

To ensure that customers were in fact in control, GM is leveraging a whole new set of tools and partnerships. GM's e-business initiatives are seeking to align functional business processes with information technology to improve efficiency and effectiveness. As shown in Figure 10–2, GM Supply Power is GM's supplier communication Web site. GM uses it to provide up-to-date information to the supplier community quickly, efficiently, and conveniently. Supply Power will help suppliers to focus on core technologies, as well as to better understand option preferences and associated capacity requirements. Supply Power also acts as a gateway to applications that are developed and implemented by groups within GM. Supply Power is used at GM's business partners (suppliers, design organizations, logistics providers, etc.) and GM's allied divisions. Other e-business applications being implemented include:

1. Purchase Power: To receive bid packages, submit quotes, and receive purchase contracts.
2. Quality Power: To share quality and warranty information, share supplier performance metrics, and participate in the Supplier Suggestion Program.

3. Engineering Power: To collaborate on vehicle design by sharing data, receive vehicle program information, and collaborate on testing.
4. Finance Power: Query invoice payment status and share information on new vehicle sales and trade discount programs.
5. Material Power: Collaborate on production capacity planning, production schedules, and share logistics information.
6. Manufacturing Power: Collaborate on manufacturing and share inventory and production information.

Other new technologies are also being adopted into GM's products and supply chain networks. OnStar is a leading provider of in-vehicle safety, security and information services in the United States and Canada, with more than 1.5 million active subscribers. This very successful effort is helping customers with 15,000 door unlocks per month, 14,250 roadside dispatches per month, and 375 stolen vehicles located per month. Covisint was created a little over a year ago and is the world's largest Internet-based virtual marketplace. Forming an unprecedented alliance, GM, Ford, and DaimlerChrysler announced a joint venture to build a network to streamline business with their vast array of suppliers. If successful, Covisint would handle much of the $240 billion in purchases of raw materials, parts, and supplies made each year by the three automakers, creating what could be the largest Internet company in terms of revenues. The venture underscores just how powerful the promise of the Internet has become to traditional businesses. The automakers believe the new B2B company will slash costs, save time, and make operations more efficient for them and tens of thousands of suppliers around the world. GM plans to do $25 billion of the corporation's total purchasing through Covisint and that number will grow. Lastly, GM formed a joint venture company called Vector SCM in December 2000 with a partner, CNF Inc, a freight-management and transport company. Vector SCM has become GM's 4th-Party Logistics Service Provider worldwide, and is bringing increased delivery speed and visibility to GM's global supply chain. This is helping GM to address the logistic challenges associated with OTD by gaining access to logistics resources globally, to drive more costs to a variable basis, to minimize structural costs, to decrease implementation time, to minimize incremental staffing/management needs, and to minimize required process/system development.

The changes occurring at GM clearly point to the fact that as internal integration improves, organizations must ensure alignment of their customers and suppliers. This means understanding the business requirements for the current supply chain structure, as well as developing a vision of the supply chain of the future. Based on this gap, leading companies such as GM are creating a set of e-business requirements that will enable them to close the gap, and are seeking technologies that have the capabilities to do so. This is an important

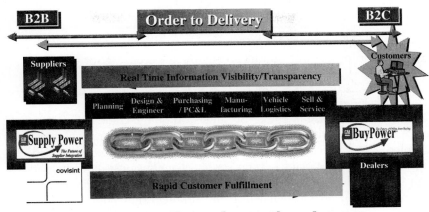

Integrating and Driving Operational Excellence

*OTD Drives a Transformation Across
All Business Processes*

Business Process & IT Transformation

Constraint Elimination

Customer Demand Sensing

Online Distribution/Consensus Process

Online Dealer & Vehicle Locator

Online Vehicle Configurator

Online Customer
Lead Management

Accessorization

Real Time Order Prioritization

Real Time Outbound Distribution Visibility

Product Delivery Date Commitments

OTD Cross-Functional Operating Organization Structure

Daily Order Scheduling & Sequencing

Assembly Plant Rapid OTD Enablers

Online Simultaneous Multi Tier Supplier Scheduling

Order Lead Time Reduction Process

New Model Part Planning Tool

Online Supplier Information
Visibility - SupplyPower

Supplier Capacity
Management Tool

Total Cost Sourcing Tool

Real Time Supplier Performance
Monitoring / Metrics

Vector 4PL Business Model Implantation

Outbound Logistics Network Redesign

Inbound Logistics Network Redesign

WIP Inventory Management Improvement Tools

Figure 10–2   GM Supply Power

criteria: many B2B e-commerce providers have failed to understand that their software and Internet capabilities must be able to meet the business requirements of their customers, and not the other way around!

CCF 9: Supply chain redesign requires organizations to explore new technologies—but build a strong business case prior to adoption.

Consider the promise of trade exchanges. Although trade exchanges were once considered the ultimate solution for many supply chain problems, many have failed. Why? Because many companies quickly realized that trade exchanges do not address many of their supply chain business requirements. Although trade exchanges are an important part of the B2B promise, little is really known about how to manage them. Although they hold a great deal of promise for commodity-type products, e-business managers at GM, and other companies, realize that not all relationships should be managed using this approach. The greatest danger to trade exchanges, which is frequently overlooked by some of the "experts," is that supplier relationships may be irreparably damaged by entering an exchange. Trade exchanges tend to ignore those important elements of supplier performance other than price. However, the value of these elements may be difficult to express to a senior executive who is only looking at the "bottom line."

Although linking customers and suppliers is important, the real challenges lie in linking suppliers beyond the first tier. Many smaller suppliers may not have the technology capability to implement EDI—in such cases, B2B initiatives must provide streamlined networks that are easily configurable and provide Web-based "point and click" solutions. Such systems should have "Wizards" that help smaller suppliers to implement and integrate their product inventory and BOMs easily, and provide complete visibility of inventory and demand information at multiple points within the supply chain on a real-time basis.

Changing the Culture for Supply Chain Redesign

At GM, the OTD initiative began as a new global business model for the company, with a new mindset about supply chain management and integration across functions of both old and new processes and capabilities. The critical question is: What has GM gotten for all its efforts? What is the impact on the business? In fact, what is happening is a complete transformation of GM's processes, systems, and business results.

Organizational Transformation

GM has changed their organization dramatically, to an integrated, cross-functional, customer-focused structure. For the first time in its history, GM's Manufacturing, Purchasing, Order to Delivery, and Vehicle Sales Service & Marketing are structurally connected, along with other supporting activities such as the production control and logistic operations at the powertrain, metal fabrication, and service parts units. That is a huge change, particularly in a company that has traditionally been very functionally focused. But this structural connectivity enables cross-functional decision-making and the elimination of silo mentality, which has paid off significantly since it was established in 2001.

GM's new organization drives common processes and systems across the regions of North America, Europe, Latin America, the Middle East, and Asia Pacific. This requires sharing common global strategy and tools from a supply operation, order fulfillment, and logistics standpoint, yet at the same time it respects the different order-fulfillment models within the different regions. This restructured organization drives implementation and accountability for performance.

Another critical component of OTD is a new set of capabilities that allows GM to give its customers their vehicle of choice with superior delivery times and reliability. This requires a large number of initiatives across different business processes, and requires significant transformation in terms of both business processes and IT systems. It also means significant supply chain process reengineering with critical IT spending to replace uncompetitive systems.

This has resulted in a significant re-design of GM's supply chain. For example, last year GM signed a contract with Union Pacific to manage all outbound rail transportation needs in the western United States. In North America, GM instituted a large number of OTD initiatives in its plants that highlight the importance of sold orders, to reduce processing times, and to reduce in process inventories. As recently as a year ago, GM faced serious dealer and customer discontent; they could not order vehicles equipped as described in its sales information. Even worse, they didn't have a method for making these constraints visible to the organization, let alone a process for eliminating them. Both of those are in place now, and GM has reduced such constraints by 70 percent in the last year.

The challenges of implementing OTD are considerable. As in many other industries, the "bullwhip effect" is alive and well within GM's supply chain. This means that as one goes back through multiple tiers of suppliers that provide materials and components to OEMs, the level of inventory increases dramatically. The root cause for this bullwhip effect is the inability of entities in the supply chain to sense demand properly; the gap between supply and demand is thus buffered with inventory. This causes last-minute production schedule changes and adds a lot of variability in the system. The ripple effect is experienced by all suppliers in the chain, who respond to the variability by holding inventory. At the other end, dealers also hold a lot of inventory in order to meet customer demand. There are times when, due to production schedule changes, suppliers are not holding the right inventory required. Suppliers become less responsive, requiring long lead times to deliver the required part, thus increasing the cycle time. There is also a possibility that their inventory will become obsolete, which drives cost into the system. Customers are unwilling to wait, and in such cases will go to a competitor.

GM's rival, Ford Motor Company, is attacking the same challenges. Ford is also taking its business to the Internet and is aggressively moving to improve its OTD capability. This has increased the urgency with which the GM OTD team has been tasked to equip its operations for real-time information sharing. GM believes that OTD is the engine that will deliver the promise of e-business to its customers and shareholders and is a critical link to its e-business strategy:

CCF 10: Value system creation requires a sweeping change in corporate culture within every business function within every enterprise in the supply chain, beginning with raw material suppliers and ending with final customers, that focuses on immediate responsiveness to change in end customer requirements.

If the OTD initiative is to become the core enabler for GM's Web-based strategy of linking customers, dealers, plants, and suppliers, then suppliers must be a big part of the process. The associated set of challenges for the OTD team is *the integrated execution of key functional activities to meet customer requirements.* Moreover, Buy Power must transfer information and provide visibility to suppliers via Supply Power. Supply Power must provide components via the OTD cycle of planning, design, purchasing, production control, inbound logistics, manufacturing, outbound logistics, sales and service, and ultimately link up to Buy Power. A primary deliverable is to cut lead times from 60 days down to 30 days or less. To date, the GM team has been making good progress, and cycle times for ordered vehicles have already been cut to 31 days. For World Wide Purchasing, progress on this initiative translates to three core objectives:

1. Define OTD requirements, based on input from suppliers.
2. Understand GM's current sourcing strategies—is it capable of meeting these requirements? If not, change sourcing patterns and schedules to enable fulfillment of these requirements.
3. Integrate OTD requirements into all future requests for quotations. Eventually, OTD requirements will simply become an entry-level requirement for doing business with GM.

Although this appears to be a straightforward task, it is not. The functional leads on the OTD project must be aligned with the Supply Power initiative. Currently, Supply Power provides access to aggregate volume schedules that are useful for helping suppliers understand broad levels of demand, but do not provide insights into specific part number requirements. Supply Power is linked to all aspects of GM operations, including design, engineering, manufacturing, production control, logistics, purchasing, sales, and marketing, etc. In addition, Supply Power provides:

- Real-time inventory status and production counts
- Real-time advanced shipping notices
- Online engineering specs
- Quality and warranty data
- Capacity planning
- Supplier communications
- Real-time supplier feedback and corrective action process
- Link to GM TradeXChange

This is a good foundation for the OTD initiative to work from, but significant challenges exist to realize complete visibility of requirements to suppliers up the supply chain:

CCF 11: Supply chain redesign is enabled by visibility of customer requirements throughout the entire supply chain in a collaborative approach.

Future Challenges

What challenges are in store for GM as it moves from a traditional bricks-and-mortar company to an enterprise within an integrated value system that responds to rapid shifts in global market conditions, technology, and customer requirements? We have already discussed a set of CCFs that document GM's transition from a traditional organization to one that is undergoing a rapid series of changes based on the redesign of its supply chain. These changes continue to occur even today. A set of five Future Challenges remain to be achieved at GM as it moves forward. These last are perhaps the most difficult to deploy—yet also remain the most critical in terms of their impact on success. GM is not the only organization that must surmount these challenges. Those who are quickest to do so will effectively be able to exploit this advantage, regardless of industry or market.

FUTURE CHALLENGE 1: Before jumping into new supply chain technologies, managers must thoroughly understand their company's existing supply chain.

A requirement for success is a fundamental redesign of a company's supply chain structure in order to apply B2B technologies across multiple tiers of customers and suppliers. To learn to crawl, walk, and then run, organizations must address the current designs of their existing supply chains and only then build applications around their pre-engineered networks. A Web-based application cannot fix the problems associated with a large and poorly performing supply base, i.e., fragmented logistics and distribution networks, adversarial supplier/customer relationships, and unwillingness to share information due to a lack of trust. To create integrated value systems, organizations must be willing to share risks and rewards and to build the underlying infrastructure to apply information technology tools.

FUTURE CHALLENGE 2: Creating an integrated value system infrastructure involves optimizing the coordination between business functions, to the point that people work together in a routine manner based on aligned functional strategies that seek to maximize customer value.

Purchasing, operations, and distribution must have aligned business strategies, performance metrics, and an understanding of where the organization is going. Basic processes such as order fulfillment, commodity strategies, and logistics flows must be analyzed and improved. Total business spending across all global units should be documented, with established commodity strategies in place for all major purchases. In addition, the fundamental network structure of suppliers and customers must be optimized (in most cases through supply base/customer base reduction).

FUTURE CHALLENGE 3: Organizations must change the nature of their alignment and collaboration not only with first-tier customers and suppliers, but also throughout their supply chain networks to create an integrated value system.

In the future, the best value systems will win. Managers must be aware of the actions and requirements for critical customers and suppliers in their network. However, it is difficult to access this information unless the scope and nature of the relationships are established. Not every relationship needs to be "strategic" and "long-term." However, the relative impact of suppliers and customers in an organization's network on value should be mapped, defined, and communicated to all parties concerned.

FUTURE CHALLENGE 4: Managers must make joint cross-enterprise decisions based on well-defined cross-enterprise performance metrics across multiple supply chain entities, based on the value elements of technology, potential for growth, and profitability.

The performance of key suppliers and customers in terms of quality, delivery lead-time, on-time delivery, and technology should be described in terms that relate to bottom-line financial impact. Key functions should be aligned with your organization's internal strategies, in order to exploit their expertise and knowledge in creating value. (For example, designers, engineers, and marketers should have an ongoing program to agree on product component and service standards to minimize unique items; a single demand forecast should be used by all participants in the sales and operations plan, etc.)

FUTURE CHALLENGE 5: Achieving true collaboration is the key to developing trust in a value system.

In effect, it is only through full *collaboration* between multiple tiers of suppliers and OEMs that *trust* is built into a supply chain network. This may at first seem counterintuitive, but it reflects some of the principles emphasized again and again in this book. Only by truly *experiencing* a relationship where people follow through on their commitments in a reliable manner, can trust occur between parties. Collaboration can occur through sharing of forecasting and demand information, leading to joint long-term capacity, inventory, and human resource requirements planning. One of the most important forms of collaboration is in product/process/service design. By bringing suppliers and customers into the design process, innovative new technologies can be combined in ways that were not previously imagined. Collaborative design can significantly reduce the time-to-market for new products, and ensure that the customers' requirements are integrated into the design from the outset. Bob Lutz, recently appointed chief of design at GM, is working hard to make this happen in GM's new line of vehicles.

Long-term and continuous supplier performance improvements will only be achieved through the following: identifying where value is created in the supply chain; strategically positioning the buying firm in line with value creation; and implementing an integrated SCM strategy to maximize internal and external capabilities throughout the supply chain. A process map for the path forward will help to identify critical commodities and products to focus on, critical suppliers and customers to work with, opportunities for improvement, and needed steps toward more effective partnering.

Creating trust among supply chain participants represents a long-term undertaking, and must be led by a Change Leader with true vision. Unless supply chain members support this vision, asking them to do things faster in response to real-time ordering systems will fail. As discussed in Chapter 9, a supplier who receives an order via the Internet, prints it out, and puts it on a stack on his or her desk is not going to be able to improve performance. When information is shared in the supply chain and made available to all parties, there will be mutual understanding about demand requirements, capacity limitations, inventory positioning, and the need for collaboration between partners. Then mutually beneficial agreements can be developed and the power of the Internet can begin to be fully exploited.

Can GM turn it around? The signs are there that the organization is moving in the right direction. Although it is still early in the journey, executives are pleased to be seeing some significant early results. Order fulfillment lead-time has been reduced 50 percent. GM continues to perform well in terms of the percentage of parts delivered on time to the assembly line station in its plants, and outbound quality from a logistics standpoint is improving. Delivery date reliability is now at 85 percent. Production and material constraints have been reduced by an incredible 70 percent—in about a year's time. And inventory and logistics costs have been reduced as well. At the same time, GM has reduced headcount by 10 percent. These early business results clearly demonstrated the power of an integrated, cross-functional supply chain network.

Other suppliers in GM's network structure have a similar view of the situation. For example, Milliken and Company, a textile manufacturer in Spartanburg, South Carolina, produces the fabric that is used in GM's Corvette sunroof tops and in many other GM vehicle interiors. Although Milliken is actually a Tier-3 supplier, they feel the immediate impacts of changes to GM's production levels, and are seeking ways to be able to access GM's forecasts in terms that are meaningful for their own planning purposes. Milliken also understands the importance of relationships. In the words of Phil McIntyre at Milliken: "Sitting down and having an honest discussion with our supply chain partners has a direct impact on our ability to perform and achieve higher market share and improved profits."

GM is making significant changes in other areas of their organization as well. The hiring of former Chrysler Vice Chairman for Product Development Bob Lutz points to the fact that new exciting vehicles will be in showrooms in the next several years. Richard Wagoner is emphasizing that although there will some short-term pain on the financing of vehicles, American consumers are going back into dealerships, and are looking at GM vehicles for the first time in many years. The potential to win new and previous customers is what everyone is hoping for.[11]

The true roots of this change lie in changing people's mindset regarding the nature of their work. The original change in GM's culture initiated by Lopez relied on a complete dedication to driving "process thinking" into an area that was traditionally "ad hoc." Tom Putvin reflecting on the importance of process thinking at GM commented:

> "In a recent consulting session with a client regarding their business with GM, I was describing the importance of "process" at GM and specifically within the WWP organization. I was telling the client that it was Lopez who introduced the WWP Process to GM in North America and that he made the issue of Process almost like a religion at GM. Once Lopez had introduced the concept of WWP there was **NO OPTION** for anyone to do things their own way—everything had to follow the WWP **PROCESS.** This, I feel, is a significant point to be made on the subject of Change Management, especially in situations where companies are contemplating radical changes. Everyone has to follow the same process—to do things the same way."[12]

GM's experience in implementing change point to a final lesson learned:

> SCM is all about people working with people and convincing them to adopt a common process for decision-making for the benefit of all supply chain members in their efforts to meet the needs of the final customer.

GM's experience applies to any organization struggling to integrate its supply chain to create a competitive advantage. Until organizations are able to effectively change the nature of their relationships with their suppliers and customers, it will be difficult to make significant progress. Although e-technologies can certainly help to enable people to communicate better, create information visibility, and establish channels of communication, in a sense there is nothing more important that a sound relationship based on trust and mutual respect for one another. Customers should have as their goal to become the "preferred customer of choice" for their suppliers; likewise, suppliers should strive to be the "supplier of choice" for their customers. This evolution may take years—but in the end, it will make the difference in the supply chains of the future. Creating supply chains that are truly high-performing value systems is a significant undertaking. It is, however, one that will reward those organizations that can accomplish it.

Endnotes

[1]Fictitious name.

[2]Mountainview Automotive (fictitious name) is a manufacturer of electronic components headquartered in Japan with sales of approximately $300 million, with 50 percent of production in Japan and 50 percent in the U.S. It is one of the largest suppliers of switch modules to the auto industry. Its annual revenue exceeds $4 billion. Mountainview is the six-time recipient of GM's Supplier of the Year Award. It has manufacturing plants in Korea, Japan, Mexico, and Europe, and produces a variety of products for the automotive and computer industries. In automotive, they build components for ignition switches, power windows, power mirrors, volume controls, and airbag harnesses in steering wheels. The latter product has a standard design that goes into virtually every automobile, but has undergone significant design changes. With the introduction of steering wheel volume controls and cruise control, the number of switches in this product has gone from 2 to 18. Mountainview produces products in all three types of GM demand streams: first-tier, directed, and order-specific.

[3]Fictitious name.

[4]Fictitious name.

[5]Brad Ross, Public Speaking Engagement, "GM Order to Delivery: A Customer-Focused Supply Chain Revolution at General Motors," March 11, 2002.

[6]This discussion of change in the Lopez era is based on interviews and discussions with several senior General Motors executives, including Tom Fabus, Bo Andersson, Tom Putvin, John Calabrese, Bob Burkhart, Anton Meurer, and L. Williams.

[7]Based on interviews with Tom Putvin on October 22, 2001.

[8]Brad Ross, Public Speaking Engagement, "GM Order to Delivery: A Customer-Focused Supply Chain Revolution at General Motors," March 11, 2002.

[9]Interview with Dick Alagna, November 27, 2001.

[10]Brad Ross, Public Speaking Engagement, "GM Order to Delivery: A Customer-Focused Supply Chain Revolution at General Motors," March 11, 2002.

[11]Gregory White, "GM's 0% Finance Plan Is Good for Economy, Risky for Economy," Tuesday, October 10, 2001, *Wall Street Journal*, p. A1.

[12]Based on interviews with Tom Putvin on October 22, 2001.

INDEX

The *Financial Times* delivers a world of business news.

Use the Risk-Free Trial Voucher below!

To stay ahead in today's business world you need to be well-informed on a daily basis. And not just on the national level. You need a news source that closely monitors the entire world of business, and then delivers it in a concise, quick-read format.

With the *Financial Times* you get the major stories from every region of the world. Reports found nowhere else. You get business, management, politics, economics, technology and more.

Now you can try the *Financial Times* for 4 weeks, absolutely risk free. And better yet, if you wish to continue receiving the *Financial Times* you'll get great savings off the regular subscription rate. Just use the voucher below.

8 reasons why you should read the Financial Times for 4 weeks RISK-FREE!

To help you stay current with significant
developments in the world economy ...
and to assist you to make informed business
decisions — the Financial Times brings you:

❶ Fast, meaningful overviews of international affairs ... plus daily
briefings on major world news.

❷ Perceptive coverage of economic, business, financial and political
developments with special focus on emerging markets.

❸ More international business news than any other publication.

❹ Sophisticated financial analysis and commentary on world market
activity plus stock quotes from over 30 countries.

❺ Reports on international companies and a section on global investing.

❻ Specialized pages on management, marketing, advertising and
technological innovations from all parts of the world.

❼ Highly valued single-topic special reports (over 200 annually)
on countries, industries, investment opportunities, technology and more.

❽ The Saturday Weekend FT section — a globetrotter's guide to
leisure-time activities around the world: the arts, fine dining, travel,
sports and more.

For Special Offer See Over

FT **FINANCIAL TIMES**
World business newspaper